A

Philip E. Lilienthal

B O O K

The Philip E. Lilienthal imprint
honors special books
in commemoration of a man whose work
at University of California Press from 1954 to 1979
was marked by dedication to young authors
and to high standards in the field of Asian Studies.
Friends, family, authors, and foundations have together
endowed the Lilienthal Fund, which enables UC Press
to publish under this imprint selected books
in a way that reflects the taste and judgment
of a great and beloved editor.

The publisher gratefully acknowledges the generous support of the Philip E. Lilienthal Asian Studies Endowment Fund of the University of California Press Foundation, which was established by a major gift from Sally Lilienthal.

Finding Women in the State

Finding Women in the State

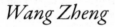

A SOCIALIST FEMINIST REVOLUTION IN THE PEOPLE'S REPUBLIC OF CHINA, 1949–1964

Wang Zheng

UNIVERSITY OF CALIFORNIA PRESS

University of California Press, one of the most distinguished university presses in the United States, enriches lives around the world by advancing scholarship in the humanities, social sciences, and natural sciences. Its activities are supported by the UC Press Foundation and by philanthropic contributions from individuals and institutions. For more information, visit www.ucpress.edu.

University of California Press
Oakland, California

Library of Congress Cataloging-in-Publication Data

Names: Wang, Zheng, 1952– author.
Title: Finding women in the state : a socialist feminist revolution in the
    People's Republic of China, 1949–1964 / Wang Zheng.
Description: Oakland, California : University of California Press, [2017] |
    Includes bibliographical references and index.
Identifiers: LCCN 2016015706 (print) | LCCN 2016017275 (ebook) |
    ISBN 9780520292284 (cloth : alk. paper) | ISBN 9780520292291
    (pbk. : alk. paper) | ISBN 9780520965867 (ebook)
Subjects: LCSH: Women—China—Social conditions. | Feminism—Political
    aspects—China—History—1949–1976. | Motion pictures—Social
    aspects—China—History—1949–1976. | Socialism and motion pictures—
    China—History—1949–1976.
Classification: LCC HQ1767 .W3895 2017 (print) | LCC HQ1767 (ebook) |
    DDC 305.40951—dc23
LC record available at https://lccn.loc.gov/2016015706

25 24 23 22 21 20 19 18 17 16
10 9 8 7 6 5 4 3 2 1

*To the memory of my parents, Li Guanghui and
Wang Yusheng*

CONTENTS

ILLUSTRATIONS

ACKNOWLEDGMENTS

This project has evolved from my original research on a Shanghai neighborhood twenty years ago. Over the past two decades I have accumulated enormous debts to numerous people who helped me in the formation of the book. My greatest debt is to everyone in China who granted me interviews and / or introduced me to more interviewees or generously shared source materials with me. I am very grateful to each one in the list of interviewees (included toward the end of the book) who illuminated opaque and complex historical processes with their highly diverse stories from various social and geographic locations. The dense files with fading handwriting in the archives became legible and meaningful when I read them with the vivid life stories of each interviewee in mind. It is well known that access to the archives of the post-1949 period in China is restricted and unpredictable. This project that investigated behind-the-scenes stories was made possible due to the generous help of many old and new friends. My deepest gratitude goes to those who gave me materials in their own collection or helped me to collect source materials, either oral, written, or visual. Zen Li, Zen Zi, Shang Shaohua, Chen Fang, Tao Chunfang, Hou Di, Chen Wenjing, Liu Jun, Lu Ming, Yang Hui, Jiang Lifen, Su Ping, Zhang Liming, Luo Suwen, Wang Qingshu, Huang Ganying, Lu Zhengmin, Zhao Wei, Liao Xinwen, Chen Xiangdong, Chen Xiangjun, Feng Mandong, Huang Zhun, Wang Yongfang, Feng Qi, Li Xiefu, Meng Liye, Chen Yan, and Yu Ningping each enabled me to construct a historical narrative with concrete evidence of socialist state feminist endeavors. I also deeply appreciate Francisca de Haan's tremendous generosity in sharing with me precious source materials on the Women's International Democratic Federation and informing me of the important roles Chinese state feminists played in it.

At a time when I still regarded my published articles on state feminists as sideline products of my neighborhood project, it was Gail Hershatter who first suggested that I should consider producing a book on feminism in the People's Republic of China. I owe the initial envisioning of the project to her. In the final stage of the manuscript, Dorothy Ko gave me valuable suggestions on the structure of the book. The highly helpful comments by her and three anonymous readers of the UC Press importantly shaped the reorganization of the final version. Grey Osterud commented on each chapter with valuable editorial suggestions that compelled me to strive for clarity in expressing complex issues to an English reading public who may not all be familiar with PRC history. Claire Moses generously offered me her editorial expertise by carefully going through each page of the manuscript and making many wonderful suggestions that enabled me to present a more coherent and clearly argued historical narrative. The book would not be in its current shape without her sharp insights in the final revision.

Many friends and colleagues have read and commented on the entire work, or on parts of it, over the long process of producing this book. I am grateful to Gail Hershatter, Dorothy Ko, Sidonie Smith, Mrinalini Sinha, Abigail Stewart, Emily Honig, the late Elisabeth Croll, the late Christina Gilmartin, Harriet Evans, Julia Strauss, Elizabeth Remick, Deborah Davis, Yiching Wu, Xiaobing Tang, David Goodman, Ellen Johnston Laing, Joan Cadden, Nikki Mandell, Carol Boyd, Deborah Keller-Cohen, Susan Siegfried, Anna Kirkland, Elizabeth Cole, Song Shaopeng, and Li Nanyang. Their suggestions and questions have either challenged me to sharpen my arguments or assisted me in exploring ways to synthesize my diverse findings from various sites. This historical narrative of socialist state feminists in China could not have been brought into existence without their tremendous support, generous help, and strong encouragement.

Colleagues at many institutions and academic meetings in and outside the United States have kindly offered me opportunities to present work-in-progress. The feedback and responses from colleagues attending conferences at SOAS at University of London; Fairbank Center for East Asian Studies at Harvard University; Pembroke Center at Brown University; History Department at University of California at Davis; Agnes Scott College and Emory University; Lieberthal-Rogel Center for Chinese Studies at University of Michigan; School for Advanced Studies in Social Sciences in Paris; Chinese Women's Research Committee in South Korea at Soongsil University; Chinese University of Hong Kong; Advanced Research Institute at Nanjing University, Nanjing Normal University; Fudan University; Women's Studies Center at Shantou University; Guangxi University; Women's Studies Center at Northeast Normal University; and East China Normal University—have helped sharpen my arguments.

Early versions of chapters 3 and 5 were presented in Chinese in China. Zhu Jian provided insightful comments on visual images in *Women of China* presented in my early piece; Liu Huiying's critical questions on Chen Bo'er urged me to trace this feminist artist's life journey; Lü Xinyu, Xiaobing Tang, Su Zhuang, and Wang Xiangxian commented on a longer Chinese version about Chen Bo'er. Their suggestions and responses helped me clarify my arguments in my English version while keeping the book's future Chinese readers in mind.

Students at University of Michigan and Fudan University, some of whom having now embarked on careers of their own, provided indispensable support for my research and technical needs. A special thanks to Prof. Chen Yan at Fudan University for recommending excellent graduate students to be my research assistants. Hou Yanxin provided unfailing professional assistance for archival and online search; Tang Chunhui made digital copies of each cover of *Women of China;* Jia Qinhan helped copy crucial archival files when I had to return to Michigan to teach; Liu Yi helped search for sources in libraries and archives and obtained permissions for some visual images; and Gao Jingwen provided technical support. At UM Ying Zhang, Sarah M. Brooks, Li Xu, Eric Couillard, Yidi Li, Yucong Hao, Joshua Hubbard, Guo Yihua, and Mi Zhao have assisted me in multiple ways through the long years when the book was in the making. A special thanks to Jidong Yang (before he moved to Stanford) and Liangyu Fu at the UM Asian Languages library, who came to my rescue numerous times when I was in urgent need of checking a source. Without their crucial assistance I would not have been able to extend the scope of the project. I also want to thank Northeast Normal University's Prof. Wang Jing for recommending her student Dong Xuejiao to assist me in collecting sources from the Changchun Film Studio; and Prof. Hu Xiaohong, who invited me to Changchun and accompanied me to the Museum of Changchun Film Studio that was built on the original site of the studio. There I was thrilled to see a life-size sculpture of Chen Bo'er in the center of the group statues of founders of the studio.

My very special thanks go to artist Hung Liu, who expressed her astute understanding and enthusiastic support of my project through her book cover design. Her tremendous generosity and artistic creativity grace this book and fulfill my wishes. I had been deeply moved by her large-scale paintings of *Daughters of China* before I discovered Chen Bo'er's crucial role in producing the original film. The kindred feminist spirit shared in our discussions on visual representation of a Chinese socialist feminist history refreshed and stimulated an author bogged down in a long writing process.

The first six months of fieldwork in China related to this project were made possible by an American Council of Learned Societies Research Award. A Stanford Humanities Center Fellowship enabled transcribing oral histories and sorting out archival materials collected as well as the writing of early versions of the first chapter. Over the years, the Lieberthal-Rogel Center for Chinese Studies at University of Michigan provided multiple research grants for my summer fieldwork in China; and a Faculty Development Fund Grant, a Research Grant of the School of Literature, Science and Arts, and a Michigan Humanities Award—all internal funding from the University of Michigan— crucially sustained the expanding scope of my research and allowed for follow- up interviews. A grant from the Associate Professor Support Fund of LS&A, a Michigan Faculty Fellowship of the Institute for the Humanities, and an ADVANCE Faculty Summer Writing Grant at UM enabled a focused writing period with needed editorial assistance that resulted in the final completion of the project. I am very grateful to friends and colleagues who took the time to recommend me to various grants: Susan Mann, Gail Hershatter, Dorothy Ko, Marilyn Young, Abigail Stewart, Mary Gallagher, and Sidonie Smith.

Although multiple grants from the Ford Foundation, the Henry Luce Foundation, and Oxfam were awarded only to my activist projects in China over the past two decades, I sincerely thank them for enabling me to be solidly situated in the evolving Chinese feminist history not only as a scholar who was writing a history about Chinese feminism but also as an activist who was doing history together with diverse communities of Chinese feminists transnationally. My activist projects in China have made a huge difference in my scholarship, in terms of expanding highly important social networks for research, gaining deeper knowledge of behind-the-scenes feminist maneuvers, and feeling the pulse of rapid changes in the political currents of both the Chinese feminist movement and the larger society. As a historian of Chinese feminism, I certainly understand the importance of the resources provided by these foundations to the continuing feminist struggles in contemporary China. I want to acknowledge the contribution of the behind-the-scenes feminists who made decisions to fund feminist initiatives.

My elder siblings in China have provided unfailing support whenever I called upon them during the long years of my archival research and fieldwork. My sisters Xiuzhi and Xiujun frequently babysat my children, together with my brothers-in-law Zhuo Zonghua and Zhang Yuanchang, and served numerous delicious meals to my children when they were still at preschool age in the beginning of this project. My brother Xiaoyou and my sister-in-law Gong Lianfang graced them with gifts and entertainments. My brother Xiyou and my sister-in-law Li Shengying warmly hosted my children when we traveled to Xi'an. Love and care from their aunties and uncles have given my children many precious memories since their childhood when they followed me to China each year and then stayed there for a couple of years, and gave me much needed time and peace of mind for research and activism. Their father, John Palmer, shouldered much of the childcare responsibility when the children were young, which allowed me to focus on my writing of early versions of the first two chapters. And I thank my children, Xiayi Palmer and Liya Palmer, for the tremendous joy they have brought to my life. Now well into adulthood, my children provide me the greatest delight when we engage in discussions on all sorts of topics, including feminism in and outside China.

I dedicate this book to my loving parents, who had passed away before I embarked on the journey of becoming a historian.

Early versions of several chapters in this book have appeared in the following publications: "'State Feminism?' Gender and Socialist State Formation in Maoist China," *Feminist Studies* 31, no. 3 (Fall 2005): 519–51; "Dilemmas of Inside Agitators: Chinese State Feminists in 1957," *China Quarterly* 188 (December 2006): 59–78; "Creating a Socialist Feminist Cultural Front: *Women of China* 1949–1966," *China Quarterly* 204 (December 2010): 827–49; and "Chuangjian shehuizhuyi nüquanzhuyi wenhua zhendi: Zhongguo funü" [Creating a socialist feminist cultural front: *Women of China*], *Journal of Nanjing University* 47, no. 6 (2010): 58–75.

Introduction

IN 1936 AN ESSAY ENTITLED "The Female-Centered Film and the Male-Centered Society" appeared in *Women's Life,* a left-oriented feminist magazine published in Shanghai. The author cautioned readers not to take the popularity of female movie stars as an indicator of women's liberation, and then proceeded to present a critical analysis of unequal power relations in a male-dominated capitalist society in which the film industry was reducing female actors to sex objects catering to male desires.[1] The author of this radical feminist political position was herself a rising movie star, the twenty-eight-year-old Chen Bo'er. In 1946, after Japan's surrender at the end of World War II, she was sent by Zhou Enlai, the vice chair of the military committee of the Chinese Communist Party (CCP), to take over the Manchuria Film Studio in northeast China. There, Chen became a founder of the socialist film industry of the People's Republic of China (PRC) and in that capacity is a protagonist in this book. Another protagonist is Shen Zijiu, the editor-in-chief of *Women's Life* who had invited Chen to write her essay, and a renowned social activist ten years Chen's senior who had founded and run the magazine with the support of her circle of left-oriented friends. Shen later became the editor-in-chief of *Women of China,* the only women's magazine circulating nationally during the early years of the PRC. Both women were elected to the Executive Committee of the All-China Democratic Women's Federation (ACDWF, later ACWF) upon its founding in April 1949; this nationwide umbrella organization brought together leading feminists of the Republican era (1912–49) who had been members of the CCP or sympathized with the Communist Revolution. This book centers on many feminists like Chen and Shen who joined the Chinese Communist Party in the course of the Communist Revolution (1921–49) and held powerful positions in the socialist state after the founding of the PRC in 1949.

The concentration of revolutionary women and men from diverse backgrounds in a political party formed amidst the cross-currents of feminism, anarchism, socialism, liberalism, nationalism, and Marxism in the early twentieth century and shaped by decades of military combat, political strife, and violent suppression by their enemies, including Chinese local warlords, imperialist colonizers, Japanese fascists, and the Nationalist government, led to messy interpersonal entanglements and left behind an extremely complex historical legacy. Revolutionary women and men with passionate convictions, if diverse visions, of a socialist modern China shaped the complicated dynamics and multifaceted struggles in the CCP's highly volatile and historically contingent experiment of establishing a socialist state. This book investigates the internal workings of the CCP in the contentious processes of socialist state formation and cultural transformation from a gender perspective and illuminates a persistent "gender line" in the struggles within high politics.

The stories in this book question the assumption of the total dominance of a socialist state patriarchy. To some extent, this study also questions conceptualizations of masculinist state power in any political system that rule out possibilities of women's subversive action in state processes. The issue here is not only to recognize women's agency but also to reconceptualize state power. Can a feminist theory of state critical of all dimensions of state power also account for sites and effects of feminist negotiation and intervention in dispersed state processes? Different from Wendy Brown's preoccupation with "finding the man in the state," *finding women* in the socialist state is the focus of this book.[2]

KEY WORD: FEMINISM

Throughout this book, I repeatedly use the words "feminist," "socialist feminists," "state feminists," and "cultural front" when naming my protagonists and their activities. I have chosen these words because they resonate with present-day usage and the relevant literature examining similar views and practices in the histories of other countries. But as with any work that relies on translating from documents and interviews in a language other than English, my wording can be viewed as arbitrary; some explanation may therefore be in order.

"Feminist" here refers to the view that women and men are equals, although the meaning and form of "equality" is inevitably the object of intense debate. In its broadest sense, feminism was one of the many ideologies embraced by educated Chinese in their pursuit of modernity and rejection of an ancient dynastic system. Sometime around 1900, the Chinese term *nüquan* began to appear in Chinese translations of foreign feminist texts, mostly Japanese that used the neologism to refer to "women's rights or power."[3] *Nüquan* was quickly adopted by those who questioned the gendered social arrangements prescribed and elaborated by ancient Chinese philosophers and male literati with the specific term *nannü*, men and women, denoting China's ancient gender system.[4] Against the Confucian ideal of *nannü youbie* [gender differentiation] and *nannü shoushou buqin* [gender segregation], Chinese feminists expressed a different imagining of a better future: a more humane society that centered on social justice and equality, a modern society that allowed individuals to break free from the constraints of Confucian patriarchal social norms embedded in kinship relations as well as from the control of an imperial polity, and / or a stronger nation that turned China from being the prey of imperialist powers into a sovereign state. Regardless of the differences in their political positions, reformers, revolutionaries, professionals, and educated women and men from elite social backgrounds who advocated various versions of feminism agreed on the necessity of changing gender practices in transforming their ancient civilization, which had fallen into deep crisis in a time of imperialist and colonialist expansion. The confluence of diverse and often contradictory ideas and practices rapidly came together to turn the neologism *nüquan* into a key word in early twentieth-century China. Related terms such as *nannü pingdeng* [equality between men and women], a Chinese rendition of the English phrase "sexual equality" that had been circulating globally since the late nineteenth century,[5] and *nüquan zhuyi* [the ism of women's rights or power] that emerged in the first decade of the Republic of China following the revolution toppling the Qing dynasty (1644–1911) were also increasingly popular.

With the birth of the New Culture Movement promoting its circulation to a wider audience, *nüquan zhuyi* as a Chinese rendition of "feminism," in particular, gained increasing currency for its advantage as a continuation of the by-then common word *nüquan* and for its explicit association of "-ism" with "women's rights or power." Marked by Chen Duxiu's publication of the *New Youth* magazine in 1915, the New Culture Movement rapidly became a rallying point for cultural radicals aiming to transform dominant Confucian morality and cultural practices in order to modernize China. Gender hierarchy, gender differentiation, gender segregation, double sexual standards that demanded chastity of women while legitimizing polygamy, and cultural practices ritualized in the service of maintaining a deeply entrenched hierarchical society that was fundamentally based on the dominance of men over women, were highlighted as the quintessential symbol of the backwardness of Confucian culture defined as "feudalist" (*fengjian zhuyi*). In turn, feminism (*nüquan zhuyi*) was enthusiastically embraced as a powerful weapon to combat this "feudalism."

The small circle of cultural radicals, which included the future CCP founders Chen Duxiu and Li Dazhao, rapidly expanded its social and intellectual influence after May 4, 1919, when college and secondary school students spearheaded a nationwide patriotic movement. Incensed by the treaty signed by world powers at the Versailles Conference that transferred all of Germany's rights in Shandong Province to Japan after World War I, the May Fourth Movement, with its vehemently anti-imperialist female and male students as major constituents, became a powerful vehicle that carried the New Culture's advocacy of anti-feudalism, including the promotion of feminism, into mainstream urban society. Women's equal educational and employment opportunities, and freedom to socialize with men that would end centuries of gender segregation, were seen as the foundation for women's liberation, *funü jiefang* (another feminist term rapidly gaining ascendance in the May Fourth feminist movement). Pursuing equality in all spheres of life and achieving an independent personhood became the hallmarks of May Fourth women's feminist subjectivities. Many May Fourth feminists—by definition, educated women and men—later played important roles in China's political, social, and cultural transformations.[6] From the two cohorts, older New Culturalists and younger May Fourth Movement student participants, emerged a small group of men and women, disillusioned with the Western liberal but imperialist powers, who formed the Communist Party in 1921, modeled after the newly founded Soviet Union, and openly endorsed "equality between men and women" in its platform.[7]

Even though many high-profile May Fourth feminists joined the CCP, the term *nüquan zhuyi*, "feminism," began to lose favor within the Party when CCP feminists came into contact with Western socialists and communists and adopted their view that "feminism" was "bourgeois"—a discursive practice that had originated out of the rivalries between radical suffragists and socialist women in the early twentieth century.[8] Nonetheless, CCP feminists

The term "state feminists" in this book specifically refers to feminists in the CCP who took on various official posts after the CCP gained control of the state in 1949. Here I am adopting the transnationally circulating term "state feminists" that social scientists first deployed decades ago to refer to feminists employed as bureaucrats in positions of power or women politicians who promoted gender equality policies in Scandinavia, and is now conceptualized to enable scholarly examinations of the institutionalization of feminism in state agencies in a variety of political and economic systems.[10] The term has also been adopted in scholarly discussions of the Chinese socialist state's gender policies but with a significant twist.[11] When applied to China it often portrays a paradoxical image of a state patriarch championing women's liberation, although with vacillation and inconsistency. Parallel to this conceptual chasm also exists a methodological difference between studies on women and the Chinese socialist state and studies on feminism in capitalist democratic states. In the latter case, documenting feminists' engagement with state power and identifying individual feminist actors in the process of shaping pro-women policies or institutions often constitute the main body of a study. Works on "femocrats" in Australia and the Netherlands are good examples of in-depth ethnographic studies of a transformative political process.[12] But studies on Chinese socialist state's gender policies are generally content with an abstract concept of the "party-state" without investigating the concrete policy-making process.[13] It is never clear how pro-women laws and policies came to be initiated and passed by a patriarchal centralized power structure.

The conceptual chasm and methodological difference in dealing with "state feminism" are symptomatic of a lingering Cold War paradigm of a "totalitarian Communist party-state" in the field of Chinese studies.[14] By ignoring fissures, contradictions, gaps, and conflicts inherently embedded in the formation of the socialist state, and by assuming the impossibility of expressions of feminist agency in the male-dominated power structure, a masculinist fixation on power struggles among top male leaders in high politics has effectively worked to erase feminist contentions in the socialist state. At the same time, feminist criticism of a centralized socialist patriarchal state has also become a blindfold that prevents us from seeing subversive women in the state and from exploring theoretical implications of gender transformations and feminist possibilities generated in the process of building a socialist state. As a result, the gendered internal workings of the "party-state" remain uninvestigated; inside feminist agitators are unknown; and conventional assumptions persist.[15]

"Socialist state feminists" are the lead characters of the history I narrate here. Although feminist officials did not call themselves "socialist state feminists," I have chosen to define my subjects in this way in order to illuminate the dynamics that shaped their work and explore its historical significance and highlight a gender line in the Communist Revolution and the PRC that mainstream narratives generally overlook. First, positioning CCP officials as *feminists* points to the tenacity with which they held to the May Fourth feminist vision of equality between women and men. Second, defining them as *socialist feminists,* I stress their goal of women's "thorough" liberation and their commitment to the "masses" of women. Third, emphasizing their positions in the *state* brings into focus the important feminist endeavors that contributed to political, economic, social, and cultural transformations in the PRC that effectively enabled the social advancement of millions of Chinese women, and whose erasure from history seriously hinders an adequate understanding of this unique period. Finally, in tracing these socialist state feminists' interactions with male officials and CCP leaders, I illuminate the historical processes in which, as depicted in much scholarship on socialist China, the socialist state appeared as a paradoxically "woman-friendly" patriarchal party-state that sporadically promoted gender equality. By investigating socialist state feminists' activities, contentions, and struggles in the formation of the socialist state, I expose diverse and even contradictory visions and actions underneath the conventional image of a monolithic party-state that was presumably gendered male, stable, and depersonalized (if not outright dehumanized). An adequate understanding of Chinese socialism and its politics, I insist, has to include the stories of these socialist state feminists who fought at multiple fronts—in their *formal* capacities as Communist Party members and state officials—toward an egalitarian vision of a socialist modern China premised on equality between women and men.

THE PAST AS PROLOGUE: WOMEN IN
THE CHINESE COMMUNIST REVOLUTION

The scope of feminists' involvement in the formation of the socialist state may be represented with a brief review of women's participation in the long

Communist Revolution. Hundreds of thousands of women from diverse social backgrounds became members of the CCP, the first cohort having joined in the 1920s. Most early Communist women were urban-based educated feminists of the May Fourth generation, and some were factory workers active in the CCP-led workers' movement. Many in this cohort died either during the Nationalist Party's persecution of Communists after the breakup of the first United Front between the CCP and the NP (1924–27) or in the subsequent military battles. The survivors of this cohort served in various official posts at the national level in the early PRC, including the two top leaders of the CCP-led women's movement who founded the ACDWF: Cai Chang, a May Fourth activist who had joined the CCP in 1923 when she was in France; and Deng Yingchao, a renowned young feminist leader in Tianjin in the May Fourth feminist movement before she joined the CCP in 1925. Other prominent leaders included Zhang Yun, vice chair of the ACDWF, and Yang Zhihua, director of the Women Workers Department of the All-China Trade Union.[16] For the surviving first cohort of CCP women, the men they married in their youth who also survived ferocious battles either on the military fronts or in political fields rose to the top of the new PRC's power structure. The young man whom Deng Yingchao married in 1925, Zhou Enlai, would become the PRC's first premier, while the young man whom Cai Chang married in 1923 in Paris, Li Fuchun, would become the vice premier.

The second cohort was mainly composed of rural women who joined the Communist Revolution when the CCP established its rural military base areas after the breakup of the first United Front. CCP membership swelled from over forty thousand in 1928 to over three hundred thousand in 1934. Many rural women were involved in guerrilla warfare and the Soviet-style local government in the CCP base areas in southern and central China. After the CCP's military defeat by the NP forces in 1934, however, only ten percent of the Communist troops survived the almost two-year-long retreat and relocation, which Mao Zedong later named "the Long March." Among the Communist women who survived the ordeal and reached the CCP's new base areas in the northwest in late 1935, several rural women guerrilla leaders from the second cohort rose to leadership at the national level, including Kang Keqing, who became the vice chair of the ACWF in 1957 and the chair from 1978 to 1988.[17]

The third cohort joined the CCP in the War of Resistance against Japan's invasion, especially after July 1937 when Japanese troops advanced beyond the borders of Manchukuo, their puppet state, seized in 1931. This military advance, a marker of the start of the second Sino-Japanese War (1937–45), ignited a full-scale military resistance, with the NP and CCP forming their second United Front to save China. Patriotic zeal for national salvation as well as dislocation caused by the war drove hundreds of thousands of urban students and young professionals to the CCP bases areas established in peripheral rural areas around the desolate rural town in the northwest, Yan'an, that was now the CCP headquarters. Party membership expanded dramatically from about forty thousand in 1937 to over eight hundred thousand in 1940. From this cohort some urban celebrities, including Chen Bo'er and Shen Zijiu, later took on leading official posts in various branches of the central government of the early PRC. Other women students in this cohort also became important in a second tier of dedicated leaders of the ACWF; a few of them, such as Luo Qiong and Dong Bian, appear in this book. In most cases educated women in the third cohort became officials at the provincial or municipal levels, and rural women with little education staffed the county governments or lower-level posts. Because women who were appointed to the leading positions at national and provincial levels in the early PRC were mainly those with a secondary or college education when they joined the CCP, they are the central focus in this study of socialist state feminists. The group of state feminists certainly includes women officials with less education working at diverse local levels.

The fourth cohort joined the CCP during the civil war between the CCP and the NP in the late 1940s, after Japan's surrender. This cohort was more diverse, including urban young students, factory workers, professionals, and rural women from both the old CCP base areas and newly occupied regions. Many in this cohort would staff the new socialist state's local governments, as well as Women's Federations at the urban district or street and rural county or township level. By the time of the CCP's victory in 1949 its membership had expanded to 4.49 million, of whom 11.9 percent were women.[18] Integrating these 530,000 CCP women into our understanding of socialist China is a crucial step toward engendering the Chinese revolution, an agenda proposed by the late historian Christina K. Gilmartin in her work on radical women of the CCP in the 1920s, which has remained largely unfulfilled.[19]

Perhaps more important than the number of Communist women are the shared characteristics of the different cohorts. Outlawed except during the brief periods when the CCP and the NP formed temporary alliances, CCP members either worked underground in urban settings with their real identity as a Communist revolutionary disguised, or resided in rural military camps that frequently engaged in battles with the Nationalist army, local warlords, or invading Japanese troops. The drive to risk their lives in a perilous revolution was most prominently explained in CCP women's memoirs and interviews by their experiences of gender oppression from childhood to adulthood. Some literally ran away from an impending arranged marriage or from an abusive husband or in-laws to the Communist camp that in a sense served as a shelter for women who had no other refuge from the blows rained down on them, all permissible in the Chinese gender system.[20] In other words, while not every Communist woman was necessarily a conscious feminist, situated in a Chinese gender system, each would feel attracted to and empowered by the CCP's slogan of equality between men and women. The strong appeal of the CCP to women was attested to by Chiang Kai-shek's perplexed lament after his Nationalist Party was driven from the mainland to Taiwan, "Why did women all go to the Communist Party?"[21] Moreover, given that ninety percent of Chinese women were still illiterate in 1949, educated women (the focus of this study) were predominantly from families with some degree of social privilege. Their choice to risk their lives by joining an embattled political force, either to pursue an idealistic dream or to escape from predicaments in their personal life as a woman, or both, indicates the presence of a clear political consciousness and commitment, as well as a strong will and inclination toward action.

How did socialist state feminists act out *their* dreams and visions in their daily practices of socialist feminist transformation of China? In what ways did enacting a socialist feminist project generate significant changes as well as new antagonisms in a socialist country? Such questions open up new vistas to a relatively recent past that has almost been sealed by a reductive and one-dimensional depiction of a totalitarian polity. Most definitely, the existence of these Communist women revolutionaries requires historians to adopt a historical perspective that does not mechanically sever the identity of the CCP as a state power holder from its former identity as a grassroots organizer and revolutionary outlaw. Embodied in these historical actors, the two diametrically opposed roles of the CCP were played out in the lives of the surviving CCP members, who (for better or for worse) endeavored to blend the two roles rather than allow them to be separated, especially since grassroots mobilizing and organizing held the key to the CCP's victory and "the mass line" was theorized as a fundamental principle of the Party. Accordingly, relying on a dichotomous sociological model of "top-down" versus "bottom-up" would be inadequate when approaching the Chinese socialist state feminism embodied in the generation of Communist revolutionaries.

Two realms of feminist endeavors are the focus of this book: the All-China Women's Federation and the film industry. Together they constitute what I refer to throughout the book as a "cultural front." Although "culture," which we normally associate with literature and the arts, may seem to be a peculiar designation for a state agency that organized women into governance structures, and "front," with its implication of militancy and struggle, may appear a peculiar designation for an entertainment film industry, in both cases the mission of providing the masses of women with representative models for a new socialist subjectivity is understood as essential to an ongoing anti-feudal revolution. Even organizationally, the two realms were not entirely distinct; for example, the founder of the socialist film industry Chen Bo'er, who introduces this book, was also on the executive committee of the ACDWF. This defies our conventional disciplinary divisions that would place an examination of the ACWF into the discipline of government and politics and Chen Bo'er into film studies. In this historical narrative tracing socialist state feminists' footprints, their agenda of cultural transformation brings together the ACWF and the film industry in their shared role in creating a cultural front that functioned to consolidate and expand a socialist feminist revolution of culture to a vast and largely illiterate population in a pre-television age via its massive institutional coverage.

The euphoria of socialist state feminists is evident in their staging of some of the earliest public events in the PRC, even before its official founding. The first was their March 1949 National Women's Congress—the very first national conference organized by any of the social groups convened in anticipation of a transfer of political power to plan for action in a socialist China. It was at this conference that it was resolved to set up a national women's organization, the All-China Democratic Women's Federation (its name was changed to All-China Women's Federation in 1957, hence ACWF), an umbrella organization that would horizontally unite all pro-CCP women's organizations and an official institution that would vertically reach all women down to the rural villages and urban neighborhoods nationwide (excluding students who would be organized in the Youth Association and workers who would be organized by the Trade Union).

Then, on December 10, 1949, only two months after the founding of the PRC, a significant *international* conference of the new socialist China was convened in Beijing. The All-Asian Women's Congress, attended by 197

FIGURE 1. Three top women leaders—Cai Chang, Deng Yingchao, and Song Qinglin—attending the All-Asian Women's Congress in December 1949. Courtesy of Hung Liu.

representatives from 23 countries, was organized by the ACDWF in its new role as a member of the Women's International Democratic Federation (WIDF) (fig. 1). Hosting an international conference on women when only about ten socialist countries had established diplomatic relationships with the PRC indicated the CCP leadership's full support for this initiative. The event not only demonstrated state feminists' conscious efforts to merge the women's movement in the PRC with socialist women's movements globally; it also revealed the crucial role the ACDWF played in the new socialist state's efforts to establish international connections. The chair of the ACDWF, Cai Chang, served as vice president of the WIDF from 1948 to 1958.[22]

Additionally, it was the ACWF (still known as the ACDWF) that was charged with promulgating the 1950 Marriage Law. CCP feminists had been working on this since late September 1948, even before the founding of the

ACWF, when the Party Central assigned the Central Committee of Women-Work a task: to draft a Marriage Law for a new socialist China. Chairing a group of six CCP feminists of the first three cohorts, Deng Yingchao provided strong leadership in drafting a feminist law, the first law passed in the PRC.[23] A central debate among the members of the drafting committee concerned the freedom to divorce. Some CCP women officials supported restrictions on divorce in order to deter male CCP officials from replacing their old wives with young urban-educated women once they moved from the rural bases to the major cities and assumed privileged positions in the new state. But Deng Yingchao insisted on removing these restrictions on the ground that the law should prioritize the interest of the vast majority of women, that is, rural women. Poor rural women who were sold to men or endured an abusive marital life needed a divorce law that could assist their escape from such predicaments.

Coordinating support from multiple branches of different levels of government, including film and other fields of cultural production, the ACDWF turned the promulgation and enforcement of the Marriage Law into a powerful mass campaign promoting women's equal rights and personal freedom. The May Fourth language of "anti-feudalism" as the expression of women's equal rights and independent personhood was widely circulated among the vast population in this period, and the Chinese term "feudalism" (*fengjian zhuyi*) quickly became a gender-inflected key word encompassing everything we today call sexism, masculinism, patriarchy, male chauvinism, and / or misogyny. Even illiterate women in rural areas could deploy the term effortlessly.[24] "Equality between men and women" and "women's liberation," popularized via state-owned media and cultural production, became household slogans intimately connecting gender equality with the authority of the new socialist state. The feminist law promulgated with socialist state power, although encountering ferocious resistance in its implementation, significantly transformed not only the marriage institution but also gendered cultural practices and discourses.

The subject of Part II of this book, socialist film production infused with feminism was also a militant in the feminist cultural front. Its significance cannot be overstated given that, before the advent of television, film was the most accessible and influential medium in socialist China, where 80 percent of the population was illiterate. The CCP had paid tremendous attention to the film industry even before they gained state power. The founding of the PRC enabled the Party to turn the now-nationalized film industry into a key location for cultural production in the process of socialist construction and cultural transformation. As such the film industry became a center of intense ideological and political struggles as well as artistic strife. From this highly unstable and fiercely contested field emerged a vast range of films centering on representations of revolutionary heroines in both war and peace that constituted a prominent feature of socialist culture.

Curiously, while some post-socialist film scholars have clearly noticed this conspicuous feature of Chinese socialist films, their examinations do not lead to an excavation of feminist endeavors behind the scenes. Relying on visual analysis of the films, they have examined how the socialist representational mode, prominently featuring revolutionary heroines in leading roles, is accomplished through a confluence of scenario, lens, angle, lighting, composition, background music, acting, editing, and so on; and how the cinematic language and narrative structures in visual representations of gender performativity were distinctively different from gender representation in classic Hollywood movies. Rather than seeing this as a puzzle calling for historical research, such distinctive gender representation in socialist film has instead served as film scholars' evidence that the representation of revolutionary heroines demonstrates the patriarchal socialist state's "masculinization" of women by erasing their "innate femininity."[25]

Few film studies scholars who have looked at socialist films have concerned themselves with the questions that this book explores: What went on behind the scenes in the production process that produced films centering on revolutionary heroines with gender representation distinctively different from conventional Hollywood modes of gender representation? Who contended for aesthetic and political control in visual representation, by what means, and for what purposes? My historical research, in a sense, questions the methodological and conceptual adequacies in the conventional field of film studies when applied to socialist cinema. An adequate understanding of socialist films cannot be separated from an investigation of the specific political context and the actual filmmakers and production crews. The production of socialist films, an openly acknowledged political act in an art form, was intimately entangled in the politics of the time, in which diverse and complicated forces were involved in intense contentions. While the final products obviously became part of socialist political culture, the fierce struggles behind the scenes were never transparent to viewers or scholars. I insist that only when we illuminate this opaque process can we understand the significance of the final products in their historical context, complicating our comprehension of socialist China beyond the prevailing assumption of a one-dimensional authoritarian state. Indeed, projecting researchers' own values and aesthetic standards shaped in a specific location and political moment onto a visual text produced in a different time and place without a historical approach—a prevalent practice in post-socialist film critiques in China as well as in film studies outside China—is among the reasons that have led to the erasure of Chinese socialist state feminists' historical endeavors of cultural transformation.[26]

How can feminist scholars maintain a critical stance that opposes masculinist power without erasing feminist revolutionaries' historical endeavors? Can we conceptualize the construction of a socialist state without reducing the state and the Party to an ahistorical, monolithic entity that conceals complex and fluid historical processes and contestations? In what ways may we avoid demonizing revolutionary ideals, including feminist revolutionaries' visions and pursuits of gender and class equality, even as we condemn the colossal blunders and actual crimes that were committed in the name of the revolution? I think contextualized historical research may help us tease out significant historical actors and actions from extremely messy and entangled processes of a Chinese socialist revolution.

FINDING WOMEN IN THE STATE

Socialist state feminists have existed in a contradictory political environment. Ideologically, the Party's platform has endorsed a feminist pursuit of "equality between men and women," and the Constitution of the People's Republic of China grants legitimacy for feminist expressions and actions as it claims to uphold "equality between men and women." Institutionally, however, the various administrative levels of the CCP's leadership have always been predominantly occupied by men, many of whose subjectivities seem to have been shaped by a pervasive patriarchal culture rather than fundamentally transformed by feminist and socialist principles of eliminating all hierarchies.[27] In practice, the presumptions and power dynamics of male supremacy could overrule the ideological and legal legitimacy of feminist actions. A masculinist in a position of authority could easily tell a woman official who proposed an action on behalf of women's interests that he also believed in the importance of this issue, but more important and larger issues deserved the government's resources and energy and thus justified disabling feminist protest.

The ACWF, in particular, was organized as a Party-led mass organization rather than an executive branch of the government, although everyone in the Women's Federation system was also on the government payroll. As this book demonstrates, the distribution of power between this gender-based mass organization and the government was a contested matter in the beginning of the new socialist state. The subsequent institutional marginalization of the WF system in the socialist state structure has conditioned the routine experiences of women officials in the WF that women-work was of lesser value, except for those moments when some item on the Party's agenda required that women be mobilized. The WF embodied a dilemma evident from the earliest days of the CCP: the institutionalized women-work in the CCP, a prominent progressive stance superior to those political parties or forces that totally exclude or ignore women, was turned into a marginalized enclave of feminists within the political system of the CCP and, later, the socialist state. State feminists had to fight for political and material resources as well as recognition of women's interests and rights from an internally structured disadvantaged position.

The institutional subordination of the ACWF in the socialist state structure gave rise to a particular institutional behavior that shared some resemblance to that of any subordinate social group in the power relations of domination. State feminists in the WF system routinely operated in *a politics of concealment* in their endeavors to promote feminist agendas. Since singularly and openly raising a demand on behalf of women would have a slim chance of receiving the support of male authorities, WF officials learned to insert feminist items into the Party's agenda in order to gain legitimacy and resources for actions that had a clear gender dimension. Articulating their strong support of the Party's "central tasks," state feminists often embedded a "hidden script" that intended to advance women's diverse interests. In other words, camouflaging a feminist agenda with dominant Party language was a major principle in *the politics of concealment.* This book provides many examples of such state feminist discursive maneuvers in shifting political contexts.

In the early PRC the central feminist maneuver hinged on a major item in the CCP's revolutionary goal, anti-feudalism. After the Communist Revolution drove out imperialist and capitalist powers and eliminated "feudal power" based in rural land ownership with its land reform, state feminists persistently waged battles on "feudal remnants," turning "anti-feudalism" into a gender-specific word full of feminist implications and declaring it an unfinished task of the Communist Revolution. Thus, the state feminist *politics of concealment* expressed both their marginalization in the power structure and subversive possibilities in the socialist state. Their discursive maneuvers launched under cover of the dominant official language simultaneously blurred feminist traces and inscribed socialist mainstream ideology with deep feminist implications.

The second principle in *the politics of concealment* was self-effacement. The first cohort of socialist state feminists had long experience of operating in a male-dominated Party that often created a perilous political environment for feminists. Historically, the label of "narrow bourgeois feminism" was used as a political club to beat down those outspoken CCP feminists who insisted on the priority of women's interests or raised a critical voice against male chauvinism in the CCP.[28] In this historical context, it was not only necessary to camouflage their feminist agenda with legitimate, seemingly un-gendered Party slogans, but also crucially important to attribute their own accomplishments in the realm of women-work to the "wise leadership of the Party." This self-effacing performance gave extra weight to women-work by appealing to the authority of the Party and, more importantly, publicly acknowledged their role as a dutiful subordinate to the Party Central, or to the various administrative levels of the Party committees that were the immediate supervisors of the Women's Federations. In sum, a women's organization that aimed to transform gender hierarchy nevertheless staged a gendered performance in accordance with prevailing gender norms that extolled the womanly virtues of modesty, hard work, self-effacement, self-sacrifice, and a lack of desire for power and fame. Acting in accordance with this gender script could most effectively ease the possible irritation or even resentment of male authorities. By glossing over their struggles behind the scenes, this self-effacing rhetoric made it difficult for outsiders to glean state feminists' struggles from published official documents that deliberately projected a façade of Party unity or an image of a coherent party-state. It ensured that these dynamic women leaders were, and remained, unknown to the public. Receding into the shadows, socialist state feminists contributed to the myth of a monolithic patriarchal party-state that sporadically showed benevolence toward women.

However, the socialist state feminists' anonymity was not entirely due to the politics of concealment. It was also the result of *the politics of erasure* in two different temporalities. In the early PRC unexpectedly tumultuous themes of the socialist revolution often overwhelmed the feminist notes. In many political storms after the founding of the PRC, state feminists were sometimes the targets of deliberate suppression or the inadvertent casualties of power politics. Even when they were not affected personally, their feminist agenda would often be brushed aside by imperatives from the Party Central that left no room for feminist maneuver. In 1964 the intensifying Maoist class struggles enabled suppression of articulations of women's gender-specific interests, and an exclusive focus on the theme of class struggle replaced the theme of a gender-inflected anti-feudalism in cultural production. Socialist state feminists' conscious and persistent endeavors of transforming a "feudalist" culture and society were seriously thwarted, if not buried altogether, by the rising sound and fury of Maoist class struggle that became the prelude of the Cultural Revolution. The ACWF, paralyzed in 1966 like other official organs in the heat of the Cultural Revolution, did not resume its function until 1978.

The second major erasure of state feminists arose in the production of historical knowledge of socialism since the late 1970s, when the CCP began to depart from the socialist course after Mao's death in 1976. In Chinese intellectuals' concerted critique of the CCP's crimes under Mao's dictatorship, Mao became synonymous with socialism. This anti-socialist discourse is both grossly reductive and openly masculinist. In post-socialist elites' efforts to dismantle not only the CCP's authoritarian rule but also socialist economic and distribution systems, and socialist egalitarian values and practices, the mainstream socialist gender ideology and institutional mechanisms that promoted equality between women and men were characterized as the Maoist state's imposition of gender sameness, a crime of the CCP that distorted women's natural femininity and masculinized them. Restoring gender differentiation was promoted in the urban elites' two conflicting proposals: embracing a Western capitalist modernity symbolized by sexualized and commoditized women in advertisements; or reviving a Confucian tradition by retrieving so-called "Oriental women's traditional virtues." Rearranging gender practices became a prominent theme in elite proposals to undo the socialist revolution. The vehemence with which these ideas were advocated was strikingly similar to their forebears' passionate agitation for change in gender practices at the turn of the twentieth century, though pointing toward a reverse direction in their imagining of a gendered future. As many scholars have observed, this initiative constituted an open and powerful backlash against the gender policies of the socialist period.

In retirement or approaching retirement, many in the first generation of state feminists engaged in hyper-energetic publishing activities since the late

1970s, producing a large quantity of personal memoirs and collective histories of the women's movement in various regions all over China. Memoir and history writing became a key site for the first generation of state feminists to resist erasure and to claim their contributions to the Communist Revolution and to socialist women's advancement in the early PRC. However, produced at a time when a neoliberal embrace of capitalist consumerist modernity was on the rise with the Party's endorsement, their memories celebrating a feminist revolution in a bygone and denigrated socialist past gained little currency.

ENCOUNTERING SOCIALIST STATE FEMINISTS

No prior knowledge of socialist state feminists led me to this project. I encountered them unexpectedly. Like most scholars in Chinese women's history, in the early 1990s my mission was to resist the erasure of women's agency in the master narrative of the CCP that portrayed women before 1949 merely as victims of the old society. In 1996, after completing a dissertation on May Fourth feminists, I began working on a social history of the socialist transformation of urban society, starting with fieldwork in the Shanghai neighborhood where I was born and grew up. When I interviewed women who had been neighborhood activists during the early 1950s, I immediately noticed a couple of phrases unfamiliar to me. One was *fudaihui,* the women's congress; the other was *jiemeimen,* sisters. Women used these phrases in their reminiscences of how officials of the Shanghai Women's Federation came to the neighborhood to organize them and other housewives and their feelings of empowerment as they became involved. Sensing feminist activities signified by these key terms, I conducted research at the Shanghai Municipal Archives to verify my oral history materials. The copious files of the Shanghai Women's Federation and the Department of Civil Affairs demonstrate a massive mobilization of Shanghai housewives to engage them in the socialist reorganization and transformation of urban society. Reading the passionate and sometimes biting comments of officials of the Women's Federation advocating for women's interests, I realized that my previous understanding of CCP-led women's liberation was devoid of knowledge about concrete historical processes.

Shifting my research focus to those historical actors who promoted women's rights and interests in socialist China, I began to interview retired officials of the Shanghai Women's Federation (SWF) and then moved on to retired officials of the All-China Women's Federation (ACWF) and secretaries of its deceased top officials, Deng Yingchao and Luo Qiong (in total, twenty-nine retired WF officials). Talking face-to-face with these senior women and listening to each one's life story changed my perception of the official women's organization, which had been distorted by post-socialist critiques of a socialist women's liberation that was supposedly imposed on Chinese women by the party-state. Vague assumptions of a faceless patriarchal party-state were gradually replaced by the vivid voices and viewpoints of women who remained articulate, forceful, and dynamic even in their old age. As a historian who has always been interested in finding people who made a difference in history but whose stories were unknown to the public, I quickly realized that the work and ideas of socialist state feminists, who were once the driving force in engendering the social and cultural transformation of a patriarchal society, were being erased amidst China's departure from socialism.

My cohort of educated Chinese women was unaware of the endeavors of the Women's Federations in part because during the socialist period we were not their constituents. The CCP mobilized diverse populations in the project of socialist construction by organizing them in specific social groupings. Students were included in the Communist Young Pioneers (7–14 years old) and the Communist Youth League (14–28 years old); urban workers and professionals were organized by the Trade Union; and the Women's Federations focused primarily on urban housewives and rural peasants, who comprised the vast majority of women in the early PRC. Young educated urban women's lack of interest in the WF reflected our non-identification with the WF's constituency. Being socialized in a gender-neutral educational system and social organizations and shaped by a dominant gender ideology of "equality between men and women" and Engels's theory of women's liberation based on women's participation in social production, my cohort of educated urban women generally regarded being a housewife as a relic of the old feudal society. Ironically, the powerful effects of socialist state feminism placed the WF in low esteem in the eyes of "liberated" educated urban women because of its association with "backward" housewives who were confined to domesticity. Investigating the history of Chinese state feminism, for me, has involved a reflective process of reviewing and critiquing my own prejudices and misperceptions.[29]

Parallel to my research in China, my feminist activism facilitated my comprehension of the strategies of feminists operating within the official system.

In 1993 a group of Chinese women doctoral students in the United States started collaborating with scholars in China who were interested in research on women. We worked together to run feminist workshops and conferences and to publish feminist texts, including translations of feminist scholarship written in English, in order to promote feminist discourse and gender studies in China. Chinese participants included both academics involved in feminist activism and officials from the Women's Federations at different administrative levels and in diverse geographic locations. My continuing activities in China have given me access to many groups of women, beyond that of a researcher, as their partner in shared activist projects, or as a specialist whose expertise could be utilized in their programs. As a participant in ongoing feminist actions, I have had many opportunities to observe how feminists in and outside the official system maneuvered to achieve their goals; I have come to see the logic and rationales in their strategies and to notice how feminists in the official system could respond to the same situation very differently from their counterparts in similar positions. Individual feminists' distinct pursuits and personalities can make a huge difference in a bureaucratic institution. These points may sound commonsensical. But in the English-speaking world, where the assumption persists that officials in a Communist party-state are robotically programmed to carry out the central command, it is necessary to highlight the importance of the human side of political interactions.

Although the feminist academics and officials I have associated with through my own political and intellectual work are very different from the state feminists of the 1950s and 1960s whom I studied, their tactics often reminded me of what I was discovering in the archives, memoirs, and interviews with those in the early PRC. The continuity in the political system despite the dramatic social, economic, and cultural transformations since the late 1970s means that *the politics of concealment* has remained viable. Whether it was transmitted to the new generation of officials of the Women's Federations or has been reinvented by contemporary feminists without any knowledge of their foremothers' wisdom and frustrations, similar strategies and tactics illuminate the presence of feminist consciousness and similar feminist predicaments, as well as persistent structural constraints of an institutionalized political culture. I have identified two principles of *the politics of concealment* in the operation of the post-socialist state feminists of the WF system: engaging in discursive battles over key words to claim legitimacy and authority for promoting women's rights and interests; and publicly representing the WF's accomplishments in a self-effacing manner.

Not all special features of the first cohort of state feminists, however, have been re-created in different historical contexts. Though never in the center of the political power of the CCP, the first generation of ACWF leaders, with their own Party seniority, and with their husbands in the top echelon of the Party, simultaneously enjoyed tremendous institutional and informal power and suffered from deep entanglement in masculinist power struggles. Indeed, unexpected and seemingly inexplicable turns of political events often resulted from unpredictable dynamics in complicated personal relations formed in the long Communist Revolution. The leading state feminists and their feminist agendas could become inadvertent casualties in power politics in the early PRC. Therefore, this story of Chinese socialist state feminism emphasizes that the political is often personal, in addition to underlining the feminist insight that the personal is political.

Although my research has benefited from the social networks I built through my activism in China, restrictions on access to the ACWF's archives thwarted my ambition to systematically document its internal workings and delineate the full scope of its activities. I have been unable to follow the clues I found into new lines of inquiry. For instance, from the ACWF's published materials, it is clear to me that, by utilizing its membership in the International Democratic Women's Federation, the ACDWF played a major role in China's diplomacy as well as the international socialist women's movement in the early 1950s, when China was denied access to many international events beyond the socialist camp. That story could convincingly disprove another enduring myth, that in the Mao era China operated in total isolation from the rest of the world. But, without access to those precious archives, I have been unable to explore the transnational dimension of Chinese socialist feminism in the early PRC, although this large global context was crucial to the state feminists and the CCP in their efforts to build a socialist China.

Looking back, my frustration that I was denied use of the ACWF files now seems like a healthy corrective that prevented me from romanticizing an institution that was deeply embedded in the bureaucratic system of the Chinese state. As an inseparable part of the Communist Party in the project of forming a socialist state, the ACWF was always entangled, embedded, or implicated in a tragically ironic historical process in which a revolutionary Party aiming to establish an equalitarian society ended up creating a huge hierarchical bureaucracy and becoming a new privileged ruling class. State feminists' innovations in creating socialist democratic practices that enabled them to serve women's interests did not provide them with an alibi in an increasingly centralized and bureaucratized CCP. In fact, the quagmire of bureaucratization combined with internal contentions in the CCP was the political reality in which these youthful, daring, and idealistic feminists were situated. Transforming a patriarchal society while resisting or complying with being transformed or disciplined by a male-dominated Party constitutes a motif in the trajectory of their feminist struggles.

CONSTRUCTING A GENEALOGY
OF CHINESE FEMINISM

Scholarship on women, gender, and feminism in China has flourished in the past several decades, though with an obvious deficiency regarding the socialist period. Without access to all of the relevant archives and with the loss of the first cohort of the CCP feminists since I started my research, this history of socialist state feminism is necessarily incomplete, only representing an initial effort toward a history of the PRC from a gender perspective. Eventually, more research will emerge out of increasing access to the official archives and, perhaps more crucially, with the coming of age of a younger generation of feminist scholars in and outside China who are discontented with the hegemonic historical narrative exclusively focusing on male power holders in a historical era when China witnessed massive social, economic, cultural, and political advancement of women in the largest numbers.

This history of a socialist feminist revolution in the early PRC is organized into two parts. Part I, "The Women's Federation and the CCP," focuses on the WF system's efforts in its institutional building and feminist cultural transformation in the process of socialist state formation. The four chapters in this part highlight feminist contentions inside the CCP, operating in *the politics of concealment,* and demonstrate intense gender struggles in and outside the Party in socialist state feminists' endeavors to transform a patriarchal society. While these chapters show constant feminist battles on all fronts and at all levels, two moments of severe feminist setbacks are the focus of particular attention, 1957 and 1964 respectively, when the internal workings and power dynamics in the CCP were laid bare. The ACWF leaders' conscious feminist transformative agendas, I argue, had to fold in 1964 when the intensifying Maoist class struggles enabled rapid development of a pernicious political environment. A Maoist concept of "class" finally suppressed state feminists' critical articulations of gender hierarchy, gender norms, and gendered power relations.

Part II, "From Feminist Revolution of Culture to the Cultural Revolution," investigates socialist state feminists' innovations in film production as an important site for the feminist revolution of Chinese culture. Chapter 5 uncovers a long-neglected feminist founder of the socialist film industry, Chen Bo'er, whose pioneering role in creating a paradigm of revolutionary heroines in socialist films moved lower-class women to the center stage in the cultural representation of women's liberation as well as socialism. Chapter 6 focuses on a male feminist leader of the film industry, Xia Yan, whose artistic creativity continued a New Culture heritage of transforming a patriarchal culture in the socialist period. In chapter 7, the narrative turns to the dense entanglement of cultural production and power politics that was a prelude to the Cultural Revolution. A critical examination of Jiang Qing's rise in the cultural realm demonstrates that her key role in framing a "two-line struggle" in the film industry led to the elimination of an anti-feudalist agenda in socialist films and in the larger cultural realm as well.

My examination of feminism in the early PRC's social, political, and cultural realms suggests a new periodization for recent Chinese history. The moment when the ACWF's pursuit of a feminist agenda was disabled, the moment when Xia Yan was removed from the leadership of the film industry on charges that he followed a "revisionist line," and the moment when Jiang Qing's endeavor to revolutionize theater received official recognition were simultaneous and occurred within the same political context. If we shift our focus from power struggles between the top CCP leaders, Mao and Liu, to the cultural realm, we can see the Cultural Revolution actually began in 1964. Moreover, in its initial stage the Cultural Revolution *was* largely about complex contentions in the cultural realm, resulting in eliminating the May Fourth New Culture heritage of "anti-feudalism" in cultural production, although tensions between different artistic and political visions of a new socialist culture had long been mired in contentious personal relationships formed through the long course of the Communist Revolution.

Continuing my investigation of the politics of erasing socialist state feminist endeavors, chapter 8 extends my critical examination of discursive contentions into the post-socialist era. Condemnations of the dominance of the CCP since the 1980s have functioned to delegitimize all socialist transformative programs and policies, including gender equality. The political maneuvers of the post-socialist masculinist elite have succeeded in demolishing many of the mechanisms of the socialist period that addressed gender and class inequality, in part by obliterating the memory of the historical actors who strove to achieve a socialist feminist vision. This book stages a feminist historian's resistance to the erasure and distortion of socialist feminist struggles for human dignity as well as presents a historical analysis of the contentious forces and contingencies that contributed to the demise of a revolution for social justice and equality.

The Conclusion brings the narrative to the present state of feminist struggles in and outside the official system in China. In a drastically changed country where "comrades" have metamorphosed into "consumers" and, except for the dominant power of the Party, much of a socialist revolution has been undone, where can we identify the legacies of socialist state feminism? What political valence could such a heritage generate in an era of capitalist globalization? And what lessons from socialist state feminists' endeavors can be meaningful and useful to a young generation of feminists? Ultimately this book expresses my aspiration to bridge a significant gap in feminist knowledge in order to inform young feminists of their foremothers' beautiful dreams, strong commitments, tenacious struggles, bitter frustrations, formidable constraints, serious limitations, and astonishing accomplishments. Reviewing and reflecting on a saga that has as yet been only partially recovered will, I hope, inspire our continuous efforts to carry on the dream of a world of justice, equality, and human dignity.

PART ONE

———

The Women's Federation and the CCP

ONE

Feminist Contentions in Socialist State Formation

A CASE STUDY OF THE SHANGHAI WOMEN'S FEDERATION

FOUNDED WITH THE ENDORSEMENT OF top leaders of the Chinese Communist Party (CCP) in April 1949, the All-China Women's Democratic Federation (later renamed the All-China Women's Federation, hence ACWF) was designed as an umbrella of existing women's organizations to lead the women's liberation movement in socialist China. Led by senior women Party members (the first cohort of Communist women) who had gained extensive experience in grassroots organization of women during the Communist Revolution, the ACWF went through rapid institutional development in the early 1950s, setting up local branches at each administrative level, reaching down to rural villages and urban neighborhoods. By 1953 there were already over 40,000 officials of the Women's Federation (WF) system nationwide working at and above the district level on the government payroll.[1] How was such impressive institutional development accomplished? What implications did it have in the formation of a socialist state in the aftermath of revolution? Archival research and fieldwork confirmed the pioneering role that the Shanghai Women's Federation (SWF) played in feminist organizing in urban areas. Focusing on the SWF activities around its creation of a grassroots organization, the women's congress, in the early 1950s, this chapter explicates the power-laden and tension-filled process of the WF system's institutional building. Gender dynamics and contentions were replete in "socialist state building," a grand program in which state feminists inscribed their visions with their innovative, though not always successful, struggles.

29

EXPLORING THE ROLE OF THE WOMEN'S
FEDERATION IN URBAN CHINA

One month after the People's Liberation Army had entered Shanghai, on June 26, 1949, the preparatory committee for the Shanghai Democratic Women's Federation (renamed the Shanghai Women's Federation later) was established. It immediately started to investigate and register existing women's organizations in order to "unify the Shanghai women's movement." Following the program set forth at the first national congress of the ACWF and inscribed in "The Resolution on the Current Tasks of the Chinese Women's Movement,"[2] the SWF identified women workers as the group it intended to organize first, followed by students, teachers, artists, professionals, and, last, housewives (*jiating funü*).[3] Establishing six contact lines to connect these various groups of women in Shanghai, the SWF intended to be an umbrella organization unifying all women, although with a clear awareness that its efforts might "bump and press" (*pengzhuang*) others.[4]

Indeed, the emphasis on workers as the primary target group of urban women-work, although ideologically correct, soon brought the SWF into conflict with the newly established Department of Women Workers (DWW) of the Trade Union, which regarded it as its job to organize women workers. This conflict must have been a nationwide problem, for the ACWF stepped in, in 1949, to resolve it, by specifying that organizing women workers would be in the realm of the DWW of the Trade Union but that the DWW would be a group member of the Women's Federation at each of the levels of their hierarchical system. Although this appeared to turn the DWW into a Women's Federation branch, by making the top officials of the DWW members of women's federations' executive committees, cooperation between the two organizations was guaranteed.[5]

This model of cooperation between the two organizations, however, created a challenge for the SWF not faced by other urban women's federations, because in Shanghai, the nation's largest industrial city with a population of more than 5 million in 1949, 170,000 women factory workers were removed from their agenda. The SWF felt compelled, therefore, to actively look for an alternative constituency, a constituency that would define and legitimate its role in socialist state building. Of the twenty-two existing women's organizations in Shanghai that had been either CCP peripheral organizations or sympathetic to the CCP before 1949, the SWF had identified six *jiating funü* [housewives] organizations and had combined them to form the Shanghai

Housewives Association on August 22, 1949. Although originally ranked last among the SWF's intended constituency, it was these housewives who by their sheer numbers—more than one million—as well as their detachment from any other branch of the CCP organizational apparatus, soon became the SWF's central constituency, with the Shanghai Housewives Association becoming the basis of further organizing at the grassroots level.

Although the strategic value of organizing housewives would seem compelling on its own, it nonetheless took some debate within the SWF before it decided to include housewives in women-work. The class standing of housewives, in the perception of the CCP, was dubiously close to bourgeois; so it was necessary for officials in the SWF to stress that of one million Shanghai housewives (all women without gainful employment at the time were lumped into this category), the majority were not "bourgeois parasites" but lower-class and poor women.[6] Appealing to Engels's theory of women's liberation, they argued that "her work is unpaid and has no significance for social production, but she is not a sheer consumer in society." A policy of preparing housewives for their liberation was articulated with mixed themes of representing both the interests of these women and the socialist state:

> The long-term goal of organizing housewives is to liberate them from subordinate positions and to engage them in social production. The immediate goal is to prepare housewives intellectually and technologically so that our society will have a large reserve labor force. Meanwhile we should raise women's consciousness and make them understand that social liberation precedes women's liberation. Therefore we should closely connect social production with our work to support the front line. We should organize housewives and send some of them to factories and other occupations. The process of organizing one million housewives will gradually enable them to participate in various production departments.[7]

The shift in the targeted constituency of the WF would have unexpected long-term ramifications. Reclassification of "housewives" would be achieved eventually in socialist China by both the Women's Federation's redefinition of the class standing of this group and the theory of women's liberation that defined those participating in social production as "liberated women." "Housewives" thus connoted not only a group of lower-class women but also backward elements (not yet liberated) in the public perception. The irony is that by identifying housewives as its main constituency, the WF failed to gain esteem in the eyes of "liberated women," urban professional women.[8]

Nonetheless, there were positive consequences from this shift in focus that cannot be underestimated. The identification of housewives as its organizational base led the SWF to explore new methods of organizing that had far-reaching implications. By late 1950 the Shanghai Housewives Association (SHA) had set up twenty-one district branches with individual housewives as members and through them intended to reach women in all neighborhoods. Thus, in late 1950 when the ACWF urged local women's federations to speed up their grassroots organizing by forming "women's congresses" like those that had been created in the CCP-liberated areas to organize rural women, the SWF had an organizational structure already in place to accomplish this. Women's congresses already existed in the villages where representatives were elected to a "congress" that in turn elected an executive committee to manage routine work relating to women. These women's congresses were representative bodies responsible for expressing local women's demands to the government and, in turn, explaining government policies to them. As such, it was hailed by CCP women leaders as the best organizational form for connecting women broadly and democratically. With the CCP's power extending to urban areas, the ACWF hoped to establish women's congresses in cities as well as a new institutional base for a unifying national women's movement.[9] The SWF was quick to see the utility of its neighborhood-based housewives associations in this endeavor. Thus the chair of the SWF, Zhang Yun (1905–1995), a Communist woman among the first cohort CCP feminists who had been a leader of women-work since she joined the party in 1925, sent out work teams of SWF officials to selected neighborhoods to explore new methods of organizing women in urban areas.

At the same time, however, the municipal government began implementing a "mode of spatial organization" to organize the unemployed, self-employed, and nonemployed and placed its Department of Civil Administration in charge of organizing residents in Shanghai lanes[10] and streets into residents committees, constituted, initially, mostly by male residents. A district government branch, called the "street office," was set up in each precinct of a public security station to supervise approximately ten residents committees. And then, in December 1950, the SWF also decided to establish its grassroots organizations in the precincts of public security stations. In less than one year, women living in 10,009 lanes elected a total of 42,900 representatives and 6,000 chief representatives, and 120 housewives committees with 1,300 members were established. Was the scene set for another "bump and press" in the neighborhoods?

At first, at least, the SWF at the neighborhood level worked seamlessly with the municipal government's efforts to organize residents committees. The CCP's creative ritual of mobilizing women was a well-developed practice in the Party's long history, dating back to the early 1920s, of mobilizing the "masses." What deserve our attention are the responses of women. The archival documents and memories of interviewees reveal that women were highly enthusiastic about participating in SWF mass rallies. In 1951 the Shanghai municipal committee requested that the SWF mobilize women for its "central work," which at the time included a patriotic campaign against American imperialist intervention in Korea, suppressing counterrevolutionaries, promoting production, and improving state finances. A municipal directive called for a mass rally and parade on March 8, International Women's Day, with the theme of protesting the U.S. re-arming of Japan, for which the SWF successfully organized over 300,000 women, of whom 250,000 were housewives. The internal report reveals that many women joined the parade spontaneously.

> Laoza District underestimated the number of participants. They thought five thousand women would come out, but actually ten thousand did. Among them were elements with complicated backgrounds such as prostitutes and bar maids, who created a sensation among the spectators. Although we originally decided not to ask old women to participate, there were also sixty- to eighty-year-old women traipsing along with the parade. There were also women parading with their kids. The spectators were so numerous that they crowded into the street and pressed the six parade lines into three lines. The police and guards were so busy keeping order that they were soaked with sweat.[11]

Although the theme of the parade was patriotism and anti-imperialism, interestingly, the report commented on its effect on women's empowerment. "Participants in the parade all felt that women have power and status now. Even men said, now women are a big deal. The Communist Party truly has its way, and even women are organized by them."[12] Leaving the praise of the Party aside, it is still clear that the parade had a gender overtone that both women and men recognized. If the CCP intended to use women to demonstrate popular support for their politics, women were also quick to utilize the new government power to cross gender and class boundaries. Parading in a public space with official endorsement, women in households and women of various subaltern groups all symbolically staged their legitimate position in the new political order. A patriotic parade carefully designed by the CCP was thus appropriated by women of different social backgrounds to produce political meanings important to them.

The parade had its special meaning for the SWF, too. From the beginning the SWF regarded it as a golden opportunity to mobilize women. Its plan for the March 8 celebration consciously aimed at combining the parade preparations with further organization of a representative system of women in residential areas. SWF's work did not rank high on the municipal agenda and ranked even lower at the district level. The municipal Party committee's attention and support was therefore a great opportunity not to be dismissed. Equipped with a mandate from the city authority, SWF officials were able to utilize district resources and assistance to extend its reach in neighborhoods and reportedly identified 5,792 new women activists in the process. Proceeding rapidly in the favorable political atmosphere, the SWF completed establishing the neighborhood women representative system and housewives committees in late 1951, which laid the institutional ground for the formation of women's congresses in the following year. Needless to say, the impressive performance of women on March 8 enhanced the stature of the SWF in the eyes of the municipal authority as well as the public. It demonstrated that the SWF had a large constituency and an important function in socialist state building.[13]

By 1952 the SWF was ready to restructure its neighborhood organization by replacing chief representatives and housewives committees with a women's congress in the jurisdiction of each residents committee (the local organization of the municipal government). Women representatives elected by women in several lanes on the same block or adjacent area (usually with about five to six thousand residents) formed a women's congress. They in turn elected a women's committee that paralleled the residents committee. By early 1953, women in Shanghai lanes and streets formed 1,684 women's congresses with 16,964 members of women's committees and about 50,000 women representatives. Since then the women's congress has remained the grassroots organization of the SWF.[14] Zhang Yun's pioneering work in creating urban women's congresses and in organizing housewives was acknowledged by her supervisors. In 1953 she was promoted to the position of vice chair of the ACWF. Significantly, in 1953 its "Resolution on the Future Tasks of the Women's Movement in the Country" emphasized that work on housewives was an important part of urban women-work. Also in 1953 the revised Constitution of the ACWF specified clearly that the women's congress in rural townships and urban streets was the basic organizational unit of the national organization.[15] Thus in the first few years of the PRC, state feminists completed the institutionalization of a women's movement led by the ACWF.

This brief introduction to the development of the SWF inevitably fails to adequately capture the intensity and excitement experienced by SWF officials and housewives representatives in those days, encouraged undoubtedly by the pageantry the SWF displayed in establishing a women's congress. In order to attract housewives to the first congress meeting and to make elected representatives proud of their new identity, the work teams would advertise the agenda of the meeting, which usually included talks by the district head and leaders of the SWF and special shows by professional performers. On the day of the congress meeting, housewives in each lane were organized to send their representatives away with fanfare. "The representatives all wore silk red flowers on their chests, walking in an orderly line, entering the auditorium. Behind them, teams of gongs and drums and *yangge* followed into the auditorium with drum beating and dancing. Every representative had a smile of pride and pleasure on her face."[16] Inside the auditorium, colorful silk flags were hanging all over and flowers were displayed on the platform. In some districts, representatives donated over one hundred silk flags and dozens of flower vases to celebrate the convening of the women's congress. But women's enthusiastic response could, at times, dismay SWF officials. One work report criticized, "Although it was the representatives' wish to celebrate the founding of their own big family, it was still too extravagant and wasteful . . . Shanghainese like to fuss in a grandiose style."[17]

FUDAIHUI (WOMEN'S CONGRESS)—A PRECARIOUS EXISTENCE

The Women's Federation, nationwide Trade Union, and Youth Association systems have usually been perceived together as arms of the centralized state that enjoyed institutional security in socialist China. The assumption neglects a history of precarious existence for the Women's Federation system, a history that sets it apart from the other two organizations and sheds light on gendered contentions in the socialist state. The story of securing its grassroots organizations—the women's congresses—epitomizes the tensions this gender-based organization aroused in the early days of state building.

The SWF's rapid development of grassroots organizations among housewives in 1951 generated ambivalent responses from different branches of the municipal and district governments. Anxiously exploring the ways of local governance in the big city, the municipal authority recognized the value of SWF's housewives associations; for when officials in the Public Security Bureau, the Department of Civil Administration, and the district governments were puzzling over whom to organize and how to approach residents, the Women's Federation at the level of each district had already hosted frequent meetings and workshops to train women representatives as grassroots activists in their neighborhoods. The gender-specific women's congresses with their emphasis on women's special needs were much more attractive to women than the early neighborhood organizations dominated by men. If a residents meeting was called by the male-dominated neighborhood organization, few women would attend; but if the meeting was announced jointly with the women's congress, many would.[18] Because male residents were an unstable force for neighborhood work due to their higher employment rates and because many had dubious political or social histories pre-1949 and were therefore considered untrustworthy, housewives became increasingly valued by the government both for being a stable workforce in their neighborhoods and for their political "purity." Thus, the municipal government emphasized the importance of mobilizing housewives for neighborhood work and recognized the SWF's large role in organizing housewives to fulfill the Party's "central work."[19] In fact, many women representatives of the women's congresses were elected to the newly established residents committees and even, in time, came to predominate in their membership.

Neighborhood work, a new term associated with the CCP's urban reorganization, encompassed all dimensions of urban management. Various orders and demands by different government branches were passed down through street offices to reach residents committees within their jurisdictions. A 1953 government report described the tasks of a street office:

> Its major work is the campaign. After the campaign concludes, there is still much work to finish. Besides that, the civil administration section requests it to work on relief and help families of military personnel and martyrs. The health section asks it to work on street sanitation, public hygiene, and immunization. The culture and education section asks it to run literacy classes and investigate the situation of school-age children. The district People's Court asks it to work on accumulated cases. The district Political Consultative Committee asks it to send out meeting notices and to report on how well representatives to the People's Congress connected with residents.[20]

The long list of tasks for residents committees also included collecting property and land taxes, rent, and scrap bronze; helping to sell insurance, local products, movie tickets, and patriotic bonds; fixing hazardous houses, dredging sewers, and repairing street lamps and wires. In short, neighborhood work covered everything in urban life except the production of commodities. Within the boundary of the miniature city—the neighborhoods—tens of thousands of housewives stepped out of their domesticity and broke gendered boundaries by engaging in all sorts of work in civil administration and public security. Many parts of the city saw an increasing physical presence of women who were "running" neighborhoods as, literally, "domesticated" social spaces—spaces that a few years earlier had been associated with gangland violence. Moreover, these highly efficient local managers worked without pay. In other words, identifying housewives for neighborhood work, the CCP found the most economical and effective way to address myriad pressing issues early in its experience with urban governance.

Nonetheless, although the SWF's role in mobilizing housewives for neighborhood work was initially valued by the government, its emphasis on women-work soon encountered problems. Facing the emergence of residents committees, the SWF's strategy in 1951 had been to place their officials in leading bodies at district and street levels doing neighborhood work and to select women representatives to work in residents committees. However, the SWF organized housewives not simply to fulfill the Party's "central work." An important component of women-work was to address women's special needs, such as women's health and childcare, and to provide literacy classes and vocational training as a means toward women's liberation. Women's congresses were the vehicle for such women-work. But to the dismay of many enthusiastic SWF officials, they soon found that male officials in street offices and district governments were reluctant to deal with demands raised by SWF officials on issues relating to women's welfare. Although the SWF emphasized that its women's congresses were parallel organizations to the residents committees and should in no way be subordinated to or controlled by the latter, the residents committees swiftly became more powerful with their direct ties to district and municipal governments and public security bureaus. The SWF officials found the territory they first entered now being claimed by someone else.[21] Wu Cuichan, who was the director of a district Women's Federation in the 1950s, recalls, "When I was in the district, I worked with pilot sites in neighborhoods. I helped neighborhood Party secretaries and residents committees with their work. Thus people in the street office would welcome you. I could not singularly work on the women's congress. If I only stressed the work of the women's congress, people would see me as a nuisance. . . . In our contact with the street offices, to use an unpleasant term, we had to act obsequiously. They had power but we didn't."[22]

Department of Civil Administration (DCA) investigative reports described the women's congress and the residents committee as competitors who "vie for cadres, for the masses, and for work. If this one holds a meeting, the other will hold a meeting, too. . . . Even when both have worked on a task, they fight over who would give a talk on the work. Each regards itself as the one who accomplished the most."[23] Dealing with the messiness in neighborhood work became high on the DCA's agenda. Apparently, women in the women's congress did not see themselves or their organization as secondary to the residents committee. Moreover, this competition at the local level was paralleled at the municipal level; although the SWF never considered its role secondary to the DCA, SWF officials were keenly aware of unequal relations at play in their daily work. Now, not because women's congresses were emphasizing women's special interests, but rather because they refused to play a subordinate role in carrying out "central work" in neighborhoods, they also became a nuisance to the DCA.

Wu's memory of an SWF official being seen as a nuisance by male officials is well substantiated by many documents in the SWF archives. On September 13, 1951, the chair of the SWF, Zhang Yun, wrote a letter to the municipal Party committee, revealing that there was already strong sentiment against the SWF's work. The letter was to report on the consequences of a talk by the municipal leader Liu Xiao, with an apparently critical tone.

> Liu Xiao in his talk suggested that the Housewives Association should concentrate on resident work in the neighborhood. We all think this is a glorious task. But because he did not make clear the relationship between work with housewives and other work, some party secretaries and directors of districts told district Women's Federation officials, "From now on you should not agitate for autonomy [*nao dulixing*]. Comrade Liu Xiao said clearly that you should concentrate on neighborhood work." Such opinion reflects that some cadres have inadequate understanding of why we need women-work, why women should have their own independent organizational system, and why we should show concern for women's special issues, and so on.[24]

More than male officials' resentment toward women-work, what was at stake here was that male officials were denying the necessity of a women's organization. Significantly, in less than two weeks the municipal committee sent back a conciliatory reply to Zhang Yun's letter. Although it largely missed the point of her protest against male officials' hostility toward the

SWF, it did instruct district committee members that if they misunderstood Liu Xiao's talk and obstructed the SWF's work, the municipal committee should be informed so as to check and correct such behavior.[25] This exchange is remarkably revealing of the relaxed political atmosphere within the Party in the early days of the PRC when women Party officials felt safe to raise criticism of their supervisors. The daring criticism by women officials would disappear shortly when political campaigns intensified, especially after the Anti-Rightist Campaign in 1957 when criticism solicited by the Party leaders for the improvement of their work would become criminal evidence of anti-Communist Party activity. In 1958 Wu Cuichan was demoted for her "rightist tendency" simply because she had complained that the district Party committee had not paid enough attention to the SWF's work.

The opportunity for the DCA to restrain the women's congresses came in 1953 when the municipal government began a campaign to "rectify residents committees." The campaign was to purge impure elements from residents committees as well as fugitives from the campaign to suppress counterrevolutionaries who were taking refuge in residential areas. The DCA used the campaign to resolve the problematic relationship between residents committees and the women's congresses. It called for "a unifying leadership" in neighborhood work and created regulations that defined women's congresses as integral but subordinate to residents committees. The chair of a women's congress should be the deputy director of a residents committee in order to coordinate work between the two organizations; but the women's congress was no longer allowed to conduct any concrete work on its own initiative beyond conveying women's demands to the residents committee and carrying out tasks assigned by the residents committee. In 1955 the municipal government formalized the DCA's regulation in an official document, "Tentative Regulations on the Organization of the Women's Congress in Shanghai Neighborhoods."[26]

It is not clear if the SWF top leadership tried to resist this redefinition of the women's congress and its relationship to the residents committee that regulated its subordinate position in the administrative structure. What is revealed in the SWF's work reports is that the major setback was taken hard by many of its officials. A dispirited sense of "inferiority" seemed to suddenly emerge, which led to the SWF leaders' repeated criticism of officials' complaints that women-work was not valued and was inferior to other work or was meaningless. Addressing women officials' "inferiority complex" (*zibei sixiang*) appeared high on the SWF's agenda. Special meetings were held to help women officials understand the "seriousness and peril in such thinking."[27]

The rising sense of "inferiority" was not only an expression of women officials' negative experience in seeing the women's congresses' role curtailed and subordinated; it was also generated by the confusion over the nature of women-work and the crisis over the SWF's identity following its defeat by the DCA. The SWF was formed for the double purpose of mobilizing women to carry out the Party's "central work" and protecting women's interests. In the first few years of the SWF, the part of women-work that served women's interests included literacy education, vocational training, formation of small-scale cooperatives, finding employment opportunities for poor women and women with skills, providing information on women's health and infant care, publicizing the new Marriage Law, mediating domestic disputes that jeopardized women's interests, and so on. By the end of 1952, 40,000 women entered gainful employment through recommendations by the SWF. By mid-1956, 69,000 women in neighborhoods had become literate and 360,000 were in literacy classes. Although the SWF's accomplishments in this aspect of women-work were impressive, its major efforts were in support of the Party's central work. Large-scale mobilization of women called for patriotic donations for the Korean war (evidently housewives' donations financed eleven fighter jets), reporting on counterrevolutionaries hiding in neighborhoods, participation in the five-antis campaign (by admonishing their husbands to be law-abiding),[28] support for the state-planned economy by not making a run on commodities controlled by the government, purchasing government bonds, and participation in the general election for the People's Congress. In order to obtain housewives' support for these "central" tasks, a major part of local SWF officials' routine work was to raise women's political consciousness. Newspaper reading groups, study workshops, and activist training sessions were regular activities organized down to the neighborhood level via the women's congresses.

This lopsided work pattern that placed more energy on the Party's "central tasks," a result of the SWF's having to follow Party directives, did not go unquestioned by women officials. In the biannual summary report on the SWF's work in the second half of 1953, the section reviewing its weakness contains a revealing paragraph:

> Because we have not done a good job on improving our cadres' work, the Women's Federation cadres sometimes do not have adequate understanding

of the important significance of raising women's political consciousness and improving their organizational capacity through campaigns. They often express doubts, such as, "It is correct to mobilize women to participate in the central political campaigns called by the Party. But what have women gained through these campaigns? What have they given to women? What can we say about our special work for women?" After discussions on the second National Women's Congress, and after repeatedly reviewing our work for the general election campaign, cadres generally have improved their understanding in this respect. Still we must educate them again and again.[29]

These forceful critical questions by women officials cited with quotation marks contrast sharply with the vague generalization of "improved understanding." Instead of presenting a routine self-criticism to its superior—the municipal Party committee— the paragraph could be read as the SWF's top leaders' euphemistic way of conveying to the Party authority women officials' critical voices and discontent about being unable to focus on work relating to women's immediate needs. At the same time, the passage confirms that it was a common strategy for SWF leadership to use the Party's campaigns of "central tasks" to consolidate its organizational building.

If the SWF top leaders had misgivings about mobilizing women for the Party's central work because it overshadowed the work for women, they had more to worry about after the DCA placed the women's congresses under the residents committees. Inside and outside the SWF, questions emerged about the necessity of the women's congresses because they performed the same tasks as the residents committees; some even suggested that the women's congresses should be incorporated into the residents committees. The SWF's emphasis on the Party's central work, therefore, turned out to prove the redundancy of the gender-based women's congresses. Seeing the legitimacy of its grassroots organizations challenged, the SWF leaders took pains to present a coherent and legitimate identity of the women's organizations while attempting to justify its concession to the residents committees. In many talks given to local women officials, the SWF leaders made great efforts to explain the necessity of having a women's organization at the grassroots level. The primary reason was what later became a familiar story to people in the PRC: that women had been the most oppressed group in the old feudal society; that even though women's lives changed rapidly in the new society, feudal remnants still remained; and that a women's organization was needed to educate women to fight against feudalistic thinking and to protect women's rights in their struggle against feudalism. "Feudalism" in this context was defined entirely in terms of oppressive and backward gender norms and practices.

The explanation of the relationship between women's oppression and the need for women's organizations often sounded negative in its depiction of women. One talk went on at length to describe how women's long-term deprivation of any rights resulted in "their narrow-mindedness, conservative stance, dependency, lack of courage to struggle independently, lack of desire for advancement, lack of common sense, slowness in comprehending new phenomena, and lack of concern for things around them." A women's organization was needed to educate them and raise their consciousness so that they would be able to become a crucial social force in the construction of socialism.[30] As the deputy secretary of the SWF Guan Jian insisted, "The residents committee is mainly to address residents' welfare issues, whereas the women's congress is a political organization that constantly fights against feudal ideology. It seeks women's thorough liberation along with the implementation of the Party's general line. This task is not what the residents committee can fulfill."[31] As one SWF official explained, "In the past there were two systems of organizations in neighborhoods. Although they seemed to be two organizations, they had the same functions. Our women's organization did not have our own routine work. Moreover, in the central campaigns women cadres just played the role of a residents committee's cadre, without thinking from women's perspectives."

The idea of an autonomous women's organization with its own distinctive role to play at the grassroots was appealing; however, that was not the direction the SWF could take because declaring such autonomy would be political suicide. So in the same talk, this SWF official had to warn against that kind of enthusiasm. "We do not mean to separate from the residents committee now. In fact, although we have two sets of organizations, we still have one set of work. What distinguishes our work is only the perspective." She went on to explain what the different perspective meant. The examples given were all gender-specific services such as providing childcare for women who joined parades (the residents committee was responsible only for mobilizing women's participation); or, when mediating domestic disputes together with the residents committee, the women officials should approach the disputes from the perspective of protecting women's and children's rights.[32] In such detailed demarcations of difference between the two organizations, the SWF gingerly but clearly advocated a woman-centered approach as the principle for the women's congress. Thus, retreating from the center stage of neighborhoods, the women's congress nonetheless acquired a more conscious gender identity.

The controversy over the women's congresses in Shanghai certainly alarmed Zhang Yun, who was now the chief executive official of the ACWF. In 1955 she organized the first national conference on urban women-work. Speaking to the delegates, she did not hesitate to directly confront the situation in Shanghai and other cities undergoing similar experiences.

> Since residents committees were established in a few cities, some male and female cadres began to think of eliminating the women's congress at the grass-roots level. This thought is not right. The residents committee is an autonomous mass organization of residents guided by the street office. The object of its work includes all male and female residents. The realm of its work relates to common issues and common demands of residents. Because the ideas and practices of valuing men over women still exist in our society, women still confront special problems in ideas, work, and personal life. Therefore, we must have a separate women's organization specialized in women-work. The women's congress is the grassroots organization of the municipal and district women's federations. Because the women's organization should not be eliminated, certainly its grassroots organization should not either.[33]

Apparently, to Zhang Yun in 1955, the women's congress in an urban neighborhood was no longer simply an organization to reach housewives but a solidly established component of the institution of the Women's Federation. The idea of eliminating the women's congress was absurd in the eyes of the top ACWF official who had worked hard to build the federation's institutional bases nationwide. Opponents of women's congresses justified their position by referring to a 1954 formal regulation on residents committees, issued by the central government, that specified formation of women-work committees as a constituting part of the residents committees. To this challenge, Zhang Yun's reply was firm and clear. If any neighborhood found setting up a women-work committee within the residents committee generated organizational repetition and waste of resources, then it meant the residents committee's women-work committee was unnecessary. "They may advise the local government not to set it up." The message was simple: whatever you do, don't mess around with the grassroots organization of the Women's Federation. Zhang Yun added authority to her defense of gender-based women's congresses at the grassroots with a quote from Lenin without specifying its source. "We need appropriate groups, special mobilizing methods, and an organizational format to conduct women-work. This is not feminism. This is an effective means for revolution."[34]

Not everyone heeded the ACWF leader's adamant words. In 1956 the branch in the Shanghai People's Congress that managed local administration formally proposed a bill to eliminate women's congresses and to set up women-work committees under the residents committees as stipulated by the 1954 Regulations on Residents Committees. The Shanghai Women's Federation appealed to the authority of the ACWF and reported the issue to Cai Chang, chair of the ACWF, Zhang Yun, vice chair, and Luo Qiong, a member of the executive committee of the ACWF, when these top women leaders visited Shanghai that year (their timely visit might have been a planned action to lend their prestige to the SWF as well as to settle the disputes over the women's congress). Cai Chang—who had joined the CCP in 1923, held a party seniority surpassing any official at the municipal level, and whose husband was Vice Premier Li Fuchun—at a meeting with the top officials of the municipal Party committee, the People's Congress, and the SWF gave a long talk on the women's congress, directly addressing three proposals: merging the women's congress and the residents committee, eliminating the women's congress, and totally separating the women's congress from the residents committee. She defended the women's congress by appealing to the Party line: "It is not only beneficial for the work of the Women's Federation; more importantly, it helps to consolidate the connection between the Party and the masses and to consolidate the basis of the people's government."[35] Following this line, the women's congress should cooperate with the residents committee while clarifying its own functions. Cai gave detailed instructions on sorting out the institutional mess in neighborhoods that further confirmed the Women's Federation's presence along with the other two major municipal branches, the People's Congress and the Public Security Bureau.

With the senior leader Cai Chang's decisive support and advice, the SWF resisted the move to eliminate the women's congress. Moreover, the SWF requested that the municipal government give the same financial support to the women's congress as it did to the residents committee and that women's congress executive committee members should receive the same subsidies as the residents committee members. The municipal Party committee might have had a better sense of the relationship between the women's congresses in Shanghai neighborhoods and the ACWF that was led by top CCP leaders' wives. It accepted the SWF's requests. But the battle was not over. In 1959, when mobilizing women in neighborhoods for the Great Leap Forward became the main job of the street Party committees, suggestions to eliminate women's congresses emerged again. The SWF had to engage in justifying the necessity of its grassroots organization all over again.[36]

IMPLICATIONS OF THE TUG-OF-WAR OVER THE
WOMEN'S CONGRESSES

What can we make of this tug-of-war over the women's congresses in the early 1950s in Shanghai? In what ways does it complicate our understanding of gender and the socialist state and "state feminism"? Most visibly, the story demonstrates that the relationship between the Women's Federation system and the Party was far from a one-dimensional story of subordination and dominance. The Women's Federation was no doubt an organ of the Party, and Women's Federation officials were firmly identified with the Party's goal of socialist revolution. However, their identification with the Party did not exclude the possibility of expressing their own gendered visions of a socialist state. Indeed, the early days of the PRC witnessed diverse visions of a new China inside and outside the Party. Women in the Party thought their long-awaited moment had finally come: women's full liberation in the new socialist China. Despite the limitations in their conceptualization of women's liberation, women Communists, especially those working in the Women's Federation, took it as their task to fulfill the Party's promise of women's liberation in socialism. The vision and methods of organizing housewives, as demonstrated here, were not granted by some abstract state patriarch but grew out of the Women's Federation officials' initiatives. The move to establish the women's congresses clearly expressed the top Women's Federation leaders' urgent sense of creating an institutional foothold for women in the incipient stage of a new state. With the Party's mandate of social reorganization, the Women's Federation grabbed the moment to make its own institutional claims in the social transformation. The landscape of a socialist state was thus inscribed with women's vision and accomplishments that are all too often overlooked or mistaken as the deeds of the state patriarch.

Exactly because of the Women's Federation officials' keen awareness of gender conflicts and gender hierarchy in the formation of the socialist state, they were constantly looking for opportunities to enhance the status of the women's organization and to gain institutional power. Understandably, the time when the Women's Federation had the most power and resources was when the organization was most useful to a particular central task of the Party. As a result, the Women's Federation repeatedly demonstrated its faithfulness to the Party by enthusiastically throwing itself into the Party's central work. This pattern, disappointing to feminist observers, was in part a result of a conscious strategy theorized by senior CCP women leaders. In this regard, Deng Yingchao (1904–1992), a feminist leader since the May Fourth era who had joined the CCP in 1925 and married Zhou Enlai the same year, demonstrated her political prudence by playing a central role as a feminist strategist in the CCP.[37] In a talk to the Central Women's Committee in 1948, even before the founding of the Women's Federation, she elaborated on this strategy of emphasizing the central task when clarifying the nature of the Women's Committee. It was to be an advisory unit with full freedom to do research and make suggestions, rather than a governmental policy making or executive branch. The committee should assist with general policies and ongoing campaigns and issues; only in this way "will our suggestions be timely and be considered by *others*" (italics mine). Timing was especially important.

> In general, we should proceed with a consideration of the effect, not with our subjective enthusiasm. When we estimate that a suggestion won't be accepted, we should rather postpone it. At the same time, we should grab the right moment. That is, we should be cooperative, have a focus, foster and prepare for the right moment. A suggestion will be effective only when the time is ripe and we calculate *others* may accept it. (italics mine)

Following these instructions, Deng gave a concrete example of an effective intervention by the Women's Committee. The resolution of the land reform conference in 1947 included the importance of women-work after a long period of silence on the subject by the Central Committee. How did that happen? Deng explains:

(1) At the time of the retreat from Yan'an, assisting in land reform, [we] asked the Central Committee in its telegram to local branches to request that they pay attention to women-work and collect material on women.

(2) Before the opening of the land reform conference, [we] first sent a notice to each representative, asking if they brought the material on women and telling them [we] hope they would include women-work in their land reform work report to the conference.

(3) [We] organized talks by representatives. Therefore, of 29 people reporting on their work, 19 talked about their women-work and mentioned the importance of women-work.

(4) [My] own speech was after the 19 representatives' talks. This is much more powerful than if I had shouted and yelled all by myself.

(5) After the land conference, [we] held a meeting of the Women's Committee, sent out a telegram drafted by five WC members, and published a newspaper editorial on the subject.

(6) To further improve and consolidate our work, [we] proposed to hold a conference on women-work in December.[38]

Significantly, in the Chinese text the sentence describing each action is without a subject, which I note in my translation with square brackets. Subconsciously or not, the speaker was covering up her manipulative role behind the scenes by leaving out the subject of action. Agency is nevertheless expressed in the Chinese text in conveying a clear sense of careful plotting, a tone of secrecy, and a marginalized subject engaged in a subversive act. Similarly revealing in Deng's language is that she often used "others" to refer to male power holders. Even though the whole talk was "politically correct," in the sense that Deng emphasized that women-work had to be a part of the whole of the Party's central work, the use of "others" obviously indicates the presence of a gender awareness of "us" vs. "them."

Similar to Deng Yinchao's manipulative moves during the land reform policy-making process, ending with a drastic increase in rural women's participation in land reform and obtaining equal rights in land redistribution,[39] the SWF's active role in the CCP's reorganization of Shanghai also resulted in a rapid development of the Women's Federation's urban grassroots organizations. These cases demonstrate the agency of Communist women doing women-work and explicate gender negotiations within the Party power structure. More significantly, these cases reveal a pattern of the Women's Federation's strategy that has so far received little scholarly attention.[40] From land reform, the 1950 Marriage Law, and paid maternity leave, to the law to protect women and children's rights in the post-Mao reform era, every pro-woman policy or legislation resulted from women officials' successful maneuvering behind the scenes, rather than from some favor granted by a benevolent patriarch. The CCP's on-again, off-again emphasis on women's interests, observed by many feminist scholars, was not because the Party was simply unable to make up its mind, but rather was the result of successful or failed feminist maneuvers within the Party. In the least congenial political circumstances, CCP feminists adopted an inactive stance on promoting women's interests and withdrew to the bottom line of survival by following the dominant Party line. When the political atmosphere changed and new opportunities emerged, they would swiftly jump at the opportunity to raise women's issues and to expand and consolidate women's organizations. "State feminism" in the Chinese socialist state, after all, is no less an expression of feminist contention within the state than it is in capitalist states.

The Women's Federation's enthusiastic work with housewives also led to redrawing gendered social spaces in socialist state formation. Historically, the local administrative system—*baojia*—had been run by men, and many neighborhoods in Shanghai had been gangsters' spheres. Mobilized by the SWF, women stepped into the male space and became managers of local governance and community service in socialist China. In 1954 women already constituted 54.6 percent of the members of residents committees and the percentage has kept increasing to well over 80 percent in Shanghai in the post-Mao era. Extending their domesticity to the management of the "socialist big family," these women turned neighborhoods into a female space.

Along with a gendered transformation of social spaces was the construction of new identities for many of the women involved. Many a lower-class woman who had been a subaltern by both gender and class became a speaking subject for the first time in her new role as a neighborhood cadre. As an example, the words of Wu Xiuying, daughter of a dockworker, expressed her meaningful experience of becoming a neighborhood cadre, "Oh, the happiest moment was when I organized residents to tour the newly built China-Soviet Friendship Palace. I was truly exhilarated! I organized several hundred residents, all housewives!"[41] Leading housewives through a prestigious public space had deep symbolic meanings for her. Both her class and her gender could no longer exclude her from entering the social space to which she could not have belonged a few years before. She also emphasized the big meetings at which she was the honored speaker. "My husband went to a conference held by the East China Bureau. I was invited to give a talk about women's liberation. . . . Many of the attendees at the East China Bureau conference were quite high-ranking cadres." Explaining her devotion to neighborhood work, Wu emphasized, "I never thought of quitting, because I felt extremely happy. We women have power now. We can speak. In the old society, other people would say, 'You step to the side! I want to talk to your man! Go back into your house!' Women had no status. No one wanted to talk to you. . . . Thinking I can speak to the leaders, I can attend all kinds of meetings, how happy I was!" Transformed from a voiceless working-class housewife who was brushed aside rudely by men to a vocal cadre who had a public presence, Wu regarded those early years in the 1950s as the most cherished time in her life.

What should be emphasized here are (1) that the WF played a large role in making women into "state subjects," a point stressed by some feminist critics in and outside China; and (2) that such state subjects, like the socialist state formation, were not made entirely according to a prescribed masculinist script (if there were such a script), but embodied tremendous contestations between gender and class at both institutional and individual levels. The contentious process produced empowered "subjects" such as Wu Xiuying. And feminists with state power were pivotal in such empowering process. In an interview with two veteran SWF officials, Wu Cuichan and Cao Shunqin, when Wu described how male officials in local governments sniffed at women-work, Cao cut in vehemently: "That is why we need a women's organization!" Cao listed various strategies the Women's Federation deployed to subvert the male monopoly of power in different branches of government, for example, creating the March 8 Flag Bearer (*sanba hongqishou*) in 1960 as a measure to break the male monopoly of "labor models."[42] "No one would fight with us over March 8," she emphasized with a cunning smile.[43]

The SWF's contestation with masculinist power was not only expressed in what they did, but also in what they did not do. Zhao Xian, who succeeded Zhang Yun as chair, mentioned her disagreement with the pronatalist policy of the Party in the early 1950s. "At the time the Party emulated the Soviet Union, calling upon women to become glorious mothers. The Soviet Union lost half of its population in WWII. But China had a large population. Women had to go out to work. How could they be glorious mothers? So we did not advocate that women become glorious mothers." (It was this interview that explained why I never came across any reference to "glorious mothers" in the SWF's files.) Unfortunately, the quiet refusal to follow the Party's policy in this case did not go unnoticed. It was listed as one of Zhao Xian's "mistakes" in 1957 when she was labeled a rightist and removed from her position.[44] Yet this meaningful example would have gone unnoticed by this historian focusing on what the SWF *did*, were it not for Zhao Xian's recounting of what meant so much to her. How many more such quiet resistances by women have been buried in history?

CONCLUSION

The WF feminists' contentions in the beginning of the socialist state formation took place in a unique political context. In the early 1950s the heritage of the May Fourth feminist discourse combined with Engels's theory of women's liberation, provided leverage for Communist women to maneuver for gender equality in their capacity as state officials led by the CCP. In contrast, in the West the emergence of state feminism was in the context of autonomous feminist social movements. Although a feminist discourse that had long been an integral part of the modernity project in China was not necessarily less powerful than political pressure from a feminist movement, the WF officials were, nevertheless, constrained by a history of the CCP's suppression of "bourgeois feminism" and an institutional structure that placed them in a subordinate position. They would always find themselves walking a fine line between advocating women's interests and being named "bourgeois feminists" for seeming to insist on the primacy of gender issues. Their intense efforts to theorize the relationship between women-work and the Party's "central work" reflected WF feminists' keen awareness of this central dilemma. In short, Communist women's legitimate fight for women's equality coexisted with the real danger of stabs in the back for that very fight.

This unique paradox largely explains the strategy of Communist women's intervention as well as the puzzle that such intervention has long gone unrecognized. To make a feminist maneuver effective, it was best to do so under the rubric of the Party's "central work" or statist projects, unnoticed by masculinist leaders. This *politics of concealment* was most clearly articulated by Deng Yingchao, who in her 1948 talk had this advice to women officials: "Because we cannot do women-work singularly or in isolation, the accomplishment of women-work cannot be expressed as a singular and isolated phenomenon either. Therefore, we should work in the spirit of a nameless hero."[45] Pursuing effective results in promoting women's interests within a male-dominated state system, therefore, required not only *disguising* feminists' real agenda but also *concealing* the actual agents who were actively and discreetly maneuvering behind the scenes. The necessity to be a nameless hero (appropriating CCP terminology again) speaks volumes about the treacherous political environment in which inside feminist agitators functioned. The clandestine behaviors consciously adopted by state feminists bear a striking similarity to subordinate groups' "hidden transcripts" theorized by political scientist James C. Scott in his study of domination and resistance.[46] But in the case of Chinese state feminists, the subordinate group based on gender situated inside the state power as part of the new ruling class further complicates the task of analysis.

A few points involved in excavating the *politics of concealment* should be highlighted here. First is the issue of discerning hidden feminist agendas embedded in non-gender-specific Party programs enthusiastically supported by state feminists. Evidence of their commitment to statist projects is abundant. Wendy Brown's caution against state-centered feminists' possible production of "regulated, subordinated, and disciplined state subjects" makes tremendous sense in the Chinese context.[47] Still, what is illustrated here is not an either / or case. The mixed effects of subversive actions coded in compliant language deserve our attention, a subject that will be further examined in the following chapters.

Second, the official discourses state feminists appropriated in the socialist period were not necessarily masculinist or anti-feminist. In fact, the CCP's discursive commitment to an egalitarian socialist goal was the source of feminists' discursive power. More specifically, CCP's agenda of anti-feudalism was most effectively deployed by state feminists in their massive contentions in and outside the state that resulted in the feminist redefinition of a key word in socialist China's political discourse. In this case, operating in a politics of concealment, state feminists nonetheless became co-authors of the dominant state discourse.

Third, the WF officials' subordinate status was not fixed but rather quite fluid contextually. Cai Chang's successful intervention in Shanghai reveals that provincial officials were subordinate to this ACWF leader in the Party's hierarchy based on seniority of Party membership in addition to the administrative hierarchy. Equipped with seniority of Party membership and informal power, the first cohort Communist women could utilize an uneven power structure with multiple hierarchies to push for their agenda behind the scenes. We will see that when second and third points listed here disappear in the post-socialist era, the dynamics between the ACWF and the Party will change accordingly, even though the institution persists.

Besides displaying concealed feminist contentions, the tug-of-war over the women's congresses can also be read as part of a process of demarcating institutional boundaries in the formation of the socialist state. Political scientist Timothy Mitchell suggests that we "examine the political processes through which the uncertain yet powerful distinction between state and society is produced." He emphasizes: "We must take such distinctions not as the boundary between two discrete entities but as a line drawn internally, within the network of institutional mechanisms through which a social and political order is maintained. The ability to have an internal distinction appear as though it were the external boundary between separate objects is the distinctive technique of the modern political order."[48]

Although Mitchell's object of analysis is the postwar capitalist state, his insights are useful for thinking about the formation of the Chinese party-state. In the initial stage of building a state apparatus, various CCP branches had to negotiate and define their territories. By specifying the subordinate role of the women's congress to the residents committee, the municipal government drew a distinct line that curtailed the institutional capacity of the SWF and defined the secondary status of this "mass organization" to government branches although they were in the same Party. The SWF's summary of its work in 1954 reveals its recognition of such institutional containment in these words: "We have now further clarified the nature of women-work and found the correct method of women-work (mainly *assisting* work [*peihe gongzuo*]). We must conscientiously work on what we should do. For that which should not be done by the Women's Federation we should suggest the concerned party do. We have reduced our blind enthusiasm in our work."[49] Regardless of its needed service to mobilize housewives and its proved capacity to work with women in neighborhoods, the Women's Federation was simply not allowed to play the leading role in local governance. This was the first hard lesson for the Women's Federation officials who were blindly enthusiastic about women's full and equal participation in socialist construction. At the institutional level, unequal gender relations in the Party were naturalized, consolidated, and legitimated by the internal distinction between the "government" and the Party-led "mass organization," a distinction full of ambiguity but nonetheless taking on "the appearance of structure" in the socialist state.

This CCP-sponsored nongovernmental women's mass organization apparently does not fit existing conceptual categories of women's organizations. It is within both the state apparatus and the local communities. It is to represent the interests of both the state and women masses. Recalling their work in the 1950s, veteran Women's Federation officials in interviews all insisted that the Women's Federation was a mass organization, not a branch of government. Wu Cuichan, who had worked both as a local government official and a Women's Federation official at different times, summarized the difference between the two most succinctly. "They had power, but we didn't." In other words, Women's Federation officials have always seen themselves as working outside the government, *assisting* the government but without governmental power. The Women's Federation officials' emphasis on their nongovernmental status is not a new pretext invented for the 1995 Fourth U.N. Conference on Women in order to attend the NGO Forum. Rather it is substantiated by a long history of producing and maintaining boundaries between the government and the "mass organizations" in the CCP's power structure.

The ambiguous location and elusive identity of the Women's Federation system paved the ground for complicated dynamics and multiple power relations operating in the daily practices of this gender-based organization that aimed to serve as a "bridge" or "linkage" between the Party and women. The impulse and heritage of mobilization of women at the grassroots to enable their democratic participation in revolutionary processes, theorized in the Party as the mass line, would be aligned in the formation of an increasingly centralized socialist state. Situated inside the socialist state structure, the ACWF nonetheless often acted like a lobbyist maneuvering behind the scenes to intervene in policy-making processes. Epitomizing a historical process full of contradictions, challenges, and contestations of moving from a grassroots-based revolutionary group on the margin to the state power holders, the ACWF had to deal with an extra dimension of conflicts that was central to its existence. When gender conflicts and masculinist authority's disciplinary power were expressed at the top echelon of the Party, that would be the real moment of crisis for the ACWF packed with the first three cohorts of Communist women with feminist consciousness. We will see that along with an accelerated tempo of socialist revolution in the following decade, these state feminists would confront grave challenges constantly.

TWO

The Political Perils in 1957

STRUGGLES OVER "WOMEN'S LIBERATION"

FOLLOWING THE PIONEERING WORK DONE by the Shanghai Women's Federation, by 1954 women in many cities had been organized into women's congresses, the grassroots organization of the ACWF. In a matter of a few years, state feminists had successfully developed this gender-based organization into the only mass organization that reached down to rural villages and urban neighborhoods throughout this vast country.[1] WF officials' burst of energy in their massive grassroots organizing endeavors expressed their long-cherished hope for the founding of a socialist country where Marxist promises of a "thorough liberation" of women would be fulfilled through the elimination of private ownership and then, with socialism achieved, the liberation of women would take precedence over other concerns.

But even in this initial euphoric stage, WF officials' dedicated work to promote equality between men and women was not without obstacles and challenges. The institutional structure that guaranteed the Party's leadership of the "mass organization" created inherent barriers to state feminists' enthusiastic initiatives. As each level of the Women's Federation was subordinate to the Party committee of the same administrative level, WF women officials often encountered Party officials who showed little interest in equality between men and women or women-work. Chairman Mao was apparently well aware of this situation. On November 12, 1952, in a meeting the ACWF leaders had requested, he instructed them on dealing with different levels of Party committees with these colorful words: *yi song* (first, submit proposals to the Party committee); *er cui* (second, push the Party committee to respond); *san maniang* (if the first two methods do not work, third, just curse and swear).[2] Apparently, though never an intentional policy, neglecting women's interests was common practice within the Party that continued into the socialist period; and significantly, the chairman's support stopped at the level of advice without offering any structural rearrangement of power relations.[3] Still, in this early stage the ACWF was able to forge ahead, mostly relying on the personal prestige and seniority of Party membership of its top leaders. Their undaunted stance can be illustrated by a high point in this period when Deng Yingchao and Cai Chang each gave a speech at the Eighth Party Congress in September 1956, reiterating the goal of women's liberation, providing critical assessment of the state of equality between men and women, and calling for promoting more women officials to leadership positions.[4]

The Women's Federation system's impressive efforts in addressing gender inequality—from implementing the Marriage Law and breaking down gender boundaries in employment to mobilizing women's participation in public affairs and local governance—constituted a large part of what was new about the new China in the initial stage of the CCP's rule. However, in 1957, at the Third National Women's Congress, the ACWF suddenly took a conservative turn, departing from its previous policy of mobilizing women to participate in production as a means of achieving women's liberation and adopting instead a new agenda known by the terms *qinjian jianguo, qinjian chijia* [diligently, frugally build the country, and diligently, frugally manage the family], or "the two diligences." In her careful study of women-work of the ACWF, Delia Davin pointed out that "a striking feature of the documents of the 1957 Congress was the unprecedented emphasis on the importance of women's family and household duties brought in under the slogan." She related this conservatism in the women's movement to conservative economic policy, while acknowledging the difficulty of finding traces that might indicate debates behind the formulation of new policies and aims for women-work.[5] Other feminist scholars have also noticed the significant change in the objectives of women-work in 1957, but so far it has remained unclear why the ACWF embraced such an apparently regressive line.[6]

Based on documents from the Shanghai Municipal Archives and ACWF's archives as well as published works including memoirs by ACWF officials, this chapter traces the process of the ACWF's alleged "change of heart" so as to illuminate internal workings of gender politics of the CCP in the late 1950s. Political tensions within the Party were played out in unexpected ways in the volatile time of 1957, a period in which scholars have examined confrontations between intellectuals and the Party, and workers and the Party.[7] Gender, I argue, no less than class, was a focal point for many in the power game. Constructing a narrative of Chinese state feminists' contentions, negotiations, and compromises in a particular historical context, this chapter sheds light on the flaws in the revolutionary leadership that did not bode well for a socialist cause.

DENG XIAOPING'S INSTRUCTIONS?

Years ago when I was working in the Shanghai Municipal Archives on a different project, among the files of the SWF I happened to see a curious document dated October 22, 1957, entitled "Notes of Comrade Luo Qiong Conveying the Relatively Important Directives on Women-work by the Leading Comrades of the Secretariat and the Political Bureau of the Central Committee."[8] It had a disclaimer at the beginning, stating that the text was put together from one or two comrades' note-taking; it had been checked by some leaders but without Luo Qiong's personal proofreading; it was just meant to be reference material for internal discussion; and it should be returned after reading. Apparently, this was an informal transmission of internal talks. To date, this document remains the only one I have found that directly quoted the top Party leaders' talks on women-work in that critical historical period. It struck me as a curious piece because it recorded those talks verbatim, but without an introduction that would explain the context. The only hint is the date, which identifies that the talks were given during the Anti-Rightist Campaign. The specific context of the talks and their meanings remained vague.

The document has two parts, one containing directives from the Secretariat of the Central Committee and the other with directives from the Political Bureau of the Central Committee. The directives from the Secretariat address three issues: *qinjian jianguo, qinjian chijia* ("double diligences" hereafter), women's liberation and equality between men and women, and methods of women-work. From these directives, it is clear that Deng Xiaoping was the one who instructed that "double diligences" should be the theme of an upcoming National Women's Congress. He gave a long talk elaborating the significance of "diligently, frugally building the country, and women's important role in diligently, frugally managing the family in the construction of socialism." With this evidence one could reach the conclusion that Deng Xiaoping had imposed the patriarchal policy on women-work and the ACWF had succumbed to the power of the patriarchal state. Case closed.

However, in her memoir published in 2000, Luo Qiong (1911–2006), one of the co-authors who drafted the report for the Third National Women's Congress and was promoted to the Secretariat of the ACWF at the conference, recalled the experience of following Deng Xiaoping's instruction forty-two years before and unequivocally expressed her deep gratitude to Deng. This is how she describes her feelings when the Political Bureau approved the final version of the report: "Holding the report draft in my hands, all kinds of emotions passed through my heart. I was deeply grateful to the guidance of the Central Committee and comrade Deng Xiaoping in the important historical moment. I was also deeply sorry that we had been unable to grasp the key to the problems at first. I will forever remember comrade Deng Xiaoping's instruction."[9] Such overflowing gratitude to Deng Xiaoping could be more a reflection of the author's mind in 2000 than in 1957. Nevertheless, given that Deng Xiaoping had just replaced equality between men and women with a double diligences policy, why would Luo Qiong be so grateful to him? What was the inner logic behind this demonstrated gratitude, past and / or present? What was so inspiring about Deng's instruction? Certainly Luo Qiong was not just talking about the double diligences policy that, in any case, was subsequently abandoned in less than a year when the Great Leap Forward began. So what valuable instruction did Deng give to the ACWF officials?

THE WORK REPORT FOR THE THIRD NATIONAL WOMEN'S CONGRESS

The Third National Women's Congress was scheduled to take place in September 1957. Luo Qiong and Dong Bian (1916–1998), both members of the standing committee of the ACWF, were assigned to draft the work report for the Congress, while the vice-chair of the ACWF, Zhang Yun, was in charge of writing the report. The work report, setting the agenda for the entire Women's Federation system for the following four years, is the centerpiece of the National Women's Congress when representatives of women from all walks of life throughout the country convene in Beijing. As such, the report is a crucial part of the preparation for the Congress. But on this occasion, the team began writing in the spring of 1957 but was unable to finalize the report in six months. According to Luo Qiong, by early August they had already revised the report ten times, yet even after much debate, still could not reach agreement. Luo Qiong's memoir does not specify what they were debating; but it does summarize in a tone of self-criticism the reasons for being unable to produce a report over such a long period. She names the following "mistakes": they did not handle well the relationship between fulfilling the Party's central task and raising women's status; they did not regard the Party's main work as the central task of women-work; they mistakenly thought that when the economic system changed to public ownership the conditions to achieve complete equality between men and women had arrived; in the draft's title they drew a parallel between building a socialist country and achieving equality between men and women and accentuated the latter in the content of the report; and finally, they confused work policy with work methods.[10]

Documents found in the ACWF's archives confirm Luo Qiong's memory. The title of the fourth draft was "Strive Further to Achieve Equality between Men and Women." Vice-chair Zhang Yun edited the draft carefully but did not change the title and its main theme. Late in July 1957 Zhang Yun conveyed the instructions of Cai Chang and Deng Yingchao to ACWF officials working on the preparation for the Congress:

> On the fundamental issue of women-work in the construction period after the victory of socialist revolution, [they] agreed to say mobilizing women in the whole country to participate in socialist construction, striving for complete equality between men and women. We will not propose striving for women's thorough liberation. Three ways of phrasing may be considered: one, mobilizing women to participate in socialist construction and striving for complete equality between men and women, paralleling the two parts; two, participating in socialist construction so as to achieve equality between men and women; and three, highlighting the mobilization of women to participate in socialist construction as the general principle, followed by concrete tasks. The two elder sisters are inclined to the third way and would like the ACWF's Party group to discuss the issue.[11]

Clearly, the focus of the debate was whether to insist on equality between men and women as a theme of the report or not. The first two suggestions by "the elder sisters" for the title already expressed compromise when compared with the title of the fourth draft, which singularly emphasized equality between men and women. Cai Chang and Deng Yingchao opted for the third suggestion, which actually removed the phrase from the title. And they made a firm suggestion not to propose striving for "women's thorough liberation." Why had pursuing equality between men and women and women's thorough liberation become problematic at this time? Why did Cai Chang and Deng Yingchao, two veteran communists and top CCP leaders' wives who had openly advocated equality between men and women at the Party's Congress only one year before, not even dare to highlight equality in the title of the work report? What was at stake behind these anxious discussions?

Any attempt to answer these vexing questions must take into account the treacherous politics of the Anti-Rightist Campaign of 1957. In May of that year Mao Zedong shifted the CCP's policy of encouraging criticism of Party officials in the opposite direction with the Anti-Rightist Campaign. Hence, anyone who criticized Party officials was in danger of being labeled as a "rightist" who opposed the CCP. The sudden change of political direction not only startled people outside the Party but also disoriented many Party officials such as the ACWF top leaders. In the eight years since the founding of the PRC, feminists in the ACWF and the whole Women's Federation system had worked very hard to advance gender equality. From implementing the Marriage Law, encouraging women to break down gender boundaries in employment, and improving women's health and literacy, to setting up women's organizations at the grassroots level nationwide, the WF officials, many of whom were young women in their twenties or early thirties, actively, even vehemently, promoted women's interests and social advancement. Many of them firmly, though naively, believed that with the victory of socialist revolution it was time for women to cash in the Party's promissory note of women's liberation. Even veteran communists such as Zhang Yun held high expectations of women's liberation in the socialist country and believed that achieving equality between men and women was a sacred mission.[12] Luo Qiong's self-criticism was to the point in that they "mistakenly thought that when the economic system had changed to public ownership, the conditions for achieving complete equality between men and women had arrived."[13]

The Anti-Rightist Campaign, unlike previous campaigns that simply required women's participation, not only diverted the ACWF's energy and resources from women-work, but also posed serious challenges to it. Since the founding of the ACWF, the rationale for the necessity of such a gender-based organization could be summarized in two points: first, socialist revolution and socialist construction required women's participation, and the ACWF was to organize and mobilize women to work for the Party's general tasks; and second, there were still feudal remnants in socialist China that oppressed women, so women needed such an organization to help them break free from feudal bondage to achieve equality between men and women. In a sense, the two-faceted rationale worked like a tacit pact between the Communist feminists and the male-dominated Party, in that each side agreed on their mutual support and mutual benefit. In ACWF official talks, publications, and training workshops for women activists, terms such as feudal bondage, women's oppression, equality between men and women, and women's liberation were most frequently articulated as a way to raise gender consciousness and to shape a sense of sisterhood in a common struggle for women's liberation, and as a result women's liberation quickly entered the new China's public discourse, deployed often by illiterate women as well. As discussed in the previous chapter, in the early 1950s when their efforts to set up grassroots women's organizations were questioned or resisted by local male officials, ACWF officials could always appeal to such rhetoric framed in a legitimate denouncing of feudalism, emphasizing the reality of gender inequality or even abuses of women so as to stress the necessity of a women's organization for the ultimate goal of women's liberation.[14]

But after the internal circulation of Mao Zedong's article dated May 15, 1957, entitled "Things Are Beginning to Change" and signaling his offensive against "bourgeois rightists," things changed rapidly. Now merely talking about problems in socialist China could qualify one as a rightist. ACWF officials were quick to realize that they could no longer say women in socialist China were still oppressed or not yet liberated. But if women were not oppressed and were already liberated, what should be the tasks of the ACWF? Or an even more troubling but logical question: Was there any need for the existence of a gender-based organization if there was no more gender oppression? The suggestion by Cai Chang and Deng Yingchao to drop equality between men and women in the title reveals their astute awareness of the new taboo. But even if the report drafters accepted this compromise, they would still have been faced with the dilemma of how to articulate the goals of the ACWF in a manner that both conformed to the current political atmosphere and justified the existence of the Women's Federation. In any case, the drafters apparently were not ready to give up the theme of equality between men and women, as Luo Qiong revealed in her memoir.

The deadline for submitting the report to the Secretariat of the Central Committee for approval was August 7, but the top officials of the ACWF were unable to reach a consensus by that date. Instead, a draft with the title "Report on Women-work'" was submitted to the Secretariat for their instruction on revision. The document had no other title, which could be read either as indicating that the drafters were too disoriented to present a clear theme or as an uncompromising compromise, that is, a vague title to gloss over what the drafters did not want to give up. By informing the Secretariat that they needed the top Party leaders' instruction on revision, the ACWF officials hoped to protect themselves from making political mistakes at this critical moment.

According to Luo Qiong, a few days after the draft was submitted, Deng Yingchao called her from Beidaihe where the top Party leaders were spending their summer, telling her that comrade Deng Xiaoping told them not to argue any more, just come to Beidaihe to discuss how to revise the report. "Elder sister Deng also told me to take with me materials on diligently, frugally building the country, and diligently, frugally managing the family."[15] Receiving the call, Luo Qiong "was elated" and immediately reported to Zhang Yun. The writing group went to Beidaihe straight away. Luo Qiong must have known that the heavy burden of producing a politically correct report had been lifted from the shoulders of the writing group.

On August 14, General Secretary Deng Xiaoping hosted a meeting of the Secretariat to discuss the draft submitted by the ACWF. Luo Qiong recalls, "Comrades Cai Chang and Deng Yingchao expressed their views first. Comrade Zhang Yun gave some explanations on the draft. All the participating comrades of the Secretariat talked, giving comments or suggestions. Not a single comrade gave positive views on our draft."[16] Even in her memoir published in 2000, Luo Qiong would not reveal what the members of the Secretariat said. What did she hide and why?

Here that curious document I found in the Shanghai Archives fills in the blank. The first part of the document was actually a set of notes on the comments of the members of the Secretariat on the draft in that meeting. It could have been from Luo Qiong's notes in the meeting since she was the one conveying the "directives of leaders of the Secretariat." A full quotation of Party leaders' comments on women's liberation and equality between men and women recorded in this document will help reveal what danger ACWF officials confronted in the summer of 1957.

The leading comrades of the Secretariat unanimously think that women are already liberated now, and men and women are already equal. They think whether women are liberated and having equality should be mainly judged by the social system. Due to socialist ownership, men and women have already achieved economic equality. Women are already participating in state politics, and the numbers are not small. Since women already have equality, why still demand equality? What else do you want? One leading comrade says: equality between men and women is a slogan of anti-feudalism. Capitalist society has faked equality. The socialist system has genuine equality. Raising [the slogan of] equality between men and women again at present will cause ideological confusion.

Leading comrades also point out: are there any phenomena of inequality? There are. These should be gradually resolved in the process of socialist construction. Therefore, in the Congress [you] should emphasize what shortcomings women still have; what efforts they themselves should make to overcome them; and how to achieve equal rights they already have. Moreover, the extant phenomena of inequality will not be entirely eliminated in a short period of time, and they are just remnants in the whole society. If [you] singularly raise the issue, it would cause ideological confusion. It is incorrect to parallel [equality between men and women] with socialist construction.[17]

Luo Qiong's notes did not name who said what in this section, a significant contrast to the way she mentioned Deng Xiaoping in a different section. Did she sense that such hostility to equality between men and women would make male leaders lose face one day if publicized? Whatever motivation she or other ACWF officials had, the anonymous way they presented these top male leaders' directives and the odd usage of the adverb "relatively" to modify "important directives" in the title of the notes for internal transmission reveal their disapproval if not disdain of the male leaders' comments. The male Party leaders' "unanimous" criticism of ACWF leaders' insistence on equality between men and women indicates their tremendous ignorance or disavowal of deeply entrenched structural inequality still existing not only in rural but also urban China, a reality that the ACWF officials had been making great efforts to publicize and to change. The stern warning against causing ideological confusion by raising the issue of equality between men and women was certainly made within the specific context of the Anti-Rightist Campaign, thereby giving it extra coercive and manipulative weight.

Following the comments by Party leaders conveyed by Luo Qiong, Zhang Yun added more in parentheses: "Comrade Zhang Yun added: inequality between men and women is the problem of class society. Some phenomena in the socialist society should be resolved gradually, and they exist because of individuals' mishandling, or problems, mistakes, shortcomings in work, not as a fundamental condition of inequality between men and women. The saying that [there is still] inequality is inappropriate."[18]

A veteran women-work official who had bravely confronted masculinist challenges in her exploration of the format of grassroots organization of women a few years before, and who possibly was the key person insisting on keeping the demand for equality between men and women in the draft,

Zhang Yun in 1957 had to convey these party leaders' "instructions" to the WF officials. Previously she had criticized male chauvinism as politically incorrect. Now, as masculinist views were shielded in the dominant hymn to socialism by top male leaders, Zhang Yun had neither the language nor the power to fight back. No record indicates her emotions or inner thoughts when she and Luo Qiong reported to other women officials these male chauvinist remarks packaged in Marxist class theory.

The male leaders did not stop at an assault on equality between men and women. They also criticized ACWF officials for complaining about working on central tasks of the Party and for "treating it as doing odds and ends." They stressed that only in the process of completing central tasks could the ACWF do a good job on women-work. In the first eight years' history of the Women's Federation, the conflict between the Party's central work and the ACWF's women-work had been an ongoing issue. The ACWF had been called on to mobilize women to work on each campaign and each task set by the CCP, in addition to directly transferring ACWF officials to work on those tasks. In most cases, those central tasks had no relation to addressing gender hierarchy or women's needs and interests. Women's Federation officials at different levels found they worked more for the central tasks than for women, and many were troubled by such a situation. The Shanghai Women's Federation's officials' discontent in the mid-1950s, discussed in the previous chapter, was a clear example. "It is correct to mobilize women to participate in the central political campaigns called by the Party. But what have women gained through these campaigns? What have they given to women? What can we say about our special work for women?"[19] Contrasting these critical questions with male Party leaders' criticism, the different gender positions of the WF and the male-dominated Secretariat are salient.

In essence, the controversy over the central tasks and women-work was a contest to make the ACWF a tool of the Party on the part of the male leaders and to make it a genuine women's organization for women's interests on the part of WF officials. Seen in this light, the title of the fourth draft of the report, "Strive Further to Achieve Equality between Men and Women," almost amounted to a declaration by the ACWF that it would focus on gender issues. The top ACWF officials must have hoped that with the completion of the nationalization of industry and commerce, the Third National Women's Congress in 1957 would mark a turning point at which the ACWF would shift its central focus to equality between men and women. However, the turning point was diverted by the Anti-Rightist Campaign. The changed political setting provided a golden opportunity for masculinist power in the Party to effectively block any feminist move, and to exert tighter control over this gender-based organization.

Cai Chang and Deng Yingchao, wives of top leaders, must have had a better sense of masculinist sentiment in the Party's leading body than Zhang Yun, who had been widowed since her twenties and thus had little chance to observe powerful men intimately. Their inclination toward the third title, which did not mention equality between men and women but highlighted the central task of socialist construction, proved to be a shrewd assessment of the current situation. Apparently, the report-writing group, including Zhang Yun, still clung to their original goal despite the drastically changed political environment. Their unyielding insistence on equality between men and women must have looked outrageous to the male leaders, arousing strong negative reaction from everyone in the Secretariat except for Deng Xiaoping. This was one of those moments that laid bare the deep gender gap within the Party.

It must have been devastating for Zhang Yun, Luo Qiong, and Dong Bian to hear male leaders denouncing their report draft in such blatant male chauvinist language. But there is no record of how they felt at that moment.[20] What we do know is that this terrible situation did not last long. This is how Luo Qiong described in her memoir what happened after the male leaders' criticism:

> Comrade Xiaoping was sitting on the side, smoking and listening quietly. In the end comrade Xiaoping gave a summarizing talk. He had a well-thought-out plan and came straight to the point. His first sentence was: "Revisions could be small, medium or large. It seems your draft requires a large revision." His second sentence was: "Your labor will not be wasted as some parts can be used in the revised version." He clearly pointed out: "It seems that you did not grasp the general task of constructing a socialist country set by the Eighth National Congress of the Party. Your Congress should be one that mobilizes women in the whole country to diligently, frugally build the country, and diligently, frugally manage the family in order to strive for the construction of socialism. Your report should use this as its title." He confirmed: "The principle of women-work in the period of socialist construction should be diligently, frugally building the country, and diligently, frugally managing the family in order to strive for the construction of socialism." He said once, and then said again with emphasis: "This principle is not wrong and it should be the fundamental principle for a long time."[21]

According to Luo Qiong, Deng Xiaoping gave a long talk on the double diligences policy and quoted Chairman Mao twice. Deng also gave detailed instructions on the structure of the report, telling them to organize it into seven parts and specifying the theme for each part. He told them how many words they were supposed to write for each part and asked them to limit the length to 20,000 characters. "From the principle and task to the structure and length, comrade Xiaoping told us everything clearly," Luo Qiong said in her memoir. Obviously, Deng Xiaoping had done his homework before hosting this meeting of the Secretariat.

Following Deng's instructions, the writing group finished revisions in one week and sent it back to the Secretariat. Besides centering on the double diligences, the revised version also included the Secretariat members' view on equality between men and women. It stated: "Because the socialist revolution was completed, women in our country have already achieved equal rights with men in political, economic, cultural and social aspects and family life. They have forever ended thousands of years of sad history of being oppressed and subjugated, and achieved women's liberation."[22] A second meeting of the Secretariat to review the report was scheduled. Luo Qiong was very uneasy on that day. But this time Deng Xiaoping was the first to talk and he said, "This version is basically fine now." Then other leaders followed to give their consent. They only offered some minor editorial suggestions before they approved it. Then the draft was ready to be submitted to the Political Bureau of the Central Committee.

Before following the draft to another setting, we should look closely at Deng Xiaoping's role in this critical moment. It is clear that he was the only male leader in the Secretariat who did not attack the ACWF that day. Instead, he had spent time beforehand working out a "politically correct" theme to break the impasse. Judging from Luo Qiong's description, Deng Xiaoping did not mention "equality between men and women" at all, either positively or negatively. We have no way of discerning his personal position on the issue. His agenda was unmistakably to propose a new principle for women-work: the double diligences. This principle was a retreat from the goal of striving further for equality between men and women since it did not address gender hierarchy but rather consolidated the gender division of labor and reinforced gender roles. It also strengthened the masculinist Party position of using the ACWF as a tool for the central tasks of the Party. As such, it received the unanimous approval of the Secretariat.

But was this proposal totally siding with the masculinist power in the Party? Why were Luo Qiong and other ACWF officials so grateful to Deng? What was the key to the problems that Luo Qiong regretted they had not grasped at first, and that apparently Deng Xiaoping had? The clues to these puzzles can be found in the second part of the curious document, that is, the part recording the discussions of the revised draft by the Political Bureau. The document set out the Political Bureau leaders' discussion under three topics. The first, on the situation of the Anti-Rightist Campaign, recorded Party leaders' discussions about how rightists attacked socialism and their suggestions on how the report should include denouncement of rightist theses by using examples from work on women and children (the final report of the ACWF included some direct quotations from leaders' discussions on this issue). The second topic, about the double diligences, expressed leaders' agreement and approval of this "very important issue." The third topic was about the question of whether the ACWF should exist or not and its function. In this crucial part, the document did not note opposing views at all, but simply quoted Liu Shaoqi's favorable view of the ACWF. The length of the quotation showed that the Political Bureau spent quite a while on this issue.

Liu Shaoqi's views as recorded in the document, apart from registering his approval of the revised report, focused on refuting the view that the WF should be eliminated:

> To the question of whether we want WF or not, I think we should not utter such words any more. Some people have thought that women's liberation was a task of one period, a task of a historical stage. As if since women are liberated, WF is not needed. In my view, not only at present, but also in the future, WF still should exist. With the existence of WF, [we] can carry out work among the women masses.

Liu repeated this subject at the meeting with a firm tone: "As to the question of how much longer WF should exist, WF should exist for a long time. Don't bring up the question of whether it should be eliminated or not any more."[23]

The political environment for the ACWF in 1957 is now clear. The contention was not simply over gender equality, but more seriously, over the very existence of the organization. This explains why ACWF officials wanted to insist on striving for equality between men and women, even though they knew that the slogan might sound problematic in that particular political context. How could this gender-based organization legitimize its existence without a gender-specific goal and function? Seen in this light, Deng Xiaoping's ingenuity comes into focus. His proposal of the double diligences provided a gender-specific function to legitimize the existence of the ACWF. And better yet, he used politically correct rhetoric to present a traditional role for women to play, rhetoric that would shield him from any possible attack.

The formulation of the double diligences first appeared in Chairman Mao's writings in 1955. When editing a volume of reports on the development of rural cooperatives nationwide, Mao wrote 104 small commentaries on more than 170 reports. The title of one report, "Diligently and Frugally Running the Co-ops," evidently inspired Mao to comment, "diligently and frugally running everything," and during the following years he would occasionally mention "diligence."[24] In the context of promoting rural collectivization, he gave a talk on rural co-ops at the Sixth Congress of the Central Committee in 1955, again mentioning diligence: "We should advocate diligently and frugally managing the family, diligently and frugally running the co-ops, and diligently and frugally building the country. Our country needs diligence first, and frugality second; we don't want laziness, and we don't want sumptuousness. Laziness would lead to decline, which is not good."[25] According to Luo Qiong, this was one of the two sayings by Chairman Mao quoted by Deng Xiaoping at the Secretariat meeting. In July 1957 Mao wrote an article that was circulated among provincial Party secretaries who were convening in Qingdao. In it he again mentioned diligently running the co-ops. But this time, he specifically mentioned women's role in diligence: "In order to resolve the issue of diligently and frugally managing the family, [we should] chiefly rely on women's groups to do such work."[26] This was the second quotation cited by Deng Xiaoping in his speech on the double diligences, followed with his own emphasis that this was the historical responsibility of WF.[27]

In early 1957 the Party Central launched a campaign of *zengchan jieyue* [increase production and practice economy] as a response to the overheated economy of 1956.[28] In publicity for this campaign, Mao's quotation of "diligently and frugally running everything" was widely circulated. In the Women's Federation system, officials at different levels began to emphasize women's role in the campaign of increasing production and practicing economy, and together with Chairman Mao's quotation, to emphasize women's role in "diligently and frugally running the family."[29] In other words, by the time of Deng Xiaoping's selection of the couplet, "diligently, frugally build the country, and diligently, frugally manage the family" had already been circulating in the official media, although not necessarily as a pair.

Deng Xiaoping did not initially decide on the theme of double diligences for the ACWF. The July instructions from Deng Yingchao and Cai Chang on the report also included Deng Xiaoping's directives. At that time, he told the ACWF that "following Chairman Mao's instruction at the meeting of provincial Party secretaries, the theme of the report should be the issue of women passing the test of socialism."[30] The term "passing the test of socialism" first appeared in one of Mao's talks in January 1957 when he said: "Some Party members have passed all kinds of tests in the past, but it is difficult for them to pass the test of socialism."[31] Mao's attention at this point was on Party members and high officials who disagreed with his collectivization and nationalization policies. Although passing the test of socialism was originally not intended for people outside the Party, in July when the Anti-Rightist Campaign peaked, it did not sound far-fetched to include women, since by then everyone in China was expected to pass the test of socialism. The ACWF followed Deng's instruction to prepare their report and other designated presentations. Consequently, Honorary Chair of the ACWF Song Qingling's talk at the Congress was entitled "Women Should Resolutely Pass the Test of Socialism."[32] The theme, however, only worked in one way, that is, it followed the political tempo. It did not help address the specific dilemma of the ACWF to legitimize its existence. Therefore, in the leading body of the ACWF the debate over the central theme of the work report continued.

Deng's instruction in July showed that he was informed of the preparation for the Third National Women's Congress and was involved in decision making. The liaison between Deng and the ACWF was through either Deng Yingchao or Cai Chang, or both. It was Deng Yingchao who informed Luo Qiong of Deng Xiaoping's request that the writing group come to Beidaihe and that Luo Qiong bring materials on double diligences with her. Deng Yingchao had obviously informed Deng Xiaoping of the dilemma of the ACWF and it was this information that made Deng Xiaoping look for a different theme for the report. We don't know how Deng Xiaoping discussed the new theme with Deng Yingchao, but when he decided to get the writing group to Beidaihe he had already thought of the new theme and had told Deng Yingchao what it concerned. By switching the theme from passing the test of socialism to double diligences, Deng Xiaoping showed astute understanding of what was at stake in drafting the report. And with this switch he simultaneously succeeded in saving the Women's Federation, appeasing masculinist power in the Party, and exhibiting his faithful adherence to the ideas set forth by Chairman Mao. At any rate, Deng Xiaoping should be credited with finding those two short quotations from Mao's many long talks and writings and applying them to practices with such creativity at this critical moment.

Interestingly, at the meeting of the Political Bureau, when Liu Shaoqi defended the ACWF, he tried to use the same strategies. He also invoked Mao to legitimize the existence of the Women's Federation. According to him, Mao at the Supreme State Conference had said: "In the old society there were matchmakers for marriage. The new society has abolished the feudal system but young men and women have difficulty in getting married, that is, they cannot find a partner. Shouldn't we have a department for introducing [partners] and [providing] guidance?" After quoting Mao, Liu Shaoqi then emphasized that issues of marriage, women, and children were pervasive social issues that deserved research so as to create healthy social ethics and common practices: "Creating lively social practices and healthy ethics is beneficial to socialism. If WF could shoulder this task, it would play a good role."[33]

Searching for a "politically correct" role for the Women's Federation to play, Liu Shaoqi, just like Deng Xiaoping, expressed narrowly defined functions for the women's organization while appealing to Chairman Mao's authority. Their support for the ACWF could be motivated by a pragmatic political concern. Where else in the Party's power structure could they place women Party members with no less Party seniority and credentials than those of the male members of the Political Bureau, the Secretariat, and each level of the Party committees if the WF system were eliminated? In any case, it is ironic, though not surprising, that these Party leaders protected the Women's Federation by placing it within the parameters approved by masculinist power. Were they conscious of the regressive nature of their proposals? Probably not. The act of appealing to Mao's authority in those circumstances seems not so much to seek protection from possible criticism of their conservative stance on gender issues as to add weight to their ingenious proposals. The practice of quoting Mao for legitimacy, which would be pervasive throughout the entire country a decade later, seemed already to be a common practice among top Party officials in the late 1950s.

Highlighting the two male Party leaders' role in this historical moment makes it possible to see a pattern of the ACWF's working strategy. The two male leaders did not jump to the rescue of the ACWF on their own initiative. Although I have not yet found evidence to establish a connection between the ACWF and Liu Shaoqi at this point, I have already shown that Deng Yingchao, who had known Deng Xiaoping since the early 1930s, played a crucial role in obtaining Deng Xiaoping's support. Informal relations are always important in the formal decision-making process. To Chinese state feminists—the ACWF officials who were used to long-term marginalization of women in the Party's power structure—informal relations were crucial channels of access to the male-dominated power center. It would not be an exaggeration to claim that in the first decade of the PRC every important state policy promoting women's interest was the result of successful maneuvers by these inside feminist agitators who deftly utilized crucial informal relations formed in the long course of the Communist Revolution.[34] The double diligences policy, seemingly a setback, should be regarded as representing one of those successful maneuvers behind the scenes, a state feminist lobbying stunt.

DISPUTES AMONG STATE FEMINISTS

Embracing the double diligences as its central principle, the ACWF thus survived 1957. It must have been a huge relief for the Women's Federation top officials that with this new principle the Third National Women's Congress smoothly sailed through the rough seas of the Anti-Rightist Campaign. But intriguingly, the leadership of the ACWF seemed to be not just relieved but also galvanized by this apparent diversion from its original goal of pursuing women's thorough liberation. After the conclusion of the Third National Women's Congress, the ACWF seriously devoted itself to the implementation of the double diligences nationwide. They even enthusiastically presented a proposal to the Central Committee to begin nationwide publicity activities on diligently and frugally managing the family, and the Central Committee approved their proposal, issuing directives to Party branches all over the country to include such publicity activities in their agenda. By the Spring Festival of 1958, the ACWF had successfully launched a nationwide campaign. Local WF officials, in rural areas especially, were enthusiastically honoring model women of double diligences, and some of these rose to national prominence with their stories of diligences and frugality appearing in *Women of China,* the ACWF's official women's magazine, and other newspapers.[35] Leaders of the ACWF were busy giving speeches in multiple locations nationwide to promote the double diligences. Significantly, "Various ministries of the government, such as Ministry of Food and Ministry of Commerce, would approach the ACWF actively, discussing how to assist our work. Money, people, meeting places, whatever you asked, they would give it to you." Luo Qiong recalled the splendid scenes of the successful national campaigns with a genuine sense of thrill even decades later.[36] Obviously, instead of being eliminated, the ACWF emerged into the spotlight, gaining support from various Party and government branches at the central and local levels. It was a rare moment for the WF system to enjoy the attention it received as a key player in creating a national campaign.

If we recall how the Shanghai Women's Federation's parade protesting American imperialists was ingeniously appropriated by women to stage their various public performances imbued with social meanings important to them, we can better grasp the unusual significance in this double diligences campaign. The double diligences provided an even better opportunity than the parade of anti-imperialism for many women's empowerment, because it directly situated the family in the center of the nation. Women did not have to go to the street to claim their newly acquired socialist citizenship. The meaning of their routine and undervalued domesticity changed overnight. In Luo Qiong's articles and speeches during the campaign, she never forgot to point out that in China at the time the great majority of women were house-wives and even many working women were housekeepers as well. "Under the circumstances, when housework has not yet become public enterprises," she theorized, "it is an indispensable labor in socialist construction." The double diligences, in her view, by acknowledging the value of women's housework, was an effective method to incorporate the great majority of women still in domesticity in the socialist nation building. "So promoting diligently, fru-gally managing the family is the important content of diligently, frugally building the country; it is simultaneously beneficial to the nation, the co-op, and the family," she emphasized.[37]

In her effort, passionately argued, to link women in the family with social-ist nation building, Luo Qiong was actually invoking the social order and normative practice of imperial China: the family is the foundation of the empire; it is a woman's key role to manage a household that often includes multiple generations and multiple conjugal units, which is the basic economic unit of an agrarian society; and celestial honors would be bestowed upon exceptionally virtuous women who persevered in dire situations. Diligence and frugality had been important virtues associated with legendary women who brought prosperity to many a poor family, or who managed to support their sons' or husbands' years of education that led eventually to a successful career as an official.[38] But in Luo Qiong's advocacy, diligently and frugally managing family is defined as "an embodiment of socialist consciousness," contributing to socialism by increasing the productivity and well-being of rural families as a crucial means to consolidate rural collectives.[39]

The top leaders' strategic maneuvers, however, were often too opaque for local WF officials to perceive, or the contradictions inherent in their theorization were too obvious to be neglected by the many WF officials who steadfastly held onto a socialist feminist theory of women's liberation. The report on the conference of provincial WF leaders hosted by the ACWF in January 1958 revealed that the ACWF leaders were pressed to clarify that the double diligences should not be mistaken as "before (we) mobilized women to participate in production; but now (we) mobilize women to do housework." The leadership insisted that the double diligences did not depart from but only enriched the ACWF's former principle of mobilizing women's participation in socialist production. Not surprisingly, local WF officials also questioned why the double diligences should be regarded as only concerning women. The ACWF leaders explained that it was because women actually did more housework than men, but the double diligences should certainly concern all branches of the government.[40]

The ACWF's promotion of double diligences, however, was soon swept aside by another even greater campaign, the Great Leap Forward in 1958. Suddenly people in the whole country were mobilized to speed up socialist construction, and women were portrayed as an important labor force in social production rather than frugal managers of families. Moreover, it seemed that individual families might be abolished very soon, as collective dining halls were set up in rural communes. Socializing housework and liberating women's productivity were in vogue. To respond to the rapid change in the Party's preoccupation, in June 1958 the ACWF hosted another national conference on women-work attended by provincial Women's Federation leaders to adjust its agenda and principles. In fact, it was a reorientation conference to shift the WF in a different direction. Documents for this one-month-long conference reveal that with the changed political environment local Women's Federation officials felt free to question the work report of the Third National Women's Congress. And they did: Was it problematic to adopt the double diligences as the principle for women-work? How come the report said women had already been liberated and had already achieved equality? Why was women's thorough liberation not mentioned? Why was socialization of housework not mentioned? And so on. Feminist consciousness was fully expressed by these WF officials who, nonetheless, had no clue of the treacherous waters the ACWF top leaders had had to navigate just barely a year before.

From a talk at the conference by Dong Bian, the co-author of the report, it becomes clear that the ACWF officials were put in the awkward position of justifying the theme of the report written less than a year before, without revealing the true reason for its regressive stance. She explained the circumstances in a vague and generalized way to local officials who clearly did not understand the pressure the ACWF had experienced at the time: "The whole country was just in the most intense period of struggling against bourgeois rightists. The circumstances required us to concentrate all our efforts to call on women in the whole country to go firmly on the socialist road." But the talk also demonstrates how the ACWF officials swiftly responded to the new political situation. Dong Bian basically broke all the taboos set by the Secretariat the year before and returned to the pre-1957 rhetoric of the existence of inequality between men and women and feudal remnants: "Women's thorough liberation and genuine equality between men and women will have to follow the development of socialism and be achieved completely in a communist society."[41]

As to the double diligences, Dong Bian explained that the productivity of the time had required that women diligently and frugally manage the family for the construction of socialism. Now that social productivity has developed, she claimed, it has became appropriate to turn individual housework into collective enterprises so as to liberate women from housework to devote themselves to socialist production, although the spirit of diligently and frugally running everything should be maintained. In the dominant craze of "running to communism," Dong Bian neither explained, nor did any official ask, how social productivity could have developed so fast in less than a year. Thus, the Great Leap Forward, according to the ACWF's new stance, enabled women to leap out of the role of a diligent housekeeper and leap back into the role of a socialist producer. Nationwide, promotion of the GLF swiftly replaced discourses and activities of double diligences with a loud call for women's liberation, though mainly defined as women's participation in social production. It is exactly against the context of the setback in 1957 that many local WF officials regarded the Great Leap Forward as the high point of women's liberation in China.[42]

When women's productivity was "liberated" (meaning when the massive mobilization of women into the labor force was accomplished) in the Great Leap Forward, however, the legitimacy of a gender-based organization was once again questioned. At the June conference, local WF officials not only criticized the double diligences, but also articulated their doubts of the necessity of the WF. Obviously the idea of eliminating the WF had been circulating for a while and local WF officials could not be impervious to it. Given the marginality of the WF, it was conceivable that some WF officials could be more than willing to be reassigned to the government branches rather than staying in the women's "mass" organization.

Facing new challenges emerging in the Great Leap Forward, the ACWF leaders sought guidance from the Secretariat of the Party Central again. Deng Xiaoping, Peng Zhen, and Liu Lantao (who was then the Secretary in charge of mass organizations) held a meeting with them on July 24, 1958, before the concluding of the conference of provincial WF leaders, and each one of them reiterated the principle of double diligences. According to Luo Qiong, Deng Xiaoping stressed his point in a serious manner, "The double diligences must be continued. Diligently and frugally managing the family should not be abandoned. At least in the next ten or twenty years, the slogan of socializing housework should not be raised." Peng Zhen added that family would exist for a long time and socializing housework could not possibly be realized in the near future. Liu Lantao also emphasized that the double diligences should be followed for the long term as the fundamental principle of women-work, and the WF should strengthen its work following this principle. "At present," he said, "it is not a matter of elimination of the WF but a matter of strengthening and improving its work. You will never be unemployed."[43]

What happened immediately after this meeting revealed the special meanings in Luo Qiong's memory of the event decades later. Rather than following the Party Secretariat leaders' insistence on the double diligences, this time the ACWF followed the "higher authority"—Mao's call to leap forward. In the long concluding report on the conference by the Secretary of the ACWF Secretariat Cao Guanqun, the double diligences were only mentioned briefly and the new direction of women-work was unambiguously and forcefully articulated. In addition to repeating the old principle of women's participation in socialist construction, the report highlighted a specific vision of women's liberation, that is, promoting women's participation in technological innovation and cultural activities. "Enabling women to have the same development as men in areas of technology in production and cultural knowledge is the key to achieve equality between men and women."[44] Also in disregard of Deng Xiaoping's admonishment not to mention socializing housework, the report called on WF officials to "actively guide the masses to organize their life toward socializing housework" while cautioning them to do so gradually according to the level of productivity.

The passionate proposal of a new direction toward women's liberation enabled by the Great Leap Forward contrasted sharply with Luo Qiong's equally passionate theorizing of the double diligences barely six months before. The report clearly indicated which feminist agendas were suppressed by the Anti-Rightist Campaign and now reactivated when the ACWF officials felt safe to do so. The huge disparity between Cao's report and Luo Qiong's advocacies of the double diligences may seem simply to demonstrate how fast ACWF top officials were able to adjust to the fluid and shifting political environment, but Luo Qiong's memory of the events in those years also reveals that there were real disagreements among the ACWF top leadership. For Luo Qiong, the double diligences provided an effective means for the WF to serve as a bridge to link the vast majority of Chinese women, that is, rural women, and the state; to empower ordinary women in domesticity; and to secure the existence of the WF itself. Her genuine support of the double diligences was also expressed in 1961. By then the Great Leap Forward had run out steam with disastrous economic consequences and the ACWF's promotion of women's leap toward liberation was criticized as a "leftist" tendency. Luo Qiong was the one who brought the double diligences back to the ACWF as the correct principle. And in her memoirs she consistently criticized the Great Leap Forward. Luo Qiong's position, to borrow the distinction made by Maxine Molyneux, could be defined as pursuing *practical gender interests,* while those WF officials who vehemently embraced a "leap" position aimed to achieve *strategic gender interests* concerning the transformation of social relations.[45] In the Chinese context, *practical gender interests* also suggest a politically less risky strategy for the ACWF that can be incorporated more seamlessly into the Party's central tasks.

REFLECTIONS ON THE POLITICAL PERILS
FACING THE ACWF

The sporadic proposals to eliminate the WF were finally put into practice in the heat of the Great Leap Forward. In some locations Women's Federations at the county level were disbanded in the second half of 1958.[46] The ACWF officials hastily maneuvered to address another crisis threatening the existence of their organization. Cai Chang appealed again to Deng Xiaoping who then had a formal decree issued in the name of the Party Central, articulating the Party's support of the ACWF's position against the disbanding of local WFs.[47] From Shanghai officials' attempts to eliminate the women's congresses in the early 1950s, to top officials' suggestions of elimination of the WF in 1957, and to the actual disbandment of local Women's Federation in multiple locations in 1958—all these cases demonstrated that hostilities to this gender-based organization emerged sporadically and unpredictably at both local and central levels.

Such a perilous political environment in a way explains Luo Qiong's deep gratitude to Deng Xiaoping as well as the ACWF's huge concession in 1957. After all, facing numerous crises, ACWF officials managed to sustain the gender-based organization. Protecting their organization was the bottom line for which the ACWF leaders were willing to compromise. In less than a decade since the founding of the PRC, the unexpected battles over the WF, a national organization set up with ACWF leaders' vision and local WF officials' tremendous hard work, indicated pervasive gender struggles in the construction of the socialist state. Enthusiastically and idealistically forging ahead with their dreams of women's liberation, state feminists at all administrative levels must have ruffled many patriarchs' feathers and rubbed many male chauvinists the wrong way. And perhaps most unexpected to them, the "many male chauvinists" were male Party officials.

For the ACWF top leaders, the chilliest moment was the summer of 1957 in Beidaihe when all the members of the Secretariat, except for Deng Xiaoping who had been briefed by Deng Yingchao, attacked the ACWF and their agenda of pursuing equality between men and women and women's liberation, an episode that epitomized the masculinist nature of the Party Central. It must have been a startling revelation to the ACWF leaders that there existed this huge ideological as well as cognitive gap between themselves and the male Party leaders. If not before, this episode in 1957 alone would be sufficient to alert the ACWF leaders to the grim reality of what a huge "feudalist mountain" they were facing within the very Party upon whose power they had to rely. The dilemma of inside feminist agitators was profound.

Significantly, the ACWF restricted the circulation of the blatant sexist remarks made by the Secretariat in the summer of 1957. It is obvious from the provincial WF officials' critical responses to the Third National Women's Congress report that they did not see the notes of the "directives" from the top Party leaders I found in the Shanghai Municipal Archives.[48] It is also obvious from Dong Bian's awkward explanation on why they produced that problematic report that the ACWF leaders had no intention of informing their feminist colleagues of the ordeal they endured during this concerted masculinist attack from the Party leaders in 1957. Why did they want to cover up the deeply entrenched "feudalism" among the top Party leaders? One plausible consideration could be their desire not to dishearten local officials with this bleak picture, since the WF officials at various administrative levels were already engaging in hard struggles on the margin of the official system. The ACWF leaders' role was to boost rather than dampen their confidence and enthusiasm in fighting for equality between men and women in socialist China.

Riding on the tide of the Anti-Rightist Campaign, the Secretariat in 1957 disciplined the ACWF by way of a gender-conservative framework within which the ACWF apparently complied in a creative way that consolidated the organization and brought women's housework to public recognition. However, as soon as the political atmosphere changed, state feminists began a robust push against the restrictive boundaries. With apparent devotion and tremendous nimbleness in their adjustment to the Party's swiftly shifting priorities, the ACWF officials managed to continue their pursuit of women's liberation in ways they saw fit. A concealed but nonetheless vibrant gender line of struggles in the CCP kept unfolding in the following years.

THREE

Creating a Feminist Cultural Front

WOMEN OF CHINA

THIS CHAPTER CHALLENGES WIDESPREAD ASSUMPTIONS that some faceless patriarchal authority—variously known as "CCP propaganda" or "Maoist gender discourse"—authored revolutionary cultural images of gender, ignoring the evidence of feminist centrality in the contested history of the production of a socialist culture. By examining the flagship publication of the All-China Women's Federation, *Women of China*, and exploring the behind-the-scenes stories, I offer an alternative account that reveals a dynamic site of feminist contestations in cultural production in socialist China and brings feminist producers of gendered "propaganda" back to the historical process.[1] Symbols, icons, and discourses created by this magazine may be most productively read in the context of multifaceted feminist struggles that were often opaque to its readers. Departing from a scrutiny of gender struggles in high politics momentarily but continuing my investigation into the politics of concealment in the cultural realm, this study is based on interviews with eight retired senior officials of the ACWF and three generations of editors of *Women of China* conducted in Beijing from 2005 to 2010, in addition to memoirs and biographies of women in the CCP and internal documents compiled by the ACWF since the late 1980s.[2]

Close attention to the ways in which state feminists identified with the Party Central's agenda, quietly diverged from its imperatives, or openly challenged sexism in the Party may help us to understand how feminist contentions figured in socialist ideological formation and cultural transformation, and further, allow us to challenge the widely held assumptions of a "totalitarian state." One example of this in practice drew on the experience of Communist women in the decades preceding the revolutionary victory, who had deployed the Party's mass line, *qunzhong luxian*, organizing at the grassroots level to create a public space that enabled diverse voices of women and men from different social and geographic locations to be heard. The ACWF continued as a mass organization, and its magazine, *Women of China*, in this sense served both as a forum created for the general public to articulate their opinions on issues relating to women and as a cultural front initiated by state feminists to engage in transforming patriarchal culture and shaping new socialist subjectivities.

Here, the notion of a cultural front refers to the cultural product, the magazine, and the physical location of the press of *Women of China* that brought Communist women together with feminist consciousness initiating socialist feminist cultural practices. Situating this unique location inside the socialist state and investigating the state feminists' agendas and strategies in their discursive practices as well as political maneuvers, I explore the meanings of the feminist cultural front in the socialist state process of the early PRC. This chapter tackles the complicated entanglement of webs of relations and dynamic interplay of contradictions by focusing on the key players in *Women of China,* the shifts in its contents, and the themes of the covers. Life stories of leading figures of the magazine are highlighted to add a personal dimension to their revolutionary performances. I pay special attention to the discrepancies between the contents characterized by changing themes, formats, and voices and the cover images representing consistent themes. The meanings of such discrepancies and disconnections present a key puzzle in my investigation of socialist state feminist efforts to build a feminist cultural front.

LEADING ACTORS BEHIND THE SCENES

Women of China[3] first appeared in Yan'an on June 1, 1939, following the decision of the Secretariat of the CCP to develop women-work in the resistance against Japan.[4] Its mission, at this point in time, was to mobilize women to join the fight against Japanese invaders and to build an independent new China, although its circulation was limited to Communist women in the base areas. The first editor, Wu Ping, solicited contributions from CCP leaders as well as women writers in Yan'an, while the well-known writer Ding Ling designed the layout for its first issue. The magazine was changed into a supplement of the Party's newspaper *The Liberation Daily* (*Jiefang Ribao*) in 1941 when Luo Qiong worked as its editor. The supplement suspended publication in 1942 but was revived in July 1949 as the monthly magazine *Women of New China* (renamed *Women of China* in 1956), under a resolution of the First National Congress of Chinese Women on the eve of the founding of the PRC, and officially affiliated with the newly established All-China Women's Democratic Federation (ACWDF).[5] The magazine's editors in Yan'an and after 1949 were mainly from the cohort who joined the Communist Revolution in the 1930s. A member of the Executive Committee of the ACWDF and director of the ACWDF's Advocacy and Education Department, Shen Zijiu (1898–1989), was appointed the revived magazine's first editor-in-chief.

Shen belonged to the May Fourth generation. From a comfortable business family in Hangzhou, she attended the Provincial Girls Normal School in Zhejiang and taught in an elementary school after graduation. She married at 17 and had a daughter, but her marriage soon ended in tragedy when after graduating from the Philosophy Department of Beijing University her young husband died of typhoid during a visit home. Rejecting the confinement to widowhood in her husband's wealthy family, she went in 1921 to study in Tokyo, leaving her daughter with her mother, an arrangement not uncommon among women of that cohort who aspired to a career. In 1925 she returned to China to teach in Huangzhou. However, she found people around her still focused more on her identity as a "little widow" than anything else, an expression of a patriarchal norm that disciplined the chastity of a widow. In defiance, she decided to "overthrow the arch of chaste widowhood" with a second marriage.[6]

Shen Zijiu's second husband was an official whose gender prejudices became intolerable to Shen and she ended the marriage in 1931.[7] Up to this point, Shen had consistently pursued May Fourth feminist ideals of gender equality and women's liberation by insisting on equality in marriage and maintaining an independent career. Her failed second marriage, the Japanese invasion in 1931, and the bankruptcy of her father's silk company prompted her to look for a new direction in life. She went to Shanghai where she was hired by the Zhongshan Culture and Education Institution to translate Japanese articles for the journal *Collection of Current Affairs* (*Shishi leibian*). She shared a rental house with her film director brother Shen Xiling and extended her circle of friends, most of whom were left-oriented young intellectuals and underground Communists in the cultural realm. After a year working as a translator she was invited to edit *Women's Garden* (*Funü yuandi*), a newly created weekly supplement of the *Shanghai Daily* (*Shenbao*). This new position marked a turning point in Shen's life.

In the initial issue of *Women's Garden* published on February 18, 1934, Shen revealed her discontent with the outcome of the May Fourth feminism to which she had adhered. Criticizing emancipated and intellectual women for their concerns with modern trends, love, and the arts, her descriptions of the hardship suffered by rural women and female factory workers expressed a strong sympathy with lower-class women whose misery she had observed in her hometown's silk industry. *Women's Garden*, she stated, was a space for women to raise their demands and to pour out their sufferings. Shen soon found herself busy receiving young women visitors who wanted to contribute to this work. The left-oriented supplement, however, increasingly came under political pressure when the Nationalist government intensified its censorship. Luo Qiong in her old age remembered her first encounter with Shen in early 1935 and how impressed she was by Shen Zijiu's remarkable courage.

When hosting a lunch meeting with a group of left-oriented feminists in a private room of a restaurant in the French Concession in Shanghai, Shen expressed her outrage at the Nationalist Party's assassination in November 1934 of the owner of the *Shanghai Daily* Shi Liangcai,[8] and informed her friends that *Women's Garden* had been ordered to reduce its space in the supplement. Her friends expressed their anger at the government censorship and their disdain for a mainstream media that catered to a consumerist culture or glorified traditional womanhood. But how, Shen asked, could they continue their fight should *Women's Garden* be closed down? Answering her own question, she told them of a plan she had come up with after consulting with "some friends."

> It seems that we have to prepare ourselves in two ways. As long as the ban from the "supreme ruler" is not issued, we will not close our *Garden,* nor will we change our tone. At the same time, we should prepare to start a new magazine, *Women's Life,* a monthly magazine with about sixty to seventy thousand characters each issue, with the same editorial principle [as the *Garden*], expressing our views freely. Let's see what those reactionaries can do to us. We have readers, progressive writers and publishers, and the support of friends who pursue justice. So while they attempt to kill our small *Garden,* we will create an even bigger garden.[9]

Luo Qiong described her feelings upon hearing Shen's comments: "She boosted our confidence . . . I genuinely admired elder sister Shen. She had a gentle and soft appearance but in fact she was very firm and strong when it came to national salvation and women's liberation."[10] Shen's reference to "some friends" was undoubtedly to underground Communists who were prepared to back a new magazine; and the lunch meeting was obviously intended to organize left-oriented feminists to write for a new magazine, *Women's Life* (*Funü shenghuo*), that would begin publication a couple of months later. As was predicted by Shen, in October 1935, the Nationalist government suspended the weekly supplement *Women's Garden*.[11]

Women's Life swiftly made Shen Zijiu a celebrity. In 1938, she attended the Lu Mountain women's meeting organized by Song Meiling (Madame Chiang Kai-Shek) for coordinating anti-Japanese resistance by women's groups. Shen then became head of the cultural affairs group in the Women Supervision Committee (constituted of leading women activists with various political affiliations). In this role, she promoted a coalition of women of different classes and political perspectives and also organized literacy classes and political training workshops for women factory workers. Shen formally joined the CCP in 1939; and in 1940 Zhou Enlai, having decided to maintain her public identity as a nonpartisan social activist, assigned her to assist Hu Yuzhi, a renowned writer, translator, and journal editor and a CCP member since 1922, working among overseas Chinese in Singapore for the resistance. Shen married Hu in 1940, and during the postwar years the couple worked together to set up the South Sea Press, publishing progressive journals to reach overseas Chinese. They returned to China in 1948. Shen became editor-in-chief of *Women of New China* and her husband was appointed the first director of the State Publishing Bureau in the PRC.[12] Lending much prestige to the new magazine, Shen's appointment guaranteed the transmission of a feminist heritage originating with the May Fourth era.

Women's Life also introduced many middle and high school girls to the CCP, some of whom became Shen's colleagues in *Women of New China* and the ACWF after 1949. Among them was Shen's successor at the magazine, Dong Bian (1916–1998). Discrimination and mistreatment accompanied Dong's childhood. The third daughter of a small landlord in Shanxi province, she was blamed for her family's failure to produce a son. She started working in the fields and taking on chores at home at the age of five. After four years of elementary school, Dong staged a hunger strike to protest her father's decision not to allow her to continue her education. Her father relented, and she went on to complete her primary and middle school education in Xin County. As the only girl in her class, she went alone to Taiyuan to take high school entrance exams and was accepted by Taiyuan Girls High School, an elite school in the capital of Shanxi province. The quiet poor student from a small village excelled in her class and dreamed of going on to

Beijing University and, like Shen Zijiu whom she had come across in the pages of *Women's Life*, of becoming an educated independent woman.[13]

Following the further Japanese military aggression in China in July 1937 after its occupation of Manchuria, Dong Bian's life decisively changed, as it did for numerous young students who rushed to join the resistance. Intellectually and politically inspired by feminism and nationalism advocated in *Women's Life*, she joined the Eighth Route Army led by the CCP in 1938. She stayed in Yan'an for eight years and excelled as a student at the Women's University and Yan'an University. She was selected to work in the Party Central Political Research Office in 1941, the only woman researcher in her group. There she met Tian Jiaying (1922–1966), a talented young writer and recent divorcé from Chengdu. Dong and Tian's romance was nurtured by their shared political and intellectual concerns, and when Tian proposed to Dong, she laid down three conditions before agreeing to marriage: "First, family affairs should be decided by the woman; second, help each other and progress together; third, feelings for each other should not be estranged because of transfer of posts." By insisting on women's autonomy on questions of reproduction and domesticity and equality in conjugal relations—her first two conditions—Dong was expressing a clear feminist consciousness. Her third condition reflected the reality that CCP couples often broke up after receiving assignments in different locations. For Dong Bian, this condition would attest to their commitment to their marriage. Tian accepted all three conditions and they married in 1942. Tian kept his promise, and when Dong decided in 1944 to leave her newborn son with a village woman in order to pursue her work, he agreed with her decision.

Dong was assigned to various posts in charge of local district Party branches or land reform work in the Jidong area of Henan Province, separated from Tian for three years. At the end of 1948 they reunited in Xibaipo, the new location of the CCP Central Committee. Tian was assigned a new post as Chairman Mao Zedong's secretary, and Dong was assigned to study at the Central Party's school. However, with her activist commitments, Dong wanted to engage in grassroots work at the local level, showing little interest in the assignment. At this point Deng Yingchao scheduled a meeting with Dong, asking if Dong would consider doing women-work. When Dong related the crucial moment in her life to her daughters in her old age, she quoted what Deng had said to her verbatim: "Chinese women sisters are oppressed most severely by the three big mountains. Fighting for women's liberation is a sacred mission for women cadres." Deng's emphasis on women's

FIGURE 2. Dong Bian, Tian Jiaying, and daughter Zeng Li in 1951. Courtesy of Zeng Li and Zeng Zi.

sufferings brought back to Dong sad memories of her miserable childhood. Dong thus accepted Deng's invitation to work for the ACWF, a decision that resulted in her fifty-year commitment to women-work.[14] She was assigned to work on the new magazine *Women of New China*, first to write editorials. Then, tutored by her idol Shen Zijiu, Dong swiftly rose to the position of deputy editor-in-chief. After Shen was transferred to the Chinese Democratic Alliance in 1956, Dong became editor-in-chief, a position to which she devoted unswerving energy until 1966 (fig. 2).[15]

During her seventeen years with the magazine, Dong Bian wrote numerous articles, initially under her own name but then, as was standard practice at the time, anonymously, as part of the "the editorial group" or "reporter of the journal" after she became the deputy editor-in-chief (similarly, Shen Zijiu's name as author appeared only once in an early issue). In an era when being an anonymous hero was the promoted behavioral norm among the Communists, Dong remained unknown to the general public. But her extreme frugal lifestyle was well known to her colleagues. For example, she preferred to take the bus to work rather than the chauffeur-driven car to which officials of her rank were entitled.[16] Her "Yan'an-style" leadership brought huge savings to the press of *Women of China*. She was also responsible for initiating the compilation of the history of the Chinese women's movement after the Cultural Revolution. During her retirement, she edited many volumes of memoirs of "elder sisters," the Communist women leaders of the first cohort who passed away in the late 1980s and early 1990s. "The pile was higher than the desk as those books were stacked up on the floor," said her daughter, describing the amount of Dong's edited volumes produced while she was old and in poor health.[17] Such prolificacy reveals her determination to resist the erasure of their hard struggles for women's liberation in the course of the Communist Revolution. But she did not leave an autobiographical memoir. Self-effacement, a characteristic "virtue" of Dong Bian and many other Communist women leaders, contributed to the concealment of these important historical actors.

MAKING A POPULAR WOMEN'S MAGAZINE IN SOCIALIST CHINA

For these activists, the founding of the PRC marked the beginning of the long-awaited moment when women's liberation would no longer be pushed to the back burner. The mission statement of *Women of New China* made it clear that the magazine aimed to "help its readers correctly and comprehensively understand the way to achieve women's liberation in new China,"[18] calling on them to actively participate in socialist revolution and socialist construction as the way to achieve women's liberation. With the double theme of "participation" and "liberation" and adopting the Party's "mass line" as its practice, the magazine soon evolved into a public forum for state feminists to express their vision of a new socialist China as well as a major site for their discursive practice in pursuit of women's liberation.

Shen Zijiu played a major role in fashioning the socialist feminist magazine in its initial stage. In her memoir, Dong Bian reveals that Shen was discontented with the initially stagnant sales of the magazine when the People's Press was managing its publishing and marketing,[19] and decided instead to establish a financially independent press run by *Women of New China* itself. Thus, the magazine would be not only financially self-supporting, but also would satisfy her vision of a feminist cultural front exclusively run by the ACWDF, not bogged down by other state-run institutions that were beyond their control. Her prior experience in running *Women's Life* in extremely difficult circumstances endowed her confidence in her ability to manage *Women of New China*; by 1953 she had succeeded in her goal and the state began to stop subsidizing the magazine. Once it had its own marketing networks, sales of the magazine rose rapidly from 10,000 copies for its first issue in 1949 to over 300,000 in 1955 and close to one million in the 1960s. In fact, by then subscriptions had to be restricted because of a shortage of paper. Some 95 percent of sales went to individual subscribers and for retail sales, and the rest went to the government and the Women's Federations. Throughout the socialist period, *Women of China* ranked among the top four magazines in circulation.[20] And when in February 1967 the magazine suspended publication, the press had a surplus of 600,000 yuan, considerable wealth at the time.[21]

What accounted for this rapid increase in circulation? What mechanisms were set up to promote the magazine's popularity besides its effective marketing? Changes in contents suggest editors' constant exploration of new ways to extend its influence. At the founding of the PRC, 90 percent of women in China were illiterate.[22] Constrained by this reality, the magazine set out to target two groups of women: those with a middle-school education and above and government officials at the county level and above. Although the magazine was primarily designed as a vehicle for women officials to exchange their experiences in women-work,[23] it also emphasized educating literate women and transforming them into new women of new China. In order to expand women's intellectual horizons and transform their worldviews, *Women of New China* allocated significant space to domestic and international political affairs (activities of the Women's International Democratic Federation were highlighted to connect Chinese women with the international women's movement and to forge global sisterhood),[24] Marxist theory, and Chinese women's history, in addition to brief reports on how women workers, peasants, and urban women students were embracing socialism.

This rather dogmatic form of education seems to have served the needs of the government officials who were expected to use articles and reports from the magazine for training materials. In fact it repeated the format of *Women's Life* that targeted educated urban women in the 1930s. But the magazine's urban focus in the early PRC also reflected the Party's new attention to urban-based industrialization after decades of rural-based warfare. The magazine's mission statement demonstrates an adherence to the Party's agenda by centering on the importance of women workers and urban industry, which soon proved controversial. In response to a request for feedback, the Advocacy Department of the Shan-Gan-Ning Women's Federation sent in two letters that were published in the May 1950 issue in a special column—highlighted in the contents in large-size font in bold—"Critical Views of *Women of New China*."[25]

The first letter stated that in order to provide suggestions for *Women of New China*, the department hosted a special meeting to collect feedback from all women officials. At the top of a list of nine concrete suggestions is its criticism that "the allocation of space in the magazine tilts more toward the urban than the rural," adding "we hope you will try your best to increase space on the rural without neglecting urban work." More interestingly, the letter devoted a large part to criticizing its own reporting on rural and ethnic minority women, noting it had only contributed four reports on women in the northwest region, and of these "not even a single report was on rural and ethnic minority women. . . . We have to seriously admit our own responsibility for this shortcoming." To redress this problem, the department set up mechanisms for submitting one report to *Women of New China* each month on women in the northwest region, and developing a grassroots network of correspondents in the whole region to enable adequate reporting on rural women and market the magazine more widely.

The second letter—signed by Li Qiyang (1918–2014)—provided a detailed analysis of the texts *Women of New China* published for teaching literacy to workers and peasants (fig. 3). The author pointed out that these were detached from rural women's lives and that the explanation of large political concepts, which may have been suitable for women officials, were beyond the comprehension of women with limited education. "In short, the texts designed for literacy classes for workers and peasants are not suitable for rural society. But in today's China the great majority of Chinese women are rural women. I think in the future it would be best if teaching materials in *Women of New China* take into consideration the great majority of women in the country."

Li Qiyang, thirty-two years old in 1950 and a Party member for thirteen years, had worked for a long time among rural women in the northwest region including Yan'an and was the director of the Advocacy and Education Department of the Shan-Gan-Ning Women's Federation (soon renamed Northwest Women's Federation)(fig. 4). It was apparently she who organized the meeting to review their own work on the representation of women in the region under their jurisdiction and made effective plans and suggestions for improving both *Women of New China* and the work of her own department. In 1951 Li also founded the first women's pictorial in the PRC, the *Northwest Women's Pictorial*, targeting illiterate rural women. Rural women could barter one egg for one copy of the *Pictorial*. In 1952 she was promoted to the position of interim director of the

FIGURE 3. Li Qiyang (with glasses on the right) and her classmate in high school in Nanjing, 1937. Courtesy of Li Qiyang's family.

FIGURE 4. Group photograph of officials of the Northwest Women's Federation in December 1952, taken to commemorate Li Qiyang's (center in the front) transfer to Beijing. To the left of Li Qiyang is Hou Di, who will become the deputy editor-in-chief of *Women of China* in 1956. Courtesy of Li Qiyang's family.

Advocacy and Education Department of the ACDWF, suggesting that the editors of *Women of New China* appreciated both her constructive suggestions and her work in the Northwest Women's Federation.[26]

What is especially notable here is that the magazine's own leadership solicited readers' criticisms months prior to the Party Central's similar action, calling for people's open criticism "of all the mistakes and shortcomings in our work in all the public occasions among the people and masses, especially in newspapers and journals."[27] It is unclear if the top Party leaders got the idea from their wives in the ACDWF who had started such action four months earlier. However, the editors of *Women of New China* felt it necessary to emphasize that they had initiated the review process long before the Party Central's decision. The August 1950 issue included a "One-year Summary of *Women of New China* Monthly Journal" by the editorial board, which stressed that editing a magazine for such a diverse readership was very challenging, and the editors knew they must have many shortcomings. Therefore, "before April this year we had already arranged review work." Now, following the Party's decision, they decided to engage in a more thorough process of criticism and self-criticism. The summary was a product of this process.[28] Their statement demonstrates that state feminists were far from passive followers of the Party Central and that in fact their agency and initiatives often placed them in the vanguard of the Party. The Party's decision in 1950, however, also reflects the ethos in the CCP at the initial stage of its tenure as a state power holder.

The magazine's most visible improvement following Li Qiyang's constructive criticism is the appearance of rural women on the cover. Beginning with the June 1950 issue, images of rural and ethnic minority women rapidly exceeded images of women workers, becoming the most prominent cover themes throughout the 1950s and the first half of the 1960s. This shift in representational orientation, preceding the central government's shifting attention to rural collectivization, demonstrates the advocacy of lower-ranking women officials in the cultural representation of women in the periphery. Although illiterate rural women and women who belonged to ethnic minorities were unlikely to read the magazine (let alone submit their opinions), local women officials did consider it their responsibility to include underrepresented women in cultural representation.[29]

The shift in representational focus in the covers of *Women of New China* brought an array of images of smiling rural and ethnic minority women holding bundles of grain or vegetables (fig. 5), carrying baskets of cotton or dirt, operating tractors or engaging in agricultural experiments, or attending the

FIGURE 5. Cover of *Women of China,* 1955, no. 11. Niu Yufen and Yuan Lianfang, members of the Red Flag agricultural cooperative in Baoding.

highest state conventions and even toasting Chairman Mao at a state banquet (fig. 6). What were emphasized were rural women and ethnic minority women's contribution to socialist construction and their political participation. When, during the Great Leap Forward, the ACWF's focus was to promote women's participation in technological innovations, the covers also highlighted ethnic minority women engaging in science and technology (fig. 7). Such repetitive subjects of visual representation contributed to the formation of a new symbolic order that unambiguously disrupted deeply entrenched gender, class, and ethnic hierarchies.[30] Although women's

FIGURE 6. Cover of *Women of China,* 1956, no. 4. Co-op leader Long Donghua toasts Chairman Mao.

diligent productive labor had been extolled by the elite literati and imperial court in ancient times, the constant visual representation of laboring women in this socialist state feminist magazine carried new social and cultural meanings. It conveyed a powerful message that women of the laboring class, or to use the widely circulated term at the time, *laodong renmin* [laboring people], were now the dignified masters of the new China.

To what extent does such visual representation reflect the reality of the time? It was obvious that most photographs were carefully composed to achieve optimal effects of lighting and composition and smiling subjects were posing for the camera. When I myself worked as a farmworker during the

FIGURE 7. Cover of *Women of China*, 1958, no. 16. A meteorologist of Yao nationality.

years of the Cultural Revolution, I certainly knew we never wore new clothes to work in the fields, let alone pretty bows in our hair while working amid dirt and dust. However, in my interview with the art editor Shi Yumei (1925–), who was the photographer of many of the cover images, she informed me that in most cases the women appearing on the covers were actually "labor models" (an honorary title for those with exceptional performance at work) from rural communities or factories, and photos were never randomly shot. Sometimes it took her a few days to follow her subject(s) around to find the best setting to stage the heroine(s). In other words, what Shi did was not photojournalism to capture newsworthy spontaneous images, but rather a kind of conceptual photography carefully designed to represent an idea, and in her specific case, to "convey the spirit of laboring women." When I commented on those pretty bows young peasants wore on their braids while working, Shi replied: "The women felt very honored for being able to appear on the cover of *Women of China*. They always insisted on wearing their best outfits for such photo opportunities."[31] The pictures, thus, did not faithfully represent these laboring women's material condition, but captured their dignity and pride at being the glorified subject of the new socialist country. In a sense, the cover images were visual representations co-authored by both a state feminist photographer from the power center and the "laboring women" on the periphery. Indeed, proudly adorned in new peasant or ethnic outfits when mixing with state officials or urban labor models, or engaging in various forms of manual labor, rural women and ethnic minority women exuded confidence and self-assurance. There was no trace of anxiety of being seen as "backward" or "rustic" (*tu*). Rhetorical schemes of "othering" by the urban elite would not become dominant until the post-Mao era when class realignment was in motion and modernity was redefined as Western. The images of rural and ethnic women prominently presented in the official media are historical evidence of a time when socialist state feminists were striving toward their Communist goal of eliminating gender, class, and ethnic inequalities in China.

To increase the appeal of the magazine, the editors also set out to organize three groups, or to use their term "three troops" (*sanzhi duiwu*), revealing a legacy of the CCP's recent military history. The first was the troop of correspondents. *Women of New China* expanded its local networks of correspondents to include women and men working at the rural county cultural centers. By August 1950 there were already over 1,300 correspondents nationwide. To raise the quality of reports from the grassroots, the magazine ran periodic training workshops. The second was the troop of readers. With the assistance of local Women's Federations, editors regularly hosted meetings of readers' groups in urban and rural areas to hear readers' feedback after the publication of each issue. Since women-dominated grassroots organizations, such as women's congresses and resident committees, sometimes used *Women of China* as their study material by reading selected articles to illiterate women in study sessions, the scope of "readers" actually encompassed much broader groups than actual literate readers. The third was the troop of professional writers and artists. The magazine regularly solicited literary and art works from renowned professional writers and artists to enhance its appeal; cartoons, for example, emerged in 1955 as a welcome device for criticizing erroneous ideas and practices. The magazine's prestige is demonstrated by the frequent contributions from famous writers and artists. Literature editor Duan Yongqiang (1932–) proudly recalls how easy it was for him to solicit articles from famous writers,[32] and art editor Shi Yumei, who graduated from the Central Arts Academy, fully utilized her social network to solicit top artists' paintings sometimes without having to pay.[33]

To guarantee the magazine's connection with the masses, a group of four editors was responsible for compiling summaries from readers' letters each month as the basis for editorial decision making for the following issue. About 80 percent of the space of each issue was designated for readers' letters and contributions from local correspondents and professional writers who produced short stories and biographies of heroines. The remaining 20 percent was for editors' articles. Editors were also required to do fieldwork in rural villages and urban factories periodically, in line with the Party's tenet "from the masses and to the masses."[34] Hou Di (1924–), who joined the editorial board in 1954 and became the deputy editor-in-chief in 1956, remembered what Dong Bian often emphasized: "Our editorial board is like a processing factory. The raw materials are in the life of the masses, which are endless and abundant. As long as we have sharp eyes, quick hands and fast legs, we will be able to obtain them. Then with elaborate design and dexterous assembling by our editorial board, the processed 'products' will be lively, vibrant, refreshing, and will meet readers' demands."[35] In my interviews with Hou Di over a span of three years, she never failed to emphasize the mass line and attributed the popularity of the magazine to the editors' persistent pursuit of "making the magazine close to the life of the women masses."

A major innovation in engaging a broad range of women readers occurred almost by accident. In 1954 Shen Zijiu, reading through submitted articles, found one reporting on the suicide of a woman official. Yang Yun had been separated from her husband by ten years of war, and committed suicide when she eventually found her beloved husband only to discover that he had just remarried. Shen decided to create a forum discussing "Why did Yang Yun commit suicide?" as a way to guide women toward a revolutionary outlook on marriage and the pursuit of the revolutionary cause. Publicizing a Party member's suicide was unprecedented in official magazines. Revolutionary couples separated by war were not uncommon and how to handle unfortunate situations in personal life was a concern to many young revolutionaries. Readers responded with vehement and diverse opinions on Yang Yun and her husband and sales rocketed from 117,000 to 340,000 copies over the five months that the debate went on.[36]

Once the format of inviting readers to participate in debate had proved an effective way to extend the magazine's influence, themes were not limited to shaping women's revolutionary outlook. A few months after the conclusion of public discussions on the suicide case, Hou Di, then the head of the editorial group for readers' letters, brought to the attention of the editorial committee a letter from a woman teacher, Liu Lequn, condemning her high-ranking official husband's affair with a young woman. Liu's case could be characterized as representative at a time when many male Communist officials were busy changing wives after they entered urban areas (replacing old with young, rural with urban, and illiterate with educated women). Hou Di, at the time 31, and her colleagues of the same cohort "all felt the tendency repulsive." She explained in the interview: "In the base areas the sex ratio was sometimes one woman to a hundred men. So those men would feel lucky to just get hold of a woman. But upon liberation they wanted to change wives. We in the editorial committee sneered at the phenomenon as 'replacing a donkey with a horse' (*qilü huanma*)." The sarcasm vividly expressed these young Communist women's contempt toward those male officials who wanted to "upgrade" their wives once they moved into new positions of power.

This sentiment was also shared by the senior cohort. After verifying the validity of Liu Lequn's accusation, Shen Zijiu approved the exposé as the focus of a daring forum—"Why was our conjugal relationship broken?"—in order to "educate people to establish Communist morality in marriage and family."[37] But when the husband Luo Baoyi learned of this, he pleaded with the editors not to publish Liu Lequn's letter, promising that he would not divorce her. The top executive official of the ACDWF, Zhang Yun, held a meeting with Liu Lequn to inform her that the ACDWF would leave it to her to assess if her husband genuinely wanted to fix their marriage or if this was just a ploy to avoid the exposé. Liu decided that it was the latter, and consequently, the sensational forum featuring Liu's original letter appeared in the November 1955 issue.

Again, readers' response was phenomenal. The number of letters soared from around 4,000 to over 8,000 each month over the eight months of the forum, and sales totaled over half a million in 1956. One thousand copies sold out instantly in front of a department store in Wangfujing, the heart of the business district in Beijing, when a shop clerk loudly hawked that *Women of New China* had printed a story on the morally degenerate assistant to the minister of international trade.[38] When asked if they had any apprehension about criticizing a prevailing phenomenon among high-ranking male officials, Hou Di replied: "No. We were young and innocent. Unlike people today worrying about this and that, we just wanted to speak out against whatever we thought was wrong. We were bold and fearless."[39] However, they could also be careful in devising strategies. The editors solicited strong support from high-ranking male officials who had stable marriages and resented the tendency to change wives since it tarnished the image of the Party. The forum included essays by Xie Juezai, the chief justice of the Supreme Court, and Xie Xuegong, the Party secretary of the Ministry of International Trade where the accused husband worked, condemning "bourgeois individualism" and calling for Party members to uphold "Communist morality." To obtain a contribution from the chief justice, an editor waited at the gate of the Supreme Court for hours until he stepped out of his office.

Rather than a one-dimensional tool for teaching women a socialist outlook, the exposé of a male official's affair highlighted another dimension of the magazine. State feminists obviously used the dominant political language (in this case "Communist morality education") to legitimize a gender critique of a rather prevalent sexual practice among male officials. This maneuver revealed the continuation of the gendered tensions in the Party that had been generated by the new Marriage Law of 1950. Many Communist women at the time had feared that the new law's radical clause of unconditional divorce would put their marriages in jeopardy; in conditions of gender inequality and double sexual standards, freedom of divorce was more likely to benefit men with power and money and place divorced women in a predicament. The trend for male officials to "change wives" in the early 1950s validated their fear.[40] Although the editors involved in the exposé all had stable marriages, their enthusiastic participation in the forum demonstrated their resentment of the Party's double standard of sexual morality. Their tactful yet conservative appeal to "Communist morality" expressed their desire to exercise some leverage in a system of unequal sexual power relations.

"EDUCATING SOCIETY ABOUT WOMEN"

In sharp contrast to the shifting themes and multiple voices of the contents, the covers of *Women of China* presented a consistently stable theme throughout the 1950s and early 1960s: the celebration of women's work in all walks of

新中國婦女
一九五四年　　　第四期

FIGURE 8. Cover of *Women of China,* 1954, no. 4. Housewife
Wang Guilan becomes a bricklayer.

life. Placing working women in the center of visual representations of socialist women has multiple meanings. It suggests the identification of women
with the project of socialist state building by highlighting their diverse public
roles, celebrates their contribution to socialist construction, and by extension
glorifies and elevates the work they perform, no matter how ordinary, thus
raising them to the rank of the leading class of the socialist polity.

The magazine's cover images of urban women during the 1950s depict
them almost always in roles previously associated with men. They include the
first woman locomotive operator Tian Guiying, the first group of women
pilots, a housewife-turned-bricklayer (fig. 8), a young woman in training for

新中國婦女
一九五四年　　　　第六期

FIGURE 9. Cover of *Women of China,* 1954, no. 6. Future woman
captain Kong Qingfen during an internship at sea.

ship's captain (fig. 9), a shipping company's electrician, the head of a shift in
a power distribution station, a woman welder (fig. 10), and so on. These
images can be interpreted in several ways. First, as Tina Mai Chen has argued,
images of seemingly emancipated women were invoked to symbolize broader
transformation in the new socialist China;[41] and second, they can be understood as a means to inspire women readers to move beyond their familiar
domestic environment to participate in industrialization. However, when we
look more closely at the political and economic context in which these images
were produced, a very different interpretation emerges: that they were part of

FIGURE 10. Cover of *Women of China,* 1959, no. 9. A woman welder.

a concerted effort by state feminists to challenge sexism inside and outside the Party.

In the early 1950s the economy was only just beginning to recover from the devastation of wars and the depletion of capital. The unemployment rate was high. Urban unemployed women, especially the lower classes who desperately needed a wage to support their families, wanted to be gainfully employed in socialist construction.[42] However, the road to women's liberation was blocked by Communist officials. The problem was so rampant that Deng Yingchao had to make a strong appeal to the Party Central to redress it. At a national conference on ideological propaganda work hosted by the Central Committee in July 1951, Deng pointed out the seriousness of "feudal thinking" that was often reflected in the minds of Party members and officials.

The primary view is that "women can do nothing." [People with such a view] use every possible means and from every possible aspect to restrict women. Its manifestation in society is discrimination against women, or using all kinds of excuses to refuse or restrict the opportunities for women to participate in employment or education. They would even distort government policies and decrees in order not to give women equal rights.[43]

To address this grave situation, Deng proposed that the Party's ideological propaganda work should "use Marxist Leninist theory and Mao Zedong thought to engage in the struggle against feudal thinking, against its various forms of restricting and confining women, resolutely break the notion that 'women can do nothing,' and replace it with the view that 'women can do everything.'" She emphasized that such educational work should first be conducted among Communist Party officials: "Only after the feudal remnants among the cadres are eradicated, will they then be able to play a better leading role among the people, and will they be able to effectively implement the Party's policies on the women's liberation movement, to bring into play boundless initiatives of the women masses and enable them to participate in all kinds of construction work for the people's motherland."[44]

The sharp critical tone illuminates the prestige Deng enjoyed as a senior Party member whose husband was Premier Zhou Enlai. However, her critique demonstrates the fissured nature of the Party. Although conceptually women's liberation had been on the Party's platform from its inception, institutionally male officials blocked women's entry into the public domain. Obviously, a deeply entrenched gender regime based on differential labor and the spatial division between women and men did not evaporate upon the CCP's assumption of state power. On the contrary, as Deng exposed, the gender regime remained entrenched in the minds of many CCP officials. A cartoon in *Women of China* in 1956 entitled "Three Women Are Not Equal to One Man" vividly captures how women often encountered dismissals (fig. 11). An arrogant male official tells the first woman: "You have too much housework. You should resign and go home!" He says to the second woman holding a sick leave request: "No, you cannot ask for rest. You should resign!" To the third woman who is pregnant, he says: "Pregnancy affects production. You should resign!" He is finally relieved when he succeeds in maintaining an all-male working environment. "Now we can guarantee our work."[45]

It was during this important talk that Deng Yingchao articulated a tenet that would become a guideline for the ACWF's advocacy: "Educating women about society and educating society about women." Party officials

FIGURE 11. Cartoon in *Women of China,* 1956, no. 8. "Three Women Are Not Equal to One Man."

became an important part of "the society" that state feminists proceeded to educate and transform. It was obviously a difficult mission to accomplish, judging from the many exposés of discrimination against women published in *Women of New China* in the first half of the 1950s. On March 6, 1957, Deng went to the CCP's national conference on ideological work to call again on Party officials to "establish the notion that the whole Party should be involved in women-work; to establish the notion that 'women can do everything' in ideological and educational work."[46] At this time state feminists still had to fight tough battles to crack open male-dominated gainful employment for women, especially lower-class women. As observed in recent scholarship, for many women the Great Leap Forward in 1958 was a watershed in Chinese women's liberation.[47] Urban women were recruited in both state and collectively owned enterprises in large numbers during this period with the strong push from the ACWF to remove gender barriers in many fields.

The intense gender struggle depicted by Deng Yingchao, in the framework of a teleological battle between rising socialism and declining feudalism, cautions us to learn to decode feminist language in order to trace state feminists' discursive maneuvers. "Feudalism" was one of the three "big mountains" that the CCP avowed to overthrow. After 1949 it could claim the accomplishment of toppling the other two, "imperialism and bureaucratic capitalism," and Deng legitimately highlighted the remaining one. However, her usage of the word "feudalism" in this context was similar to what we mean today by a combination of "sexism," "patriarchy," "masculinism," and "misogyny." Once this is understood, socialist state feminist texts can be read in a different light. Rather than deviating openly from the Party line, state feminists invoked an item still on the agenda of the Party, anti-feudalism, to legitimize their gender-specific claims. It is in such simultaneous congruence of rhetoric and deviation in meaning that state feminists were most effective in inserting their own agenda or transforming and expanding definitions of Party lines. The rapid adoption of "feudalism" (*fengjian zhuyi*), "feudalist thinking" (*fengjian sixiang*), or the abbreviation "feudal" (*fengjian*) with a gender inflection in everyday speech even by illiterate rural women attested to the considerable success of state feminists' discursive strategy in socialist state propaganda.

Deng's talk as well as many articles and cartoons in *Women of China* indicates that images of women overcoming gender barriers in employment were a representational device of state feminists to "resolutely break the notion that 'women can do nothing.'" The cover of the magazine was a cultural site in which state feminists deliberately engaged in a gender struggle by representing women as versatile and capable socialist constructors. This understanding helps explain the huge discrepancy between a single-minded focus on celebrating women's accomplishments in social production and the diverse subjects responding to women's needs in daily life in the contents of the magazine. Cover images rarely showed women caring for children or old people or serving food. When such images did appear, they would always depict women in the context of collective facilities such as daycare centers or canteens, mostly in the Great Leap Forward, expressing the ACWF's advocacy of socialization of housework.

When I asked Hou Di why the covers never showed women's domestic life during the Mao era, she replied instantly: "At that time we never thought about that. It is hard to imagine how low women's status was at that time!" She recalled a letter from a reader who challenged the magazine's promoting of equality between men and women by saying "women are like flying a kite under the bed" (that is as high as they can go). "That saying incensed me so much," Hou Di emphasized, "that I still remember it clearly today."[48] So much was at stake in visually representing women that the editors used the precious space of the cover as a window display to convey the important message "women can do everything, and do well in the public arena!" This motive was also behind their decision to use photographs for the covers, a practice conspicuously different from other journals at the time. In Hou Di's words: "Real people and real deeds have stronger impact on people in our advocacy."

Hou Di's unhesitating reply that the editors never thought about visually representing women in a domestic setting deserves further probing. At one level, it illuminates the primary understanding of women's liberation by this cohort of state feminists. Women's liberation, according to Engels, was based on women's participation in social production in an economic system of public ownership. But more recently, over the past three decades, feminists both in and outside China have criticized the applicability of this simplistic thesis to the practices of Chinese women's liberation in the socialist period. However, in the specific cultural context of the new socialist China, socialist state feminists confronted two interlocking imperatives: the move from the control of private ownership of a patriarchal family to an autonomy enabled by financial independence through socialized productive work, and a revolution to destroy a gender regime based on the spatial differentiation of *nei / wai* [inner / outer]. Socialist public ownership did not automatically undo the gender regime, and undoubtedly male officials' blocking women's entrance into the public domain had less to do with economic profitability than with maintaining the gender order. In other words, a Marxist project of women's "participation in social production" generated powerful locally grounded dynamics and resistance. Lacking analytical tools other than the all-encapsulating term "feudalism" to confront mounting challenges and obstacles, socialist state feminists forged ahead with their innovative daily practices, including grabbing any representational space available to promote women's accomplishments in the public arena.

The radical implications of repeated visual representations of laboring women can be further explored with reference to recent scholarship on women and gender in China. Joan Judge locates the disruption of "the regime of feminine virtue" of the Qing Dynasty at the turn of the twentieth century, when women of the elite class ventured outside the domestic confines by attending girls' schools, going abroad, and becoming involved in revolutionary activities. The public appearance of elite women changed the gender norm that associated chastity, the highest virtue for women, with domestic seclusion.[49] Louise Edwards demonstrates how elite women used their privilege of education to legitimize their demand for equal rights to political participation in the first part of the twentieth century, since historically the right to rule was linked with the privilege of education of male literati.[50] These and many more works on the Republican era have shown clearly that elite women successfully challenged gender segregation, gaining respectability in public domains in metropolises. But for lower-class women, both rural and urban, the gender regime of feminine virtue continued when the PRC was founded. As Gail Hershatter and Lisa Rofel demonstrate, performing manual labor outside the home, either in the fields or in the factory, jeopardized a woman's chastity and reputation.[51] Within this context, the meanings of socialist state feminists' exclusive visual representation of laboring women in the public domain become clearer. It manifests their keen sensitivity to what trapped the great majority of Chinese women: an intertwined regime of gender and class that placed women doing manual labor outside the home at the bottom of the social hierarchy. Thus it was inconceivable for that cohort of feminists to use images that located a woman *inside* the home as a signifier of women's liberation.

MEANINGFUL DISCREPANCIES

The gap between the contents and the cover of the magazine had another dimension. The cover did not always keep pace with the political tempo, while the contents generally followed Party imperatives by assigning at least an editorial in each issue to discuss major government decrees. An example of visible dissonance can be found in 1957. The Anti-Rightist Campaign charged ferociously through urban China beginning in mid-May 1957. On May 22, the ACWF held a meeting to inform all the officials and staff in the headquarters of the significance of the campaign.[52] The cover of the June issue belied this new political agenda, featuring a baby girl looking at a little chick (fig. 12). The ACWF followed the Women's International Democratic Federation decision to make June 1 International Children's Day in China, and the June cover of a baby was also an indirect expression celebrating motherhood.

If the June cover had a prerogative reserved for children, what about the following issues when the Anti-Rightist Campaign intensified? The cover of the July issue portrays a smiling woman hairdresser serving a young girl. Readers would have been totally unprepared for the intense animosity and

FIGURE 12. Cover of *Women of China,* 1957, no. 6. So cute!

harsh condemnation of rightists in the contents. Throughout the political storm of the campaign, the magazine steadfastly adhered to its principle of visual representation, celebrating women role models in all walks of life. Only the cover of the November issue diverged from this theme. It is a painting of a Russian girl and a Chinese girl jointly saluting the image of Lenin to commemorate the fortieth anniversary of the Russian Revolution. The cover's attention to international political events makes the indifference to domestic politics even more puzzling.

The art editor Shi Yumei solved the puzzle when I asked her about the editorial decisions that led to the cute baby picture in June 1957. First she told me proudly that she took the picture and the baby was her neighbor's child. Then I questioned her further:

WANG: It was June 1957. What did the editors-in-chief say since they made the final selection on cover images?

SHI: Oh, the leader [Dong Bian] dashed to the picture, saying excitedly "that's it, that's it!" The leaders totally adored the picture.

WANG: But it was 1957 and the struggles against the rightists were intensified. Didn't the magazine have to follow the political issues of the day?

SHI: Well, to tell you the truth, at that time I did not like those struggles. I have an art background and my job was to make the magazine aesthetically appealing. My top priority was to give beauty to the magazine. Matching political tempo was not so high on my agenda. If you had class struggles and fighting on the cover, people would not like it and would not buy it.

This instance of the omission of a rampant political campaign in the magazine's visual representation thus largely reflects Shi Yumei's personal tastes and political position, which were shared by the editors-in-chief who had the final say on the cover. It is worth noting that the absence of the Anti-Rightist Campaign was also a feature of the covers of *Youth of China*, the Communist Youth League's journal, though its covers generally demonstrated a conscious effort to follow the Party's main agenda.

Meaningful discrepancies can be found when comparing *Women of China* covers with those of *Youth of China*. The covers of four issues of *Women of China* in 1952 used a charcoal sketch portraying the trio of the worker / peasant / soldier, a familiar subject in a familiar format. However, all three figures on the covers of *Women of China* are female (fig. 13). The absence of men in this otherwise familiar trio reveals a clear feminist rejection of male-centered visual representation in socialist China. The trio in *Youth of China* are usually men, and if a woman is included she unfailingly represents the peasant, standing either on the side or behind the male worker.[53] Her gendered subordination is conveniently deployed in representing the subtle hierarchy among the leading classes of the proletarian socialist state. The image was so prevalent and pervasive that no one could imagine what it would look like if a woman replaced the male worker who was always positioned in the center. Hence the all-women trio on the covers of *Women of China* represented a significant feminist challenge to the hegemonic symbol of the Mao era, a symbol that simultaneously signifies a conscious transformation of the class order and an unconscious continuation of gender hierarchy.

FIGURE 13. Cover of *Women of China,* 1952, no. 4. Female worker / peasant / soldier.

Further evidence of a Chinese socialist feminist consciousness comes from photographs of women militias on the covers of both magazines. Such pictures became popular after the publication of Mao's poem on women militias in 1961. The militia photographs in *Youth of China* always portray the women under the guidance of men, highlighting their subordination (fig. 14).[54] But covers of *Women of China* consistently place women militias in the center and autonomous (fig. 15). When I showed the images from *Youth of China* to Shi Yumei, she responded immediately, "Hmm, giving prominence to men again. I would never select such a picture. And even if I did, our leaders would never approve of it. Our magazine is *Women of China.* We gave prominence to women. On this issue we [Shi and the editors-in-chief] held identical views."

FIGURE 14. Cover of *Youth of China,* 1965, no. 17. Instructing a militia woman.

Before the Cultural Revolution, editors of *Women of China* controlled the magazine as their turf, a space where they created a distinctive socialist feminist visual culture. It was not until mid-1966 that they discontinued the representational device of extolling women's diverse accomplishments. When I asked Shi Yumei why Chairman Mao's images replaced women labor models, she replied: "For the sake of safety. Even top Party leaders were frequently condemned. We could not guarantee [the political stability of] any labor model. So it was the safest thing to do to put images of Chairman Mao on the cover. Besides," she added candidly, "I very much worshipped Chairman

FIGURE 15. Cover of *Women of China,* 1964, no. 8. Militia woman Zhang Guijiao.

Mao, too. I had experienced the old society and was very grateful to him for the changes in new China, despite my own political frustrations."[55] Shi's explanation shed light on the phenomenon of Chairman Mao's images swiftly taking over every inch of visual space during the Cultural Revolution. It was not just an expression of blind worship but also a pragmatic tactic for the sake of political safety. However, the images of Chairman Mao that thereafter monopolized the cover of *Women of China,* a prominent example of how state feminists followed the political norm of the Cultural Revolution, can now be seen as announcing the collapse of the feminist cultural front created by state feminists of the ACWF.[56]

CONCLUSION: STATE FEMINISTS AND GENDER DEMOCRACY

Shen Zijiu, editor-in-chief of *Women's Life,* a marginal women's magazine in the Republican era, and editor-in-chief of *Women of China,* the only women's magazine dominating the market in the early PRC, and her cohort as well as a younger cohort of feminist colleagues upheld the May Fourth feminist agenda of anti-feudalism in their pursuit of a proletarian women's liberation in socialist China. The creation of a socialist feminist cultural front, *Women of China*, was only one area of state feminists' massive engagement in a grand project of transforming Chinese culture, society, and people. The micro case, however, epitomizes the complexity of socialist state feminists' multifaceted endeavors as state architects who shaped the configuration of a new socialist China.

The micro case also serves to remind us that the goal of revolutionary transformation was not the same for all revolutionaries. Communist women's personal experiences in a patriarchal culture decisively conditioned their passionate pursuit of a revolutionary transformation of gender hierarchy and patriarchal norms. Although egalitarian socialist principles were the source of the discursive power of state feminists, it fell to them, often to them alone, to insure that gender equality would be included in the conceptualization of a socialist state and in social and cultural practices. It should not surprise us that a thorny situation would arise in their revolutionary efforts: state feminists' pursuit of women's liberation very soon brought them into conflict with masculinist power within the Party. Battling against "feudalism" and upholding "Communist morality," the first two cohorts of state feminists did not hesitate to include male Party officials among their targets. They effectively deployed the Party's ideology and agenda as discursive resources in their gender struggles. In such discursive maneuvers they also redefined and transformed the Party's ideology and agenda, making a gender inflected anti-feudalism prominent in the socialist transformation of society and culture, and lower-class laboring women central to dismantling gender, class, and ethnic hierarchies.

As an organizing principle, following the Party's "mass line" also facilitated their development. During the Communist Revolution the mass line had proved an effective method for the CCP to connect with and mobilize the masses; and following the revolutionary victory, the Party continued to emphasize it for state building. Defined as a mass organization, the ACWF shouldered the responsibility to put the principle of the CCP into practice in its women-work. In the case of *Women of China*, state feminists' faithful implementation of the mass line resulted in the rapid development of a feminist cultural front that connected with writers, artists, readers, grassroots-based correspondents, WF local officials, local cultural halls, and marketing sites throughout the vast country. State feminists' practices and innovations enabled democratic participation of socialist citizens, especially previously marginalized and disadvantaged women, in the formation of a women-centered discursive space close to the power center, at a time when the Party was consolidating its centralizing power. Moreover, the dominant discursive power of the feminist cultural front based on participatory democracy was secured by the monopoly of *Women of China* in socialist China's publishing market for women's magazines. These parallel, paradoxical, and contradictory developments were the social reality experienced by socialist citizens, which were vividly captured in *Women of China*, a rare window for us to perceive the multiple contradictions, conflicts, and contentions in socialist transformations.

The state feminists' simultaneous involvement in the Party's political imperatives and discreet pursuits of a feminist transformation were often entangled messily in tension in their daily work as Communist officials. Their discursive strategy of camouflaging their gender-specific struggles with dominant Party language further shrouded their distinctive feminist initiatives and agenda. To delineate Chinese socialist state feminists' maneuvers requires a gender-sensitive conceptualization and an ethnographic approach. Stories behind the scenes enhance the ability to decode key words and tease out concrete gender conflicts from multiple sources. In order to achieve a more complex understanding of the internal workings and dynamics of the socialist state, we must pay close attention to state feminists' visions and strategies, and the differences they made. Especially because state feminists operated in a *politics of concealment*, constituted of their conscious discursive strategy of a "hidden transcript" and a self-effacement that erased themselves as authors and active agents, it requires extra investigating and decoding efforts of historians in research. My investigation of a major shift in the history of *Women of China* in the next chapter will further illustrate the politics of concealment and its limitations.

FOUR

When a Maoist "Class"
Intersected Gender

IN THE OCTOBER 1964 ISSUE of *Red Flag,* the Communist Party Central Committee's theoretical journal, an essay entitled "How Should We Deal with the Women Question" was published under the direction of Chen Boda, the editor-in-chief of the journal. After the appearance of the article in *Red Flag,* it was reprinted in the CCP's newspaper *People's Daily* on October 30, 1964. The double appearance of the article in the Party's key publications suggests its unusual importance, since women did not often enjoy such attention. Why, in the midst of a political storm swirling around the question of class struggle generated by Chairman Mao in his campaign against revisionism and capitalist restoration, would women suddenly appear at the center of the CCP's media? Before we start the investigation, it is necessary to offer a disclaimer: this chapter has little to do with feminist theorization of the intersection of gender and class. Rather, tracing and unpacking diverse meanings and usages of these words lead us to the morass of entangled power relations between the personal and political in high politics in 1964.

WOMEN OF CHINA UNDER FIRE

The article directed by Chen Boda, who had served as Mao's secretary for decades and in May 1966 would become the head of the Cultural Revolution Group of the Central Committee, openly condemned the state feminist magazine *Women of China,* specifically targeting the two recent forums in the magazine that had received much public attention.[1] The editors of *Women of China* were stunned by the attack; in their later recollections of the strongly worded condemnation, they emphasized not only their surprise but also that they found the charges entirely unwarranted. For example, the then editor-in-chief Dong Bian, writing in the 1990s, gave this account of the unforgettable incident.

> After investigation, research and thorough preparation, we organized two forums on outlooks on life and marriage in the magazine. The forums attracted vast attention from women in all walks of life. Letters and articles poured in and debates were very heated. The sales of the magazine were rising rapidly. Just as we were thrilled by the wonderful situation, the October 1964 issue of *Red Flag* published an article entitled "How Should We Deal with the Women Question," attacking the forums in *Women of China.* The listed crimes include, one, "deviating from the class analysis and absence of class perspective," and two, "leading women to fall into the mud pit of bourgeois humanism." These were huge hats befalling us [that is, severe political accusations were brought down "on our heads"]. The sudden blow smacked me into dizziness. I had totally no clue what went wrong.[2]

And in an essay commemorating Dong Bian, then deputy editor-in-chief Hou Di mentions the event in a similar vein:

> In the October issue of 1964, *Red Flag* suddenly published an article entitled "How Should We Deal with the Women Question." The article condemned the two forums in *Women of China,* "What Should Women Live For?" and "What Are the Standards for Choosing a Lover [*airen*]?"[3] The article accused the two forums of being enshrouded in a veil of tender feelings, "using sex to cover class distinction and erase class struggle," and "leading women in the degenerating direction of capitalism and revisionism." On October 30 of the same year, the *People's Daily* reprinted the article. Indeed, at that time both the Party's journal and the Party's newspaper were aiming their guns at *Women of China.*[4]

Recalling the event, both Dong Bian and Hou Di highlighted the memory of experiencing a "surprise attack" and being enraged at the accusation. Their surprise is in itself illuminating; evidently the editors-in-chief had had no doubts about the political correctness of their forums in that political context, let alone anticipated condemnation. It was certainly an unprecedented experience for *Women of China,* the official magazine of the ACWF, to be accused by the Party's official publications. At the least, the memoirs reveal a huge chasm in the perspectives of these state feminists and the attacker who appeared to represent the Party. What were the differences between them? What made these women editors so furious beyond that the attack was unexpected? Let's first turn to the *Red Flag* article for some clues.

"How Should We Deal with the Women Question" opened the long text with a phrase by then already an authoritative cliché, "Comrade Mao Zedong has taught us: never forget class struggle." Although Mao had first enunciated the political dictum at the Tenth Plenary Meeting of the Eighth Central Committee in September 1962, the deteriorating relationship between the CCP and the Soviet Union that climaxed in 1963 added greater urgency to his preoccupation with taking preventive measures to guard China against a revisionist road (the Soviet way) and capitalist restoration. The *Red Flag* article demonstrated the author's intimate knowledge of both the political context and the ascending political discourse. Indeed, published in the CCP's most prestigious theoretical journal, the article projected an air of theoretical authority by frequently quoting from Mao and Lenin in addition to engaging in a lengthy discussion of historical stages in which women of different classes evolved. Concrete criticisms of "problems" and "mistakes" in *Women of China* took less than one third of the space, sandwiched in between quotations from authoritative proletarian leaders and totalizing descriptions of human history.

A breakdown of the first eight paragraphs may illustrate the structure of the article and how the use of quotations in particular elevated the article to the high political ground, leaving little room for the accused to defend themselves. Each of the first four paragraphs begins with the words "Comrade Mao Zedong," and then summarizes Mao's key points on class struggle in socialist society and the importance of class analysis. The repetitive use of "Comrade Mao Zedong" powerfully constructs a visual image of the highest authority presiding over the issue being discussed. And beyond invoking his name, the relevance of Mao's teaching to each issue makes it nearly impossible to dispute. Here is an example from the second paragraph:

> Comrade Mao Zedong ... points out that socialism is a very long historical period. Throughout this historical period, there exist struggles between bourgeoisie and proletariat, the question of "who defeats whom" between the way of capitalism and the way of socialism, and the danger of capitalist restoration. In order to guarantee the victory of socialism and to prevent the restoration of capitalism, we must continue socialist revolution on political, economic, ideological and cultural fronts to the end.[5]

These words read like prophecy today. And their truth-claiming power was even stronger for Communist Party members in 1964. *Women of China* in 1964 also frequently warned about class struggle domestically and internationally; the editors of *Women of China* had no disagreement with Mao's emphasis on the necessity of continuing socialist revolution in order to prevent capitalist restoration. Then what was in dispute?

It is in the sixth paragraph that the key polemic in Chen Boda's attack appears:

> Marxism and Leninism told us, the thorough liberation of the mass of laboring women is an extremely important component part of the whole proletarian revolutionary cause; raising and solving *funü wenti* must be subordinate to the interest of the whole proletariat's class struggle. This is still the fundamental principle from which we can never deviate when examining *funü wenti* in socialist society. Deviating from this principle, treating *funü wenti* only from the perspective of sex [*xingbie,* connoting biological sex], erasing class distinctions among women, and severing the connection between women's liberation and the whole proletarian cause, are the so-called women's perspective of the bourgeoisie.[6]

I leave *funü wenti* untranslated in this quotation because the Chinese term contains a significant ambiguity that cannot be conveyed by either one of the two English renditions ("the women question" or "women's problems"). Indeed, I'm tempted to use both translations—"raising the women question and solving women's problems"—for the Chinese *funü wenti de tichu he jiejue,* but such clarity in the English expression would only distort a deliberate fuzziness in the author's argument about *funü wenti.* If his point is that women's problems are social problems, it would follow that nothing social could be free of class, that is, class struggles are also embedded in women's problems. The author does elaborate on this point in the fifth paragraph; but his attack hinges more on the concept of "the women question," his goal being to prove that the act of *raising* "the women question" in itself expressed a bourgeois position, which made even naming gender issues and talking about women's problems a political mistake. The ambiguity in the term allowed the author to move deftly from the definition of women's problems as embedded in class to *defining the act of raising "the women question" in the framework of class struggle.*

Thus, the author could move directly to the seventh paragraph with a vague claim that infuriated Hou Di. "The women question can easily be enshrouded in a gauze curtain of tender feelings, and hence easily deviates from class analysis, facilitating the propagation of bourgeois ideas." After this significant transposition from "women's problems" to "the women question," the author revealed his real target in the eighth paragraph. "It should be pointed out, currently in some of our magazines there exist some wrong concepts that deviate from historical materialism and class analysis in dealing with the women question. For instance, a certain magazine has raised such questions as 'What Should Women Live For' and 'What Are Standards for Choosing Lovers' with no discussion of the concept of class."[7]

After pinning down his target, Chen Boda elaborated on how outlooks and worldviews could only be distinguished by class but "never by sex" nor by "differentiating what is 'women's' from what is 'men's' outlooks and worldviews." He then presented a lengthy discussion on how in different historical stages women in different classes had different class consciousness, different views on life goals, marriage, and love. The conclusion of this part of the argument is that there are no abstract women and men. So raising a question that represented an abstract woman deviated from Marxist and Leninist class analysis. But even more serious than raising a non-Marxist question, the forum questions, according to the author, were actually diverting women's attention from current political tasks and class struggle to questions like "family happiness, lover's salary ranks, and what women should live for."

For the historian, Chen Boda's attack evokes a long history of masculinist practices of suppressing feminist voices within the CCP, which also in turn reflects the political heritage of the international Communist movement. Since the early twentieth century, feminists in international revolutionary camps who dared to raise issues about sexuality and gender hierarchy in intimate relations and reproductive work were accused of being "bourgeois feminists" by their male comrades. Such issues were defined as individualistic and personal matters that diverted attention from proletarian collective struggles that would lead to women's liberation via their participation in productive labor. Chen Boda's reiteration of the old Communist thesis served to establish political parameters in a new political context with an irrefutable authoritative male voice, no matter how biased the voice was. The jarring logic that shifted from women's liberation being "an extremely important component part of the whole" to *funü wenti* having to "be subordinate to the interest of the whole" could be retained without being seen as jarring because the author treated the "component part" as an "extremely important tool" to the subject of the "whole," the subject that the author presumed to represent and to own. The unquestionable authoritative tone that demanded the subordination of the "part" of "women" to the gender-unmarked "whole" enunciated a quintessentially male-centered political order that threatened to punish any transgressors.

Chen concludes his article with a long rambling argument that it is inconceivable that husband, children, and family could be problems troubling revolutionary women, citing Mao and Lenin on the importance of educating women to focus on political struggles. The last paragraph of the article delivers its menacing verdict:

> We are confronting intense and profound struggles between two classes and two roads. All the anti-socialist capitalist forces are adopting all kinds of means to promote bourgeois ideas and concepts. They are most good at using the talisman of humanism, creating confusion deliberately, spreading among women individualism and hedonism, often using issues such as "family happiness" to divert women's attention, destroying laboring women's socialist consciousness, damaging their revolutionary will, and making them degenerate into the direction of capitalism and revisionism.[8]

Such an explicit identification of *Women of China* with capitalist and revisionist forces would certainly incense all the editors working for the magazine and alarm the top ACWF leaders as well. What went wrong in *Women of China* that attracted such severe fire from the Party's official publications? Which part of the accusation in the devastating article actually did hit some politically erroneous spots in the women's magazine? These would be logical questions to ask after reading the condemning article. But they will prove irrelevant questions when we carefully examine the "file" of the accused, which therefore requires a different direction of exploration. The investigation of the puzzle eventually sheds light not only on gender politics but also on destructive flaws in high politics of the CCP that crucially contributed to the demise of a socialist revolution.

SOCIALIST STATE FEMINIST DISCURSIVE PRACTICES

It appears that the very format of the magazine's forums was at the root of its vulnerability to masculinist attack. Remember that the format of forums was the result of the editorial group's efforts to develop more accessible forms and relevant topics that might attract readers to participate in public discussions. Designed as an effective and democratic method to guide and educate readers (women and men) toward revolutionary worldviews (shaping revolutionary subjectivity), the forum became a significant public space that incorporated more diverse voices from among its readers.

The topic for each forum was carefully selected through reviewing readers' feedback. Typically one reader's letter would be selected to start a forum on a particular subject. The subsequent issues would print more letters responding to the issue raised in the first letter. Selecting diverse viewpoints was an editorial principle that enabled the debate to continue. The duration of a forum was determined by readers' enthusiasm for a particular topic, with the longest running for eight monthly issues. A forum would usually be concluded with an editorial summary commenting on the scope of readers' participation and their diverse views, before explicating the editors' position.

While the official magazine of the All-China Women's Federation never failed to devote a few key articles or editorials to the Party's central agenda or major world events, the forum was a designated space for the voices of the general public. Of particular interest to historians is that these "voices" spoke in the discourse of their moment, denoting its distinctive historical context. However, even though deeply immersed in the political ethos of the time, this public space nonetheless often engaged in issues remote from the Party's imperatives in a particular moment but close to many readers' concerns in their everyday life. It was because of its relevance to readers' difficulties, frustrations, confusions, and conflicts in everyday life that the forum gained its popularity. Forums with popular topics drove the sales from 10,000 copies in the magazine's initial stage in 1949 to 900,000 copies in 1964 when the two most popular forums came under attack by *Red Flag.*

The topics for the forum from 1954 to 1964 range widely, reflecting editors' diverse concerns about and responses to a particular issue at a specific moment. As discussed in the previous chapter, two early forums with quite sensational titles— "Should Yang Yun Commit Suicide?" (1954) and "What Broke Our Conjugal Relations?" (1955)—did not hesitate to condemn sexism (coded in terms of "feudalism" or "bourgeois morality") among CCP members and articulated diverse views on socialist norms for conjugal relations. A few topics reflected the editors' efforts to shape readers' consensus on the ACWF's priority at a specific time, such as "How Should Housewives Serve Socialist Construction Better?" in 1955 when the ACWF realized that it would be a while before most women could enter gainful employment; "Is My View on Diligently and Frugally Managing the Family Correct?" in early 1958, which reflected the ACWF's Third Congress's theme of diligently and frugally managing the family and building the country;[9] and "Is a Job in the Service Industry Lowly?" in 1958, when the Great Leap Forward opened up job opportunities for women especially in the service industry.

Most topics, however, addressed readers' concerns on conjugal relations, spousal selection, love, divorce, education of children, and juggling work, study, and domesticity. The great majority of forum participants were educated urban women, including many women officials of the WF system who were faithful readers of the only women's magazine in China at that time. The forum, like other columns of the magazine, expressed the editors' sensitivity to women's gender-specific needs in their efforts to shape new socialist subjectivity among diverse groups of women. Rather than subsuming gender to class, the editors of *Women of China* consciously built a women-centered discursive space with their socialist feminist vision of women's liberation in China.

What motivated the editorial committee to start the two forums that proved to be popular among the readers but unfortunate for the editors of the magazine? According to the editor's commentary that introduced "What Should Women Live For" in the sixth issue of 1963, readers' enthusiastic responses to two articles in the fourth issue, "On Revolutionary Women's Outlook on Life" and "Giving Priority to the Revolutionary Cause," led to their decision. From numerous letters sent in by women officials in the government and in the Women's Federation system, the editors selected three for the opening forum because the questions they raised reflected many women officials' concerns. The questions included: How should a woman cadre handle the relationship between revolutionary work and family and children? When there are conflicts between work and family, what would be the best way to resolve them? What should a revolutionary cadre pursue in life? Should establishing a perfect nuclear family be seen as the greatest happiness of a woman cadre? Does shouldering the responsibility of child rearing reduce one's responsibility for socialist construction? The editor invited women officials' feedback to these questions and emphasized that the discussion related to the central question of how to establish a revolutionary outlook on life.

Dong Bian further revealed the reasons behind the editorial decision on the forum in her essay written in 1990, commemorating Cai Chang, the chair of the ACWF in the early PRC:

In the three difficult years, some women cadres did not perform well at work but were comfortably content with managing their nuclear families. Therefore, our magazine published Sister Ou Mengjue's article "Women Cadres Should Establish a Revolutionary Outlook on Life," which was popular among readers who sent in a lot of letters. Comrades in the press did many surveys and decided to start public debates on the issue of outlook on life.[10]

Dong Bian's recollection is confirmed by the letters they selected for the forum in 1963. Apparently, many women officials who had joined the revolution in their teens during the wars shifted their preoccupation to marriage and domesticity a decade after the victory of the Communist Revolution. "The three difficult years," referring to the economic disasters following the Great Leap Forward in 1958, might have dampened the revolutionary passion of many young Communist women especially if they were starting a family just then. The readers' letters published in the forum indicated quite high fertility rates among many women officials working at the county level of government or in the Women's Federation. Three children would be mentioned in a matter-of-fact tone and five children were not unusual, either. Burdened by many children, these women officials' job performance understandably would be vastly different from the time when they were single, fighting in the wars shoulder to shoulder with men.

In fact, the changing climate among women officials had appeared before the "three difficult years." In her 1990 essay, Dong Bian recalled a visit to Cai Chang in 1956. The two were delighted at the effects of Cai Chang's advocacy for promoting women cadres in the Party. The number had increased from 150,000 in 1951 to 764,000 in 1956. But Cai Chang was not content with this rapid increase in number, evidently because the actual percentage of women cadres dropped from eight to four, and few women cadres were in leadership positions or in the fields of science and technology. Moreover, Cai Chang was concerned about challenges these women cadres faced in terms of juggling work, study, and domestic responsibilities. Dong Bian agreed with Cai's concern and pointed out a big difference between now and then in the war years while revealing her wrenching personal experience to Cai.

> After we entered the city, the situation became different from that in the Liberation War years. At that time women comrades were young and most unmarried. Even if they were married and had children, they would give the children to local people to raise. In 1944 I gave birth to a baby boy and I gave him to the daughter-in-law of the village head of Zaoyuan xigou village. Her name was Wu Guihua. I wrote a note, promising never to ask for the return of the baby. That decision was made for the need of revolutionary work. It is impossible for today's people to understand it.[11]

Hearing this revelation, Cai Chang inquired with concern about the baby and if Dong Bian had ever contacted the baby. Dong Bian's reply was, "I wrote the note promising never to ask for his return. We must make people

trust our words. So let him be a peasant." Then the two continued their discussion on how to relieve domestic burdens of women cadres.

Dong Bian's recollections shed much light on the editorial decision
regarding the forum. If, in 1956, it had already been hard for people to understand Dong Bian's decision to give away her baby for the sake of revolution,
it would be even less likely for people to understand it in 1963. Dong Bian was
using her personal story to illuminate a significant shift in the revolutionary
camp. A whole cohort of young Communist women who entered marriage
and childbirth in peacetime no longer exhibited the same degree of devotion
to the revolution as the previous generation of Communist women had done
in wartime. For Communist women like Dong Bian who had made tremendous sacrifices for the revolution and never questioned the priority of the
revolutionary cause in a revolutionary's life, women cadres' waning devotion
to the revolution and increasing passion for domestic life, or confusion about
which one should come first, revolutionary work or family, were worrisome
signs that the revolution was running out steam, which would ultimately
threaten the sustainability of the revolutionary cause.

The forum was decidedly a well-planned pedagogical device to educate
Communist women officials. In Dong Bian's recollections the title of the
forum came from talking to Cai Chang in 1963. When she reported to Cai
Chang on the plan to start a forum on how women cadres should establish a
revolutionary outlook on life, Cai Chang agreed that it was a good question
for discussion. Cai added:

> We should address the question of for whom we work. This is an ideological
> issue. Women cadres' outlook on life is also a question of for whom one lives.
> Is our existence for the nation and the masses of people, or for individual
> self-interest? Only when we approach the question from the ideological level
> and understand that we should serve the people, will our lives have meanings
> and value, and will we be able to achieve a firm position of being people's
> servants. Women carry a double burden. We should rebalance the relations
> between the cause and the family and give priority to the revolutionary
> cause.[12]

Cai's talk provided Dong Bian with a central point, that is, the heart of establishing a revolutionary outlook on life is to address the question of serving
whom and living for whom. Hence, the title for the forum, "What Should
Women Live For?" which met with the approval of the Secretariat of the
ACWF.

This forum, as mentioned before, was a continuation of a consistent editorial approach for fulfilling its mission of shaping a revolutionary outlook among women with a democratic pedagogy. Instead of writing "authoritative" articles lecturing women readers, as the *Red Flag* article did, *Women of China*'s editors used readers' debates and life stories as a pedagogical device, that is, having readers themselves educate readers. To reach this goal, the forum deliberately selected letters with diverse and opposite viewpoints. Thus we see one letter claiming that since women are doomed to never advance in their work ("women engaging in a career is like flying a kite under the bed"), they might as well focus on domesticity. Another letter—this one from a husband—proposed that "women should do more housework" because his wife had less ability and a lower social position than his. Then letters refuting these and other "erroneous" views would be printed in the following issue. A male reader criticizes the husband's idea for being male chauvinistic, an expression of the feudal patriarchal idea of men being superior to women, and selfish behavior in the conjugal relation.

Before the final concluding essay, the editors would advance their own position, albeit with subtlety, by arranging letters with contradictory views side by side or by giving prominence to articles advocating devotion to the revolution. For example, a letter describing one WF official's contentment with her happy family life is placed alongside other women officials' comments on her life. Some think her life, with a good husband, comfortable living situation, nice children, and her good management of domesticity, defines happiness for women. Others disagree, pointing out her visible lack of interest in work and low job performance at work. "How can a person without lofty ideals and who cares little for her work be considered happy?" But this reader hesitates to criticize the domestic choice, instead concluding with her questions, "what kind of happiness should a revolutionary woman pursue in this era, [and] is it problematic to be content with a cozy nuclear family life?" Beneath this letter, the editors placed a few succinct quotations from the diary of the recently deceased young soldier Lei Feng—all on how he thought of happiness. One of the quotations reads, "A revolutionary should give priority to the interests of the revolution. Contributing everything one has to the cause of the Party is true happiness." Mao's propaganda campaign to "learn from comrade Lei Feng" had been initiated just three months before. It was a timely and nice touch to both prove one's loyalty to Chairman Mao and respond to the reader's question.

According to Wen Jie's recollection of the editorial group's work on the forum, nothing was actually left to chance. Her description of the division of labor in the five-person editorial group is telling. "Yang Yun took the leadership role. Gao Qi and I were responsible for selecting articles and reading readers' letters. Hu Bangxiu and Huang Yecai went out to interview and write reports on progressive people, using positive examples to assist the advocacy of the central idea 'women should give priority to the revolutionary cause.' The whole editorial group collaborated closely and wholeheartedly. The forum discussion was extremely lively."[13]

Wen Jie also recalls proudly how demanding their editorial work was. Working through nights was common. Months-long fieldwork trips were frequent. They were all married women with children and housework. "But at that time we thought we should give priority to the revolutionary cause. We had little time to manage our family. We ourselves, children and husbands all had meals in the canteens. Our life was very simple. Certainly we women comrades were very tired, but spiritually very gratified. Because at the time the social climate was positive, no one complained. We were happy, no matter how hard or how tiring our work was." The editors apparently identified with the perspective on revolutionary work that they advocated.

Hu Bangxiu, whose report on Zhang Lizhu, "Giving Priority to the Revolutionary Cause," stimulated enthusiastic responses that initiated the forum discussion, recalls her interview with Zhang Lizhu, a highly respected gynecologist who was the head of a gynecological / obstetric hospital. Zhang did not talk about her career accomplishments, but instead spoke emotionally about what worried her. Before 1949, Zhang had experienced sexual discrimination in her medical career that frustrated her aspiration to become a surgeon; but after 1949 she obtained the right to work like men, an equal right she cherished tremendously. All she wanted was to fully use her knowledge, skills, and ability in the service of the people. But she worried that many young women graduates assigned to the hospital did not share her aspiration but rather were "wasting their precious youth in endless emotional entanglements and distractions of domestic affairs. Years have passed and they are still mediocre, without any accomplishment and without any special expertise."[14] Zhang strongly wished that each young woman would "hoist the sail of their careers and make their lives brilliant and colorful." Obviously Zhang shared the concerns of Dong Bian and other editors about the changing climate among a younger cohort of career women. Hence the report on

Zhang was selected as one of the two feature articles to generate debate. Zhang's story provided a powerful testimony that invited women readers in various posts to review their own lives accordingly. Hu recalls unexpectedly large numbers of readers' letters filled with candid and emotional descriptions of their difficulties, frustrations, and aspirations. "It was as if *Women of China* hosted a discussion session in which thousands of people participated."[15]

In Hu Bangxiu's assessment, the forum reached its pedagogical goal:

> Creating forums for discussion in the journal is the best method for the masses' self-education. There is no need for editors to put on long faces and preach. Let the masses express their own opinions and debate among themselves. The truth would emerge clearly via debate. Being a woman in the new society, how should we live? Should we drift with the currents, our lives mindlessly passing? Or should we establish a correct goal in life with aspirations and pursuits, being a useful person for the people and for society? The answer is evident and the reason is not obscurely profound. But with personal testimonies of absorbing interest from each female teacher, female actor, female engineer, female doctor, female nurse, female prospector, and women-work cadre, the reasoning is so vividly presented and so convincing.[16]

Like her other colleagues, Hu took significant pride in having hosted the influential forum that "provided a lively ideological education class to the masses of women." The strong faith in the significance of the debate demonstrates that the editors were, in a sense, promoting their own revolutionary outlook on life through the forum. Hu Bangxiu reveals a deeper emotional source in editors' strong commitment to the revolutionary cause. "One deeper driving force was, they could never forget those comrades who had been killed on the execution grounds and battlefields, to whom they owed their own lives. Thus, what else can one not give up today? For that generation, their conviction was devotion and commitment, devoting everything to the people and to the Party. That was their conviction and pursuit in life."[17]

All of these lengthy quotations from various editors' memoirs and magazine articles should be ample evidence of the solid revolutionary subject position of these socialist state feminists and prove the falsehood of Chen Boda's accusation that *Women of China* led women toward capitalism and revisionism. But there is one more piece of historical evidence that will not only demonstrate the editors' dedication to the revolutionary cause but also help us understand the differences between these socialist state feminists' discursive practices and Chen Boda's rhetorical deployment. Penned by Luo Qiong who at the time was already a member of the ACWF's Secretariat, suggesting the tremendous importance of this forum to the ACWF, the eight-page-long editorial entitled "Be a Strong and Thoroughgoing Revolutionary Woman Soldier Resolutely" appeared in the second issue of 1964. The summary of the seven-month-long forum amounted to a manifesto of socialist state feminists in the 1960s. As the title loudly declared, the article was an explicit enunciation of the state feminists' position on the question of how women should live and a vehement urging of Communist women to continue their devotion to the socialist revolution and construction. The term "revolutionary woman soldier" revealed the presence of the subject position that Communist women embraced in the war periods. The language clearly situated the editorial in the political discourse of the early 1960s. Instead of deviating from class analysis and Marxism and Leninism, the ACWF's major theorist, Luo Qiong, who upheld the Marxist theory of women's liberation, demonstrated no less familiarity with the political rhetoric of the day and no less knowledge of Marxism and Leninism than Chen Boda. And yet, their citations of proletarian leaders and applications of class analysis revealed significant differences.

The striking differences in style and content between the editorial of *Women of China* and the article in *Red Flag* provide telling evidence of different gendered subjectivities in the Communist Party. Unlike Chen Boda who appealed to powerful male figures to establish his authority in laying out his argument against *Women of China,* Luo Qiong mostly relied on ordinary women for justifying her position in her article summarizing the forum. Her style was consistent with the style of the forum and the magazine, educating women with positive examples from the women masses and thereby demonstrating a proletarian-based revolutionary outlook. Luo Qiong was good at amplifying, highlighting, and exalting the presence of a revolutionary subject as a way to empower all those women striving hard in various localities as well as to set up concrete role models for the rank and file to emulate. Luo Qiong quoted at length from over ten women's letters and articles to illustrate how women in a wide range of posts and geographic locations were performing extraordinary tasks in their devotion to socialist construction. She took a sentence from the story of a woman head of a commune-level Women's Federation, Mei Jiwen, as a subheading for the section that elaborated the necessity for women cadres to continue their commitment to the revolution. When Mei's husband tried to stop her from participating in her work, Mei reportedly said, "Unless the sun rises from the west, I will never give up revolution!"[18]

The editorial had four succinct one-sentence quotations from Mao, Lenin, and Stalin, all with citations in the endnote. Unlike Chen who punctuated his article with a set phrase, "Marxism and Leninism told us," Luo Qiong had no intention of projecting a pretension of masculine power by assuming a male authoritative voice. The four sentences by Communist leaders were placed at the end of different paragraphs to highlight a point. Most importantly, all four quotations emphasized women's contribution to and agency in revolution. "Chinese women are a force that determines the victory or defeat of the revolution" (Mao). "Women in China are a great human resource" (Mao). "In human history there has been no great movement by the oppressed masses that achieved success without the participation of laboring women" (Stalin). "Laboring women's liberation should be laboring women's own affairs" (Lenin). To the last quotation, Luo Qiong added one sentence, "They cannot rely on other people's charity."[19]

Indeed, explicating women's agency in women's liberation was the major thesis of the editorial. The linkage between women's liberation and revolution was a constant theme in state feminist discourse. Different from the male-centered demand to subordinate the "part" to the "whole," as illustrated in Chen Boda's article, the relationship between the socialist revolution and women's liberation expounded in the editorial was symbiotic rather than hierarchical. These socialist state feminists' eagerness to call for women's participation in the socialist revolution was grounded in their keen understanding that women's liberation "cannot rely on other people's charity." Luo Qiong argued that women's full participation in the revolution was an integral part of the process of achieving the goal of women's liberation. It enabled women to obtain the equal rights granted by the socialist state. And it enabled women to further transform the traditional views and customs of valuing men over women. Women would have to "achieve women's thorough liberation through their own struggle." "Traditional old ideas passed down by thousands of years of history have deeply rooted influence on women and the society. They cannot be washed away in a brief fifteen years."[20] Clearly, in the view of state feminists women's liberation was an unfinished revolution, which provided a political ground for their identification with Mao's call for continuing revolution. Luo Qiong's exposition on the need to continue revolution evidently showed such identification:

> The people's revolution in our country has already won the victory. Our country has been liberated for fifteen years. But there still exist class and class

struggle in the socialist society. The ruling class that has been overthrown would never be willing to die. The question of who will defeat whom between the proletariat and the bourgeoisie has not yet been settled for good. We cannot relax a bit but must continue our vigilant struggle.[21]

Contrary to Chen Boda's accusation, the editorial engaged in a distinctive class analysis in examining various positions expressed in the heated discussion of the forum. Having summed up the major views, the editorial stated, "This debate reflects contentions of different classes' worldviews and outlooks on life in our society, and reflects that some cadres have not established a solid revolutionary outlook on life. Some have even vacillated."[22] Luo Qiong presented her class analysis more prominently in the middle section with the subheading "Don't Be Duped by Feudal and Bourgeois Ideas." She opened this section with a phrase strikingly similar to the one in Chen Boda's article. "To the question 'what should women live for,' different classes will have different viewpoints and different answers, just like [they do] for any social questions." But following this claim, Luo's class analysis departed from Chen's in a major way. While Chen denied any significance of gender by stressing that only class mattered, Luo Qiong centered on gender oppression embedded in class power relations in these terms:

Based on their class self-interest, the feudal landlord class oppressed women, subordinated them to men, made them tools for waiting on their husbands, and gave their husbands children to inherit feudal property. Likewise, out of their desire to squeeze out high profits, the bourgeoisie also drove women workers and peasants out of their families to capitalist factories, oppressing them to sell their labor cheaply to the capitalists. At the same time, the bourgeoisie tried hard to maintain the feudal tradition of valuing men over women, creating bourgeois nuclear families, keeping their wives and daughters in "cozy and rich nuclear families," treating them like "little birds" in the gold threaded cage to play with at their will, and making them reproduce progeny to inherit their capital.

These feudal and bourgeois ideas have been constantly critiqued in the past fifteen years since the Liberation. But class struggle reflects itself from various angles. On this issue, feudal, bourgeois, and all the old customary forces have much deeper foundations. Under the new circumstances, [the old forces] try to use various sayings in disguise in order to influence revolutionary women cadres with their worldview and outlook on life. We must not lower our guard against feudal and bourgeois ideas.[23]

Thus in Luo Qiong's analysis (which revealed her mastery of Engels's theory), class struggle was expressed in various attempts to confine women to domesticity, exploit women's productive and reproductive labor, treat women as inferior beings and sex objects, and subordinate women to men. The roots of these gendered class struggles were deeper than those of other class struggles. Therefore, it was more urgent for revolutionary women to be vigilant in order not to be seduced by feudal and bourgeois ideas to "withdraw into the family from the way of the revolution." To illustrate the existence of intense gendered class struggles, Luo Qiong selected several sayings from readers' letters. Besides that phrase "women engaging in a career is like flying a kite under the bed," some readers also claimed "women should live for producing children," and "for serving men." "Women's biological constitution determines that they can only produce children," and they should "do more housework." She criticized such views as representing feudal and bourgeois thinking, and "aiming to seduce women cadres to withdraw from the revolution road and retreat to family." On the women question, Luo Qiong asserted, "just like with any other question, we must insist on keeping the purity of proletarian ideas, seriously critiquing feudal and bourgeois ideas, and unambiguously making a clean break with them."[24]

Her stern position recommending the importance of carrying on gendered class struggle extended to conjugal relations. Discussing how to use a revolutionary spirit to solve practical difficulties, she advocated equal comradeship between husband and wife. Those husbands who embraced "three fulls and one down" (sanbao yidao) at home (eating three full meals, then laying down in bed) were the ones who were deeply poisoned by feudal and bourgeois ideas and should receive serious criticism. The theme of revolutionizing conjugal relations in the editorial would be extended to the second forum, "What Are the Standards for Choosing a Lover?" that started in the fourth issue of 1964. The focus on choosing a spouse and conjugal relations in the second forum indicated that these were major concerns reflected in readers' letters that poured out women's confusions and frustrations in dealing with multiple tensions in marriage, family, and work. Conflicting values and gender norms troubled many young women who turned to Women of China for help.

Responding to readers' urgent needs, in addition to carrying on the second forum, the Women of China press swiftly published in August 1964 a volume of reports selected from Women of China and other newspapers about model husbands entitled Between the Couple (Fuqi zhijian).[25] Eight exemplary husbands were featured either for their shouldering a large share of housework to support their wives' work in socialist construction or for taking good care of wives who were afflicted with serious long-term illnesses including one who was blind and another who was paralyzed. Its introduction was printed in the tenth issue in 1964, "What Kind of Attitudes a Husband Should Have in Treating His Wife."[26] Advocating a new norm for conjugal relations that specifically required husbands to treat their wives as comrades and equal companions, the introduction explicitly criticized "feudal and bourgeois thinking" expressed in husbands' infidelity, or refusal to share housework, or treat their wife as a "nurse."[27] The highlighted topic and swift printing of the volume demonstrated a clear awareness of the editors after months of public debates on the outlook of women that a serious obstacle to women's pursuit of a revolutionary career might be their spouse. Transforming conjugal relations thus became a focus in the second forum, while the gendered class struggle was consistently identified in both forums.

Luo Qiong's class analysis had one more dimension that was not gender related but rather articulated her strong concern over the effects of bureaucratization. The first forum discussion exposed the phenomenon that some women officials were becoming a privileged group enjoying all the benefits granted by the bureaucratic system but having little commitment to work. "Having been endowed with trust from the Party and people, they eat meals provided by the people and take money from the people, but they do not work. Rather, they enjoy 'cozy nuclear family life' under the cover of their job." With these descriptions conveying her sense of outrage, Luo Qiong warned them not to be corrupted by bourgeois ideas to stray from their revolutionary missions.

What should be emphasized here is that the target of Luo Qiong's critique was women officials rather than ordinary women "masses." It was the obvious gap between the daunting task of eradicating "feudalism" and women officials' declining interest in such hard work, work that they were paid to do, that worried Luo Qiong. Hence she vehemently called on women officials to "Be a Strong and Thoroughgoing Revolutionary Woman Soldier Resolutely." Luo Qiong's identification with Mao's agenda of anti-bureaucracy (that is, opposing the new bourgeoisie in the Party, in Mao's definition) and continuing revolution was genuine, although she adhered to her own understanding of the primary goal of revolution.

In short, in the context of the Party's dominant discourse of class struggle in the early 1960s, the editorial penned by Luo Qiong presented a distinctive class analysis that centered on gender hierarchies embedded in class relations as well as in conjugal relations. Without available language to name "gender," she heavily relied on a Marxist terminology to explicate unequal power relations between women and men. At the same time her analysis was not at all constrained by a rigid class framework that attributed everything to economic status and mode of production. She consistently used the term "feudal ideas" to denote gender problems in or outside class relations and over diverse modes of production. This usage by Luo Qiong and other state feminists articulated a locally grounded understanding of a persistent gender system in China's long history as well as reflected a May Fourth New Culture feminist heritage of anti-feudalism. For them, the fact that abolishing private ownership did not entail the eradication of gender hierarchy made the tenacity of "feudal ideas" salient. Fighting against the effects of "feudal ideas" rather than explicating material and institutional bases that produced and sustained such "feudal ideas" constituted the main efforts of the first two cohorts of state feminists.

"Feudal ideas" as a coded phrase for gender hierarchy, patriarchy, or sexism may lack explanatory power for today's readers. But in the context of a Marxist conception of linear history, the word "feudal" connoted an outdated historical remnant that should be swept into the dustbin of history. It was a major task of the Communist Revolution to do away with anything feudal so as to enable the ancient nation to catch up with the teleological process of human progress. Moreover, since the New Culture Movement of the 1910s, radical cultural critics' condemnation of "feudalism" had often relied on cases of gender oppression in Chinese culture. When the CCP promoted the slogan "overthrow the three big mountains" (imperialism, feudalism, and bureaucratic capitalism), the term "feudalism" was already inflected with gender, reflecting the discursive power of New Culture feminism. Continuing this New Culture heritage, state feminists' appropriation of the word further consolidated the gender connotation of "feudalism." In a time when the other two "big mountains" had been removed with the success of the revolution, "anti-feudalism" helped situate state feminists' gender struggle in the center of the Communist revolution with full legitimacy, at least discursively. And Luo Qiong was obviously sensitive to Chairman Mao's new political thrust of class struggles between the proletariat and the bourgeoisie. She almost always paired "feudal" with "bourgeois" in defining gendered class struggles.

By no means did *Women of China* reveal any trace of leading women toward capitalism. Quite the contrary, the editors' firm conviction and tremendous efforts to consolidate women officials' revolutionary outlook on life should place them at the vanguard of Mao's project of continuing revolution, albeit theirs was more of a feminist revolution aiming at empowering all laboring women and eradicating gender hierarchy.[28] The gender preoccupation in state feminists' identification with Mao's new agenda of anti-revisionism, anti-bourgeoisie, and continuing revolution could have been the reason to raise the eyebrows of Chen Boda. However, in the condemning article, he did nothing to tease out how a gendered class analysis might differ from the class analysis proposed by Mao, and he totally ignored the magazine's professed "anti-feudal" agenda, a legitimate agenda that would have been difficult to argue against. Instead, the article focused on accusations of how *Women of China* intended to seduce its readers on to a revisionist and capitalist road by advocating the pursuit of "family happiness" and "hedonism," when actually the editors were doing exactly the opposite and criticizing these attitudes. Statements of how women enjoyed family life were selected from readers' letters in *Women of China* as evidence of the editors' advocacy of a bourgeois outlook. Clearly, Chen Boda had no intention of engaging in a serious intellectual debate. But, with the solid evidence of black words on white paper contrary to his accusation, why on earth would Chen Boda distort reality and fabricate crimes to frame *Women of China?* What did he intend to accomplish by this slanderous attack? Before we turn to these key questions to the puzzle, let us first examine how this attack affected *Women of China,* since the responses of state feminists to the *Red Flag* article provide some clues to the mystery.

A SERIOUS SETBACK IN TRANSFORMING GENDER RELATIONS

The damaging article in *Red Flag* threw the ACWF into crisis. Since *Red Flag* represented the higher authority of the Party Central, the ACWF top leadership decided that the editors-in-chief of *Women of China* should prepare a self-criticism to be published openly. When Hou Di, then the deputy editor-in-chief, was on overnight duty, the chair of the ACWF Cai Chang called her office at five o'clock in the morning, inquiring whether they had completed their self-criticism. In her commemorative article for Dong Bian, entitled "One Does Not Have to be Magnificent to be Noble," Hou Di wrote a detailed account of Dong Bian's remarkable response when confronting tremendous political pressure. "Facing the threatening surprise attack, Dong

Bian was furious. But she acted in a calm manner. She neither succumbed to the pressure, nor hid her own views, nor complained."[29] In three separate talks to the staff of the press about the *Red Flag* article, Dong Bian never mentioned that the decision of the forums had been approved by the Secretariat of the ACWF, nor did she mention the responsibilities of the editorial committee of the press and editorial group for the forums. She emphasized only that, if in the end the Party leaders decided that the two forums had made political mistakes, she would take all responsibility upon herself. Clearly, Hou Di did not think Dong Bian's being willingly to undergo this coerced act of self-criticism was an expression of "succumbing to pressure," but rather a courageous act of self-sacrifice in order to protect her colleagues.

Hou Di's appreciative remarks on Dong Bian's noble character inadvertently revealed dynamics within the ACWF in a time of political crisis. Apparently, the top leadership of the ACWF neither requested a higher-level Party supervisor to investigate the accusations made by the *Red Flag* article nor stepped up to take responsibility for having approved the "problematic" forums and written the concluding editorial. Although the top ACWF leaders, including Cai Chang, had all supported the forums, now they made Dong Bian the scapegoat responsible for the accused forums. One could interpret such timid moves as a strategy to avoid open confrontation with the Party Central, which might have negative consequences for the ACWF. But whatever considerations they might have, the ACWF leaders' response to the crisis spoke volumes on the power relations between the male-dominated Party Central and the gender-based "mass" organization, as well as the political climate in 1964. From the perspectives of the ACWF leaders, at least, the possibility of arguing against *Red Flag*'s condemnation simply did not exist. Just how drastic the changes in internal political dynamics were becomes all the more evident when we compare the inaction of Zhang Yun, by then the executive chair of the ACWF, to her action when, as chair of the Shanghai Women's Federation back in 1951, she had candidly criticized her Shanghai Party leader's inappropriate remarks on women-work.[30]

The crisis was resolved in an unexpected manner. In early 1965, the ACWF submitted a report to Peng Zhen, a member of the Politburo, one of whose responsibilities was to oversee women-work.[31] The report stated that the ACWF accepted the criticism from *Red Flag* and planned to publish a self-criticism. Dong Bian, assigned to draft the self-criticism, was totally at a loss over a self-criticism that she was loathe to write when she was called to attend a talk by Peng Zhen. After the talk, Peng Zhen asked Dong Bian and the secretary of the ACWF Secretariat to remain behind, and then told them that he had read their report and it was not necessary to write an article of self-criticism. Dong Bian, thrilled by this not-guilty verdict, went directly to Cai Chang's home. The great news made Cai Chang smile, too. For the time being, the incident was ended.[32]

But the ramifications of the incident did not stop there. Most prominently, *Women of China* dropped the discussion forum format after the *Red Flag* attack. Since Chen Boda's accusation that *Women of China* promoted a bourgeois mentality was based on the diverse views selected from readers' letters, understandably, the magazine's editors concluded that it was no longer safe to present "politically incorrect" views, even for the purpose of critique and debate. Hence the debate format folded. Although *Women of China* retained columns on education of children, marriage, family, birth control, and women's health, after Chen's article, most of the themes appearing in the magazine's contents concerned major political issues of the day. Public debates on gender-specific issues were replaced by articles highlighting women's enthusiasm for studying Chairman Mao's works and women's devotion to the revolution including educating children to be revolutionary successors. The editors were still able to sustain their major theme, that is, celebrating remarkable accomplishments of laboring women in all walks of life. However, the magazine moved away from its former adherence to the "mass line" that emphasized the importance of listening to women's voices and thereafter abandoned a reader-driven focus on tensions in women's multiple roles and gender relations. It was still recognizably a women's magazine, albeit with women "talking" strictly within the parameters set by the dominant political discourse and expressing little interest in gender relations. An autonomous state feminist space had been severely diminished by male-dominated Party politics in 1964, two years before the Cultural Revolution engulfed the ACWF.

The two unfortunate forums would be dug out again in the Cultural Revolution as evidence of Dong Bian's "crimes." Starting with the seventh issue in 1966, *Women of China* created a special column condemning "a member of a black gang, Dong Bian." The column was continued for three issues. Of the many accusations of Dong Bian's allegedly counterrevolutionary deeds, one stood out: Dong Bian was accused of harboring a deep hatred toward women who studied the works of Chairman Mao. The "evidence" was that from 1961 to 1965, *Women of China* had published only thirty-three articles on how women workers, peasants, and soldiers studied Chairman Mao's works, constituting a terribly low 2.3 percent of the total number of articles. And in 1964 Dong Bian had made the press publish two "big poisonous weeds" (*da ducao*) but refused to print the planned volume on women models of studying Chairman Mao's works. The two "poisonous weeds" were, first, the volume entitled *What Should Women Live For,* which was a collection of the forum debates, and the other, entitled *Between the Couple,* a companion volume to the second forum targeting husbands for a revolutionizing transformation in conjugal relations. Clearly, before Chen Boda's attack, Dong Bian had felt no qualms about allocating resources to the circulation of texts on gender issues even when the rising political trend was to praise the magical power of Chairman Mao's works. With all this hard evidence, we can quite confidently pinpoint the *Red Flag* incident as the crucial moment when state feminists' efforts to transform gender relations not only in public but also in domestic life, especially conjugal relations, were suppressed.

A REVEALING INCIDENT

But who actually suppressed state feminist endeavors with such overwhelming power and for what purpose? Although *Red Flag* undoubtedly represented the authority of the Party Central, it was actually not the Politburo that authorized the *Red Flag* article: Peng Zhen's lenient response to the ACWF's report suggests that. Judging from the way he dismissed the case when Dong Bian went to talk to him about it, it is reasonable to assume that Peng Zhen himself disagreed with that article, or was even annoyed that an article criticizing *Women of China* by the Party's authoritative journal was published without his approval. After all, he was officially the highest authority in the Party charged with supervising women-work.[33]

Would it be possible that the article was approved by a higher authority, Mao, since Chen Boda was his secretary? The evidence, puzzlingly, suggested otherwise. Mao Zedong wrote a new inscription for *Women of China* in August 1966, bestowing great honor on the very magazine that had been condemned by *Red Flag* two years before. The act effectively removed him from the list of suspected attackers of *Women of China*. He might have been totally unaware of the incident when Cai Chang, the younger sister of the best friend of his youth, Cai Hesen, asked him for an inscription on the rostrum of Tiananmen where hundreds of thousands Red Guards were cheering below. In a politically volatile time, when top officials were brought down one after another as "capitalist roaders" by Mao, obtaining an inscription from Chairman Mao was tantamount to receiving an amulet that provided immunity from political attacks. The event was instantly celebrated by the ACWF in fanfare fashion with women officials doing drumrolls and dancing in an impressive celebratory parade in front of Zhongnanhai.[34] Although the effect of the amulet did not last long (the ACWF would soon be paralyzed just like other state organs in the storm of the Cultural Revolution), Cai Chang's maneuver, revealing her lingering worries over *Red Flag's* attack, was still brilliant.[35]

But if the attack on *Women of China* was not part of a concerted plan of the Party Central, even though the damaging article was published by the most authoritative journal of the Party, what motivated Chen Boda to make the political move on his own? Dong Bian provided a clue to the riddle in her commemorative essay for Hu Qiaomu, along with her husband another of Mao's secretaries. After seeing the *Red Flag* article, Dong Bian searched for, but could not find, a clue to the grounds for Chen Boda's accusation. One day, Chen Boda came to visit her husband, Tian Jiaying. Seeing Dong Bian, he said, "The criticism in *Red Flag* was not just pointing at you. It mainly pointed at Hu Qiaomu. He should just take care of his own illness. Why should he give you ideas?"[36] Recalling this episode, Dong Bian emphasized, "It dawned on me that the article was Chen Boda's roundabout way of attacking Hu Qiaomu."

It turned out the article was just the tip of the iceberg of internal politics at the top echelon of the CCP, or—deploying another metaphor for what was going on beneath the surface of the "political"—a small sample of the muddy ground of entanglement of the political and personal that would bog down even a revolutionary veteran such as Dong Bian. In 1942, in Yan'an, around the time when Dong Bian married her young colleague Tian Jiaying, Tian met the person who would become his mentor and closest friend, Hu Qiaomu. Serving as Mao's secretary since 1941, Hu was a famous "pen" (ghostwriter) for Mao. In 1948 Hu recommended Tian Jiaying to Mao and Tian served as Mao's secretary until May 1966.[37] Hu Qiaomu, Chen Boda, and Tian Jiaying, enjoying the reputation as the "three pens" of Mao, were responsible at different times for drafting and editing Mao's articles and talks, collecting documents, writing footnotes, and proofreading the *Selected Works of Mao Zedong*. They were also involved in drafting some work reports and Party Central policy guidelines as well as the constitution of the PRC.[38] The three secretaries' different involvement in tasks of more or less importance and prestige often reflected the degree of trust by Mao, which would lead to jealousy and competition between Chen and the other two who shared a close friendship.

The unpredictable winds of politics in the early PRC created deep animosity among the three men who were closest to the top authority, Chairman Mao. While Chen Boda proved to be quick to figure out Mao's intentions, Hu, suffering from depression due to intensified power struggles among the top leadership as well as his increasing difficulty in identifying with Mao's views and practices after the failure of the Great Leap Forward, asked for a long sick leave in 1961. Then in 1962, Tian Jiaying, the youngest of the three, after being sent by Mao to conduct investigations in rural villages, made a colossal mistake by suggesting the household responsibility system as an expedient measure to relieve rural poverty and stimulate productivity, a direct challenge to Mao's insistence on collective rural economy. In Mao's words, "We should practice the mass line. But sometimes we cannot entirely listen to the masses. On the issue of household responsibility, we cannot listen to them."[39] Tian lost Mao's trust as a result and was reassigned to edit Mao's manuscripts. Hu and Tian maintained their friendship and shared contempt toward Chen, as revealed in Hu Qiaomu's comment, "Jiaying and I observed from daily interactions that Chen never dared to raise any different views in front of Chairman Mao. Whenever there was any [controversial] issue, he would try hard to let us speak up."[40]

But why would Chen Boda even bother to attack Tian Jiaying or Hu Qiaomu when he had already gotten the upper hand in 1964? A most likely reason is that the latter two still maintained their communications with Mao in various ways, and thus continued to generate insecurity in Chen. Highly irritating to Chen was that Tian had initiated re-editing and revising footnotes for the published three volumes of Mao's works, a project approved by Mao in 1962. Before the completion of the project in 1965, Tian's role as Mao's secretary, even though it was largely limited to this work, allowed him to occasionally meet with Mao. But Chen had been the one in charge of editing the original three volumes of Mao's works. He had openly expressed his resentment at Tian's revising his editing, once accusing Tian of "critiquing Chairman Mao's *Selected Works*."[41] Chen knew perfectly well that the two old rivals were no longer in any position to defend themselves when confronted with such a roundabout attack from him. Dong Bian's daughter's memory of Chen's visit to their home proves Tian Jiaying's fury and powerlessness. "It was a Sunday. Both mom and dad were home. As soon as dad saw Chen Boda coming in, he angrily went to another room. Thus Chen Boda said those words (that Hu

Qiaomu was the target) to mom. Mom was angry, too, treating Chen with an unpleasant expression. Feeling awkward, Chen left shortly."[42]

Closely observing Mao's political moves, Chen certainly understood in 1964 that Mao was looking for entry points to engage with his own "class enemies" in the Party. Linking a public discussion on women's life and work with class struggle could also be Chen's (mis)calculation to present Mao with such an entry point, although he should have understood that Tian Jiaying and Hu Qiaomu were too junior in the ranks for Mao to care, and the ACWF had never been considered even a remote political target by Mao.[43] In fact, Mao's own theorization of a dichotomous class struggle and two-line struggle in the 1960s never involved women and gender hierarchy, reflecting his preoccupation with struggles within the masculine Party headquarters. It was the "Marxist theorist" Chen Boda's invention to extend a gender-blind class analysis shaped by masculine power struggles to the realm of women-work. However, this "theoretical" excursion apparently did not move in the direction to which Mao was heading. Even though it had been highlighted by a double appearance in *Red Flag* and *People's Daily,* Chen's article nonetheless failed miserably to make a splash in the political center that was about to fall apart.

However damaging to the ACWF and the discursive space its magazine had offered to the mass of women, the cruel irony is that the events brought on by Chen Boda's condemnation of *Women of China* were hardly noticed by people outside the ACWF. And yet, the *Red Flag* episode nevertheless shed valuable light on PRC politics at a critical moment in the formation of the hurricanes of the Cultural Revolution. It epitomized the main characteristics of the CCP power center in the mid-1960s. Political tensions entangled with personal animosities, personal ambitions mixed with political insecurity, debased desires blended with sublime ideals, unique dynamics generated in a politically charged hyper-volatile environment—all became potent materials for a pernicious political drama. Political framing based on Mao's theory of class struggle would soon become a widespread practice, pursued by people with various motivations, some being sincere believers in Mao's insights on the dangers of capitalist restoration. Here lies the tragedy of Mao's class struggle. His dichotomous class analysis both stimulated and overlooked desires and motivations that did not neatly align with political categories of either bourgeois or proletarian, and / or capitalist or socialist. Those who professedly followed Mao's proletarian and socialist line, sadly, also had the capacity to destroy serious pursuits of social and cultural transformations such as those embodied in state feminists. Overused, abused, manipulated, and manipulating, Mao's class struggle would hasten the demise of the Chinese revolution rather than prevent it.

The other hidden reality revealed in this episode was no less chilling: the marginality of state feminists in the Party machine. Although the ACWF was packed with senior Communist women officials, their glorious revolutionary records and seniority in the Party did not earn them comparable political power in the power center of the socialist state. The gender-based mass organization had hardly any institutional leverage in high politics. A groundless accusation from the Party's publication could generate a real crisis in the ACWF and powerfully derail their discursive practices, while no other Party official or Party branch even paid attention to an article on the "women question."[44] The fact that Chen would not hesitate to fabricate crimes of *Women of China* and that such a malicious public attack on the ACWF went unnoticed by the Party Central in 1964 spoke volumes of the masculinist nature of the power center in the Mao era. After all, *Women of China* was not even significant enough to be Chen Boda's real target. It was just a casualty of male power struggles in a dysfunctional political system.

Women of China had been left alone in creating a feminist cultural front since 1949 exactly because the realm of women-work was a designated jurisdiction of the ACWF. Merely an auxiliary branch of the Party instead of a real player in high politics, the ACWF was never in a position to be coveted by any male high-ranking official. Receiving more neglect than attention from the Party Central was the norm, a situation that gave rise to a major tenet of the ACWF, "to actively seek the leadership and support of all levels of the Party committees." In other words, the gendered institutional structure of the Party had granted the ACWF both marginality and "anonymity," so to speak. It was exactly from that marginal and unnoticed position in the power center that state feminists had been able to create social spaces with their own pervasive institutional development and produce socialist feminist discourse with their influential popular magazine.

CONCLUSION

"The tree wants to remain quiet, but the wind won't stop." This is an ancient phrase that became famous when Mao quoted it to suggest the inevitability of class struggle in a class society. The phrase, ironically, could be a fitting analogy for the state of the ACWF in the Mao era. Located on the periphery of the CCP polity, the highly assertive women revolutionaries in the ACWF had effectively created their own institutional bases and a feminist cultural front. To be left alone to concentrate on their women-work and transformation of gender relations and norms, however, proved to be a luxury in the first fifteen years of the PRC history. Unwanted attention to women-work by male authorities often created obstacles to state feminists' efforts at gendered social and cultural transformation. We may recall local male officials' objection to the institutional development of Women's Federation at the local level in early 1950s,[45] the claims of some male leaders in the central government in 1957 that Chinese women were already liberated and therefore did not need a women's organization,[46] and now the *Red Flag* article on the women question in 1964. Although none of those male officials represented the Party Central, each episode presented serious challenges to the ACWF and caused setbacks. The unpredictability of assault from male authorities and the asymmetrical power relations between male authorities in any of the state branches and the ACWF are best captured by the metaphor of wind and tree.

The intensifying storm of a Maoist class struggle in 1964 so severely bent the "tree" of ACWF that state feminists were compelled to cease advocating the transformation of gender relations, even if it were articulated in the trendy terminology of class struggles. The suppression of feminist gender concerns by Maoist class struggles shrouding various motives was thus accomplished when the feminist cultural front, *Women of China,* had to close down a crucial public forum for debating gender issues and critiquing "feudal" ideas and practices that had sustained a gender-inflected anti-feudalist discourse. The ensuing political hurricane of the Cultural Revolution eventually engulfed the ACWF, and publication of *Women of China* was suspended at the end of 1966.

PART TWO

From Feminist Revolution of Culture to the Cultural Revolution

FIVE

Chen Bo'er and the Feminist Paradigm of Socialist Film

THIS CHAPTER PRESENTS THE LIFE and work of the feminist revolutionary artist Chen Bo'er. My historical narratives in this and the following two chapters intend to highlight an integral part of state feminists' endeavors to transform a patriarchal culture with a socialist feminist cultural production. While the ACWF used the popular magazine *Women of China* to engender cultural transformation, feminists working in film production were pursuing the same agenda with no less enthusiasm but with a more powerful medium. Film, in this context, was envisioned by them as a crucial tool in their feminist transformation of an ancient "feudalist culture," and is used here as a central site for an investigation of the politics underlying reproduction, transformation, dissemination, and eventual discontinuation of a May Fourth New Cultural feminist heritage in a socialist cultural revolution. Delineating state feminists' distinctive contentions in the cultural realm, this part of the narratives parallels the stories of the ACWF's struggles in Part I in terms of chronology and historical contexts. The life of Chen Bo'er, a pioneer of a socialist feminist cultural revolution, serves to illuminate this obscured historical process.

Chen Bo'er's life history is emblematic of the erasure of the socialist feminist cultural front. Film studies in and outside China have shown remarkably little interest in her, despite the fact that she was one of the most important figures in the film industry in the early PRC. A famous movie star and renowned feminist social activist during the 1930s, Party secretary of the CCP's first state-owned film studio in 1946, director of the art department of the Central Film Bureau and the founder of the Beijing Film Academy upon the establishment of the PRC, Chen Bo'er played a major role in shaping socialist filmmaking in revolutionary China.[1] Moreover, she left a rich body of visual and textual records. Scholarly inattention to such an important figure in the history of socialist film is symptomatic of deeper problems that go beyond the obvious gender bias in knowledge production in a post- (or anti-)revolutionary age. The causes of her systematic erasure will be analyzed further in a later chapter, along with all the socialist feminists who have claimed our attention in this volume. I turn here to her life and work with the certainty that Chen Bo'er merits the historian's attention.

THE RISE OF A LEFT-WING MOVIE STAR

Chen Bo'er, originally named Chen Shunhua, was born to a wealthy merchant's family in Anbu, a small town in Chaoan County, Guangdong, in 1907.[2] Although Chen was the darling of her parents, her mother, as the first concubine of her father, was treated with disdain by Chen's grandmother and her father's wife, which was a source of unhappiness throughout her childhood.[3] The troubling disparity between being a beloved daughter of a locally revered and wealthy merchant and her subaltern position in the hierarchy of a large, polygamous family fostered in Chen both a strong will and an empathy for the sufferings of the lower classes, especially among women. She expressed a daring spirit in her early teens when, with a few other girls, she cut off her long pigtail in emulation of women soldiers in the 1911 revolution, which was a scandalous act in her small town. Benefiting from her father's wealth and reflecting the practice among the elite families to gain social status by sending their daughters to missionary schools, Chen was able to escape the confinement of the small town by going to Nanjing and Shanghai for high school.[4]

In school Chen Bo'er demonstrated multiple talents. She was respected as a good essay writer, a violinist, and an actor who usually played the leading role in amateur dramatics. A native speaker of Cantonese, she learned Mandarin in middle school, which became crucial for her career on stage and screen. She also became fluent in English, as her high school in Shanghai was run by U.S. Southern Baptists. After joining protests against the Nationalist Party's massacre of Communist-affiliated union workers in Shanghai in 1927, she was expelled from her high school.

Back in her hometown, she encountered two young men who would play a large role in her political and personal life. Mei Gongyi[5] and Ren Posheng[6] had been cadets in the Huangpu Military Academy but left after the split between the Nationalist Party and the Communist Party in 1927. The left-oriented young men taught Chen Bo'er about the Soviet Revolution and Marxism and suggested that she return to Shanghai for college. To save some money for school, Chen worked as a teacher for a year in Hong Kong, where her father had residency and a business. In 1928 Chen, along with Mei and Ren, enrolled in the Shanghai Arts College, a hub of left-wing artists and writers run by the underground CCP. There she became involved in the Shanghai Art Drama Troupe (SADT). Founded in October 1929, the SADT was the first drama troupe organized by Communists who were involved in the avant-garde performing art as a form of politically engaged activism.[7] Chen played the female leading roles in two of the five new spoken dramas it staged. Acting in these plays shaped her future career, inaugurating her reputation as a fine actor and connecting her with social networks of left-wing artists who shared a belief in the transformative power of art.

At the time, the Nationalist Party (NP) was intensifying its censorship and persecution of the left, and when, on February 7, 1931, it executed twenty-three underground CCP members, including five members of the Left-Wing Writers Association,[8] Chen and her lover Ren Posheng, also a left activist, decided to retreat to Hong Kong where in April 1931 they married.

Chen Bo'er taught English in a middle school in Hong Kong and gave birth to two sons in a span of three years. Subsidized by both their wealthy merchant families, the couple enjoyed a comfortable life. But national crises made the public-minded young mother restless. Japan invaded Manchuria in September 1931 and attacked Shanghai in January 1932. Although a truce was reached in May, the danger of Japanese domination and colonization of China loomed large. Chen felt the urge to leave the British colony and return to social activism in Shanghai. In early 1934, she gladly accepted the invitation from her friend Mei Gongyi to teach English in the new school he opened in Shanghai, leaving her young sons in the care of her natal family. Her teaching career was brief, however, as the government soon shut down Mei's school. Chen then began to earn a living by writing essays for the city's largest newspaper, the *Shanghai Daily* (*Shenbao*).

In these essays Chen clearly articulated her feminist position and patriotic concerns. In the 1930s Shanghai already had a substantial number of women students and professionals as a result of the promotion of women's education by both the public and the government since the late Qing Dynasty. These educated women, who were among her friends, classmates, and colleagues, were Chen's primary readers. Writing mostly on the topic of "the women question," Chen expressed both her inheritance of a May Fourth feminist discourse and her evolution since her exposure to socialism that led her to criticize what she understood as the limits of May Fourth feminism.

> History tells us explicitly that women have been bullied in society. Yes, we have attributed this problem to the harmful social institutions of the past. Therefore, from the toppling of the Qing emperor to the May Fourth movement, calls for women's emancipation have been quite loud in public discourse, which created an opportunity for women's self-emancipation. However, the sound wave has, after all, remained only a sound wave. It has not actually enabled women to achieve real emancipation and gain equal social status.[9]

Discontented that the movement for women's emancipation remained at the discursive level rather than generating structural changes, Chen held educated women responsible for failing to push for substantial social changes. She was most disappointed in those women who enjoyed the class privilege to acquire a higher education and were called "new women" but chose to return to domesticity rather than engage in social change. In examining these privileged women, she adopted a Marxist class analysis to approach "the women question." Unlike most May Fourth feminist writers who treated women as a homogeneous group without making distinctions among them, Chen differentiated the privileged ladies of the rich from poor laboring women:

> *Taitai* and misses[10] have material abundance and enjoy a romantic and luxurious life. Their life cannot be described as tragic, but represents self-degeneration. Therefore, I place the laboring women masses at the center [of "the women question"]. Their life is too dark to be imagined by others. They are downtrodden by feudal power and abused by men. Under these multiple oppressions, what would the future of Chinese women be? Only to bury their lives in death day by day![11]

As early as 1934 Chen declared that her concern was not with the emancipation of women of her own class but women of the working class. Her writings, however, were mostly in line with the framework of the May Fourth feminist pursuit of human rights, which could also have been a response to NP censorship of revolutionary advocacy in a mainstream newspaper. Her language located her safely in mainstream May Fourth feminism: "Women must stand up to fight. We should believe we are human beings, not slaves. We are not born to be possessions of men, let alone their toys!"[12]

But what was the relationship between educated women and the suffering women of the laboring class? In these writings Chen aimed to raise the consciousness of privileged women by making them aware that their own educational and career opportunities did not mean that women were already liberated. They had to pay attention to "the great majority of women who are still groaning under multiple oppressions." While continuing her consciousness-raising effort, she contended that "because so-called liberated women have directly received the education of bourgeois society, they are not aware of their own status, let alone of the numerous other women by their side who are awaiting freedom and liberation!" She did not think that educated bourgeois women would undertake the liberation of the majority of Chinese women. This disappointment with women of her own class made her look for other allies for the grand task of achieving equality between men and women, which "is related to the entire human race's freedom and equality."[13]

In her writings during this period, Chen unambiguously expressed a women-centered vision of human emancipation and a solid identification with lower-class women, though in her perception the women of the laboring class were passively "awaiting" their liberation through others' actions rather than their own agency. This stance reflects left intellectuals' self-conception and their attitude toward the lower classes, that is, left intellectuals themselves as the enlightened vanguard of human emancipation. Chen Bo'er eventually changed her position on this matter. A strong feminist, she was attracted to the CCP in her search for a political force that shared her dream of an equalitarian society and demonstrated capacity for bringing actual social change. "Animated by a spirit of mutual help for the sake of human race, we should unite in order to shoulder a task of such magnitude." Chen wrote with a conviction in the unity of like-minded idealists who aimed at the grandiose task of building a new world for the human race.[14]

The obstacles that radicals faced within Chinese society were formidable, and the situation was further exacerbated by Japan's threat to colonize China. The second most frequent topic of Chen's essays was national salvation. In her accounts of political events of the early twentieth century, she recounted proletarians' struggles against capitalists and intellectuals' struggles for democracy and against imperialism. She emphasized the spirited activism of people of different walks of life in their struggle against various forms of domination, revealing how much she herself was inspired by retelling these stories. Chen deplored imperialist invasions and described the sadness of Chinese people under Japanese occupation. "Our country is about to perish,"

Chen exhorted her readers. "To be slaves is hard. With a heart filled with grief and rage, we should shout loudly, 'It's time to roar, China!'"[15]

It is difficult to detect the author's gender identity in these essays on politics. The strong emotions conveyed by the deliberate choice of dramatic language generate an image of a man arousing huge crowds in a public square with his magnificent voice and theatrical gestures. Nothing in these writings would lead readers to imagine the author as a young woman with a petite physique. Chen meant to convey the May Fourth feminist ideal that a woman should not be confined to her feminine body in her social actions. To be human was to live an androgynous life outside the constraints of gender boundaries. In confronting national crises, she would definitely not retreat and leave the front to men. By performing in a traditionally masculine domain, Chen and her cohort of feminists sought to demonstrate that women could be equal political actors. In assuming a male voice, Chen was expressing more than her nationalist sentiments; she was also demanding an equal place in the public sphere.

Publishing political essays on national salvation, Chen's simultaneous writings on the women question demonstrate that at no time did the agenda of national salvation subsume her gender-specific concerns. Fighting for national salvation and fighting for women's liberation were not mutually exclusive, but intrinsically interrelated. Chen and other feminists who eventually joined the CCP shared a common understanding that full participation in public affairs was an integral part of women's liberation. Women's empowerment and development could not be separated from their integral involvement in social transformation, unrestrained by their gender. Moreover, for a feminist identified with the CCP, national salvation was part of a revolution that promised to lead to a new independent China; women's liberation was central to this vision.

As Chen earned a precarious livelihood through her writing, her friend Mei Gongyi suggested that she might find an acting job in Shanghai's film industry. Underground CCP artists were infiltrating film companies in order to transform film production and recruiting left-oriented young actors for films scripted by left-wing writers.[16] Initially Chen hesitated; she liked acting but hated the media's sexist treatment of women film actors. Persuaded by her close friend and a left-wing former professor, Chen decided to join their efforts to transform film as part of their revolutionary activism.

In late 1934 two films with Chen playing the leading female roles catapulted her to stardom. *Fate of Graduates* (*Taoli jie*) the first Chinese film with

FIGURE 16. Chen Bo'er in the early 1930s. Courtesy of the Beijing Film Academy library.

comprehensive sound effects produced by the underground CCP–run Diantong Film Company, was an instant hit. Allegedly, the film brought many students to the Communist Revolution. It depicted how two idealistic young students' lives were destroyed in a capitalist society replete with injustice, inhumanity, and corruption. By 1938 Chen had made three more films, in the last of which she played a role based on a real young heroine Yang Huimin, who bravely delivered a national flag to the besieged Nationalist troops in the battle against Japanese in Shanghai in 1937.[17] A journalist commented in 1940: "Chen Bo'er's acting and style occupy a very important position in the heart of youth who love freedom and pursue a bright future. As with the roles she plays, Chen herself has a persistent and brave character. She has determination. She is fearless. She dares to speak out and to act. Whatever she promises she will deliver."[18] Chen was regarded as a role model for left-oriented youth, in addition to being a movie star adored by her many fans (fig. 16).

What made Chen Bo'er stand out among all the movie stars during this period? The films in which she acted presented critical social realism, a new artistic genre introduced by left film producers who portrayed social relations in capitalist society in a critical light. More importantly, because she took acting as part of her revolutionary pursuit, Chen never limited the scope of her intellectual, political, and social activities. In between her acting roles, she continued to contribute critical essays to women's magazines and film journals.

In "The Female-Centered Film and the Male-Centered Society," published in *Women's Life* in 1936, Chen presented an important feminist critique of the film industry in capitalist society. She analyzed the relationships among marketing, the public adulation of female stars, and patriarchal culture. Rather than proof that women were becoming the center of a modern industry, Chen argued that the promotion of female stars showed that the capitalist film industry used women's bodies to make profits. After asking "[Why] the audience extols female stars rather than male stars? Why their desire toward female stars centers on her mystique, her hot seductiveness, or beautiful face and physique?" Chen articulated a concept of "the male gaze" that, in interesting ways, anticipates British feminist film scholar Laura Mulvey's famous theorization in 1975 that explicated a passive / active and spectacle / spectator relation in the sexist cinematic apparatus's representation of women and men.[19] With none of the psychoanalytical tools Mulvey took from Freudian and Lacanian theories, Chen nonetheless emphasized the psychological effects of unequal gender power relations on women viewers of films.

> In a male-centered society, politics, the economy, and all the ruling powers are in men's hands. Thus all the laws, morality, customs, and norms are shaped by men's biased positions. Aesthetic views are no exception. They too are shaped by men's biased preferences. . . . Women in such a society have unconsciously conformed to its demands. For instance, using makeup was not originally in women's nature, but in order to cater to the preferences of a male-centered society it has become female nature. This explains why female audiences have similar views toward female stars as that of male audiences. The difference is that the male audience's view expresses the direct preference out of a dominator's psychology, while the female audience's view arises from the psychology of the dominated to unconsciously cater to the preferences of the dominator.[20]

The power relations between the dominator and the dominated, in Chen's analyses, explain women's conformity and consent to masculine aesthetic standards. Refusing to naturalize femininity, she detailed the social construction of women in a male-centered society. But her greatest effort in this piece was to dispel the mystique of female movie stars and admonish women not to take the market-packaged movie stars as a model for advancing their social status. Although she herself was already a movie star, Chen ended her essay by suggesting that if film could not be revolutionized it should be abandoned. "Women's pursuit of freedom and equality requires the efforts of all walks of life. If film cannot shoulder the responsibility of guidance but is mistaken as an ideal haven and leads people to escape from reality, we would rather have no film!"[21]

This conclusion was somewhat ironic, given that Chen had gained social recognition and discursive power precisely through her stardom. But by stripping away the aura surrounding her, the essay revealed the author's honesty and audacity. More importantly, this essay by a young movie star unambiguously expressed a critical feminist stance against a patriarchal capitalist society and enunciated Chen's vision of film playing a transformative role in changing the male-dominated society and advancing *all* women's pursuit of freedom and equality. This "manifesto" of a feminist movie star would be put into practice when she became a leader of socialist film a decade later.

Chen's critique of the leading female role she played in *Revolutionaries* (*Shengsi tongxin*) enables us to understand the attractions of the Communist Revolution to Chen and her cohort of feminists. Zhao Yuhua, the protagonist Chen played, follows her lover to join the Nationalist Revolution in the mid-1920s when the NP and CCP were allied. Chen criticized the May Fourth theme of "love revolution" in the film as outdated and called on her audience to join in the salvation of their country.[22] Educated women in cosmopolitan cities like Shanghai already enjoyed autonomy in their love life and choice of spouse, which had been a prominent goal of the May Fourth feminist agenda. Now, with Japan's escalating aggression in China, national salvation, rather than love and sexuality, must become central in many young feminists' engagement. This shift in focus was historically contingent, and its gender implications were surprisingly progressive.

Although many feminist scholars define nationalist movements as predominantly masculine, the massive participation of Chinese women in the national salvation movement destabilizes this gender definition. Modern women sought to transgress gender boundaries and claim equal rights in what had historically been an exclusively male space. When high-profile women played prominent roles in the national salvation movement in China, they rewrote norms for gendered space as well as reshaped their own gender subjectivities. In the political arena, Chen and other elite women staged gender performances in multiple forms and media riding on the vehicle of the nationalist movement.

Chen participated in a wide range of public activities before she joined the CCP. In 1935 she worked with other women celebrities in Shanghai to establish the Shanghai Women's National Salvation Association and Young Women's Club. At the end of 1936, she organized and led a group of women to visit the troops at the Suiyuan front, bringing donations from Shanghai citizens and performing street theater.[23] Upon returning to Shanghai from the trip north, Chen joined Song Qingling and other celebrities in protesting the NP government's arrest of the seven leaders of the National Salvation Association of All-Walks in 1937.[24] Chen went with Song Qingling, Shen Zijiu, and nine other celebrities to the Suzhou Court demanding to be arrested for the "crime" of being patriotic.[25] In addition to such performance acts staged in public spaces that attracted extra attention because of their gender transgression—their leadership in political events—Chen also took on inconspicuous traditional feminine tasks to support those at the front. As Shen Zijiu reported in *Women's Life,* Chen would go to He Xiangning's home after shooting her scenes in the film studio to do voluntary work.[26] "We could often see this dazzling star quietly sewing winter clothes for soldiers, or deftly rolling gauze with two hands, or kneading tiny cotton balls. In the evening she would follow the group and climb onto the truck sending these goods to the brave soldiers on the battleground in the east."[27] Here Chen was praised for crossing class boundaries by engaging in manual labor generally done by household servants in elite families. With quite wide media coverage by women journalists who portrayed her with respect and admiration, by 1937 Chen Bo'er had emerged as a multifaceted celebrity on the national stage.

Her private life was mostly concealed from the prying tabloids that gossiped about her husband's wealth and his abandonment of her. No one guessed that Ren Posheng was involved in the CCP's underground work, which required his frequent absence and low profile. A profound tragedy in Chen's personal life was buried even more deeply. In early 1935 when Chen was in Hong Kong with her husband and two young sons, the hot-tempered Ren beat their one-year-old child to death.[28] The heartbroken young mother took her remaining son with her back to Shanghai and hired a nanny to care for him. Their friends were told that the baby had died of a sudden illness. This inexplicable tragedy left a deep scar on her marriage.

Chen continued working as an actor, writing political essays, and agitating for national salvation. She forged an identity as an independent social activist, artist, and woman warrior while shouldering the responsibility for her son with the help of his nanny. Her life was now entirely independent from her natal family, her husband's family, and her marriage. The large-scale movement of educated women like Chen Bo'er from their secluded inner chambers to the outer public space was simultaneously inspired by and acted upon feminism and nationalism, the two ideologies that powerfully combined to produce new subjectivities of women in early twentieth-century China. But for Chen, Marxism provided a critical lens for her to understand the world around her and to envision her role in it. *Transformation* and *resistance* are two key words that lent coherence to the various ideological strands she embraced and to her existence as a revolutionary feminist.

THE MAKING OF A REVOLUTIONARY ARTIST

Chen Bo'er was formally but confidentially accepted by the CCP in August 1937.[29] At the end of 1938 the Party sent Chen to Yan'an, the base area regarded by many left-oriented young people as the center of resistance against Japanese invaders and the embryo of a new China. Chen had been longing to go to Yan'an ever since she watched a documentary film of life in Yan'an made by Edgar Snow in early 1937.[30] To work on a special assignment of the Party, Chen sent her young son to a boarding school in Chongqing and went to Yan'an alone.

Chen was to lead a "Group Inspecting Women and Children in the War Zones" with the ostensible mission of establishing connections between women in the war zones and those in the rear. The six young Communist women traveled through war-affected areas in northern China for fifteen months, collecting information, conducting educational workshops among rural villagers, and involving themselves in local resistance work. Despite the danger, hardship, and fatigue, Chen managed to write several reports and articles, three of which reached the journal *Women's Life,* which had moved from Shanghai to the wartime capital, Chongqing. These writings illuminate a profoundly transformative experience.

In "Impressions of Three Representatives with Bound Feet," Chen described with excitement and admiration how rural women "have shouldered the double tasks of national restoration and women's liberation" and "walked out of their extremely feudal rural families with their heads held high."[31] She focused on three village women in their mid-fifties who led local resistance work despite their bound feet. Chen conveyed the immediacy of these illiterate women's voices with lengthy quotations from their speeches at rallies and her interviews with them. Her reportage serves as an ethnographic record of the transformation of gender norms in rural villages taking place when social institutions, including the family, had been reorganized by the resistance movement. It demonstrated that CCP feminists' insistence on "double tasks" of national restoration and women's liberation in their organizational work at the grassroots mobilized and empowered rural women.

Zhang Shufeng, one of the three women leaders with bound feet, declared: "Before the resistance, I did not know what constituted a human being. . . . The resistance war is really wonderful. It has brought out the human spirit of many villages. I am one of those who benefited. . . . My status has been improved since a wife who cooks and raises children now has something to do for the country. No one calls me old woman (*lao pozi*) any more. They all address me as director, chair."[32] Geng Ruzhang, another leader, told Chen: "Now women in north China are liberated and freed. . . . You can see women involving themselves in all kinds of activities, treading on mountain paths and climbing over the mountains. . . . Women of north China have all come out of their straw huts."[33] Zhang Qingyun, the third leader, commented that the tasks the Women's Salvation Associations performed "are not inferior" to men's tasks, which "smashes the views of those who have always shown contempt toward women and girls."[34]

From her distinctive feminist perspective, Chen communicated the way in which rural women took resistance activities as a golden opportunity to break out of gender constraints in patriarchal families and villages, to "come out" to enjoy the spatial and social mobility that had formerly been solely the prerogative of men. Their effortless deployment of terms such as "being a human being," "women's liberation," "freedom," and "resistance war" showed their active embrace of a political language that fused May Fourth feminism and a CCP version of nationalism that combined national salvation with social and interpersonal transformation. They articulated new subjectivities shaped by the CCP's "women-work" for the war effort in the rural base areas. In exuberant prose, Chen described not only the transformation in these rural women's lives and minds but her own transformation as well.

Encountering these strong, capable, and heroic rural women with a clear political consciousness profoundly affected Chen, who had grown up in the

FIGURE 17. Chen Bo'er photographs rural women militias. Courtesy of the Beijing Film Academy library.

urban elite that had habitually imagined lower-class women as passive victims waiting to be liberated and uplifted by better-educated women. With undisguised euphoria, Chen turned her reporting into a paean to rural women. Many touching episodes in the three women's lives were described visually, as if they were movie scenes. For instance, these women with tiny and deformed feet had great difficulty walking on icy dirt roads and snow-covered mountain paths. To attend an important meeting far away, they tripped and fell again and again, and finally had to crawl on the frozen ground and roll down the snowy slopes, arriving at their destination with injuries all over their bodies. These scenes were etched so deeply in Chen's mind that she later represented them visually in her *Daughters of China* (1949), the first film featuring revolutionary heroines. In her report, she expressed her admiration: "Indeed, the unbreakable spirit demonstrated by these rural women, with bound feet, throughout their hard struggles constitutes the most precious poetry in the resistance war. They have written the most brilliant chapter in the history of the women's movement" (fig. 17).[35]

Baptized in the unbreakable spirit of rural women in the resistance war, Chen developed the strong conviction that artistic representation should faithfully render the emerging subjectivities of heroines who would otherwise be unknown beyond their local communities. The report on the three women with bound feet signified this urban elite artist's conscious facilitation of the entrance of subaltern subjects into mainstream discourse. Several years later she found in film a more powerful medium to carry out her mission and express her passion.

In 1940 the Inspection Group arrived in Chongqing, where Chen picked up her eight-year-old son and brought him back to Yan'an. This second period in Yan'an marked a new chapter in Chen's life. She became a lively and prominent figure in Yan'an's cultural life by staging new dramas for which she worked as director and playwright. The most influential play produced in Yan'an, *Comrade, You Are on the Wrong Road!* (1942), depicted political struggles inside the Communist Party for the first time. Director Chen Bo'er introduced several innovative practices in producing a play on a military and political subject. Pursuing a mass line in artistic creativity, she recruited 90 percent of the actors from soldiers or officials who had extensive experience in warfare and were from working-class or rural backgrounds. Besides acting out their own lives on the stage, the amateur actors were invited to revise the play whenever they saw fit, including its language. She also experimented with collective directing by forming a group of directors with the participation of military officials. This mechanism was intended to transform artists' tendency toward individualism. The mass line and collectivism seemed to enhance the play's artistic quality, and it was recognized as the first spoken drama in which soldiers did not walk and talk like urban intellectuals. Directing the play provided Chen with a valuable learning experience, particularly with regard to enabling amateur actors recruited from the lower classes with little formal education to express themselves in artistic representation.[36] Her pioneering practices in cultural representation of the soldiers and peasants were emulated by cultural producers in the early PRC.

Chen won multiple awards for artists and Party members in Yan'an. The recollection of the writer Ding Ling, who was also in Yan'an, provided an explanation of Chen's popularity other than her stardom. "She was in poor health, and yet her meals came from the big pot shared with all (some artists had meals from the pot of middle size). Nevertheless, she took it naturally and joyfully. I never heard anybody say that Chen Bo'er complained about the life there. That was very rare among artists or intellectuals who had come to Yan'an with some social status."[37] The movie star lived in a cave in Yan'an like everyone else and had no special privileges. She had heart disease, which the

前排左起：康生、凯丰、任弼时、王稼祥、徐特立、博古、刘白羽、罗烽、草明、田方、毛泽东、张悟真、陈波儿、朱德、丁玲、李伯钊、瞿维、力群、白朗、塞克、周文、胡续伟。

From the Front Left: Kang Sheng, Kai Feng, Ren Bishi, Wang Jiaxiang, Xu Teli, Bo Gu, Liu Baiyu, Luo Feng, Cao Ming, Tian Fang, Mao Zedong, Zhang Wuzheng, Chen Bo'er, Zhu De, Din Ling, Li Bozhao, Qu Wei, Li Qun, Bai Lang, Sai Ke, Zhou Wen and Hu Jiwei

FIGURE 18. Group photograph of the participants in the Yan'an Forum on Literature and the Arts in 1942. Courtesy of the Beijing Film Academy library.

rudimentary medical system in Yan'an was unable to diagnose or cure. Chen fainted several times during rehearsals, but once she was back on her feet she would continue working intensely. Although this community of artists and intellectuals was often entangled in personal grievances, no memoirs or recollections show any trace of resentment toward her. On the contrary, her name usually would draw instant praise from my interviewees. Lu Ming, who had known Chen Bo'er since he was a young boy in Yan'an, even claimed, "Chen Bo'er was a flawless person!"—a comment made in the context of his emphasis that there was no gossip about Chen in Yan'an.[38] The group picture taken after Mao gave his famous talks at the Yan'an Forum on Literature and Arts in May 1942 makes her respected status in Yan'an evident. The petite paragon Chen Bo'er was placed in the center, along with a woman artist named Zhang Wuzhen, between Chairman Mao and General Zhu De (fig. 18).

Today, both in and outside China, Yan'an is largely remembered for the CCP's rectification campaign, in which many Communists were punished or persecuted for "incorrect" views. Mao's Yan'an Talks are often highlighted for his alleged agenda of disciplining intellectuals and regulating artistic creativity. Chen Bo'er's story reveals the flaws in the dominant narrative. Rather than being forced by Party leaders to undergo a political and personal transformation in order to represent workers / peasants / solders in literature and the arts, a frequent charge lodged against Mao's Talks during the post-socialist period, Chen's sense of herself and society had been shaped during her affiliation with left-wing artistic pursuits in Shanghai and been further transformed by her fifteen months of fieldwork in the war-affected rural villages before hearing Mao addressing the subject. She had consciously changed her own subjectivity in order to shoulder the task of transforming the world. In writing about revolutionary rural women, she had anticipated Mao's views for artistically representing the new subjectivities being forged in the crucible of war and revolution.

Chen's practices of cultural representation of the voiceless were integral parts of her revolutionary effort to transform hierarchical power relations that were deeply embedded in Chinese society and culture. Indeed, these practices could only be created by artists who had faith in the transformative power of cultural production. As literary scholar Liang Luo shows in her study of Tian Han, one of the founders of Chinese spoken drama, the Chinese avant-garde artists initiated socially engaging performance art since the early twentieth century, and "going to the people" was an intrinsic principle in their aesthetic and political pursuits.[39] Xiaobing Tang in his recent work on a history of the street theater movement in China delineates the emergence of "public theater" as a "paradigmatic development" in the 1930s, particularly in the resistance war against Japan. He emphasizes: "A fundamental commitment to the nation in crisis thus underlay the street theater movement and many other artistic activities during this historical period. This commitment also determined that a genuine artistic avant-garde in modern China must aspire to transform its audience as well as its practitioners through the same dynamic creative process."[40]

Having been immersed in the avant-garde artistic ethos of the early twentieth century, Chen Bo'er was by no means a singular case, except for the fact that her strong feminist consciousness allowed her to pay more attention to lower-class women among "the people" and direct more energy to transforming a gender-inflected "feudalist culture." In any case, during the early 1940s Communists were still on the political, military, and cultural fringes and very far from attaining state power that could suppress artists' "free expression." Situating Mao's Talks in the trajectory of artist Chen Bo'er's epistemological development and subjective transformation offers us an understanding that is close to that historical milieu, rather than an interpretation motivated by the desire in the post-Mao era to condemn the CCP's authoritarian state. The Yan'an Talks were by no means a monologue singularly produced in the great leader's mind for the purpose of controlling Party members and harnessing artists' creativity, but rather Mao's theorizing of Communist cultural producers' innovative practices. He cogently articulated a vision of cultural revolution that had long been shared among revolutionary artists such as Chen Bo'er.[41] In this sense, he was preaching to the converted who had voluntarily abandoned their urban privileges to reside in the caves of a desolate rural periphery for the sake of realizing a dream of transforming China, regardless how many variations of the dream there might be. For the Communist artists in Yan'an, subscribing to the familiar tenets of Mao's Talks on literature and arts that articulated a clear sense of mission functioned as a confirmation of their identity in a community, imagined and / or real, of revolutionary cultural transformers. The effects and significance of Mao's Talks necessarily vary when the audience and the context against which they are transmitted change, a point to which the following chapters will return.

CREATING A FEMINIST PARADIGM FOR SOCIALIST FILM

After the CCP took control of the northeast region upon Japan's surrender, Zhou Enlai sent Chen Bo'er to join the takeover of a Japanese film studio in 1946. The Northeast Film Studio (NFS), later renamed Changchun Film Studio, became the first state-owned film studio of the PRC. The Party also sent to the NFS Chen's old friend and partner in three films, the renowned filmmaker and actor Yuan Muzhi, who had just returned from studying film in the Soviet Union. Chen was appointed Party secretary of the NFS and put in charge of the Department of Art, while Yuan became the director of the NFS. Chen's estranged husband, Ren Posheng, had long been remarried to another woman in the CCP, but the news did not reach Chen Bo'er until 1946.[42] In 1947 Chen and Yuan married, much to the delight of their friends and fans.

With the full support of Yuan Muzhi, Chen energetically organized the production of documentary films and feature films.[43] She was heavily

FIGURE 19. Chen Bo'er in Xingshan. Photo taken in 1947 when Party leader of the northeast region Zhang Wentian and his wife Liu Ying visited the NFS. From left to right: Zhang Wentian, Wu Yinxian, Chen Bo'er, Liu Ying, and Yuan Muzhi. Courtesy of Lu Ming.

involved in the production process from screenwriting to final editing, though as a matter of principle she did not list her name in the credits. All of her contemporaries emphasized Chen's central role in this early stage of exploring a socialist film paradigm that represented workers / peasants / soldiers as Mao's Yan'an Talks directed.[44] As Lu Ming told me in our 2012 interview, "Chen Bo'er was the soul of Xingshan."[45]

In Mao's original enunciation, the workers / peasants / soldiers who were the subject of revolutionary cultural representation were genderless. In patriarchal societies, however, gender-unmarked subjects are commonly understood as men, setting a norm for humanity against which women are defined as deficient. Expressing her feminist vision in filmmaking, Chen Bo'er initiated a women-centered representation of workers / peasants / soldiers by promoting the production of films featuring revolutionary heroines. In 1946 the filmmakers in the NFS were predominantly young Communists from Yan'an who had little experience or even exposure to filmmaking.[46] Chen's artistic expertise and political power gave her full authority over the entire process of film production, from training young scriptwriters, cinematographers, and directors and selecting scripts for production to adding the final editing touches to a film. Within one year of intensive training and creative work in a euphoric atmosphere, eight new scripts were selected for production, two of which portrayed revolutionary heroines.

The process of producing the first revolutionary heroine film *Daughters of China (Zhonghua nüer)* was not a smooth one. A young Communist woman from Yan'an, Yan Yiyan, with no experience in screenwriting, was assigned to write a script about the Communist resistant force in the Northeast areas in the war. After two months of fieldwork in the military force, Yan collected numerous stories about heroic soldiers. One—about eight women soldiers of the Northeast Resistance Troop—touched her deeply but she could not find enough source material. Apparently, in a battle against Japanese troops, in order to protect the main force from the Japanese attack, the women decoyed the Japanese troops away. Being chased to the riverbank, they heroically resisted capture by jumping into the roaring Songhua River. The legend of eight women martyrs was depicted in an oil painting, but Yan could only find the real identity for one of the eight women who had been a schoolteacher before joining the resistance. Chen Bo'er strongly encouraged Yan to follow this finding to do more research. Yan spent another three months collecting material. In the end Chen Bo'er and Yan co-authored the script by incorporating many heroines' stories that Yan had collected. While Chen Bo'er regarded it as her responsibility to provide hands-on training to young scriptwriters and directors, she also insisted on letting their names appear in the credits rather than her own. Yan was credited as the sole scriptwriter of the film.[47]

The finished script depicted an international community of women, including two Korean women, who demonstrated remarkable strength and courage in fighting Japanese fascism. Yan Yiyan had originally hoped to give equal treatment to each of the eight heroines but the director Ling Zifeng rejected the idea.[48] The two got into a heated argument until finally Chen Bo'er was called in to mediate and helped revise the script, following Ling Zifeng's suggestion that just one of the eight women should become the major protagonist and to develop a central narrative line around her life story.[49] Chen Bo'er portrayed this main character, Hu Xiuzhi, in the image of those courageous rural women she had encountered and even created a long scene in which a wounded Hu Xiuzhi tenaciously crawled on the mountain in order to return to the troop's campsite, a way for Chen to visually commemorate the deeply etched memories of those bound-feet rural women representatives in the resistance war.

FIGURE 20. *Daughters of China* (1949). Hu Xiuzhi carries her martyred comrade toward the roaring river.

Ling Zifeng was also a first-time young director who loved the Soviet Union's films that the NES used as models for teaching young filmmakers. He imitated the Soviet classic *Chapaev* (1934) that portrayed a Soviet Red Army commander who became a hero in the Russian Civil War. Transposing its setting to a Chinese scene and its cinematic language for a hero to depict a Chinese heroine, Ling Zifeng inadvertently accomplished a significant subversion of Hollywood classical representation of women that objectified women in the male gaze. As film critic Dai Jinhua comments, "The new classical revolutionary film genre successfully dispelled the particular discourse inherent in Hollywood's classic cinematic narrative mechanism (that is, the shot sequence of male desire / female image and male gaze / woman as object of gaze) when it eliminated the narrative of desire along with the language of desire."[50] The heroines in *Daughters of China* stood tall, full of autonomy and courage. Absent of sexual desires and the male gaze, the sublime subject of war heroines was constructed to induce viewers' admiration and awe (fig. 20).

Viewers responded enthusiastically to this first film portraying revolutionary heroines. Many women revolutionaries perceptively grasped its gendered significance as celebrating women's contribution to the revolution. They were relieved to see that revolutionary heroines' extraordinary sacrifices in the war were commemorated. "Their names are forever engraved in history," a woman viewer declared.[51] Male viewers were also deeply moved by heroines' patriotic devotion to national salvation. As one film critic wrote: "The whole film, especially its climax and ending, exudes a profoundly solemn and tragic tone through its natural simplicity, which induces in the audience an aesthetic of the sublime."[52] Having just emerged from wars that had involved the participation of numerous women, China in the 1950s did not yet have a social context for fearing women's "masculinization," hence the public's enthusiastic praise of women's heroic sacrifice in the fight against fascism.[53] The first revolutionary heroine film was appropriately dedicated to the first international women's conference the PRC hosted—the All-Asian Women's Congress convening in Beijing in December 1949.

In 1950 the NFS finished another thirteen feature films, three of which portrayed revolutionary heroines. Of the five films featuring women's leading roles, four were based on life stories of actual Communist women.[54] Chen Bo'er thought that film was the best medium to faithfully represent the history of the Revolution, including women as well as men activists whose "magnificently glorious stories must be made known in all corners of China and to the whole world."[55] She constantly instructed young filmmakers to portray real people and events: "The most touching scene is a real scene."[56] Her own encounters with remarkable women during the war had convinced her that what ordinary people could do in an extraordinary time went far beyond anything artists could imagine. Thus it was of paramount importance for filmmakers not to create stories from their own imagination but to portray real historical figures as faithfully as possible. In order to facilitate realistic representation, she required filmmakers to conduct a period of fieldwork among the people they were about to represent. This practice, called *xia shenghuo*, entering the life, was later institutionalized in China's socialist film industry in order to reduce the gap between the knowledge of educated artists and the lived reality of workers / peasants / soldiers.

Representing revolutionary women as the main protagonists of films also expressed Chen's astute grasp of the new subjectivities that had emerged among Chinese women during the course of the Communist Revolution and the resistance war. A socialist feminist who prioritized the transformation of a patriarchal culture and the disruption of the mutually reinforcing and oppressive power relations between gender and class, Chen saw representing women workers / peasants / soldiers as powerful historical actors as an indispensable revolutionary cultural practice. In a talk on her efforts to create a new paradigm for socialist film, she emphasized: "The backward reality is gradually receding to the past. New and beautiful characters full of vitality are emerging in large numbers in front of us. We must affirm that these are the people our film should represent."[57] Revolutionary heroines were prominent among them. Chen's emphasis was entirely consistent with Mao's Yan'an Talks in terms of who should be the subject of revolutionary cultural representation, but her artistic embodiment of the new revolutionary subjectivity placed women at the center of the silver screen. In sharp contrast to the major mode of visual and literary representation of Chinese women as victims of oppression by left-oriented artists since the May Fourth era, Chen's films of revolutionary heroines articulated a new feminist perspective that showed women on the historical stage initiating actions for social and personal changes rather than merely waiting to be rescued.

In July 1949 Chen was transferred to Beijing for a new appointment as director of the art department of the Central Film Bureau (CFB); at the same time, her husband, Yuan Muzhi, became head of the CFB. As one of the key leaders of China's state-owned film industry, she pushed for the wider circulation of films showing heroines, both in China and internationally.[58] Of the twenty-six films produced under her direction by state-owned film studios nationwide in 1950, she insisted on selecting the two films with revolutionary heroines produced by NFS, *Daughters of China* and *Zhao Yiman*, to enter the Karlovy Vary International Film Festival in Czechoslovakia in 1950.[59] But in the CFB's debate about which film to send to the festival, there was resistance centered on these films' artistic quality. Some authoritative figures deprecated *Daughters of China* as a documentary film rather than an "art film." Chen defended the film passionately and reportedly threatened, "How can we face the Party and the people if such a film as *Daughters of China* is not allowed to be in the film festival! I will have to resign from my position as the director of the Art Department!"[60] Chen succeeded in sending these two films to the festival.

The awards that followed, the first international prizes won by films made in the PRC, served as a high appraisal of Chen's artistic vision in creating a new paradigm for socialist film and consolidated her leadership. *Daughters of China* won the Freedom Fight prize and the star of *Zhao Yiman* won the Best Actor prize. The prestige garnered by these international prizes swiftly silenced any critiques of the films and confirmed Chen's artistic judgment and political vision. The enthusiastic public acceptance of both films also sent a strong message to Chinese filmmakers who might previously have not shown much interest in revolutionary heroines that this subject was well received internationally as well as domestically.[61]

Then a totally unexpected critique of a film by Chairman Mao in May 1951 created new dynamics in the film industry. *The Life of Wu Xun (Wu Xun zhuan)* made by a private film studio in Shanghai, was a biographical treatment of a historical figure in the late nineteenth century. An illiterate poor man, Wu Xun was committed to building schools for poor boys and begged to accumulate the necessary funds. A well-known figure in his hometown, Wu Xun had been commemorated by generations of officials and elite men as an exemplary figure for promoting educational opportunities for the poor. Touched by Wu Xun's life story, director Sun Yu began writing the script in 1948 and had completed most of the shooting when the CCP took over China in 1949. Sensing that the original story line no longer suited the new political environment, he made many revisions and turned the story into a tragedy of a poor man whose dream of equal opportunity for education was co-opted and manipulated by the feudal ruling class. The film was screened in February 1951, warmly received by many Communist leaders including Zhou Enlai, and highly acclaimed by both film critics and general public.

Just as director Sun was elated by the huge success of the film, Mao's severe criticism of *The Life of Wu Xun* appeared in the Party's newspaper *People's Daily*. Obviously unaware of the specific process in which the film was produced, he criticized filmmakers for not studying the new class forces, characters, and ideas that had emerged in the past century in China as the basis for deciding what to praise and extol. He especially condemned CCP members for "totally losing their critical faculties in the face of such a film promoting feudal culture and even surrendering to reactionary ideology." "Reactionary bourgeois ideas have already eroded a militant Communist Party. Isn't this a reality?"[62] Mao's harsh attitude toward a film by a nonparty member director and approved by most CCP leaders shocked everyone involved. But no one challenged the great leader, who, after all, had just led the CCP to victory over the NP. The film industry was the first to experience a political campaign in which confused artists and Party officials frantically tried to figure out a politically correct socialist production of film.[63]

In contrast to those "fuzzy headed" filmmakers and officials, Chen Bo'er's insistence on representing new historical forces and new characters who were powerfully embodied by revolutionary heroines was now appreciated in a new light. Chen herself joined the critique of *The Life of Wu Xun,* expressing her dislike for a poor man who behaved obsequiously in front of the rich and the powerful. Considering her passion for powerful heroines who dared to take up arms to fight against oppressors, her negative opinion of Wu Xun and her disapproval of the film may have been a genuine expression of her deeply held convictions rather than merely a political performance. Her political analysis of the director and actor in their artistic creation of the role of Wu Xun revealed her identification with Mao's thesis that artists should first transform their subjective world in order to create proletarian art. Her stern criticism of filmmakers' petty-bourgeois positionality was openly published in the July issue of the film magazine *New Film.*[64]

It was unclear whether Chen felt uneasy about the effects of her harsh criticism of her old colleague and friend in Shanghai or whether she sensed the political pressure that Mao's critique imposed on filmmakers. In any case, in November 1951 on her way back from an official trip to Guangzhou, she insisted on making a special stop in Shanghai to meet with filmmakers there, even though she was seriously ill. Chen was warmly welcomed by a large group of admiring filmmakers when she entered the conference room. She started to address the audience in an extremely weak voice, "Comrades, I am here to hear your criticisms of our work." Everyone realized instantly how tired she was. Filmmakers at the meeting knew that whatever political pressure they were enduring did not have much to do with this leader from the Central Film Bureau. They replied that they had no criticisms to offer and insisted that she rest rather than keep talking. Chen tried to speak, but her voice faded away entirely. In a few hours she died of heart failure in hospital.[65]

After her death, a larger-than-life figure emerged as Chen Bo'er was elevated from her obscure, altruistic position behind the films she produced. Memorial speeches and articles were published widely in Party newspapers and film magazines. At the memorial services held by the Shanghai municipal government in Shanghai and central government in Beijing, her colleagues, friends, and students poured out their profound grief over the loss of their beloved "comrade Bo'er," eulogizing her as a gifted artist, a devoted revolutionary, and a magnificent soul. Young filmmakers swore to take Chen Bo'er, the people's artist, as their model. Chen's old friend Xia Yan, who was now in charge of culture and art in Shanghai, characterized Chen Bo'er in his memorial speech with these perceptive words: "Chen Bo'er's passing is a colossal loss for the cause of Chinese people's film. Revolution is never a smooth journey. When people from a petty bourgeois background embark on this journey, they tend to encounter frustrations, failures, or loss of direction. In this respect, comrade Chen Bo'er's spirit of never succumbing to difficulty and forever sticking to the right direction is profoundly valuable for all of us to emulate."[66] Amidst the political campaign critiquing *The Life of Wu Xun*, Chen was identified and commemorated by her peers as an exemplar of the correct direction for a film industry in disarray.

Chen's feminist endeavors behind the scenes were recognized and openly acknowledged by her long-term feminist friends in the CCP. Deng Yingchao, the deputy chair of the All-China Women's Federation, articulated a gender agenda as she expressed her grief: "Just as the new China's film industry is developing rapidly, and just as we were expecting you to make more and bigger contributions, my dear comrade, you suddenly departed. This is a loss to our party, people, and women!" Deng enumerated all the activities in which Chen had been involved on behalf of women and children: "When you became the director of the Art Department of the Central Film Bureau and the associate chair of the Art Committee, you strongly insisted on making more films extolling remarkable Chinese women. We will never forget all these things."[67] Shen Zijiu, the editor-in-chief of *Women of China,* described Chen's recent meeting with her and Kang Keqing, another leader of the ACWF, to ask for their help in producing scripts. "We had tremendous expectations of comrade Bo'er. Women and children in the new China need her films to help lead and organize the cause of women's liberation and children's education."[68] In addition to losing a dear friend, these senior feminists mourned the loss of a feminist leader who held a powerful position in their concerted efforts to transform patriarchal culture in socialist China.

CODA

In the years after Chen Bo'er's death, strong heroines were featured as leading protagonists not only in films but also in operas, plays, posters, and other cultural forms. Images of strong women workers, peasants, and revolutionary leaders were ubiquitous in socialist China, sweeping away the cultural representations of women as sexual objects or as passive victims of feudal or capitalist oppressions that had predominated before 1949. These images of heroines highlighted their unfailing devotion to the revolutionary cause and socialist construction. The dominant mode of gender representation became the basis for post-socialist critics' arguments that women in the PRC were made into "statist subjects" or masculinized by assuming male roles and conforming to male standards in the public arena, which meant they became alienated from their supposedly innate femininity.

Various post-socialist critiques of practices relating to women and gender in the socialist past share a common conceptual framework: that the authoritarian patriarchal socialist state manipulated its citizens in order to consolidate its power, and that cultural representation, under the rubric of "party-state propaganda," was a major means of manipulation or brainwashing. It assumes that men were the sole authors of that complex revolution, dismissing the existence and even the possibility of socialist feminist visions and practices aiming to empower the oppressed. A profound lack of interest in investigating women's participation in historical change, which is a typical characteristic of masculinist thinking, is ironically embedded in these condemnations of an all-mighty patriarchal power. Even studies on feminist activities in the PRC do not depart from the conceptual framework of a seamless patriarchal party-state. Chinese women in the socialist period thus appear only as victims, puppets, or tools of a manipulative dictatorship in the global production of a hegemonic anti-socialist discourse—in short, an objectified "other."[69]

The lack of interest in a feminist founder of Chinese socialist film by post-socialist scholars contrasts sharply with Chen Bo'er's peers and students who have made repeated efforts to keep her memory alive. Essays recalling Chen's life appeared in the early 1990s when the ninetieth anniversary of the birth of Chinese film was approaching. Several of her male colleagues who were retired officials in the film industry expressed their wishes to see a biographic film of Chen Bo'er (unaware that revolutionary heroines had long been an obsolete subject in post-socialist cultural production). Activities to commemorate Chen culminated in 1995 when a memorial conference dedicated to her was held in her hometown of Chaozhou, where gray-haired veterans of the socialist film industry unveiled a newly erected statue of Chen Bo'er with Xia Yan's inscription on the memorial tablet: "People's artist comrade Chen Bo'er is immortal."

In the early twenty-first century, when China is even further removed from its revolutionary past, significant efforts to remember Chen continue. On a snowy day in December 2011 a group of women and men in their eighties gathered at the Beijing Film Academy for a conference commemorating its founder. These were the early graduates of the Institute for Performing

Art, which Chen Bo'er established in 1950 and later developed into BFA. When I asked conference organizer Chen Wenjing why she devoted so much effort to organizing the conference and compiling a volume of memoirs by Chen's students, the frail 82-year-old woman described the strong and complex sentiments that drove her to take action, even though she herself was very ill. First, she could simply not tolerate the erasure of the founding figure of the BFA by its current male leaders, who commemorated only their male predecessors. Alongside this distinctive feminist statement, Chen Wenjing articulated an "outdated" socialist sentiment with a sense of legitimacy and passion. "Chen Bo'er told us, first be a revolutionary and then be an artist. China today needs the spirit of Chen Bo'er. We now lack the concept of being a revolutionary!"[70] At a time when the Communist Revolution has been totally derailed and demonized in an age of global capitalism, those who had experienced it felt an urgent need to present their own testimony. In this context, a feminist revolutionary devoted to eliminating inequality and pursuing social justice, Chen Bo'er symbolizes the revolution with which her students identified. Chen's early death kept her revolutionary identity intact, for she bore no responsibility for the subsequent metamorphosis of the Party from a leader of resistance movements to an entrenched bureaucratic ruling class leading China into a form of state capitalism. Remembering the revolutionary spirit of Chen Bo'er is tantamount to a tacit declaration of the necessity of a socialist feminist revolution that would embody her radical vision of overturning all unequal power relations and social hierarchies.

Significantly, a year after the conference, Chen Wenjing's persistence in pressuring the BFA leaders to commemorate Chen Bo'er's pioneering role in both film industry and film education triumphed. On December 22, 2012, the all-male BFA leaders unveiled four bronze busts on campus to commemorate the BFA's founding figures. Chen Bo'er was listed as the first, followed by the other three male leaders.[71] Chen Wenjing succeeded in her resistance to the erasure of Chen Bo'er from the BFA history. But now, ironically, *her* tremendous efforts behind the scenes are erased in the Academy's official visual and literal representations that only credit the current male leaders of the BFA for remembering its founding members. The erasure of women's key roles in engendering important changes is a routine practice in a male-dominated society.

SIX

Fashioning Socialist Visual Culture

XIA YAN AND THE NEW CULTURE HERITAGE

CHEN BO'ER'S PIONEERING WORK FEATURING revolutionary heroines provided the model to lead the film industry out of the abyss from which it had plummeted following Chairman Mao's criticism of *The Life of Wu Xun*. Although no artists or officials were punished, the association of a film on a historical figure with reactionary ideas deterred filmmakers from moving ahead on projects they feared could bring official censure on them. Film production declined precipitously from fifty-six films in 1950 to one short film in 1951 and four feature films in 1952. Concerns for political safety overrode desires for artistic creativity for many in the film industry who were unsure of how to function in the new political environment.

The story of the industry's recovery takes us beyond film criticism to questions of political culture. How did the feminist paradigm Chen had created become the hallmark of socialist visual culture in the years that followed her death? How did her legacy live on to inspire the filmmakers who reanimated their industry? Which historical actors contributed to fashioning a socialist visual culture with feminist implications? Archival research and interviews allow me to examine such questions and probe the social relations and political dynamics behind the silver screens in the process of film production that are lost to today's film critics who base their analyses mainly on the final products.[1] Examining filmmakers' pursuit of a revolutionary cultural agenda illuminates significant contradictions, dilemmas, and tensions within socialist cultural production, which, I argue, paved the way for the onset of the Cultural Revolution.[2]

My investigation of filmmaking in the PRC after 1951 centers around a key figure in the film industry, Xia Yan (1900–1995), whose life serves as a linchpin connecting multiple facets of this historical narrative. The choice to focus on Xia Yan disrupts the simplistic but tenacious dichotomy that pervades much of the scholarship on socialist films in which the Party signifies a totalitarian entity and artists represent the will for freedom, for Xia Yan represents both sides of the false dichotomy.[3] A major Communist artist of the twentieth century, a feminist immersed in the literature of May Fourth New Culture and European socialist feminism, a leader of the left-wing cinema of the 1930s, and a leading cultural authority in the PRC's film industry until 1964, Xia Yan had a long and prolific career that in many ways embodies the cultural history of the CCP. This chapter begins with a brief biography, which also traces the heritage of the New Culture and May Fourth feminism in the PRC and then explores the dynamics of Communist artists' pursuit of a revolutionary agenda in creating socialist visual culture.

THE RISE OF A COMMUNIST CULTURAL AUTHORITY

Xia Yan appears in every major English-language study of Chinese films in both the Republican and socialist eras, and films made from his screenplays are featured in the analyses they offer. In film histories in Chinese as well as in English, Xia Yan is given credit for his pioneering realism in the 1930s with his two early screenplays, *Wild Torrents* (1933) and *Spring Silkworms* (1933).[4] Drawing only on published material without utilizing official archives, however, English-language studies generally neglect Xia Yan's central role in the socialist film industry.[5] But government archives record Xia Yan's prominent leadership in building a socialist film industry as well as his entanglement in political struggles culminating in the Cultural Revolution. Filmmakers' memoirs and historical source materials published in the past two decades have also shed much more light on Xia Yan's significant role in socialist filmmaking.[6]

Xia Yan[7] was born into a déclassé family of scholar-officials in Hangzhou as Shen Naixi and brought up by his widowed mother along with five surviving siblings.[8] His life situation had much in common with that of others in his cohort of cultural radicals. The rapid dissipation of an elite family's wealth was a common story in the lower Yangzi area in the aftermath of the Taiping Rebellion. The premature death of a male head of a household would further accelerate the impoverishment of a declining family, leaving the widow to struggle on her own to continue the tradition and aspirations of a scholarly family with little means at her disposal. A widow's heroic efforts and the hardship and pain she endured would leave indelible marks on her son's psyche.[9] In his old age, Xia Yan recalled his mother with deep affection, acknowledging her important role in molding his character and taste.

At fourteen, after graduating from upper primary school, Xia Yan left school because of poverty. His mother was reduced to pawning her holiday clothes and a silk quilt that had been put aside for special occasions.[10] Fully aware of his mother's predicament, the young boy decided to look for a job. Understanding that this decision would not please his mother, he searched for a job behind her back. When he finally found an apprenticeship in a dye-works, he carefully explained its temporary nature and benefits to his mother. The full weight of his decision was revealed in his description of his mother's response.

> Listening, mother remained silent. After a very long while, she slowly opened the trunk, picking out a few clothes for me to take. Her face was full of sadness and misery. I could not think of a word to comfort her. After I went to bed, I heard her talking to herself, ". . . the end. No other way. Generations of book fragrance [a scholarly family heritage] end in my generation. Both brothers have become apprentices."[11]

The younger son's turn to manual labor did not, in fact, end the Shen family's prestigious scholarly heritage, but it did mark a turning point in Xia Yan's life. Xia Yan's hardship as an apprentice at the dye-works only lasted for six months, but the experience had an enduring impact. As he emphasized in his memoir, "The dye-house workers' lives and work, especially the honey-comb-like calluses in their palms, have forever been inscribed in my heart."[12] The downward mobility of elite families demoted their sons to the world of manual laborers, a social group whose miseries they would otherwise have had no chance to experience. These experiences in the young men's formative years generated empathy with laboring people, which laid the groundwork for their later adherence to a socialist vision and Marxist theory.

Xia Yan's memoirs and those of many other male writers of his cohort highlight their widowed mothers' crucial role in the survival of their families after catastrophes.[13] It has been a tenet of folk wisdom in China that sons of widowed mothers tend to show the greatest filial loyalty. But Xia Yan's story also suggests that the desperate aspiration of a mother to maintain a scholarly family heritage in a crumbling world could imbue her son with complex desires and emotions. Even when the dream of scholar-officialdom was shattered by institutional changes, many a son remained ambitious and appreciative of his mother's sacrifices and strong character in trying times. Here

I suggest a psychological linkage between a mother's role in a déclassé elite family and the emergence of a cohort of educated men who showed a remarkable sensitivity to the plight of women in the early twentieth century.[14] Throughout Xia Yan's career, he portrayed diverse women, from indentured workers and prostitutes to revolutionary heroines, with deep sympathy and admiration.

When the Deqing County government started a fellowship for selected students to be educated in modern technology, Xia Yan, the top graduate from his upper primary school, was funded to attend the No. 1 School of Industry in Zhejiang Province. During his five-year course of study there he continued to excel academically while becoming known as an activist in the political events leading to the May Fourth Movement in 1919. He was one of the founders of the student journal *Zhejiang Xinchao* [The New Tide in Zhejiang], and one of his articles was praised by the leading New Culturalist, Chen Duxiu, in *New Youth*.[15] These years witnessed Xia Yan's decisive transformation from a boy who was discontent with the status quo to a young man who was convinced of the necessity of transforming Chinese society through political action. After graduation, he was selected by his school to study in Japan with public funding even though the school authorities disapproved of his activism.

In Japan from the fall of 1920 to May 1927, Xia Yan majored in electrical engineering. But his interests shifted decisively to literature, the social sciences, and politics; and as with many overseas Chinese students studying in Japan in the early twentieth century, he was further radicalized by reading newly translated socialist literature. The idea of saving China by promoting industry rapidly lost its appeal after his encounter with Marxism. In 1924 he joined the Nationalist Party (NP) after meeting with Sun Yat-sen, who was on his way to Beiping (Beijing). But after the breakup of the First United Front between the CCP and the NP, Xia Yan returned to China and joined the CCP's underground cell in Shanghai in 1927 in a moment when the NP's crackdown on Communists caused many to quit their CCP memberships.

While participating in CCP underground activities, Xia Yan became known publicly as a translator. He had become proficient in English and German as well as Japanese while in Japan, where he had translated some socialist literature to submit to Chinese journals. Unemployed upon his return to Shanghai, he took a friend's advice to do translations to make a living. He translated books for Kaiming Bookstore, which was founded by the well-known feminist advocate, Zhang Xichen, who had been the editor-in-chief of the *Ladies Journal* in the May Fourth era and was now the publisher and editor of *New Women* magazine and several other popular magazines that continued the May Fourth New Culture agenda.[16] In 1927 Zhang asked Xia Yan to translate August Bebel's *Women and Socialism,* even though the Nationalist government was already imposing severe censorship on socialist literature and persecuting Communists.[17] With no access to the original German edition, Xia Yan spent six months translating from two Japanese versions that were based on German and English versions respectively.[18] Before the Nationalists' official ban on left-oriented books and authors in 1934, *Women and Socialism* had already gone through several printings. Xia Yan's translation became the best-known and foundational text for the development of Chinese socialist feminism.

Given that socialist feminist texts had been circulating in China since the beginning of the twentieth century, Bebel's thesis would not be entirely unfamiliar to Xia Yan, who had been exposed to such texts in the May Fourth period and later in Japan. But as Zhang Xichen emphasized, this translation presented the first comprehensive explanation of the relationship between a socialist revolution and women's liberation to Chinese readers. Although Bebel centered on the European and U.S. past in developing his critiques of antagonistic and unequal relations between classes and sexes in capitalism, we can imagine Xia Yan being drawn especially to Bebel's optimistic vision of the future, with its promise of a victorious socialism and Bebel's insistence that socialism's victory was inseparable from the liberation of women. As Bebel asserted, "The Socialist Party is the only one that has made the full equality of women, their liberation from every form of dependence and oppression, an integral part of its program, not for reasons of propaganda, but from necessity. *For there can be no liberation of mankind without social independence and equality of the sexes*" (italics in original).[19]

In the following decade Xia Yan seemed to devote himself to answering Bebel's call: "It is the duty of the men to help [women] cast aside all prejudices and to take part in the great struggle."[20] Taking it as his mission to disseminate socialist feminist ideas, he frequently contributed to women's magazines,[21] offered *Women and Socialism* to educated women working in the media,[22] and translated texts with a focus on women's issues. His biographers observed the importance of *Women and Socialism* in Xia Yan's life: "It was through the translation of this book that Xia Yan established a women-centered perspective in examining social issues. . . . Women's thorough liberation and equality between men and women are the ultimate goals of cultural development that no power in the world can stop, which was one of his basic value standards in judging social issues."[23] Exposing the oppression and exploitation of working-class women in colonialism and enabling the voiceless to speak became identifiable themes in his literary creativity and filmmaking in the 1930s. His widely read report, *Indentured Women Workers,* written in 1936 after months of fieldwork among textile workers in Japanese-owned factories, clearly articulated the underground CCP member's socialist feminist analysis of the existence of an enslaved class in colonial Shanghai. The suffering of those most downtrodden women, in Xia Yan's analysis, resulted from the institutionalized interlocking oppressions of capitalism, colonialism, and patriarchy.[24]

Xia Yan's first play, *Sai Jinhua*, written in 1935, which brought instant public attention to the emergence of a new playwright upon its publication in 1936, expressed a strong New Cultural heritage against dominant sexual norms as well as his defiance of the powerful. The controversial satirical drama portrayed a courtesan, Sai Jinhua, in a positive light for the first time and in contrast to cowardly men in power. Sai Jinhua was a famous figure in the late Qing dynasty for her alleged efforts to stop the occupying German soldiers' violence against Beijing residents in the aftermath of the Boxer Rebellion in 1900 by utilizing her relationship with the commander of the German troops, Alfred von Waldersee. The play insinuated Chiang Kai-shek regime's nonresistance confronting Japan's aggression as mirrored in Qing officials' obsequious submission to imperialist occupiers, which was clearly understood by the audiences on the left and right. But the controversies were not limited to the major political critical thrust. Many critics focused on the play's glorification of a courtesan who had allegedly slept with a German commander. Xia Yan refuted such views openly in his invited contribution to *Women's Monthly*:

> I do not want to hide my sympathy for the female protagonist. I sympathize with her because among various kinds of slaves of that time, comparing her with those who could speak in the royal court, she more or less retained some humanity! . . . It cannot but be a laughable act to persistently demand a prostitute to preserve national dignity but not to condemn those with knowledge and state power in her time and in the same event.[25]

Directing a political criticism against the ruling class, Xia Yan also revealed his subversive agenda to rewrite an "infamous" woman, a daring feminist stance in cultural production welcomed by his cohort of May Fourth

New Culture artists who eagerly staged the play. But the Nationalist government banned the play shortly after it gained tremendous popularity. The ramifications of *Sai Jinhua*, however, went beyond what Xia Yan could have imagined, which will be discussed in the next chapter.

Restricted by censorship, Xia Yan was unable to fully elaborate his socialist ideas of women's emancipation in *Indentured Women Workers* and other essays and plays, or the many films that he participated in making during the 1930s. Still, his conscious advocacy of socialist feminism remained consistent in his works, either implicitly or explicitly, depending on the degree of censorship in different times and at different publishing sites. In a preface to a reprint of his script *Qiu Jin* in 1944, his second play that represented the famous early twentieth-century feminist revolutionary martyr,[26] Xia Yan enunciated his socialist feminist position while deploring that many May Fourth "new women" had become

> madames and *taitai* (wives) of officials, content with raising a virtuous son and having a prestigious husband. Some have even become Buddhist believers devoted to copying scriptures and chanting the name of Buddha. When feminism and sexual equality are used by a few as stepping-stones, "the women's movement" is suffocated. But the real women's movement and the real new women have emerged among the people who do not debate terminology such as equality. Here there is no hero, and there are no glorious speeches and theories. They (她们) just want and they just do. They treat themselves as human beings. . . . a member of the new China, a human being of indomitable spirit.[27]

"The real new women" in Xia Yan's definition were those Communist women who devoted themselves to action rather than empty talk. "Doing" revolution was *the* way to women's emancipation. Xia Yan's criticism of the elite new women also expressed a socialist conviction of the importance of the common people. In the same piece on Qiu Jin, he emphasized: "We cherish the outstanding people and heroes who emerged from our nation. They are the glories and treasures of our nation. But we also think that if the entire nation's culture can be raised just one inch higher, that would be more valuable than the glory of one or two people."[28]

In an essay commemorating International Women's Day in 1948 entitled "Strength, Your Name Is Women," Xia Yan criticized Shakespeare's verse in *Hamlet,* "Frailty, thy name is woman!" He presented a brief review of women's heroic actions in revolutions, anti-fascist movements, and workers' movements around the world, arguing that the essence of women's movements was the essence of revolution. "Fighting women forever stand on the side of the oppressed, justice, and revolution. Therefore, what is heartily supported by women will surely triumph, and what is heartily opposed by women will surely lose." The reason for women's inherently progressive orientation, Xia Yan emphasized, is that in feudal and capitalist societies women are a "doubly oppressed class."[29] As a May Fourth intellectual who embraced Marxism, Xia Yan consistently highlighted gender oppression embedded in Chinese patriarchal cultural norms and social institutions, and its interweaving with class oppression in the global context of capitalism and colonialism.

Although he published a large quantity of translated texts and his own essays, Xia Yan did not join any literary societies in Shanghai until the Party Central Committee decided to transfer him from the workers' movement group to the cultural branch to prepare for the establishment of the Left-Wing Writers Association in 1929. Because of his formal training in electrical engineering, up to that point he did not see himself as a writer. The new task he received from the Party propelled his emergence as a major literary artist in twentieth-century China.

Japan's escalation of its aggression in China in the early 1930s intensified the sense of national crisis. In a rapidly changing political climate, Xia Yan and two other members of the Left-Wing Writers Association, Qian Xingcun and Zheng Boqi, seized an opportunity to infiltrate the film industry.[30] The three, with the permission of the Cultural Committee of the CCP, served as script advisors to the Mingxing film studio and convinced the company to make "progressive films," meaning left-oriented films, to appeal to an interested public. In 1933 Xia Yan became the leader of the newly established Film Group led by the Cultural Committee, infiltrating film studios as well as Shanghai's print media to circulate leftist film criticism and film theories translated from Russian. Regarding the Party's choice of Xia Yan for this important role, film scholar Laikwan Pang comments:

[M]ost would agree that the major reason for the Party to assign the young Xia Yan to such a crucial position was that he was on good terms with almost everybody, a very rare figure in the Chinese cultural world at a time when factionalism was rampant. After taking up the responsibilities of the Film Group, Xia Yan resigned from the Writer's League and concentrated his energy on cinema. His amiable and tolerant personality helped him to make many noteworthy friendships in the film industry; this encouraged the expansion and diversification of a film movement which otherwise might have been much narrower and less influential.[31]

For Communists, the decade between the breakup of the First United Front and the beginning of the Second United Front, from 1927 to 1937, was a period of "white terror," a term that originated in the French Revolution. The Nationalist government severely censored left-wing publications and destroyed many underground Communist cells. In 1931 twenty-three Communists, five of whom were left-wing writers, were arrested and executed. Xia Yan went into hiding several times between 1933 and 1935, and each time he produced a major new work.[32] Using many pseudonyms, Xia Yan and his Communist colleagues were able to work for private film companies that were eager to cater to the audience's new mood.

As film scholar Yingjin Zhang observes in his study of cinema in the Republican period, "The leftist scriptwriters managed to tap the anxieties of the Chinese audience not by injecting any blatant political ideology (due to censorship) but by bringing a new narrative mode at the story level. . . . [F]ilm stories begin to incorporate and to foreground the experiences of the small men and women of rural origin or characters who are increasingly victimized in the urban environment."[33] Film scholar Zhang Zhen traces "the transformation of a thoroughly commercialized film industry into an increasingly politicized enterprise" in the early 1930s. Her examination of "the rise of a socially engaged and patriotic cinema and its interaction with urban modernity and a mass culture of consumption and entertainment" delineates the complexity of the cinema world in which left-wing writers conducted their covert activities.[34]

In 1934 underground Communists were able to set up a film company in Shanghai that gathered many Communist or progressive artists, including famous actors, directors, composers, and scriptwriters.[35] Many artists, such as Chen Bo'er and Yuan Muzhi, rose to fame by participating in progressive film production. Films produced by progressive filmmakers (who were not necessarily CCP members) became increasingly influential, gaining popularity with many theme songs, one of which later became the national anthem of the PRC. At the same time, the audience expanded from a limited elite to a more popular audience. Social criticism became an accepted function of cinema, and realism held the key to the popularity of patriotic films. The Marxist concept of class and a left-wing critique of social inequality were introduced to the Chinese public, often through visual representations of economically and / or sexually exploited women. The first film that openly presented the entanglement of class and gender issues was *The Cries of Women* (*Nüxing de nahan*)(1933), written and directed by Shen Xiling, the younger brother of Shen Zijiu who founded the feminist journal *Women's Lives* in 1935 to which her remote relative Xia Yan was a frequent contributor. The film was based on Xia Yan's notes from his research on indentured textile workers in Shanghai.[36] Other famous left films on women include *Three Modern Girls (Sange modeng nüxing)* (1933), *The Goddess (Shennü)* (1934), and *New Women (Xin nüxing)* (1935).

Communists and progressive filmmakers during the 1930s took filmmaking as a serious social praxis that had transformative effects. Despite political persecution by the Nationalist government, the underground Communists were able to create a left cultural realm prominently marked by their influential films and film criticism. Perhaps more important for the future of CCP's cultural production, Xia Yan and his film group formed a large circle of artist friends in and outside the CCP in the 1930s. Because of their background as writers and critics informed by the New Culture's emphasis on the importance of revolutionizing the forms and contents of literature, scripts assumed an important position in filmmaking and scriptwriters enjoyed high prestige. Xia Yan became famous in artistic circles for his screenplays, plays, and a wide range of essays published under one of his numerous pen names. His real name, Shen Naixi, was rarely used.

After Shanghai fell to the Japanese army in November 1937, Xia Yan left for Guangzhou to continue his work for a resistance newspaper, following a direct order from Zhou Enlai. In the following decade Zhou Enlai formally assigned him to run newspapers promoting resistance discourse while utilizing his social networks to gain financial and political support for the CCP. Party members like Xia Yan, who supported himself and his family with his royalties, had formal professions to cover their CCP identity. Living outside the heartland of the film industry, Xia Yan relied on payments for his plays and newspaper essays. In the early 1940s when a larger number of artists gathered in Chongqing, the wartime capital, several dramas written or adapted by Xia Yan were staged there, consolidating his prestige as a prominent literary figure among the Chinese elite regardless of their political orientation.

With the Communist liberation of Shanghai in May 1949, Xia Yan was assigned to be in charge of literature and art in the Shanghai municipal government and the East China region. From 1949 to 1954 he led the transformation of Shanghai cinema from a private to a state-owned industry and from a market dominated by Hollywood to one dominated by socialist films, whether Chinese or international.[37] In 1955 he took the position of deputy minister of culture in charge of cinema in China, which he held until 1964. Even while working as a high-ranking official in Shanghai and in the central government, he kept producing his own scripts and revising others' scripts without his name appearing in the credits, just as Chen Bo'er had.[38] His knowledge of various film theories acquired from his decade-long work in translation and his expertise in scenarios as a renowned scriptwriter since the heyday of leftist films in the 1930s, in addition to his official position, made him the number-one cultural authority in the film industry. With his reputation as a "doctor of scripts," Xia Yan's editorial advice was eagerly sought. Filmmakers privately referred to him fondly and jokingly as "The Old Man" (*lao touzi*), a Chinese colloquial term for the head of an underground gang, conveying the intimate relationship between Xia Yan and artists who revered his cultural authority.[39]

This illustrious Communist was just one of a large group of artists of the May Fourth cohort or younger who joined the CCP in the 1920s or 1930s and became power holders in the PRC. For this group, 1949 meant a radical political and spatial shift that moved them from the underground or marginal rural base areas to the center of power. Culturally, however, they continued to espouse their previous May Fourth New Culture and left-wing literary frameworks, practices, and artistic tastes. This orientation proved a source of tension, for the great majority of Party members shared neither their cultural background nor their artistic sensibilities. More than two decades of warfare against warlords, the Japanese, and nationalists had turned the CCP into a predominantly military camp with peasants as its rank and file. When the founding of the PRC brought the rural-based military mainstay and the urban-based underground cultural workers together, the two groups hardly shared a common language.

In his memoir, Xia Yan vividly described a moment of mutual incomprehension in this encounter. After the Communist military took over Shanghai, Xia Yan was required to fill out a form with the help of an official from the Party's personnel department.

> After I filled in the blanks for name, birthplace, sex, and dates when I joined the Party and army, I stopped at the blank for "rank." I had been a Party member for over twenty years but I had never known my rank. The personnel cadre felt that was very strange and asked me to think again. I had to say, "I really don't know." He asked, "Well, then, how many *jin* of millet do you receive each month?" I replied, "I have never eaten any millet, nor have I ever received any." He was even more perplexed. "Then, who provides for

your living, such as meals and house . . . ?" I said I had lived on payments for my writings and royalties. Except for an airplane ticket the organization gave me when I was required to withdraw from Guilin to Hong Kong, and some traveling money when Zhou Enlai asked me to go to Singapore in 1946, I had always relied on myself, on selling my writings. . . . Absolutely incredulous, he took my form and left.[40]

The anecdote reveals a huge cultural gap as well as institutional difference between the rural military camp and the urban underground cells. The military established a hierarchy that was visibly measured by unequal material distribution among comrades, while the cells were mainly based on the self-reliance of individual underground members who were mostly professionals and artists and did not assume a hierarchical order. The interaction between an official from the military camp who was entirely unaware that millet was not the staple for people in the south of the Yangtze River and, indeed, that "eating millet" connoted "being rural" to Shanghai urbanites, and a sophisticated cosmopolitan intellectual who remained clueless about his own Party's hierarchical formation was chillingly comical. After submitting the form, Xia Yan was given a rank of "corps" (*bingtuan ji*), a military title that he neither understood nor wished to identify himself with. The accumulation of numerous instances of incongruity was unsettling. In his memoir, he recounted many experiences that contributed to his sense of alienation at that time: "Entering a new society, I felt I was encountering more perplexing things than ever."[41] An unprecedented socialist revolution led by a Party filled with internal differences and deep contradictions tested this senior Communist artist-official whom, like his Party, was to go through a thrilling ordeal of identity change.

THE MISSION OF SOCIALIST VISUAL REPRESENTATION

The first rectification campaign in the cultural realm following Mao's criticism of *The Life of Wu Xun* in 1951 set the parameters for cultural production in socialist China and generated persistent tensions among cultural producers in and outside the Party. Xia Yan became entangled in this political storm involuntarily during his early tenure as the top official in charge of Shanghai's cultural realm. In late 1949 when his old friend, the director Sun Yu, lobbied him for government funding to complete *The Life of Wu Xun,* Xia Yan expressed his concern about producing such a film on a questionable historical figure in the new era. Sun Yu pleaded that the film should be finished, given the financial crisis of his company and the unemployment of many film workers. In the end, following Xia Yan's suggestion, Sun Yu obtained both funding and approval from the Committee on Culture and Education of the Central Government. The finished film received high acclaim from CCP top officials and the general public.

Mao's vehement condemnation of the film was a bolt out the blue for everyone except Jiang Qing, his wife, who claimed to be the first to notice the political problem of the film and brought it to Mao's attention.[42] Mao's unexpected reaction, however, had its own logic and consistency. The film proved to Mao the heightened relevance of his talks in Yan'an in 1942 on the cultural field in the new China. To Mao, nine years after his major talks and rectification campaign in Yan'an, the fact that a film paying tribute to a dubious historical figure who sought to maintain feudal culture was well received by Communist artists and officials revealed "ideological confusion" and demonstrated the necessity of continuously reforming bourgeois tendencies in the Party.[43]

The criticism of *The Life of Wu Xun* in 1951 could be seen as Mao's first post-Revolution campaign in the proletarian cultural revolution he had theorized in Yan'an. Given that the CCP had just taken over state power and was at war with the United States in Korea, his attention to a film revealed the importance he gave to questions of cultural representation, as well as his perception of the gap between the ideal of a proletarian culture and a Party whose cultural front was dominated by the educated elite largely shaped in a semicolonial urban culture. Mao's critique was conceptualized in dichotomous terms, as struggles between old and new, bourgeoisie and proletariat, and oppressors and oppressed, leaving no room to accommodate the complexity of diverse cultural heritages, social issues, artistic sensibilities, and actual practices in the film industry where functional filmmakers were mostly pro-Communist and left-oriented. His either / or conceptualization was intended to keep his Party vigilant against an ill-defined enemy, presumably "the bourgeoisie," but it also contradicted the Propaganda Department of the CCP that in 1948 had instructed officials not to be too strict in their censorship in the early stage of developing socialist film: "As long as they are not anti-Soviet, anti-Communist, or anti-people's democracy, they should pass."[44] Although Mao's conceptualization of cultural production drastically narrowed the scope of visual representation, his views went unchallenged by his comrades. But to mitigate any damage Mao's harsh condemnation of the film might cause to the relationship between the Party and artists outside the CCP, Zhou Enlai and Chen Yi, the mayor of Shanghai, made great efforts behind the scenes to ease filmmakers' apprehensiveness. The charismatic premier's way of buffering the tensions generated by Mao's interventions, which became a pattern through the following fifteen years, played a crucial role in maintaining non-CCP artists' allegiance to the Party.[45]

The six-month-long rectification campaign in the cultural field following Mao's criticisim has been largely omitted from political histories of the PRC, perhaps because Mao's attack on the film was not obviously motivated by the kinds of power struggles that historians like to address; nor did it lead to any shuffling of Party officials. But for this historian, the very absence of a power struggle makes Mao's consistency in pursuing his agenda of a cultural revolution centering on cultural representation all the more salient. By overlooking this event, historians of the PRC have generally missed a key link between Mao's Yan'an Talks and the Cultural Revolution and thereby lost sight of Mao's *cultural* agenda in their interpretations of the Cultural Revolution.

The rectification campaign effectively established Mao's Yan'an Talks as the guidelines for cultural production in socialist China, a huge extension of their impacts beyond the original target group of artists in the CCP. From this point on, filmmaking was tied closely to the Party's agenda. All the Communist officials involved, from Zhou Enlai to Xia Yan, undertook self-criticism for failing to identify the "reactionary nature" of *The Life of Wu Xun*, and everyone in the cultural field pledged their allegiance to Mao's line on literature and art. Through a process of study, discussion, self-criticism, and soul-searching review of their lives and works, artists and officials, whether Party members or not, memorized—but did not necessarily internalize—the major tenets of Mao's Yan'an Talks: art should follow politics; art is a weapon in the proletarian revolution; representing workers / peasants / soldiers is the top priority of revolutionary art; and bourgeois and petty-bourgeois intellectuals have to remold their subjective world in order to transform the external world and serve the masses. The demand that intellectuals engage in the transformation of their subjectivity was linked with the imperative of extolling workers / peasants / soldiers in socialist revolution.

To guarantee that new films would follow Mao's line of socialist cultural production, in 1953 the Film Bureau of the Ministry of Culture drafted a list of suggested subject matter for films to be made in the next several years. The categories included: (1) Communist revolutionary struggles; (2) the development of industry and workers' lives; (3) the development of agriculture and rural villages and peasants' lives; (4) the Korean war and defending peace; (5) the People's Liberation Army's role in protecting and constructing the country; (6) ethnic minority people's lives; (7) other subjects including public security personnel, scientists, teachers, medical workers, students, children, and fishermen; (8) historical figures, especially peasant rebels, patriotic heroes and heroines, and artists and scientists; and (9) adaptations of literary classics and Chinese mythologies. Each category contained more detailed suggestions for topics. While women were assumed to be included in all these categories, rural women were highlighted under the rubric on rural life:

> Reflecting how rural women strive for equal rights with men in all aspects of political, economic, cultural, educational, and social life; representing how they broke the confinement of feudal thought, raised consciousness, established a firm commitment to serve the people, obtained the support of the masses, got elected as heads of townships, districts, or government committee members, and how they fought against social discrimination and all kinds of difficulties in work and accomplished outstanding results in their work in the state; representing how they overcame obstacles of family, society and their own thinking and actively participated in patriotic production, mutual aid, and collective movement, demonstrating women are an indispensable potential force in agricultural production.[46]

The passage could be mistaken for *Women of China*'s guideline. In fact, the Women's Federation, like other branches of the state, was required to propose subject matter for films. The top officials' speeches at Chen Bo'er's memorial service reveal these senior state feminists' conscious efforts to put women at the center of cultural production. The topics on rural women not only reflect their following the state's directives to mobilize rural women to participate in agricultural production but also convey their genuine excitement over the dramatic transformation of Chinese society that was manifested most powerfully by changes in rural women's lives. The inclusion of rural women breaking away from the control of patriarchal kinship and taking up independent social roles in socialist filmmaking reflects the heritage of "anti-feudalism," the hallmark of the New Culture Movement, since rural women had been seen as the most oppressed in feudalism. The emphasis on rural women's agency and their struggle for equal rights also indicates the agenda of state feminists who in the early 1950s were promoting the Marriage Law as a crucial move toward their visions of women's liberation. In 1956, the film *Liu Qiaoer*, based on a true story of a rural woman fighting for her right to choose her husband, with the WF officials' heavy involvement in its production and promotion, became an instant hit, facilitating the promulgation of the Marriage Law in rural areas. Chen Bo'er would have been pleased to see that her feminist friends continued her vision and practices in socialist filmmaking.[47]

MAKING FILMS FOR
WORKERS / PEASANTS / SOLDIERS

After Chen Bo'er's death, Yuan Muzhi took a long sick leave and never returned to his leading post in China's film industry. In 1954 Xia Yan was appointed deputy minister of culture in charge of the film industry and foreign affairs in the cultural field.[48] The revival of film production in the following years witnessed Xia Yan's efforts to meet complex demands from diverse parties and interests in and outside the Party. He and his large network of artists, either CCP members or non-Party members with May Fourth New Culture heritage and from left-wing filmmaking traditions who constituted the core of the film industry, agreed with Mao's instruction that art should be an effective weapon in the revolutionary struggle to create a new socialist culture. They still found that the suggested topics left plenty of room for exploration and self-expression, as well as occasion for disagreement, sometimes intense, over what constituted proletarian literature and art and what contents and forms best served the interests of the masses and the Party.

Central to the debates over what constituted a socialist film were issues of subject matter and the relationship between a film's artistic quality and its political function. Should socialist films *only* represent workers / peasants / soldiers, or could other social groups be portrayed? Should films only depict important themes and events in the Communist Revolution and socialist construction, or could lighter subjects in daily life be represented? Should socialist films concentrate on portraying the heroic deeds of workers / peasants / soldiers as a means to construct socialist subjectivity, or could films also cover historical subjects? Should films serve politics by representing particular state policies or by broadly reflecting the goals and ideology of socialism? Should socialist films pursue a combination of revolutionary realism and revolutionary romanticism, or could critical realism be adopted in depicting socialist scenes? How could socialist films be both educational and entertaining? These and many more concrete issues were sources of incessant disputes, sometimes explicitly and sometimes implicitly, depending on the political climate at a particular moment.

Underlying filmmakers' contentious debates was a volatile mix of ideas and emotions: excitement about the mission of creating a new culture; perplexity about how to approach new subject matter and new forms of representation; anxiety and reservations about political demands to create stories and images they were personally unfamiliar with and did not find interesting; and conscious or unconscious resistance to the increasingly narrow definition of proletarian art and socialist films proposed by Mao and the group of radicals around him.[49] Artists with diverse political orientations, tastes, and talents were expected to respond to a political environment that was constantly changing. Besides all these shifting and unstable dynamics, the socialist state created institutionally based contradictions. All the artists were on the government payroll regardless of whether they were able to deliver the goods the new state paid for.[50] State policy required intellectuals and artists to identify with workers / peasants / soldiers to create a proletarian new culture, while maintaining the filmmakers' privileged material life by paying them ten to twenty times more than the masses. The payment of 5,800 yuan in 1964 for a single film script written by Yang Hansheng, a famous writer and high-ranking official, was equivalent to fifteen years' wages of an average worker.[51] While attempting to proletarianize the subjectivities of creative artists and requiring them to use their talents and expertise to create an egalitarian new culture, the socialist state at the same time was actually consolidating their elite socioeconomic class standing. There were numerous ironies along these lines during the early socialist period.

Xia Yan's experience after 1949 epitomized tensions and contradictions in artists' conscious efforts to create socialist films. On the central issue of serving workers / peasants / soldiers, Xia Yan chose to follow Mao's Yan'an Talks, which listed the urban petty bourgeoisie and intellectuals as the fourth category included in the "masses" to be served in cultural production.[52] In spite of Mao's criticism of *The Life of Wu Xun* in which he suggested that only representations of workers / peasants / soldiers could qualify as proletarian art, Xia Yan on many occasions emphasized that writers could write best only about familiar subjects, implying his reservations about the restriction on subject matter. And despite his journalistic exposé of the enslavement of women workers in Shanghai in 1936, Xia Yan never again produced any work on the working class in socialist China. For an artist who had pioneered social realism in filmmaking and deftly used film and drama as weapons of social critique against the socioeconomic systems under the Nationalist regime and colonial dominance, Xia Yan apparently could neither refocus his critical lens on Communist rule nor shift from realism to romanticizing workers / peasants / soldiers. In his old age Xia Yan revealed that he had disagreed with the combination of revolutionary realism and revolutionary romanticism that came to be the dominant formula in the late 1950s: "There is not a bit of romanticism in my writings and my very being."[33]

XIANGLIN'S WIFE: TRANSMITTING A NEW CULTURE AGENDA

Keenly aware of the constraints of a new political environment, Xia Yan nevertheless explored his own modes of artistic creativity. In his productions his interest in an anti-feudalist agenda was manifested in his deft adaptations of New Culture literary classics. His most renowned screen adaptation, *The New Year's Sacrifice,* may best illustrate his sense of mission with respect to the feminist cultural transformation of a "feudalist" society.

The emergence of Xianglin's Wife as a quintessential symbol of victims of feudal oppression in the dominant gender discourse of the socialist period has a complicated history. Xianglin's Wife is the protagonist in a short story, "New Year's Sacrifice," written by the prominent May Fourth New Culture writer Lu Xun (1886–1936) in 1924. A widow who ran away from her mother-in-law's scheme to sell her into a second marriage, Xianglin's Wife worked as a servant for a wealthy family before she was kidnapped by men sent by her mother-in-law. After resisting capture through a futile suicide attempt, Xianglin's Wife accepted the second marriage, even though it stigmatized her as an unchaste woman according to the gender norms of her time. After a few years of married life, new tragedy befell her: an illness killed her hardworking husband, and a wolf devoured her young son. She returned to her old master's home to resume her service, only to find that as an unchaste widow who had lost two husbands she was forbidden to serve food at the New Year's sacrifice. Even her devoted Buddhist practice could not cleanse her unclean soul. Driven to insanity, she became a homeless beggar and died in the street on a snowy New Year's Eve.

Lu Xun created the poignant fictional character as an indictment of the inhumane cultural norms and oppressive institutions that were seen as characteristic of Chinese society, a typical critique launched by a leading cultural rebel during the May Fourth New Culture era (1915–25). Victimized women and oppressive gender practices served as common literary tropes in New Culturalists' writings, becoming a hallmark of their feminist stance. Condemning gender oppression under the "old" Confucian culture was a major performative act constitutive of a "new" identity of modern intellectuals for that generation's educated elite. Xianglin's Wife, who was mired in "traditional" cultural practices and social institutions, represented cultural radicals' burning desires to create a new culture in an ancient land. With the New Culturalists' discursive power, critical feminist voices entered the mainstream from the 1920s on.

Lu Xun's short story was first turned into a performance in 1946, when underground CCP members in Shanghai worked with left-oriented artists to stage an adaptation of "New Year's Sacrifice" called *Xianglin's Wife* as a Yue opera, a form of opera that originated in Shengzhou, Zhejiang Province.[54] As a commemoration of the tenth anniversary of Lu Xun's death, the Yue opera *Xianglin's Wife* became a rallying point of left-wing artists in Shanghai when they were facing intense persecution from the ruling Nationalist Party. In the context of the political battles between the Nationalist Party and the Communist Party in the post–World War II period, the staging of the Yue opera *Xianglin's Wife* gained a new political meaning as resistance to Chiang Kai-shek's dictatorship. In 1948 the Yue opera *Xianglin's Wife* appeared on the silver screen for the first time, indicating the success of the Yue opera's adaptation of Lu Xun's famous short story.

After the PRC was founded, many adaptations of "New Year's Sacrifice" were performed by local operas, but Xia Yan was the first to adapt the short story directly for the screen. It was his first screen script after he became the deputy minister of culture.[55] The decision to produce a feature film based on Lu Xun's short story was made to commemorate the twentieth anniversary of Lu Xun's death. But there were dangers in this choice of story, requiring more than artistic creativity to negotiate the political challenges. The changed historical context demanded a reworking of the New Culture text, which could alter its meanings. As a renowned New Culturalist who knew Lu Xun and the historical and cultural context of his literary creativity well, Xia Yan strove both to be faithful to the original story and also to address the demands of the contemporary period. A prominent change in socialist cultural production was in the representation of women. Full of agency and political consciousness, revolutionary heroines in socialist films were antithetical to Xianglin's Wife, the quintessential image of the abused and powerless woman who suffered under feudal oppression. Devoting substantial state resources to the production of such a symbol of women's oppression was anomalous in the context of Maoist cultural dictums. Some justifications would be required beyond the legitimacy lent by the film's commemoration of Lu Xun's death.

As the top official of a film industry that had just emerged from the storm of *The Life of Wu Xun,* Xia Yan had more than a keen understanding of the paradigm shift in visual representation. Although Xianglin's Wife was not a supporter of feudal rulers, but rather a victim of feudal society, the theme had nothing to do with "extolling new class forces" as Mao advocated. It required political courage for the new deputy minister to take on the task of making any version of *New Year's Sacrifice* in 1955. Understanding the political context is crucial to our understanding of the changes Xia Yan made in his adaptation.

Three important changes are relevant to this discussion. First, the film presents an honest, kind, and hardworking man as Xianglin's Wife's second husband, He Laoliu. After Xianglin's Wife's suicide attempt failed at her wedding, she was touched by He Laoliu's kindness and accepted him. In the original story, Xianglin's Wife said that her second husband took her by his superior physical strength, which explains her "submission" to the marriage. Xia Yan's explanation for the alteration was that he wanted to portray some "sympathy and understanding between the poor." Her momentary enjoyment of a good marital life, in Xia Yan's view, would contrast more sharply with her subsequent tragedy. Besides, Xia Yan revealed, "I think it would be difficult to depict his 'physical power' on screen. It could easily appear vulgar; and it would impair the character of an honest and kind hunter, He Laoliu." [56] The erasure of a sexual violence committed by a poor man reveals not only Xia Yan's artistic taste but also his political astuteness. Xianglin's Wife could be presented as the victim of feudal systems, but not of the sexual violence of a proletarian man. Rather, socialist cultural representations should highlight the fundamental goodness of laboring people. Operating within the political parameters of the time, the film dimmed the sharpness of Lu Xun's depiction of the relationship between gender and class, but simultaneously advocated new ideals of marital relations.

The second major change was that Xia Yan added a dramatic act of resistance by Xianglin's Wife that was not in the original short story in order to claim for her the capacity to revolt against the oppressive institutions. In the film, after Xianglin's Wife had realized that donating her hard-earned money to the Buddhist temple did not help to wash away the stigma of marrying twice, she chopped the threshold of the temple with a cleaver in utter indignation. This addition proved particularly controversial among film critics, who argued that such an act of rebellion did not conform to the logic of the protagonist's character, suggesting Xia Yan had sacrificed realism for political expediency. One may wonder, of course, if it were rather that the critics were biased in their belief that a lowly woman like Xianglin's Wife was incapable of such a rebellious act.

Xia Yan was judicious in his response to their criticism; in an essay published in the magazine *Chinese Films* in 1957, he explained that the resistant act was not his invention. It had first appeared in the film of the Yue opera *Xianglin's Wife* in 1948 and then in many other local operas on stage as well. By claiming that the revision he included in his film pre-dated Mao's criticism of *The Life of Wu Xun,* he implicitly refuted the charge that he was merely conforming to socialist principles of cultural production. But more significantly, he emphasized that he was guided by artistic judgment, by adding that when he had watched those operas, the scene of Xianglin's Wife's rebellion never failed to move him, which was why he decided to keep this scene in his film adaptation. He cited a passage from Lu Xun's original story depicting Xianglin's Wife's ferocious physical fight against her kidnappers that ended with her banging her head into the corner of a table in a suicide attempt, which he argued showed that Xianglin's Wife's rebellious character had been depicted in the original story. He contended, "On the surface, Xianglin's Wife is obedient, timid, and believing in gods and ghosts. But these should never become the grounds for one to conclude that a timid soul would never have thoughts and commit actions of revolt" (fig. 21).[57]

Xia Yan perceived correctly that at the heart of this debate was the question of whether an oppressed woman like Xianglin's Wife was capable of any expression of agency. He obviously differed from some of the male critics in his cohort; his prolific literary production consistently demonstrated his appreciation of strong female characters. In an essay on Chinese women written in 1944, he explicitly stated that from early childhood on he had been attracted to heroines who violated gender norms in Chinese operas and literature and was impatient with passive or conformist female characters.[58] Although Xianglin's Wife's resistance to a second marriage could be easily interpreted as conforming to the gender norm of chastity, Xia Yan's decision to take it as an externally meek woman's expression of her strong character did not depart from Lu Xun's multifaceted depiction of Xianglin's Wife.

Still, Xianglin's Wife was not a revolutionary heroine, and the story certainly did not celebrate women's agency, even with the addition of the act of revolt. How then did he justify the cinematic production of *New Year's Sacrifice* in socialist China? The third major change provides the answer. Xia Yan added

FIGURE 21. *The New Year's Sacrifice*. Xianglin's Wife works as a servant (1956).

a voice-over by a male narrator at the beginning and end of the film. When the opening scene of a rural mountain area unfolds, a narrator's voice emerges: "For the youth today, the story happened long, long ago. It was more than forty years ago, around the time of the Xinhai Revolution, in a mountain village of east Zhejiang." Explaining the story's historical context and location in plain language was Xia Yan's strategy to make the film accessible to the large audience who had not read the story, especially those who were illiterate. The second time the narrator's voice is heard is when the final scene depicts Xianglin's Wife collapsing in snow: "A diligent and kind woman, Xianglin's Wife collapses and dies after having endured numerous miseries and mistreatments. This happened over forty years ago. Yes, this was an event in the past. Fortunately, those times have finally passed and will never return" (fig. 22).

The tension in his representing Xianglin's Wife as simultaneously both fictional and real reveals the complex goals of this Communist artist who wanted to create an artistic film that had high educational value for the masses. Adding an upbeat voice-over to the film's tragic ending left ample room for interpretation.[59] Taking it at face value, we may say that the narrator's comment on the visual image was meant to remind the audience that the CCP was the liberator that ended the misery of Chinese women, thus

FIGURE 22. *The New Year's Sacrifice.* Xianglin's Wife in her old age, down and out.

lending legitimacy to the Party's rule. With the wide circulation of the film *New Year's Sacrifice,* Xianglin's Wife was solidly established in public discourse as *the* symbol of women's oppression in "the old feudal society" or "before liberation," two common phrases demarcating the historical era before the CCP took state power in 1949. In this sense, we may say Xia Yan made a major contribution to the hegemonic gender discourse in the Mao era that represented Chinese women as victims of a feudal society who were liberated by the CCP in 1949.[60]

A rich and powerful literary text visualized by such sophisticated artists as Xia Yan and other filmmakers, however, necessarily contains multiple complex meanings. The film does more than inscribe a vivid image of an oppressed woman of the old feudal society in the public's mind. It illustrates in painstaking visual detail what the abstract term feudalism meant and in what specific ways and in which specific sites the oppression of laboring women was enacted. Indeed, the film could be read as a didactic visual text to teach the general public what institutions, social norms, and power relations were feudalistic and were responsible for Xianglin's Wife's tragic life. Arousing emotive sympathy from the audience necessitates a rational rejection of all the inhumane institutions and practices so powerfully represented in the film.

The film's passionate indictment of feudalism, in fact, makes Xia Yan's Pollyanna-like declaration that all those inhumane practices had now entirely vanished sound highly disingenuous. To say the least, as a high official of the CCP, he would have an intimate knowledge of the ferocious patriarchal resistance to the implementation of the 1950 Marriage Law drafted by social-ist feminists. In 1953 an investigation by the Ministry of Justice estimated that, nationally, 70,000 to 80,000 women had "been murdered or forced into suicide" annually since 1950 as a result of family problems and mistreat-ment.[61] Many women were persecuted and punished either by their husbands' families when they demanded a divorce or by their natal families when they resisted an arranged marriage. In the early 1950s, when a feminist marriage law profoundly shook the patriarchal society and exposed the persistent power of deeply entrenched patriarchal institutions, norms, and practices, the decision to make a film of *New Year's Sacrifice* had more implications than simply commemorating Lu Xun. Fundamentally, it was more a camou-flaged attempt to advance a feminist agenda of anti-feudalism than a celebra-tion of the CCP's supposed eradication of feudalism. The film introduced to the general public a highly gender-inflected definition of feudalism and con-firmed the legitimacy of a feminist agenda of transforming a patriarchal culture in the PRC. The feminist significance of the supersign Xianglin's Wife can be found in state feminists' frequent invocations of the term "rem-nants of feudalism" in their speeches and publications when insisting on the necessity of a continuous struggle against misogynist and discriminatory gender practices in socialist China.[62]

New Year's Sacrifice, the first feature film in color produced in China, was an instant hit upon its release in 1956. Directed by the talented Sang Hu (1916–2004), who had risen to fame before 1949, and with a top-ranked cast, the film won a special prize at the Karlovy Vary International Film Festival in Czechoslovakia in 1957 and a Silver Cap prize at the Mexico International Film Festival in 1958.[63] The wide circulation of the film made Xianglin's Wife a household name in the PRC. The high illiteracy rate in the 1950s made print media an ineffective way of reaching the masses; but the general public could easily recognize an oppressed woman in feudal society brilliantly por-trayed by the famous movie star Bai Yang (1920–1996). The tremendous popularity of *New Year's Sacrifice* effectively exerted its discursive power to represent the oppression of laboring women as the Other of socialism. A poignant condemnation of a feudalist past was in this sense simultaneously a clear demarcation of what a socialist today was not—or should not be.

CONSOLIDATING THE PARADIGM OF
REVOLUTIONARY HEROINES

Among Xia Yan's highly acclaimed adaptations were also scripts based on life stories of real revolutionary heroines. The two films made from his adaptations in a biographical genre furthered the paradigm of revolutionary heroines created under Chen Bo'er's leadership and crucially consolidated a dominant gender discourse of the socialist period that celebrated women's remarkable strength and pervasive contribution to revolution. *A Revolutionary Family* (1961) and *Eternity in Flames* (1965) were both based on highly popular autobiographical literature by underground Communists.[64] The original text *My Family* was a memoir by Tao Cheng, who described her transformation from an ordinary, traditional wife to a committed Communist who brought up a family of revolutionaries and guarded the CCP's underground headquarters in Shanghai.[65] Despite the loss of her Communist husband and sons, she never gave up her commitment to the cause; indeed, she fostered a surrogate family of underground Communists.

Like the heroine of *My Family,* many women bravely cared for and sustained a revolutionary family of underground workers who otherwise suffered from isolation.[66] The life story of such ordinary revolutionary women touched Xia Yan, whose adaptation reworked the original narrative in a way that both expanded the historical context and narrowed the story line to focus on the revolutionary mother Zhou Lian (the heroine's name in the film).[67] With the realism that was the hallmark of his style, in this unassuming, yet heroic woman, Xia Yan projected his own memories of the underground years as well as his high esteem for those whom he had characterized as the "real new women" who performed inconspicuous tasks in the everyday life of the revolution camp. Artistically representing the interiority of a traditional wife and mother who quietly experienced subjective transformation in the vicissitudes of the revolution, *A Revolutionary Family* was an instant hit and has remained a classic of revolutionary film (fig. 23).[68]

Eternity in Flames further evidenced Xia Yan's unreserved fondness for revolutionary heroines. The original novel, *Red Crag,* was based on three male authors' experiences, portraying a range of Communists' hair-raising experiences as underground workers operating in a complex and dangerous political environment and their heroic struggles after being thrown into Nationalist prisons in Chongqing in 1948.[69] A hugely popular novel devoured by every literate person for at least two generations, it eventually sold over 10

FIGURE 23. *A Revolutionary Family* (1961). A mother of three children, Zhou Lian sees off her revolutionary husband.

million copies. The novel caught the attention of Yu Lan, the actor who had started her film career by playing the leading role in one of Chen Bo'er's first in a series of revolutionary heroine films, *Soldiers in White Coats,* and also played the mother in *A Revolutionary Family,* for which she won the Best Actress Award at the Moscow Film Festival in 1961. Deeply moved by the novel *Red Crag,* Yu Lan decided to turn it into a film. With the support of her colleague, Shui Hua, who had directed *A Revolutionary Family,* she invited the original authors to work on adaptation collectively.

The task was particularly challenging because the novel had so many extremely moving characters that the authors, as well as Yu Lan and Shui Hua who would direct the film, had trouble eliminating any of them. The adaptation they produced had a story line focused around two male characters, Xu Yunfeng and Cheng Gang, but it retained so many characters and such dense depictions of their revolutionary activities that the screen script turned out to be flat and dry and failed to be approved by the Beijing Film Studio. In the winter of 1963, Yu Lan and Shui Hua asked Xia Yan, "the doctor of scripts," for help. After reading their adaptation, Xia Yan asked: "Why don't you focus on the story of Sister Jiang? You should not just write about Xu Yunfeng. You should parallel him with Sister Jiang. The story of Sister Jiang is very touching. She had a husband and a child. Her story reaches people's emotions. You should focus on her."[70] Yu Lan hesitated a little. She also found Sister Jiang especially appealing and wanted to play the role herself, but as a Communist artist she sought to avoid making this project seem self-serving. In contrast to *A Revolutionary Family*, *Red Crag* had a constellation of heroes and heroines.[71]

Besides this personal reservation, Yu Lan worried about the political implications of a script focusing on Sister Jiang. Several events at that time signaled the intensification of "class struggle." In March 1963 the Party Central approved a Ministry of Culture recommendation to ban all dramas portraying ghosts. In May Mao stated that capitalist and feudalist forces were launching rampant attacks on socialism. Late in the year, the deterioration of Sino-Soviet relations was publicized with the CCP's open critiques of Soviet revisionism.[72] Cultural producers were on notice to represent class struggles and guard against revisionist influences. The fact that the original adaption of *Red Crag* centered on revolutionary activities rather than depicting characters' personal lives or emotions reflected writers' anxiety that they could be criticized for advocating *bourgeois humanism,* a label for serious political blunders that served as a powerful deterrence in that moment. But that did not seem to concern Xia Yan, who had survived the storm of *The Life of Wu Xun* in 1951 and the Anti-Rightist Campaign in 1957 with the strong backing of Zhou Enlai. Seeing that no one was opposed to focusing on Sister Jiang, he said, "Ok, I will work on it. Don't bother me for a week." In just a few days he gave them an adaptation that was ready for filming.[73]

Sister Jiang, whose real name was Jiang Zhujun (1920–1949), was in the Communist underground in charge of the circulation of an underground journal in Chongqing. After her husband was killed while leading a guerrilla band, she decided to become her husband's successor among the guerillas and left her baby son in the care of her husband's first wife. Before long an underground Party member was arrested and revealed Sister Jiang's identity to his Nationalist captors. Seized and imprisoned, Sister Jiang steadfastly refused to betray any of her comrades despite horrific tortures. She was executed by the Nationalists right before the People's Liberation Army captured Chongqing. Xia Yan's representation of Sister Jiang expressed both his artistic ability to reach the audience and his own sympathies for underground Communist women with whom he had shared comradeship in times of danger. The fact that he never produced a single script representing male revolutionary heroes,

FIGURE 24. *Eternity in Flames* (1965). Sister Jiang bids farewell to her comrade in prison.

with whose experiences in the underground he was also familiar, is evidence, it may be argued, of his steadfast commitment to the thesis of *Women and Socialism.* The rewritten adaptation centering on Sister Jiang should be viewed as his tribute to women revolutionary martyrs, depicted with realistic details from his profound knowledge of the subject.[74]

Yu Lan also benefited from Xia Yan's knowledge of underground workers and artistic vision in creating a heroine who would stand out among a constellation of revolutionary heroines in films. When she was perplexed about how to portray this distinctive revolutionary heroine, given that she had already played quite a few others by then, Xia Yan advised her to emphasize Sister Jiang's identity as an urban-educated underground Communist, not a military heroine on the battleground. Following his advice, Yu Lan portrayed Sister Jiang as a gentle woman with a remarkably strong will and as an ordinary woman of extraordinary deeds. Portraying a character with such gripping contrast that played out seamlessly and subtly, Yu Lan's Sister Jiang captivated viewers (fig. 24).[75]

Eternity in Flames was a huge success. As Xia Yan predicted, Sister Jiang's story so entranced the audience that they projected their admiration for the heroine onto Yu Lan. The overwhelming expression of love from the audience even compelled Yu Lan to feel that she had to live her life in the spirit of Sister Jiang.[76] In fact, many young viewers took Sister Jiang as their role model as schools routinely incorporated such revolutionary films in their pedagogy. Like Xianglin's Wife, Sister Jiang became a household name in China.[77]

The films sponsored and marketed by the socialist state augmented the influence of revolutionary heroines and powerfully transformed gender norms in socialist China. Pervasive images of brave, selfless revolutionary heroines, much like the images of lone, individualistic masculine heroes produced by Hollywood, entered the mainstream in film production, permeating the psyche of at least two generations of Chinese women born and growing up in socialist China, especially those in metropolitan areas with easy access to cinemas.[78] The cultural landscape of China was profoundly reshaped by the diverse and numerous heroines in socialist cultural production.

By the time the crew completed *Eternity in Flames* at the end of 1964, however, the deputy minister of culture was already under fire from radicals surrounding Mao for his allegedly revisionist line in the film industry. Xia Yan used a pen name in the film credits, just as he had done before liberation when he had to protect himself from reprisals from the Nationalist government. He could never have imagined that this would be the last time he would appear on a credit line, even under the cover of a pen name.

SEVEN

The Cultural Origins of the Cultural Revolution

THE FILM INDUSTRY WAS DEEPLY enmeshed in politics from the beginning of the PRC, as the criticism of *The Life of Wu Xun* indicated. Indeed, one might justly argue, as I do here, that the cultural realm was the most contentious site in the CCP's struggles to build a socialist China. What constituted socialist new culture and how to artistically represent proletarian revolutionary forces in cultural products were sources of incessant debates and disputes. In addition, complex relationships among the Communists who operated in the cultural realm often played out in unexpected ways once they came to occupy positions of power. Contentious visions of a socialist revolutionary culture were often mixed with expressions of different ideologies, artistic sensibilities, political ambitions, and personal animosities.

Gender dynamics figured prominently in such complex contentions. Feminist leaders with a New Culture heritage consciously pursued an agenda of transforming patriarchal culture, a preoccupation not necessarily shared by all involved parties. This chapter brings the story of socialist feminist filmmaking to the moment of its eclipse in the Cultural Revolution. Xia Yan continues to play a key role in this chapter, but now he shares the stage with his allies and with opponents who attacked the film industry. The rise of Jiang Qing, the wife of Chairman Mao, parallels the downfall of Xia Yan and socialist feminist filmmaking. An analysis of the sources of their antagonism illuminates the entwined and always messy arena of culture production, politics, and personal relations, and ultimately, the contentions underlying the metamorphosis of mainstream discourse in the mid-1960s when the socialist feminist agenda of transforming multiple systems of oppression was reduced to a single-minded preoccupation with a Maoist class struggle.

INNOVATIONS AND CONTENTIONS IN THE FILM INDUSTRY

In his role as the top authority of the film industry, Xia Yan demonstrated far less originality than what he did as an artist. As deputy minister, Xia Yan, like other artist-officials, joined each political campaign without expressing any dissenting views. He was forced by his old friend Zhou Yang, deputy director of the Propaganda Department of the CCP, to undertake a self-criticism in the campaign against *The Life of Wu Xun,* when Zhou admonished him that as the top leader in the cultural realm in Shanghai he should take the responsibility even he did not personally approve of making the film.[1] In 1957 he condemned "rightists" in the film industry, refuting their charge that films produced in the new China were of low quality.[2] He also staged an attack on Feng Xuefeng, who had been an underground leader in Shanghai in the 1930s and was implicated in the estranged relationship between Xia Yan and his associates and Lu Xun.[3] Obviously intoxicated by the ethos of the time, Xia Yan promoted the Great Leap Forward in film production,[4] setting the unrealistic goal that "every province should have a film studio; every county a cinema; and every commune a projection team."[5] Cultural authorities from Yan'an and Shanghai were eager to demonstrate their identification with the Party Central, sometimes at the expense of their colleagues who had less political power. When he reviewed his life in his old age, Xia Yan wrote: "Self-reflection is painful. That we, who had been baptized by the May Fourth movement, should have gone so far as to drift with the currents and gradually become 'obedient tools,' totally losing the courage of independent thinking."[6] As a senior Party member and high-ranking official, Xia Yan was among those who had the decency to admit their own share of responsibility in the destructive mistakes made by the CCP.

But Xia Yan's self-criticism should not blind us to his many achievements. It was not "obedience" that compelled him to actively explore novel cultural practices, but rather a genuine identification with the Party's imperative of creating a new proletarian culture. Many innovations were institutionalized in the nationalized and centralized film industry, becoming hallmarks of socialist film culture. For example, the practice of *xiashenghuo* or fieldwork, which had been initiated by Chen Bo'er in the Northeast Film Studio, was adopted by all the film studios. Filmmakers, including actors, were required to live with workers / peasants / soldiers for a period of time in order to faithfully represent their lives and vividly capture their characteristics on film.

The Shanghai Film Bureau's internal report on senior filmmakers describes how the political consciousness of famous movie stars Shangguan Yunzhu and Wang Danfeng had been raised by participating in manual labor with workers and peasants for an entire year. "Before, Wang Danfeng only liked to play the role of urban petty-bourgeois intellectuals. But now she is actively looking for opportunities to create images of workers / peasants / soldiers."[7] The report also commented that *xiashenghuo* allowed filmmakers to make friends with workers and peasants, provided inspiration for their creative work, and facilitated the transformation of their worldviews. From the perspective of officials, fieldwork served to reduce the gap between filmmakers and the main subjects of their visual representation. Some actors genuinely appreciated the opportunity to mingle with working-class people. Top-ranking star Qin Yi formed a deep friendship with a model laborer in a textile factory, Yang Fuzhen.[8] According to Xia Yan, the fieldwork requirement improved acting and made socialist films superior to the left-wing films of the 1930s that were produced in the absence of contact with the people.[9]

To accelerate the process of producing scripts more accurately reflecting the lives of workers / peasants / soldiers, the Film Bureau of the Ministry of Culture organized scriptwriter workshops to provide professional training to amateur writers recruited from the masses. Li Zhun, the scriptwriter of *Li Shuangshuang,* which won the 1963 "Hundred Flowers Prize" for best picture, best script, best actress, and best supporting actor, was a graduate of one of these workshops.[10] His encounters with rural women activists during his fieldwork enabled him to perceptively depict the socialist transformation of villages through a nuanced representation of subtle changes in gender relations and the rise of a charismatic woman leader in rural collectivization. Li Zhun, an ethnic Mongolian, a beneficiary of a state policy that trained cultural producers from previously marginalized social and ethnic groups, became a renowned and prolific writer and scriptwriter whose works focused on rural life.

A revolutionary cultural work required innovations in the process of production as well. Serving the masses involved taking a mass line in filmmaking: that is, the masses were expected to participate in the making of a film relating to their life, a practice first initiated by Chen Bo'er when producing a play in Yan'an. If it were a film about wars, military officers would be invited to provide feedback and suggestions on the script and rushes. For a film about women, the Women's Federation would be consulted. Democratic participation in cultural production was especially accentuated in the Great

Leap Forward, when the originality and creativity of the masses were extolled and collectivism became a guiding principle of social organization. Collaboration among film studio officials, filmmakers, and the masses, called *sanjiehe,* a "collaboration among the three," was promoted as a model of the mass line in filmmaking. The masses in each film studio—that is, the workers and staff of a film crew—were included in the review and revision of scripts and daily rushes. This unprecedented practice enabled workers / peasants / soldiers to play an active role in the formation of cultural representation, in addition to being the subject of that representation.

Understandably, the requirement for a collective approach to artistic creativity could be vexing to artists for whom creativity was intrinsically embedded in individual exploration and experimentation. A scriptwriter at the Shanghai Film Studio complained about both the practices of the mass line and officials' intrusive role in the production process:

> The first problem can be called "imposing suggestions." [Leaders] talk to you repeatedly to ask you to accept their suggestions. The second problem is making unpredictable changes constantly. A subject can be written in about a hundred ways. Today they point to the first way, tomorrow they point to the second way, and the day after tomorrow they point to the third way. The question is, how to revise? The third problem is "you talk while I listen." Many people are gathered together all at once, all expressing their views while the scriptwriter is supposed to just listen. The scriptwriter cannot talk.[11]

Making films accessible to workers / peasants / soldiers was an even greater concern, since film was regarded as the most effective pedagogical tool to educate the masses. Filmmaking was profoundly affected by this goal. Shifting the focus from the urban audience concentrated in semicolonial coastal cities before 1949 to rural peasants in the new China required filmmakers steeped in Hollywood traditions to explore a cinematic language that would appeal to Chinese peasants. The great majority of peasants had never been exposed to film before the founding of the PRC, and their artistic tastes had been formed by various local operas based on traditional Chinese classics. This shift in artistic style required a push from cultural authorities. Xia Yan, despite his work in translating Western literature and Soviet film theories, identified with Mao's position on creating literature and art with a Chinese national style and urged filmmakers to break away from the frameworks and representational styles of Western films. Admonishing filmmakers for making many films that peasants neither understood nor liked, he stated emphatically in a 1960 article: "Premier Zhou has exhorted us repeatedly that films have to be understood by the masses; stories should have a beginning and an end; the story line should be lucid and explained clearly; don't flash back and forth; the characters should speak the way Chinese speak; and every sentence should be audible to the audience." He criticized some filmmakers for "lacking the mass viewpoint of being responsible for five hundred million peasants."[12] The imperative to cater to Chinese peasants' tastes led filmmakers to "Sinify" their works, a trend accelerated especially after China broke away from the model of the Soviet Union.[13] It also led to the flourishing of a new genre, films of traditional Chinese operas.[14]

Enabling workers / peasants / soldiers to watch more films was a less challenging task. Rural projection teams were rapidly set up to reach villages, and new theaters were built in working-class residential areas in cities. In 1949 there were over 600 cinemas nationwide but no mobile projection teams. By 1959 the number of projection units, including both movie theaters and mobile projection teams, had risen to 15,400. Films were shown in rural villages and in urban parks, workers' clubs, universities, and factories, in addition to regular theaters. Watching film became a major part of cultural life in the cities.[15] The number of film viewings jumped from 1.75 billion in 1957 to 4.5 billion in 1959.[16] Part of Xia Yan's Great Leap Forward goal for the film industry was to set up a projection team in each rural commune, but this ambitious project was curtailed by the shortage of steel.[17] Officials lamented in 1964 that each peasant only got to see a film 2.8 times a year on average. In many poor and isolated rural areas peasants may never have been exposed to film. When a film was shown in a Shandong village in 1964, the villagers had prepared to "invite the people in the film to dinner."[18] The accessibility of film could well be used as a measure of the reach of socialist ideology in a vast and diverse country.

Because film was such an important means of reaching peasants, authorities in the film industry took great care to make sure that the messages in films were communicated to their intended audience. Filmmakers were instructed to take into consideration the poor screening conditions in rural areas, and actors were instructed to enunciate lines clearly to allow the audience to comprehend every word. When stories of innovative projectionists who offered translation and explanation to audiences who belonged to ethnic minorities reached industry officials, they decided to set up workshops nationwide to train local projectionists to translate for audiences who did not understand Mandarin. Government attention inadvertently gave greater

authority to local projectionists, who shouldered the role of cultural translator and ideological interpreter. The state-sanctioned ideology had to be fil-
tered through them. In one rural commune during the Cultural Revolution,
when a Soviet revolutionary classic *Lenin in 1918* was screened, many urban
youths who had been sent to the countryside flocked to see the film. The
film's special attraction was a scene in which Soviet Red Army soldiers were
watching the ballet *Swan Lake* on stage. But in the eyes of the local projectionist, the scantily clad white swan in the embrace of a man scandalously
breached the sexual norms of the local society, so he covered the lens with his
hand when the film came to this part. Alas, the young people in the audience
who had walked hours on the mountain paths from surrounding villages for
just this one scene had to be content with the fleeting, broken images leaking
through the projectionist's fingers.[19]

At the national level, an affirmative action policy was instituted in
cultural production. In order to guarantee the making of films on
workers / peasants / soldiers, women, children, and ethnic minorities, local
film studios' annual production plans began to carry quotas for subject matter
and had to be approved by the Ministry of Culture. The implementation of
this policy had impressive results. Of the 185 feature films produced between
1958 and 1960, 100 represented workers / peasants / soldiers.[20] However, when
the balance in subject matter became a priority of cultural production, it
sometimes overrode concerns for quality, especially when the gap between the
artist's interest and the required subject had not been closed. Qu Baiyin, a
scriptwriter, director, and the deputy director of the Shanghai Film Bureau,
expressed the dismay undoubtedly felt by many artists when he lamented:
"When we talk about our accomplishments, we often emphasize subject
matter. . . . But we don't examine whether [filmmakers] are able to express
their agency and creativity, or the quality of these products."[21] For Qu, who
was not a Party member, exploring original and innovative means in visual
representation was the essence of cinematic art and should neither be
sacrificed to focusing on subject matter nor be replaced by a formulaic pre-
scription of the ways in which revolutionary characters should be portrayed.

In 1962, Qu published a critical article, "Monologue on the Issue of
Innovation in Film," that considered the tensions and constraints in pursuing
artistic innovation in socialist filmmaking.[22] A draft of the article had been
read by many artist-officials in the film industry and been carefully edited by
Xia Yan, who obviously shared Qu's concern for artistic creativity. In an ideal
scenario Qu's article could have been an opportunity for filmmakers to

discuss and debate how to further exploration of artistic forms of representation in socialist film after affirmative action in cultural representation was implemented. Unfortunately, soon after its publication a group of radicals in the Party began to target the cultural realm as a major battleground for class struggle. Qu's "Monologue" was condemned as evidence of Xia Yan's revisionist line in the film industry. In this new situation, Xia Yan's delicate balancing act, which involved complying sufficiently with shifting political currents, maintaining his pursuit of artistic creativity, and exploring the development of socialist films, proved impossible to maintain.

THE RISE OF JIANG QING AND THE "TWO-LINE STRUGGLE" IN THE FILM INDUSTRY

Multifaceted contentions in socialist filmmaking were increasingly framed as manifestations of class struggle. On December 12, 1963, Chairman Mao gave a critical directive on literature and the arts: "The socioeconomic base has changed, but the arts as part of the superstructure that serves this base still remain a serious problem. Hence we should proceed with investigation and study and attend to this matter in earnest. . . . Isn't it absurd that many Communists are enthusiastic about promoting feudal and capitalist art but not socialist art?"[23] Like his sudden criticism of *The Life of Wu Xun* in 1951, Mao's renewed attention to literature and the arts reflected his wife Jiang Qing's vigilance against class enemies in the cultural realm. While in 1951 Jiang Qing was alone in bringing *The Life of Wu Xun* to Mao's attention, according to what she told American historian Roxane Witke and was confirmed by Xia Yan decades later,[24] by 1963 she had formed a cluster of radical allies based in Shanghai who were eager to identify and fight against class enemies in the cultural realm, especially after Mao's emphasis on class struggle at the CCP's Tenth Plenum of the Eighth Central Committee in September 1962.[25] The subsequent framing of a "two-line struggle" between the proletarian and the bourgeois in the film industry, a prelude to the Cultural Revolution, was the expression of the entwined ideological and personal motives of these political allies.

Jiang Qing (1914–1991) had served as Mao's secretary since they married in Yan'an in 1938.[26] In the early 1950s, she held the title of director of the film section of the Propaganda Department of the CCP and was a member of the Film Guidance Committee of the Ministry of Culture, appointments related to her previous career as an actor in Shanghai. These were minor appointments, however, and did not give her real power to affect cultural production in either the film industry or the cultural realm at large. Situated right next to the most powerful man who commanded a male-dominated Party, Jiang Qing had an acute sense of being slighted by the powerful men around Mao. Although it was difficult to consider her minor position in the government a result of sexism, given the powerful position Chen Bo'er held at the same time, Jiang Qing may nevertheless have been discontent with this assignment. According to one of her biographers, she also held grudge against the male authorities in the Ministry of Culture, since they did not invite her to participate in the first national conference of the Association of Literature and Arts upon the founding of the PRC, although other top-ranking female artists were included in the prestigious event.[27] In any case, in the extensive interviews she granted to American historian Roxane Witke in 1972, when she was already hailed as the vanguard of the Cultural Revolution, Jiang Qing confessed that she had found the snubs she experienced and the tough political battles she had had to fight just to establish her authority outrageous. In the 1977 biography *Comrade Chiang Ch'ing,* Witke highlighted this strong-willed woman's position as one of China's top leaders, a status that was "attained by no other woman of her times," and perceptively depicted Jiang Qing's "ultimate goal" as "a revered masculine type of political power."[28]

Jiang Qing's political moves were based on her keen understanding of her husband's revolutionary vision and political agenda, her will to carve out a niche of her own in the historical process, and her desire to take revenge on those who had slighted her in the past. After Mao, in 1962, called for increased vigilance against capitalism and revisionism in order to continue the socialist revolution, Jiang Qing identified the cultural realm as the superstructure that lagged behind the economic base in socialist transformation and sought to shape its future direction as well as get rid of her political rivals and Mao's. Shanghai mayor Ke Qingshi and director of the Propaganda Department Zhang Chunqiao became Jiang Qing's staunch supporters in her efforts to transform Peking operas and ballets as well as in her struggles against officials in the film industry.[29]

It may be that the Shanghai leaders' original grudge against Xia Yan and Chen Huangmei, the director of the Film Bureau of the Ministry of Culture, resulted more from a competition for authority built into institutional overlap than actual ideological differences. The film studios in Shanghai were under the leadership of the Shanghai Party Committee but, rather than looking to the city officials, Shanghai filmmakers preferred the suggestions and opinions of Xia Yan and Chen Huangmei at the Ministry of Culture. The confusion in having two levels of administration, which in this case involved authorities with and without artistic clout, necessarily created frictions and even animosities. Such tensions also seriously affected innocent filmmakers. The famous actor Zhao Dan once asked Chen Huangmei, "On the issues regarding art, who has the final say?" Chen replied, "Of course the Shanghai Party Committee." Zhao Dan then said, "I wish there were no problems between you and Xia Gong, and the Shanghai leaders. Then our lives would be easy."[30]

Shanghai filmmakers' sandwiched position is also confirmed by actor Huang Zongying, whose husband is Zhao Dan. In 1959, at a dinner that Jiang Qing and mayor Ke Qingshi hosted for this movie star couple and the famous director Zheng Junli and his wife Huang Chen, the guests were perplexed by Jiang Qing's curious remark out of the blue, "I hope you will listen to us, not to them." At that time none of the guests could figure out what she meant by "us" and "them."[31] Jiang Qing's political recruitment of Shanghai filmmakers was not successful, though her efforts to utilize the animosities between Shanghai leaders and authorities in the film industry would eventually prevail.

In January 1963 mayor Ke Qingshi declared that literature and the arts should represent "the thirteen years" of the socialist revolution since the founding of the PRC, a response to Mao's recent comments that there were too many operas on ancient subjects in feudal times.[32] Ke's proposal stimulated a heated debate in the film industry. At a meeting on literature and the arts in Beijing in April 1963, top officials in the Ministry of Culture argued vehemently against such a drastic reduction of subject matter. Premier Zhou Enlai also supported the cultural authorities' contention that socialist literature and the arts should not be so narrowly construed as to include only works representing people during the socialist period.[33] However, supporters of Ke's thesis did not give up but further debated against Chen Huangmei at a national conference of leaders of film studios in January 1964. They argued that the task of socialist literature and the arts was to oppose capitalism, while the subject of anti-imperialism and anti-feudalism belonged in the historical stage of new democracy, a stage that socialist China had already left behind.[34] Chen and authorities in the Ministry of Culture felt increasing pressure from this reductive theorization of socialist cultural production, while remaining insensitive to the political implications of such debates. The debates signaled a deepening of the fracture between the authorities in Shanghai and the Ministry of Culture as well as the increasing support of Mayor Ke and Zhang Chunqiao for Jiang Qing.

In the sixty hours of interviews she granted to Roxane Witke in 1972, Jiang Qing never disguised her enmity toward Xia Yan. Witke observed: "There was no figure in modern Chinese history she despised more than the courtesan Sai Chin-hua [Sai Jinhua]. Nor was there a modern writer and cinematographer she resented more than Hsia Yen [Xia Yan], who wrote the highly successful (by public, not by Chiang Ch'ing's standards) play about Sai Chin-hua, first produced by the Nineteen Forties Society in 1936."[35] Why did Jiang Qing hate both the playwright and the play's protagonist? Witke recorded Jiang Qing's memory of the staging of the play *Sai Jinhua*:

> One of the first plays they put on (in November 1936, at the famous Golden City Theater) was Hsia Yen's *Sai Chin-hua*. The title was the name of the notorious beauty of the Boxer era who became the mistress of a German general. Chiang Ch'ing was furious at seeing a Chinese actress portray the despicable Sai, a woman who, in her opinion, had prostituted the cause of Chinese nationalism. Her outspoken opinion of Sai so enraged the other members of the Nineteen Forties Society that they actually threatened to *kill* her, she declared, her voice shrill with emotion.[36]

Witke did not have an independent source to verify Jiang Qing's claim, though she vividly captured Jiang Qing's raw emotion thirty-six years after the episode. Since Jiang Qing's fall in 1976, many published histories have presented a very different story. Apparently, instead of opposing the play, the twenty-two-year-old Lan Ping (Jiang Qing's name at that time) fought against another actor, Wang Ying, for the role of Sai Jinhua. The director and producer did not know how to handle the intense competition between the two young women, so they appealed to the playwright for help. Xia Yan knew both of them, as well as the two male actors who were eager to play the leading male role. Placed in an awkward position, he suggested that the four be paired in two groups, designated by the letters A and B, and take turns appearing on stage, with Lan Ping and Zhao Dan in group B. On hearing the decision, despite the fact that the two pairs would be treated equally, Lan Ping stomped out of the rehearsal room, yelling and crying in protest, "Why should I be in group B? In what way is she better?"[37] The unexpected scene stunned Wang Ying and Jin Shan, the pair in group A. They decided to split from the drama troupe and form another one, the Nineteen Forties Society. Its staging of *Sai Jinhua,* obviously with the consent of the playwright, was a great success. The contest between Lan Ping and Wang Ying over the role of Sai Jinhua generated a great deal of controversy in Shanghai's theatrical circle and attracted the tabloids' attention as well.[38]

Neither Xia Yan nor any other left-wing dramatists of the 1930s realized how deeply Jiang Qing had been wounded by that episode. Twenty-seven years later, in 1963, they misjudged Jiang Qing again, this time underestimating her power to bring on a virtual hurricane in the cultural realm. Although Xia Yan's vulnerability by then made the outcome inevitable, the precipitating incidents came from three political "blunders" that enabled Jiang Qing and her allies to claim that the film industry under the leadership of Xia and Chen was following the so-called "revisionist and bourgeois line," or, for the sake of brevity, the "Xia-Chen line."

The first blunder concerned the publication in February of film scholar Chen Jihua's *A History of the Development of Film in China* that highlighted the left-wing films of the 1930s. The second concerned the Chinese Film Archives, which from October to December hosted screenings of "Excellent Films of the 1930s" for a new generation of filmmakers and film students. Both occurrences implicitly honored Xia Yan, for they recognized accomplishments under his leadership in the 1930s. Although Xia Yan was not directly involved in either of the two projects, he did not forbid his subordinates from working on them.[39]

The third blunder was that Xia Yan played a major role in revising the script for *Early Spring in February,* an adaptation by director Xie Tieli of the left-wing writer Rou Shi's 1929 novella *February.* The film portrays a male intellectual's frustrations after the failure of the Nationalist Revolution in the 1920s. The protagonist Xiao Jianqiu goes to a small town to take a teaching position but finds himself entangled in emotional relationships with two women, one of whom is an uneducated widow. Gender and sexual norms in the small town, however, are such that his sympathy for the widow becomes the center of gossip that eventually leads to her suicide. Suffocated by small-town culture and society, Xiao finally leaves to pursue a new life as a revolutionary. Endorsing this film based on a piece of New Culture literature infused with left-wing implications was an act of defiance against Mayor Ke's proposal that films focus on "writing the thirteen years of socialism." Out of tune with the dominant political chorus, the film, completed in October 1963, was criticized as advocating bourgeois humanism.[40] These three new "blunders" were added to the one committed in 1962 when Xia Yan edited and supported Qu's essay, "Monologue of Innovation."[41]

With information collected by Jiang Qing, Mao issued a second set of directives on literature and the arts in June 1964, accusing the authorities in the cultural realm of failing to work closely with workers / peasants / soldiers and to represent socialist revolution and construction, alleging that "in recent years [they] have even fallen to the edge of revisionism."[42] Mao's new charge threatened the Ministry of Culture to such an extent that the frightened leaders decided to make the film industry the target of the rectification campaign following Mao's directives. They behaved like terrified sailors who toss a sacrifice into the roaring sea in the hope of calming the wrath of the sea god and saving their toppling boat.[43] Xia Yan was forced to make a formal self-criticism on July 16, 1964. By the time he was formally removed from his position as deputy minister of culture on April 7, 1965, he had made three lengthy self-criticisms, and his immediate subordinate in the film industry, Chen Huangmei, had also made a lengthy self-criticism. These confessions, together with the "evidence" of their crimes, were circulated throughout the film industry as educational material on how to criticize the Xia-Chen revisionist line. Significantly, praising the films of the 1930s was not treated as evidence of Xia Yan's immodesty or egotism, as one might have assumed, but worse, as promoting bourgeois and petty-bourgeois films made in the 1930s against the historical context of socialist revolution, a move that, it was claimed, was intended to promote a return to capitalism. Even more seriously, Xia Yan confessed: "Indeed it denigrated the great significance of the unprecedented Yan'an Talks, that is to say, it attempted to uphold the films of the 1930s as orthodox in order to resist the direction pointed out by Chairman Mao that literature and the arts should serve the workers / peasants / soldiers."[44] After months of hearing and reading condemnations, Xia Yan was reduced from defiance to parroting his accusers' incriminating fabrications, an obedient behavior that would torment him greatly late in his life.

Mao's theory of the two-line struggle enabled the practices of identifying counterrevolutionary crimes, however arbitrarily. These are the terms in which Jiang Qing framed her case against Xia Yan. If *Early Spring in February* revealed Xia Yan's penchant for writing about petty-bourgeois characters in a feudal era (a charge he did not deny as he revealed that he felt akin to the protagonist Xiao Jianqiu), what about the revolutionary heroine Sister Jiang in *Eternity in Flames*? What interiority or consciousness did the creation of this character manifest? Here, Jiang Qing shifted her accusations to a different realm:[45] the film, she declared, "went against Chairman Mao thought and distorted the historical reality by depicting the rural struggles as having been led by the urban sector."[46] Along this line, she also condemned *A Revolutionary Family* for glorifying the Party's urban underground work rather than celebrating its military struggles in rural areas—a stance that, she emphasized, was an expression of two-line struggles. Yet, even while denouncing *Eternity in Flames,* she was organizing a group of artists to adapt the original book *Red Crag* into a Peking opera, trying to make Sister Jiang a more prominent heroine, and allegedly saying she was prepared to spend ten years on the adaptation and production.[47] Obviously, she was also under the spell of both the character and the novel. And there was yet another group of artists—these in the Art Troupe of the Political Department of the Air Force—who were adapting the novel into an opera titled *Sister Jiang,* which made a huge splash on its debut on September 4, 1964. Mao and all the top leaders of the Party went to see the opera and praised it highly. Mao did not seem to worry about the glorification of the urban underground workers.[48] The first couple's political moves were not always synchronized.

The downfall of Xia Yan and the rise of Jiang Qing were complete in 1964. Xia Yan's condemnation brought an end to a leadership in the film industry that had attempted both to fulfill the revolutionary mission of cultural trans-formation and to satisfy diverse social interests and artistic tastes in cultural production. It also signified the abandoning of the May Fourth New Culture heritage of anti-feudalism as a prominent theme in cultural production. At a deeper level, the radicals' criticism of Xia Yan as mired in the feudal and capi-talist period while history had moved into a socialist era exposes the gulf separating the radicals from those still devoted to May Fourth ideals. The May Fourth cohort understood that China did not shed its past merely by becoming a socialist state, regardless of how much significant change socialist revolution and construction entailed.[49] The radicals' teleological conceptu-alization of the task of cultural production at the socialist stage, especially their rejection of representations of a "feudalist past" even in a critical light, actually prevented cultural producers from scrutinizing conservative and patriarchal customs and practices that persisted in socialist China. Significantly, most of those practices and ideologies in the "feudalist stage" were profoundly gendered, as *Early Spring in February* illuminated. Thus, shutting down critical cultural representation of gender-inflected "feudal-ism" seriously inhibited the effort to transform a patriarchal culture that still permeated socialist China.

The downfall of Xia Yan also marked the end of an era in socialist film-making.[50] After the ensuing "rectification campaign" in the film industry that condemned most films produced under the "Xia-Chen revisionist line," the industry was once again in disarray.[51] The reshuffled film industry was now under the supervision of the "leading group of the Cultural Revolution" established on July 7, 1964, after Mao's stern criticism of the cultural realm.[52] But Zhou Enlai obviously showed great concern for the film industry. He gave instructions at a meeting of the new authorities of the film industry in the Ministry of Culture on August 5, 1965,[53] and then six days later gave a long speech at the national conference of leading filmmakers gathered in the People's Hall in Beijing. This talk was full of coded language, while his specific suggestions revealed a significant agenda that was absent in the talks of new officials of the film industry at the same conference.[54] After the usual cliché about studying Chairman Mao's Yan'an Talks, he oddly elaborated at length on current international tensions and an imminent war between U.S. imperialism and China. Having vividly depicted an ominous scenario, he got to the point: filmmakers should engage in extended *xiashenghuo,* fieldwork, rationalizing it partly by reiterating the old principle of learning from workers / peasants / soldiers, but more for self-protection in the coming "war." "If you don't go now, when the bombs drop on your head in the future you will have to go to the people. Why not go now? . . . If the American imperialists do not come, it is still good that you can settle among workers / peasants / soldiers. If they do come, isn't it far better that you go down right now to settle there?" pleaded Zhou.[55]

Following the threat of war, he emphasized how long the filmmakers should expect to spend on fieldwork: about three-fifths of their time over the next five years! And just to be certain they didn't miss his point, he then stressed, "In the following five years, we don't expect you to produce a lot of films but expect you to learn from fieldwork."[56] What is more, he also instructed that filmmakers should replace the production of feature films with documentaries of artistic quality. Zhang Ruifang, the movie star who was a close friend of Zhou Enlai and Deng Yingchao, in her old age reflected, "It took us forty years to realize how Premier Zhou had wracked his brains to protect us in the field of literature and the arts!"[57] In 1965 Zhou Enlai already perceived the cause of the troubles for filmmakers. Rather than resisting Jiang Qing and her associates' attack on the film industry, the premier chose to disperse filmmakers and disable the perilous realm of cultural production in order to avoid further casualties in the rapidly escalating storm.[58]

JIANG QING'S LEADERSHIP IN REVOLUTIONIZING
THEATERS

In July 1964 at the Festival of Peking Opera on Contemporary Themes organized by the Ministry of Culture, an extravaganza that showcased thirty-five new operas presented by twenty-nine troupes from nineteen provinces, Zhou Enlai invited Jiang Qing to give a speech on the transformation of Peking opera. The premier's unprecedented gesture indicated his awareness of the rising importance of Mao's wife in the shifting political milieu.[59] In her first official speech, "On the Revolution of Peking Opera," which marked her political ascendancy, Jiang Qing emphasized the significance of transforming Peking operas and other local operas in the socialist revolution. She gave two numbers to illustrate her point: there were more than 2,800 opera troupes nationwide, but almost all the repertoires were about "emperors, princes, generals, scholars and beauties, and on top of these, ghosts and monsters. . . . There are well over 600 million workers, peasants, and soldiers in our country, while there is only a handful of landlords, rich peasants, counterrevolutionaries, bad elements, Rightists, and bourgeois elements." She asked emphatically, "Shall we serve this handful, or the 600 million?"[60]

Unlike film, an imported art form that had a short history in China, operas were locally grounded forms of performance with long histories in diverse regions, and hence had accumulated huge repertoires of old subjects. Efforts to reform local operas with contemporary themes and modern forms did not start with Jiang Qing. Since the 1920s, Chinese artists in various fields had experimented with modernizing Chinese traditional operas.[61] But it was Jiang Qing's specific attention to the gap between the most pervasive cultural representations and the goal of socialist revolution that advanced the agenda of socialist transformation in this cultural field. Her dichotomous classification of the handful versus the 600 million deployed a Maoist concept of class that reduced the complexities of social groups as well as confusing class distinctions with arbitrarily defined political categories such as Rightists and bad elements. But her appeal to serving the majority was morally persuasive, even though it was problematic to assume that the old operas did not serve the majority and that the workers / peasants / soldiers would be content only by watching representations of themselves. As a matter of fact, both Jiang Qing and Mao loved old Peking operas. At fourteen Jiang Qing had run away from her uncle's home to join a local Peking opera company, giving performances in small towns in Shandong for one year.[62] In Yan'an Jiang Qing caught Mao's attention when she was playing a leading role in a classic Peking opera. Late in Mao's life, after his wife had succeeded in eliminating the performance of old operas through the Cultural Revolution, he missed the old, supposedly "feudalist" operas so much that first-rank Peking opera singers were summoned to make films of traditional performances for his exclusive viewing. Even Jiang Qing herself secretly ordered a Tianjin troupe to perform traditional Hebei operas for her in June 1974.[63]

Moreover, although Jiang Qing appealed to artists' "conscience" and exhorted them to *serve* the workers / peasants / soldiers who fed, clothed, and protected artists, her emphasis was on *changing* the consciousness of the masses. The conceptual slippage was common among Communists, who were supposed to be simultaneously servants to and vanguards of the people. In her speech at the 1964 festival, Jiang Qing was clear on this point. "Theatres are places in which to educate the people."[64] In subsequent years, backed by abundant state resources as well as the legitimacy granted by Mao's directives condemning the Ministry of Culture and placing her in the leading role as a pioneer of proletarian culture on the turbulent political stage, Jiang Qing acquired full authority in leading a revolution in the cultural realm.[65] She worked tirelessly with first-class artists chosen from diverse fields to revise and polish a selected cluster of Peking operas, ballets, and symphonies and make them "model theatrical works" for the whole cultural realm to emulate. What are generally regarded as Jiang Qing's "Eight Model Operas" were just the first batch of theatrical works; by 1975, seventeen works in whose production Jiang Qing was directly involved had been completed. Most of these "model works" were made into films for national circulation, exposing many rural peasants to Peking operas, ballets, and symphonies for the first time.[66]

Starting in 1964, Jiang Qing engaged in parallel maneuvers in the cultural realm: condemning and banning socialist films produced under Xia Yan's leadership, including films that celebrated revolutionary heroines; and promoting revolutionary theatrical works that often presented revolutionary heroines in the leading position. The suppression of films made under Xia Yan as well as any other performing arts produced under the so-called revisionist line of the Ministry of Culture effectively removed competitors from the cultural market, enabling her theatrical works to dominate theatres and cinemas, especially after 1966 when she was promoted by Mao to become the number-two leader in the reconstituted Cultural Revolution Leading

Group.[67] The revolutionary heroines in model operas became the best-known artistic representations of women, simply because few alternative works were available. Most of the Cultural Revolution cohort was able to sing many parts in these operas because radios everywhere played them all the time and contests for amateurs singing model operas were organized widely in both urban and rural areas.

The important role Jiang Qing played in promoting theatrical works with revolutionary themes and the intimate relationship between her efforts in the cultural realm and the Cultural Revolution were captured in a set of fifteen paper cuts produced by a group of young artists in Foshan, Guangdong, in the late 1960s.[68] It narrates a history of the Cultural Revolution that began with Jiang Qing and her first group of model theatrical works. Her artistic efforts in transforming performing arts are identified as the inception of the Cultural Revolution, as the caption at the bottom right of the first paper cut in the set explains. The central figure, Jiang Qing, is adorned in a military uniform, indicating the military's crucial role in launching her leadership in the cultural realm as well as signifying her militant leading role in the battleground of culture. Most of those surrounding her are characters from the first eight model theatrical works. The two figures on the far left side represent famous cultural products in the Yan'an period after Mao's famous talks, suggesting an inherent connection between the two periods in terms of creating proletarian culture. The female peasant and male factory worker in the top right and left corners and the old Uyghur man in the lower left corner symbolize the Maoist proletarian line in cultural representation that centers on workers, peasants, women, and ethnic minorities (fig. 25).

Given Jiang Qing's emphasis on the transformative role model operas should play, what gender norms did these omnipresent revolutionary heroines attempt to shape? Except for Li Tiemei in *The Red Lantern,* who is situated in a surrogate family, the leading female protagonists in Jiang Qing's selection of Peking operas all share one conspicuous commonality: they have no familial relationships, let alone romantic love interests. Fang Haizhen, Party secretary in *The Harbor,* is unambiguously single; Aqing's Wife, underground Party member in *Shajia Village,* has an absentee husband who is supposedly away on business in Shanghai;[69] Ke Xiang, the guerrilla leader in *Azalea Mountain,* had a husband who was martyred for the Revolution; and Jiang Shuiying, brigade Party leader of a rural commune in *Song of the Dragon River* (Jiang Qing changed the gender of the leader from the original play), may have a husband serving in the military, which is inconspicuously

FIGURE 25. Paper cut. *The Inception of the Great Proletarian Cultural Revolution.* Courtesy of the Lieberthal-Rogel Center for Chinese Studies, University of Michigan.

indicated by a sign of honor normally posted on the houses of military families. They all shouldered important leadership tasks with the necessary support of their comrades but not male kin. Their own superb capacities and commitment to the Revolution defined their identities, just like the heroes in other model operas. These heroines were not only situated squarely in previous men's turf as leaders but also absolutely detached from familial responsibilities and kinship relations. Once these personal relations were gone, gender was no longer relevant. Their female embodiment of femininity did not have significant effects on the heroines' interactions with people around them, though Peking opera has its own gendered formula for roles, singing, costumes, and kinesics that distinctively marks each actor's gender and age, as Rosemary A. Roberts in her semiotic analyses of these theatrical works clearly demonstrates.[70] In other words, rather than the "masculinization of women," a widely popularized criticism of the "model works" by postsocialist literary critics applying an essentialized notion of femininity and masculinity,[71] Jiang Qing created a theatrical fantasy in which gender-marked women could function in a men's world almost free from the effects of gender hierarchy.[72] The combination of revolutionary romanticism and revolutionary realism that she advocated as the principle of revolutionary cultural representation allowed her to depict her ideal type in her fantasy that revealed her desires rather than having to bring her protagonists close to social reality.

How did Jiang Qing's heroines differ from earlier revolutionary heroines? On the surface her heroines were a continuation of previous female protagonists from Chen Bo'er to Xia Yan, as well as from the heroines depicted on the covers of *Women of China;* all these socialist representations of women celebrated their strength and accomplishments in the public domain. But previous stories of heroines touched upon gender to some degree, showing how gender and class oppressions prepared the conditions for the heroine's revolt, how a heroine broke away from traditional gender roles, or how a heroine had to choose or juggle between her commitments to motherhood and to the Communist cause. In fact, until 1962 a significant number of films had specifically addressed patriarchal norms and practices as residues of "feudalism" that should be criticized and discarded in socialist China, and some specifically criticized gender inequality in domestic settings.[73] In this regard, the heroines in model operas presented a new paradigm that departed from previous representations. Gender contention was not just subsumed by class struggle; it entirely disappeared.[74]

Jiang Qing's creation of this highly romanticized ideal woman had contradictory implications. She favored women-centered stories, which became an implicit mandate that compelled many writers to produce women-centered screen scripts and plays in the Cultural Revolution.[75] Moreover, she was keen on placing heroines in positions of power as leaders whose wisdom and courage outshone the merits of their male colleagues. The explicit challenge to male supremacy could not be missed by anyone in the audience, sending the public a strong anti-sexist message or, indeed, launching an open visual attack on the deeply entrenched patriarchal cultural belief that men are superior and women are inferior. With their striking images of powerful women, the model operas furthered socialist state feminist advocacy of combatting male chauvinism and empowering women, especially given Jiang Qing's political clout in the Cultural Revolution.

But at the same time, her strong desire to empower her heroines coexisted with her avoidance of openly engaging with gender hierarchy and sexism, despite her intimate knowledge of their presence in the CCP and society.[76] It was not simply Jiang Qing's embrace of a Maoist class concept that restricted her conceptual understanding of gender problems in socialist China. Fundamentally, it was her aspiration to operate in the center of a man's world like a *man* that made her consciously conform to masculinist values and norms. In a masculinist framework, any reference to women would signify lesser value and importance and therefore be detrimental to the portrayal of a powerful heroine. Jiang Qing internalized this framework, which was openly displayed in her interviews with Witke. For example, she conceded that Deng Yingchao and Cai Chang were senior revolutionaries; but, she emphasized, "they are restricted to women-work and can only talk to you about the women's movement. I am different. I am much broader. I can talk about war, the military, politics, literature and the arts, and the Cultural Revolution."[77] Her theatrical heroines, just like herself, had to be detached from the "lesser" realm of women and gender in order to compete with masculine heroes on and off stage in "broader" fields.

Jiang Qing's paradoxical political aspirations were expressed not only in heroines who were exclusively preoccupied with "larger issues" such as class struggle and national salvation but also in her large project of revolutionizing the theater and, by extension, the whole realm of cultural production. She indicted traditional operas because they were immersed in feudal culture and insidiously emitted poisons that would pollute the minds of a socialist people. Certainly she would have recognized the lasting power of "feudalism," an emphasis that was shared by socialist state feminists with a May Fourth New Culture heritage. Combating pernicious and pervasive feudalist influences, one would assume, should be a logical and legitimate subject matter in socialist cultural production. Unfortunately, Jiang Qing's political agenda of marking a distinctive "proletarian line" in the cultural realm that would support Mao's two-line struggle in the political arena required that she indict other works as politically retrograde. She and her allies therefore condemned works with "anti-feudalist" themes as a manifestation of the producers' backward-looking worldview, or even worse, as an expression of bourgeois artists' refusal to represent new socialist characters. Even works such as *Li Shuangshuang,* which celebrated the transformation of gender relations in socialist collective agriculture, were condemned for not depicting class struggle.[78] An exclusive focus on class struggle became a measure of distinguishing works following a "proletarian" line from those following a "revisionist" line. Ironically, in this dichotomous classification that reduced history and society to a two-line struggle, there remained no way to represent and thus condemn gender-inflected "feudalism."

THE IMPLICATIONS OF MODEL THEATERS

The model theaters reveal more than Jiang Qing's conscious drives and unconscious desires. The cluster of model operas also epitomize the strengths and weaknesses of socialist state feminism in the early PRC. Facing a society that was still characterized by hierarchical gender divisions that relegated women to an interior domestic setting, socialist state feminists concentrated on breaking gender barriers in the public domain and transforming gender norms that constrained women's entrance into the public sphere. Their promotion of women's participation in all aspects of socialist China was powerful and effective largely because it dovetailed with the demands for human resources in the socialist modernization project as envisioned by the CCP leadership. This process was accomplished by profound institutional and cultural changes in gender norms and gendered subjectivities, a process in which state feminists' conscious and visionary efforts in cultural production played a significant role.

Yet socialist state feminists rarely engaged in comprehensive evaluation and theoretical critique of masculinist expressions in socialist China. There were many moments when they would name deeply entrenched masculinist mentality and behaviors as "feudalist"; however, the tumultuous history of the Communist Revolution and socialist state formation did not grant them the political and intellectual space to further that line of criticism and develop conceptual frameworks for analyzing the problems inherent in a male-dominated socialist revolution, including their own relations to the male-dominated power center. Participation in socialist revolution as the road to women's liberation was rarely problematized at a conceptual level from a gender perspective, though tactics to combat sexism in and outside the Party were frequently generated in everyday practices. When a gender-inflected "anti-feudalist" agenda in socialist cultural production was discontinued and denounced in the first-couple's project of "continuous revolution," the possibilities of a sharp feminist critique of patriarchal masculinity became even more remote. The heroines represented in film and theater succeeded in occupying center stage in socialist China, just as Jiang Qing did. But without a profound feminist cultural transformation of masculinist minds as well as the rules of the game sustaining a masculinist power structure, these strong heroines and the powerful Jiang Qing stood on shaky grounds.

The vulnerability of Jiang Qing and her theatrical heroines became apparent once her powerful husband exited the scene. In a political coup in

October 1976, less than a month after Mao's death, Jiang Qing was arrested and imprisoned while the Party Central had a mausoleum built for its departed chairman and vowed to uphold Mao's banner. She became a convenient scapegoat, bearing responsibility for crimes committed by many people, including her husband and herself but extending far beyond their circles, during the Cultural Revolution. The accumulated masculinist hostility toward powerful women, whether in real life or on stage, came to full expression in the subsequent years as intellectuals' condemnation of socialism was marked by a prominent backlash against socialist women's liberation. As the next chapter demonstrates, socialist feminist representations of strong heroines were condemned as symbolizing the CCP's ultra-leftist "masculinization" of Chinese women. Instead of reviving a gender-inflected "anti-feudalist" agenda that was suppressed by Maoist class struggle, reactionary efforts promoted "real femininity" and gender differentiation in public discourse to achieve a decisive departure from socialism and the fervent embrace of a capitalist modernity.[79]

EIGHT

The Iron Girls

GENDER AND CLASS IN CULTURAL
REPRESENTATIONS

THE IRON GIRLS, A POWERFUL female icon that emerged in 1964 and quickly became a supersign of socialist women's liberation, takes on a very different meaning in post-socialist China. As this chapter demonstrates, the rapid transition of the Iron Girls in the 1980s from positive to negative symbol of Chinese womanhood parallels the shift from socialist to capitalist ideals of gender, class, and ethnicity. This examination of the symbolic meanings of the Iron Girls in the two periods intends to shed light on both socialist state feminist accomplishments and post-socialist class realignment and social reconfiguration, for the Iron Girls encapsulate not only gender, but also other categories of social disparities: class and place (rural / urban spatial hierarchy).

Moreover, I argue that the fact that socialist state feminists' struggles are largely unknown in the post-socialist world is only partially explained by the politics of concealment practiced by them in the socialist period. Rather, I intend to bring into full view the effectiveness of a political assault against socialist women's liberation launched by urban elites to further their gender, class, and urban interests, in which the Iron Girls became the symbol of "masculinization" of women in the socialist period. This discursive maneuver powerfully operated in a *politics of erasure,* erasing a socialist feminist history, and constituted a crucial part in the production of a post- (and anti-) socialist hegemonic discourse that enabled China's dramatic turn to capitalism, a process marked by the naturalization, legitimation, and reproduction of class, gender, and rural / urban hierarchies.[1]

THE MEANINGS OF THE IRON GIRLS IN
SOCIALIST CHINA

Although the Iron Girls are best known as symbolic figures, they were by no means fictional characters, but rather actual young women who took on physically demanding work in either agriculture or heavy industry during socialist construction. This name was initially chosen by a brigade of adolescent girls in a model village of collective agriculture, Dazhai, and then emulated nationwide when it was promoted by the socialist state. The first Iron Girl Brigade appeared in Dazhai, Shanxi Province, in 1963, when the village suffered severe destruction by a flood.[2] Twenty-three adolescent girls ranging in age from thirteen to sixteen formed a youth task force to join male villagers old and young in salvaging crops, rebuilding collapsed cave houses, and restoring destroyed terraced farmland around the mountain village. On an exceptionally cold day when they were at work restoring collapsed terraces, their village head, Chen Yonggui (1915–1986), told the girls to go home early. But the girls replied, "Since the men do not go home, we will not go home, either. Why should we go back first?" Their strong determination and their remarkable ability to endure hardship won them a compliment from Chen Yonggui: "You girls are made of iron!"[3] The praise circulated among the villagers, and the girls proudly named themselves the Iron Girls Brigade. That year Dazhai had a big harvest despite the severe natural disaster, thanks to the collective efforts of villagers.

Long recognized as a local model village in socialist collectivized agriculture, Dazhai rose to national prominence in 1964 after the Shanxi provincial head reported to Mao on Dazhai's stunning accomplishments. Mao was deeply impressed with the Dazhai farmers' self-reliance in transforming the poor mountainous village into a thriving collective community without material support from the state, as well as the remarkable leadership capacity of their illiterate leader, Chen Yonggui. Mao announced that agriculture production everywhere should model itself after Dazhai, that is, emulating Dazhai villagers' tenacious self-reliance.[4] When Dazhai became the national model for agriculture, it was featured in national publicity. The stories of the Iron Girls Brigade played a prominent part in these depictions of Dazhai's amazing accomplishments, and the seventeen-year-old brigade leader Guo Fenglian instantly became a national celebrity. Photos of energetic adolescent girls engaging in various physically demanding farming tasks defined the phrase "Iron Girls" in the public mind (fig. 26).[5]

FIGURE 26. The Iron Girls Brigade in Dazhai. Courtesy of Dazhai.

As Gail Hershatter's work on rural women in northern China during the 1950s demonstrates, poor women often had to take on tasks normally reserved for men when able-bodied men were drafted in large numbers in times of war.[6] But, because traditional gender norms associated women's domestic seclusion with chastity, poor women who had to work in the fields were doubly degraded by the intertwined social hierarchies of class and gender. Across China's vast geographic area and its diverse ethnic cultures, the gender division of labor varied tremendously. But physical labor performed by women—or even by men—historically marked a lower-class standing, especially among the majority Han Chinese.

Socialism transformed the meanings of women's involvement in agricultural work by glorifying their participation in collectivized agriculture and rewarding those who demonstrated the capacity and skills to take on tasks that were locally defined as male, a significant transformative process initiated by socialist state feminists. As discussed in previous chapters, the ACWF's magazine *Women of China* had played a pioneering role in using media to acknowledge rural women's contribution to socialist construction and to promote women's entrance into traditionally male spaces and occupations. Before the emergence of the term Iron Girls, women's task forces in rural collective agricultural work most commonly adopted the names of legendary heroines who had excelled in the performance of male roles, mostly in military affairs, such as Hua Mulan and Mu Guiying. Such stories were often featured in *Women of China* as a common discursive practice to combat social hierarchies of class, gender, and rural/urban distinction. Socialist filmmaking also paid increasing attention to rural women's remarkable role in collectivized agriculture.[7] The 1962 award-winning film *Li Shuangshuang,* an artistic representation of a rural woman activist in collectivized agriculture based on the stories of many rural women activists, made the protagonist a household name in China.[8] Li Shuangshuang literally became a role model for many rural women who admired her courageous devotion to developing socialist villages. This was the cultural milieu in China when the teenage girls in Dazhai expressed their enthusiasm in collective work and refused to be taken as lesser than men.

The socialist state feminist vision of breaking down gender barriers through women's full integration into all spheres of life dovetailed with the state's need for female labor in rural development, especially during the Great Leap Forward when many rural men moved into industrial work. "Liberation of women's productivity" as a slogan was promoted by the major official media beyond *Women of China,* and resulted in a "great leap" in women's participation in agriculture. As Hershatter emphasized, rural women's labor continued to be an indispensable part of socialist construction through the Mao years, as well as the foundation of economic growth in the post-Mao era. In short, by 1963 rural women commonly took on strenuous physical labor without being stigmatized. Rather, rural women's work lives were celebrated and their agency highlighted in dominant socialist cultural representation.

Dazhai had a somewhat different historical trajectory since women there had a high level of participation in agriculture at least since the 1930s–early 1940s, when the war of resistance against the Japanese invasion required most of its able-bodied men to join the war effort. One of the Iron Girls, Jia Cunsuo, recalled: "Why were the Iron Girls so famous? What happened to male youth? . . . Those whom the Japanese killed and drafted were all young men. After the liberation, those who joined the army or went out to work were also mainly male comrades. . . . Therefore, female comrades in Dazhai seemed more prominent than male comrades. Actually, most male comrades left the village for employment outside."[9] In this village women had long been playing the major role in farm labor as well as in all kinds of economic activities in and outside the household. What changed in this village was not women's involvement in physical labor but the meanings of working in fields collectively.

The remarkable strength and tenacity that Dazhai women exhibited in performing physically demanding farmwork made a vivid impression on county officials who had been required to work in the fields for one month each year during the 1950s. Zhao Mancang remembered leading a team of male county officials in 1959. They followed men in the fields for about ten days but then became physically unable to continue. So Chen Yonggui suggested that they work instead with the women. Zhao vividly recounted the episode:

> Originally we thought working with women in the fields would be less strenuous, but actually women's labor was more intense. . . . Dazhai women had a particular habit while working in the fields. They did not chat and often continued working without any break. So following women in the fields for one week was even worse than before. Some in our team had such severe bodily pains that they could not sleep at night. Our county judge did not even have the strength to hold his bowl after a day's work in the fields. He dropped his bowl in the canteen.[10]

Performing challenging physical labor in the fields was the norm for Dazhai women who were responsible for their family's survival in the poor mountainous area. Decades later, the leader of the Iron Girls Brigade, Guo Fenglian, recalled their goals at that time: "To work hard to produce more grain so that we would be able to fill up our stomachs; and that would also be our contribution to socialism."[11]

What made the Iron Girls special was the national attention bestowed upon them by the socialist state after Mao's call to learn from Dazhai. Guo Fenglian was rapidly promoted, especially during the Cultural Revolution when promoting young women from the working class was a more pronounced practice, a response to Jiang Qing's prominent role in the power center. When the head of their village, Chen Yonggui, was promoted to the position of vice premier of the State Council in 1973, Guo succeeded him as

FIGURE 27. Guo Fenglian (holding Zhou's right arm) meets Zhou Enlai in 1973. Courtesy of Dazhai.

the head of Dazhai and then was placed on the county, provincial, and national leading bodies. She was received by Mao three times and met Premier Zhou Enlai many more times (fig. 27). Letters of admiration from all over China flooded her home, and she had to ask her team members to join her in replying to each of them. Signifying the new socialist identity as a rural woman who was no longer confined by her traditional kinship obligations or her lowly peasant social position, but instead defined by her superb contribution to collective agriculture and her excellent leadership capacity, the Iron Girl Guo Fenglian became a symbol of rural women's double liberation from gender and class constraints. Other groups of young women, including those in heavy industry, emulated the Iron Girls Brigade, consolidating the theme

FIGURE 28. Cover of *People's Pictorial,* 1976, no. 1. Guo Fenglian and her team member.

of challenging gender boundaries and transforming gender and class hierarchies as well as the rural / urban distinction that had been promoted by socialist state feminists since the founding of the PRC.[12] The widespread formation of Iron Girls brigades in this sense can be seen as the coming-of-age of a generation of women whose subjectivities were interpolated by socialist state feminism (fig. 28).

Gayatri Chakravorty Spivak in her famous essay "Can the Subaltern Speak?" delineates the power dynamics involved in "muted women's" entry into the system of signification and posits the many barriers that subaltern speech encounters.[13] The representation of Chinese rural women in the socialist period also involved multiple power relations and heterogeneous agendas. Rather than claiming that socialist representations of rural women conveyed the unmediated voices of subaltern subjects, I argue that the subaltern was not passively inscribed with official language but actively authorized the efficacy of socialist state feminist language, such as equality between men and women and women's liberation, which facilitated their entry into the socialist symbolic system as well as empowered them in everyday practices.[14] Moreover, the positive representation of laboring women in the official media had empowering effects on women who had previously been absent from cultural representations of China's drive for modernity. The difference between the image of a female victim of feudal oppression like Xianglin's Wife in Xia Yan's film discussed previously, which stood as the Other of the modern, and the Iron Girls, who signified women's agency and prominent role in socialist modernity, is significant. So is the fact that the story of Xianglin's Wife was written and rewritten by men to represent their desire to modernize Chinese society, while the Iron Girls both embodied a new socialist feminist gender subjectivity in the pursuit of socialist modernity and with their own bodies further authorized their inscription in the development of socialist feminist ideology. The fact that they physically *owned* the symbol of the Iron Girls makes a post-socialist denigration most problematic and revealing.

GENDER AND CLASS IN POST-SOCIALIST CRITIQUES OF SOCIALIST WOMEN'S LIBERATION

The CCP's Third Plenum of the Eleventh Central Committee in 1978 marked a major turning point in Chinese history, bringing to an end the Maoist socialist revolution. With this the symbol of Iron Girls took on new meaning. No longer glorified, the Iron Girls were now disparaged as representing the "masculinization" of Chinese women. Because in their politics of concealment, socialist state feminists had rarely if ever claimed the authorship of their projects, policies, and practices for gender equality, it was easy for critics to label all socialist gender practices as the deeds of the authoritarian rule of a Maoist state. In fact, such a monolithic conceptualization of the Maoist state has predominated not only among Chinese intellectuals but also in the field of Chinese studies outside China. Its persistent power suggests how power relations and political interests are intimately entangled in knowledge production. The criticism that denounces socialist women's liberation in the framework of anti-Maoism illustrates the workings of political and class interest groups to cover up an extremely complex historical process.

Responding to the CCP's call for "ideological emancipation," Chinese intellectuals and artists, in an extraordinary proliferation of literature, films, artistic performances, and polemical essays, voiced their condemnation of the Cultural Revolution and the CCP's "ultra-leftist line." In 1979 a comic dialogue performance (*xiangsheng*) entitled *The Iron Girls* gained instant popularity as it relentlessly mocked those young women who had excelled at physical labor and enjoyed prominent media attention prior to the end of the Cultural Revolution. Signifying a dramatic shift in the public discourse of women's liberation, the comic dialogue ushered in a powerful backlash against revolutionary gender ideology and practices of equality between women and men and advocated the replacement of so-called gender sameness with gender differentiation.[15] Gender again loomed large as a pivot at a major historical turning point.

In the name of condemning the Maoist "ultra-leftist line," the attack on the Iron Girls conceals the intense contentions over gender and the class realignment that marked China after 1979. Seemingly initiated by intellectuals and artists on their own, the attack on the Iron Girls was nevertheless a response to political changes mandated by the Communist Party's Central Committee. Deng Xiaoping had called for a "thorough denunciation of the Cultural Revolution" and the abandonment of rural collectivization, including the flagship village of Dazhai; this gave the green light to the expression of gender sentiments drastically opposed to the views of socialist feminists. At no time did the Party condemn the Iron Girls openly, although Guo Fenglian, an inconvenient reminder of the glory of Dazhai, was removed from all her leading positions in 1980 and disappeared from the limelight for almost two decades.[16] The choice of a specific gendered target, the Iron Girls, and the accusation of women's masculinization, if not "official ideology," were the expressions of intellectuals of the post-Mao era and its meaning is uncovered by examining their class and gender interests in the social-historical context of that particular moment.

It is clear that the image of the Iron Girls aroused fear and anxiety in many urban elite men. As the actor in the comic dialogue *The Iron Girls* declared, he would never dare to marry an Iron Girl because he would be afraid that she might flatten him with a random swing of one of her overly muscled arms.[17] Proclaiming their aversion, rather than attraction, to the strong women depicted in socialist visual and literary culture soon became a popular theme in urban men's writings. Literary men would proudly confess that while watching socialist films or reading socialist novels they had never been attracted to the revolutionary heroines who could perform extraordinary tasks but whose sex appeal was downplayed. Instead, they found themselves attracted to the sexy female spies or other counterrevolutionaries, which made them feel uncomfortably guilty. One even claimed that being unable to openly express his attraction to sexy women, who were represented as reactionaries or degenerates, was a form of sexual repression by the socialist state.[18]

In their study of changing gender discourses during the 1980s, historians Emily Honig and Gail Hershatter point out that the backlash against the Iron Girls was primarily "manmade." A group of male scholars attending a meeting on the status of women in 1986 declared themselves particularly revolted by the idea that women should be masculinized and become "iron women." According to these male scholars, "A woman who becomes masculine is a mutant. Capable women should be different from men. They have their own special charm, for example exquisiteness and depth of emotions, and well-developed imagistic thinking."[19] Educated urban men's heterosexual desire was not merely unfulfilled but seemingly threatened by prevailing images of strong women who could outperform men. Condemning the Iron Girls is thus only a sign of the entangled dynamics of sexual, gender, and class politics set in motion by the socialist revolution. In contrast with elite men's call for strong women "with the character of men" at the start of the twentieth century,[20] we may treat late twentieth-century elite men's stated fear of strong women as an index of historical change in which a critical mass of strong women had actually emerged in the public realm rather than merely existing in men's fantasies about modern women.

Elite men's complaints extended beyond the so-called masculinization of women, however, to the claim that men had also been "de-gendered," in their case by emasculation. Literary scholar Xueping Zhong, in her path-breaking study of Chinese elite men's representation of masculinity in the 1980s, analyzes the myth of *yinsheng yangshuai,* that is, a widespread discursive construction of a "women-are-too-strong-and-men-are-too-weak phenomenon" and identifies a male "marginality complex."[21] In the 1980s, she argues, literary men's writings centered on their painful experience of "castration" by the Maoist regime, which made intellectuals "impotent" politically, economically, and sexually.[22] Male intellectuals' protest against a Maoist authoritarian political system was often charged with sexual imagery, and pursuing sexual potency became a major performative act of the elite in the effort to achieve a masculine identity. Indeed, because the Maoist state monitored the sexual mores of citizens, taking on a sexual libertarian stance also indicated their avant-garde, anti-authoritarian, and anti-socialist position. Ironically, with the mandate of dismantling Maoism in the name of moving China toward modernity, elite men's blatantly misogynist language and sexist proposals were justified as a progressive stance against the so-called ultra-leftist imposition of gender equality on the Chinese people by an authoritarian regime.

Literary men were not alone in condemning this putative masculinization of women and emasculation of men. Social scientists joined them in this discourse when advancing their arguments for a state-commanded market economy. Starting in the 1980s, many male sociologists and economists engaged in concerted attacks on socialist equal employment policies and promoted a restoration of gender differentiation (*nannü youbie*), that posits that women's roles as mother, wife, and daughter are expressions of their "natural femininity."[23] The double deployment of a key principle in Confucian social hierarchy, that is, gender differentiation, and a key principle in some Western scientific texts that had been translated into Chinese in the early twentieth century, that of an essentialized "femininity" (*nüxing tezhi*), epitomizes the reactionary outlook of many male intellectuals in the late twentieth century. But these conservative and outdated gender ideologies were repackaged as bold challenges to an egalitarian gender regime in a dictatorial state, gaining them an avant-garde status in "ideological emancipation."

In an article published in the prestigious academic journal *Sociological Studies,* Zheng Yefu argued that contemporary China was falling far behind developed countries in terms of the level of a knowledge economy, as well as the level of social and material wealth. At the same time, he pointed out that Chinese women's liberation surpassed all countries in the world in terms of women's equal employment and equal pay. Deploring what he viewed as a cause-and-effect situation, Zheng offered a critique that condensed key elements in the backlash against socialist women's liberation:

> The immediate consequence of a government-enforced women's liberation "outpacing" [*chaoqian*] socioeconomic development is dysfunctional family relations. . . . We have failed to explore a new gender division of labor in family life **because, through supporting the weak and suppressing the strong, a strong administrative power has interfered and destroyed the normal division of labor between the strong and the weak in the family.** It has even made the weak mistakenly think they are not weak, and made the

strong lose confidence in themselves. **Ultimately, it has deprived Chinese society of "real men." . . . A women's liberation promoted by politics has also made China lose its women.**[24] (bold in original)

Zheng Yefu was among many vociferous male intellectuals who expressed a strong interest in reviving "normal" gendered power relations that had been disrupted by socialism. Other arguments condemning gender equality circulating widely include examples such as these: "equality of outcome should be the natural consequence of equality of opportunity and its realization should not rely on social movements" (Pan Jintang);[25] socialist women's liberation "outpaced" the low level of productivity; because women's physical characteristics made them less adaptable to various job requirements, excessive employment of women reduced enterprise efficiency; the helping that women took from the socialist "big rice pot" exceeded the value of the quantity and quality of their work (Chang Leren);[26] the "egalitarian" ideal of equality between men and women violated the law of value, thus it ought to be abandoned in the commodity economy; a new equality between men and women should not be expressed in rights and distribution but should be in the exchange of value between men and women; females can best express their values in the service sector, as secretaries and in public relations (Zhang Xiaosong);[27] in order to pursue the principle of efficiency, the social division of labor should be determined according to sex differences between men and women; for the sake of national development and the "takeoff" of China's economy, Chinese women should learn from Japanese women to return home and sacrifice themselves for the nation (Feng Chujun).[28] Male elites' concerted demand to restore pre-socialist gender norms compelled a male sociologist, Pan Suiming, to give this explanation: "Since 1980 society has promoted a good-wife-and-virtuous-mother and harmonious family ideal because during the prior thirty years, especially under the attack on society in the Cultural Revolution, Chinese men tenaciously guarded the family and protected women; now they request compensation from women."[29]

Just as Xueping Zhong's analyses of novels written by men in the 1980s demonstrate that criticisms of the authoritarian state were saturated by men's desires for an imagined masculinity, condemnations of socialist egalitarian ideology and gender equality policies by male sociologists and economists were also charged with their desires to restore elite men's gender and class privileges. That view was expressed unambiguously by Zheng Yefu, who used the American economist George Gilder's *Wealth and Poverty* to echo his own ultimate concern: "In the welfare culture, money has become not something earned by men's hard work but a right to women offered by the state.... Nothing can be more damaging to men's value than increasingly recognizing that his wife and children could live better without him." Resisting the "damage" inflicted by a socialist welfare state legitimized a righteous condemnation of a draconian form of women's liberation that "beat men back into the family to become 'housewives' and drove women into society to become 'strong persons,' and eventually destroyed men's masculinity and women's tenderness, degenerating into a 'neutered' or 'asexual' state."[30] Restoring women to domesticity would not only improve productivity but, more importantly, guarantee the strengthening of masculinity.

The dominant masculinist sentiment propagated since the 1980s not only expresses a backward-looking desire to revive Confucian spatial gender differentiation (*nanzhuwai, nüzhunei*)—men should manage "the outside," or public space, while women should be in charge of "the inside" domestic space—but also articulates a new brand of nationalism by promising to enhance China's potency in the world. "Where Are the Masculine Men," the theme song of a popular TV show *Husbands' Variations* (*zhangfu bianzouqu*) written by a famous male playwright, Sha Yexin, in 1990, declared that taking on any household chores diminished Chinese men's masculinity. "If a country has no masculine aspiration, how can it shake the world?"[31] Thus the crucial mechanism for realizing the dream of China's shaking the world is to remove women from gainful employment and send them back to the kitchen. While none of these intellectuals had any concept of gender as an analytical category, their schemes of grandeur of a powerful China were nevertheless imbued with gender ideologies. A new nationalist dream was charged with desire for a hypermasculine sexual and political potency, as well as for gender privileges, as male elites eagerly immersed themselves in global capitalism. As an inconvenient symbol that signified the dismantling of both gender and class hierarchies, the Iron Girls acutely disturbed this elite masculine dream, so it was banished, along with an egalitarian social and economic system permeated with socialist feminist practices.

Perplexingly, some educated urban women also condemned the Iron Girls and Chinese women's "masculinization," although their critique of socialist women's liberation was not a wholesale negation. Educated urban women in the late twentieth century generally insisted that Chinese women were more socially advanced than women in Western capitalist countries and admitted that they were the beneficiaries of socialist gender equality policies.[32] Their criticisms centered on the measurement of women's liberation against male standards, as the often-quoted saying of Mao illustrates: "The times are different now. Whatever male comrades can do, female comrades can do, too." As these women saw it, socialist gender equality was defined as gender sameness to the extent that women's "natural femininity" was suppressed. As a consequence, women were no longer feminine, but became desexualized and neutered (*feixinghua, zhongxinghua*). Moreover, that which injured "delicate" female bodies was not only the double burden of paid labor and household chores but also the demanding—and demeaning—physical labor required of women as epitomized in the campaigns promoting emulation of the Iron Girls.

A popular short story by a woman writer, Zhang Xinxin, entitled "Where Did I Miss You?," published in 1980, depicts an educated urban woman's painful realization of her "masculinization" through the eyes of the man she loved but failed to attract. In this story of complex and contradictory meanings, the author unambiguously attributed her process of "masculinization" to her having performed physically demanding work in a rural village. Contrary to Pan Suiming's claim that men gallantly protected women, Zhang deplores the lack of "strong men." Alluding to her experience of being sent down to a mountain village during the Cultural Revolution, Zhang used these vivid flashbacks to describe the protagonist's "masculinizing process":

> She carries water on the tortuous path along the mountain cliffs, the slightest loss of balance would spill the water into yellow dirt without a trace. . . .
> She carries a gunnysack over fifty kilos toward a stack, moving up step by step with all her strength, her teeth set. . . .
> In a decade when one was most attentive to one's appearance, she had only a few blue clothes to change into; and worrying about growing increasingly busty, she deliberately hunched her shoulders.[33]

If Guo Fenglian and her team members were reading these memories in 1980, they would recognize them as a realistic description of their daily hard work and poverty during the 1960s. Guo Fenglian did not even have decent clothes without patches in 1965 when Zhou Enlai made the first visit to Dazhai. She had to borrow a new blouse from her friend in order to host the national leader. These Iron Girls might also agree with Zhang's description of covering one's breasts, which reflected a traditional notion of women's chastity that demanded concealing both a woman's body and expressions of sexuality. But they would not have imagined the cultural meaning Zhang gave to these "realistic" flashbacks, although Zhang's meaning would have been instantly recognizable to educated urban women in the 1980s.

Literary scholar Li Xiaojiang articulates the significance in such literary representations: "The image of masculinized women often appears in contemporary women writers' works. They do not eulogize it, but express their secret anguish. On the one hand they interrogate the tendency toward women's masculinization; and on the other hand they imply condemnation of the ultra-leftist ideologies and an era of no-females."[34] Here we discern a criticism shared by women and men writers of the supposed "ultra-leftist masculinization of women." In strikingly similar language to that used by Zheng Yefu, Li follows Zhang's argument to identify the "damage done to a whole generation of women" in a "twisted era." The similarity stops there, however. The damage to women was not to their sense of value, like the damage to men's self-esteem in Zheng Yefu's portrayal. For Li Xiaojiang, it was rather that "women experienced their adolescence without youth, and experienced a hard life without pursuing beauty and without experiencing tenderness. Now the loss of youth and emotional life of adolescence was imbedded in their deep psychological structures, affecting their courtship, marriage, and even family life."[35] "A hard life," therefore, constituted a crucial factor in depriving the femininity of "beauty" and "tenderness" of the unspecified generic "women."

It is important here to consider a particular kind of criticism of socialist women's liberation that since the 1990s has gained wide circulation among feminist scholars outside China, especially among those in the field of China studies. Feminist academics in the United States, while making conscious efforts to deconstruct Eurocentric or U.S.-centered knowledge production, are now paying special attention to "native voices," especially in the so-called "Third World." Informed by post-colonial criticism, this well-intentioned feminist agenda may nonetheless overlook the specific historical context within which women's "native" voices are articulated and the locally situated power relations in knowledge production. With neither a critical awareness of the historical context in which the Chinese elite produced knowledge nor a critical framework to delineate the intense class reconfiguration going on in China's historical turn from socialism to capitalism, a feminist respect for what are imagined as native voices has led to an uncritical facilitation of the global circulation of some Chinese educated urban women's thesis that women have been masculinized by an authoritarian state's strategy for women's liberation. Unfortunately, this has become an accepted truth both in and outside China, constituting a major theme in the public memory of socialism. English-language scholarship on women in China often adopted problematic terms such as "gender erasure" and "the masculinization of Chinese women" to define the effects of socialist gender policies, rather than treating them as signs of discursive maneuvers that emerged in an era of intensely contested power relations between and among gender and class that needed to be unpacked and interrogated.[36]

What was the historical context within which some urban women literary scholars and novelists embraced the notion of masculinization? On what grounds can I claim that these concepts were an urban elite's discursive construction? The original Iron Girls, Guo Fenglian and her team members, never used the term masculinization to describe the effects of their heavy manual labor. Women shouldering physical labor in the fields as well as domestic toil has been the norm of Chinese rural society in the PRC, at least since the beginning of the Great Leap Forward. Women's physical labor has been associated with their earning capacity (earning more or fewer work points in the era of collectivization, or producing more or fewer agricultural commodities in the recent era of privatization and marketization), and hence an important factor contributing to their family's financial status.[37] There is no evidence that rural women and men have ever worried that women would be masculinized by performing physical labor, even though women have increasingly taken on previously male tasks out of sheer necessity in a changing economic environment.

Indeed, the evidence shows that rural women have continued to express pride in being able to do "whatever men can do" in total unawareness of the urban elites' discourse of masculinization. A 1995 feminist intervention project in Yunnan distributed digital cameras to village women so they could take photographs of scenes and subjects that interested them. The resulting photo album powerfully conveys Yunnan rural women's demanding physical work in both agricultural production and domestic reproduction. Most agricultural tasks women performed in this region demand great physical strength but are obviously regarded as women's normal work. The captions of several photos specifically note that now women can do things that previously only men were allowed to do, such as fishing, threshing grain, and driving an ox cart. Even as the photos recognize that rural women experience hardship, the photos also emphasize women's important contribution to the rural economy and family livelihoods.[38] The outcry against women's masculinization by taking on men's jobs and the language of "masculinization" were definitely not shared by, or even transmitted to, millions of rural Iron Girls.

Even more revealingly, urban elite women and men have not expressed any concern about *rural* women's "masculinization" during the accelerated feminization of agriculture in recent decades with the privatization of rural economy and outmigration of rural men. The silence today on rural women's burdensome responsibilities in a privatized economy contrasts sharply with the outcry in the 1980s against the "masculinization of women" by the socialist state policy of gender equality. This striking contrast has two possible explanations. First, the intensity of rural women's physical labor may never have been the concern of those urban elite who worried about women's masculinization, so there is no contradiction in their current silence. Second, the thesis of the masculinization of women was situated in the political context of anti-socialism, and the decisively changed economic, social, and cultural milieu in twenty-first-century China has eliminated the motivation to continue this discursive device that, after all, has already effectively done its work to reshape the dominant gender discourse. In any case, the 1980s discourse protesting the masculinization of Chinese women should be situated and interpreted in relation to debates regarding gender and class relations in the elite pursuit of a capitalist modernity.

Chinese women's bodies have always been a focal point of elites' contention at moments of drastic social change. From the late Qing reformers' agitation against foot-binding, the early Republican-era feminists' endorsement of physical education as a way to strengthen women's bodies, the 1930s feminists' and nationalists' advocacy of robust beauty, to the PRC socialist state feminists' promotion of strong, heroic women that culminated in the celebration of the Iron Girls in the mid-1960s and heroines in the "model operas," physically strong women remained the ideal type in dominant discourses of Chinese modernity. Moreover, after the initial eugenic emphasis on producing healthy sons, the primary rationale for building up women's physical strength was to enable them to enter what had been an exclusively men's world.[39]

What, then, made the post-Mao urban elite women reject this heritage by deploying an essentialist notion of sex to disparage women's performance of physically demanding tasks? If the discursive device was directed at an authoritarian state's monopoly of gender policies, why were other lines of analysis of the shortcomings of socialist women's liberation foreclosed? What political context enabled this particular critique, rather than other narratives about socialist women's liberation that were available at the same time, to gain traction domestically and transnationally? We must take a closer look at the political context of women intellectuals' discursive practices at that time.

Women intellectuals in the 1980s certainly shared the political agenda of deconstructing the Maoist state with their male counterparts. The "ideological emancipation" campaign was a discursive maneuver by which post-Mao intellectuals broke free from a Maoist class categorization that had defined intellectuals as "class enemies" during the Cultural Revolution. With the end of the socialist revolution, senior or newly minted intellectuals who offered various proposals to steer China away from authoritarian socialism were not only condemning the CCP dictatorship under Mao, but also paving their material passage to social ascendancy. While their condemnations of the damage caused by Mao's (mis)use of class in political struggles were mostly pertinent, their total rejection of the utility of class as an analytical category for examining deeply entrenched social hierarchy and power relations in Chinese society, coupled with their passionate commitment to demolishing an egalitarian ideology and redistribution system, reveals their class standing and their desire to revive intellectuals' privileges as a social elite. In place of the now-detested Maoist class struggle, intellectuals propagated a myth of a value-free scientific knowledge as the panacea to cure the ills of a socialist system and to move China onto the track of "global"—or, rather, neoliberalist—modernity. Demonstrating their full collaboration with the new CCP leadership's agenda to depoliticize a severe political rupture, intellectuals' widespread deployment of "scientific theories" in all fields successfully reinstated their elite position as experts while camouflaging a historical process of class realignment replete with power dynamics of gender, place, and ethnicity.[40] It was against this particular background that naturalizing femininity and masculinity emerged as a scientific truth from biology and psychology (constituted largely of translated texts published before 1949 and discredited in the West in the second half of the twentieth century) that would help Chinese to recover the "human nature" that had been distorted by the Maoist dictatorship.

For some women intellectuals, theorizing a biologically determined femininity prior to and beyond the realm of the social and political was also a political strategy to detach gender issues from a Maoist class analysis.[41] Joining male intellectuals in abandoning class as a valid analytical category, women intellectuals also had no qualms about presenting natural femininity as well as their discursive claim on it as free of class inflection. By condemning a patriarchal state's suppression of gender issues with a theoretical pillar of a naturalized femininity, women critics produced a discourse of universal womanhood bound by biology.

Women intellectuals' complicity with male elites in redefining the Iron Girls as the symbol of socialist masculinization of women did not simply pry open a discursive space to discuss gender issues free from Maoist class dominance. It also became part of the process of *class* realignment at that moment of profound political rupture. Class tensions and power dynamics in the socialist period were conveniently glossed over by a "scientific" accusation of masculinization. Urban elite women's aversion to the recent experience of being sent to villages or factories to take on manual labor found an elevated feminist expression in denouncing the socialist state's suppression of women's femininity and erasure of sexual difference. A telling moment to illustrate this point can be found in a documentary film when an urban woman adopts the dominant language to claim that she was so masculinized by years of hard work in the rural areas that she even "grew muscles on her arms." [42] The ability to claim a delicate and tender natural femininity has signified a privileged social status that shields a woman from physical labor, conventionally a prominent marker of lower-class status. Some educated urban women deployed the language of "masculinization" not only to perform a newly defined femininity but more importantly to differentiate themselves from the women who still had to engage in physical labor. Co-opted by a market economy, their naturalized femininity has also been pervasively expressed in women's ability to consume dazzling feminine products. In post-socialist China, gender differentiation has resumed its historic function as a marker of class distinctions manifested in a woman's relationship to physical labor and consumption.

CODA

When being interviewed by a Beijing TV talk show host in 2012, Guo Fenglian, now the CEO of Dazhai Conglomerates with assets over 1.7 billion yuan, attempted to refute urban elites' denigration of the Iron Girls by saying, "We are also made of flesh and bones, not iron." She never deploys the term "masculinization," a fact that suggests her rural identity and her conscious rejection of the hegemonic gender discourse in the post-socialist era. With an ironic twist, the Iron Girl who was silenced for over twenty years has triumphantly returned to the limelight with a new identity as the CEO of a major enterprise. Owing much to the cultural capital Dazhai gained in the socialist period, as well as her personal reputation and leadership capacity honed since adolescence, Guo led Dazhai from a rural village of collective agriculture to a diversified conglomerate owned by Dazhai villagers collectively. Hailed by the media as accomplishing a "magnificent turn from an Iron Girl to an Iron Lady," [43] Guo's success in the market economy enabled her to resume her membership in the Standing Committee of the National Congress and gain discursive power in an era when power is the prerogative of the rich. [44] In interviews on TV and in print media, she has consciously utilized her regained discursive power to inform the public of a glorious history of Dazhai's collectivization and the Iron Girls' tremendous contribution to the village's development, tactfully refuting all the public denigrations launched against both Dazhai and the Iron Girls in the post-Mao era. Even when the young TV host, cast in the typical image of sexualized modern femininity, exclaims, with a tinge of condescending sympathy, that Guo's hands feel hardened and coarse, Guo is unapologetic about this proof of the hard physical labor she performed in her youth. With dignity and pride, she presents a powerful narrative of a meaningful youth. [45] The reemergence of the real Iron Girl with discursive power presents a significant crack in the long-solidified discursive sediment regarding the "socialist masculinization of women." [46]

By the time Guo Fenglian reappeared in public, both gendered discursive terrains and social practices had changed in significant ways. Gender differentiation has become the hallmark of a market economy in which abundant feminine commodities lavishly package a modern femininity embodied in omnipresent images of young sexy women celebrities. Gender differentiation has also been prominently displayed in gender stratification in employment, with millions of young rural women at the bottom, toiling in sweatshops for the global market, while men predominate in managerial positions. While a rapidly expanding and feminized service industry has provided new employment opportunities to some women, the lack of opportunity for women to rise to positions of power and wealth has led to a dramatically enlarged gender gap in average incomes. The ratio between women's and men's incomes has declined from 0.84 to 1 in 1988 to 0.65 to 1 in 2011; women now earn just two-thirds of men's earnings. [47] Although the result of complex factors, the increasingly gendered class disparity indicates the concrete socioeconomic effects of the elite's discursive demolition of socialist gender equality ideology and practices since the 1980s.

The masculinist discursive maneuver in the 1980s also paved the way for the emergence of a hegemonic masculinity in China's merger with global capitalism. The rapidly rising economic power of China has relieved the male elite of its previous inferiority complex. The dramatic amassing of power and resources in the hands of elite men—Party and state officials, entrepreneurs, and intellectuals—has made the elite men's dream of "potency" come true. One visible indicator of masculine potency is the booming sex industry, as well as the new norm (or rather a revival of polygamy) of keeping multiple mistresses as a sign of success. Through the revelations of Xi Jinping's recent anti-corruption campaign, the public now gets to see that all fallen officials are in possession not only of massive amounts of wealth but also numerous women. Male commentators, either from the right or left, generally express a sense of disgust toward those corrupt officials. But relevant questions about the formation of this particular type of masculinity have not yet emerged in any analysis of the pattern of corruption among male officials. And even though critical reviews of the intense discursive struggles in the 1980s have recently emerged among some Chinese literary scholars, it is still rare to see a self-reflective interrogation of the politics of post-socialist knowledge production in and outside China with critical lenses focused on both gender and class.[48]

Against this intellectual background, the erasure of a history of socialist state feminists is particularly poignant. Iron Girls either continue to symbolize masculinized women under the rule of a Maoist state, or are simply forgotten. For young Chinese women growing up in the post-socialist era, their knowledge of the history of Chinese socialism is basically constituted of the anti-socialist master narrative produced by the urban elite since the 1980s. Chinese socialist state feminist struggles, like the Iron Girls, are either misunderstood or forgotten. A distorted and denigrated recent past can hardly offer anything meaningful to a new generation of Chinese feminists. The consequences of this are revealed in a recent action staged by young feminist activists. In January 2015 a young woman, Ma Hu, sued the Beijing Postal Office for gender discrimination because managers there rejected her job application on the ground that women could not deliver packages.[49] In publicly demonstrating their feminist support of Ma Hu's courageous action, the activists had no Chinese figure or symbol to invoke. In total unawareness of their Chinese feminist foremothers, they turned instead to an American model: Rosie the Riveter!

Conclusion

SOCIALIST STATE FEMINISM AND ITS LEGACIES
IN CAPITALIST CHINA

EXPLORING THE ROLE AND ACTIVITIES of socialist state feminists in China's socialist revolution brings a long-obscured feminist history into relief against the backdrop of dramatic socioeconomic and political transformation. Yet, this study entails more than restoring feminist actors to their rightful place on the historical stage; by examining the historical process during which Chinese women made tremendous social advances in a male-dominated socialist state, we raise new and difficult questions about the power dynamics within the socialist revolution itself and reveal its contradictions, tensions, and antagonisms, as well as the intrinsic flaws in the political party that led the revolution. Feminist aspirations to build a society based on equality and justice in order to achieve women's liberation generated significant transformations in gender norms and gendered subjectivities, but also encountered determined resistance and ferocious hostility. Antagonism along gender lines, a pervasive reality both in social life and in high politics, was among the principal causes of the failure and eventual abandonment of the socialist revolution.

The complexities of that period and severe restrictions on the accessibility of archives defy any attempt at a metanarrative of socialist history. Approaching that era with an analytical focus on how gender functioned in the nexus of power relations, however, is quite productive in peeling away some of the protective shell surrounding the power center and enabling a glimpse of its internal workings. The critical lens to examine the internal struggles centering on gender is no doubt also sharpened by the hindsight of a historian who has observed the tremendous conflicts and power struggles occurring in China over the course of the past three decades since the CCP abandoned its revolutionary agenda. The fierce post-socialist contentions over knowledge production about socialism, and the powerful effects of the dominance of neoliberalism and capitalist consumerism with the endorsement of the ruling CCP, make reexamining socialist state feminist endeavors all the more urgent. This conclusion summarizes the special features of socialist state feminists' struggles in the early PRC, highlights the symbolic meanings of the fall of the feminist cultural front, and reflects on the legacies of socialist state feminism in today's China.

A FEMINIST REVOLUTION ENABLED AND OBSTRUCTED IN SOCIALISM

The first fifteen years of the People's Republic of China witnessed two prominent processes that were made possible by socialist state feminists: the conscious perpetuation of a gender-inflected anti-feudalism agenda that state feminists inherited from May Fourth New Culture feminism, which was manifested in both socialist feminist institutional development and cultural production; and the shift in the feminists' status from revolutionary grassroots organizers to positions within the bureaucracy, even if remaining marginal in the formal power structure of the socialist state. These parallel processes transformed the Chinese society and the Communist Revolution in important ways.

First, the persistent agenda of anti-feudalism was expressed both in the Women's Federation officials' women-work and in the efforts of artist-officials who had been shaped by the New Cultural discourse in their formative years. To generate cultural transformation through cultural production was passionately pursued by a large cohort of May Fourth New Cultural rebels who became power holders and major producers of the socialist cultural apparatus. Not all were consciously feminists, but in the important cultural realm of film industry I have identified two strong top leaders with a clear feminist consciousness, Chen Bo'er and Xia Yan. The transformative cultural production by these and many more feminist artists corresponded with the ACWF's feminist efforts in cultural transformation. Launching concerted battles in different realms, targeting patriarchal gender norms and practices in a grand vision of eliminating a gender-inflected feudalism, socialist state feminists infused an inherited New Culture gender critique with a class consciousness heightened by the theoretical study of Marxism as well as by their revolutionary experiences among the lower classes, whether mingling with women factory workers in the cities or struggling alongside peasant women in the rural areas in wartime. The significant transformations that occurred in gender practices and gendered subjectivities during the first fifteen years of the socialist revolution were as much a result of the institution of gender equality laws and policies and practices in education and employment, especially for urban women, promoted by state feminists, as they were the creation of a socialist gender ideology that aimed to eliminate both gender and class hierarchies by making laboring women the major subject of cultural representation. Revolutionary heroines, who became the paradigm of socialist cinematic and theatrical production, performed powerful ideological work in combating deeply entrenched and long-held cultural assumptions of male supremacy. Extolling Iron Girls in this context was both a continuation and a celebration of the success of socialist state feminism that hailed a young generation who displayed socialist feminist subjectivities by proudly embracing their identity as rural laboring women in socialist construction. The double jeopardy of gender and class was eliminated discursively at least, owing much to socialist state feminists' persistent efforts in empowering laboring women.

The continuation and modification of a May Fourth New Culture agenda of cultural transformation with an anti-feudalist focus expressed feminist officials' and artists' deep understanding of the dominant Chinese gender system signified by the *nannü* [men and women] hierarchical divide. One of their prominent predecessors, the early twentieth-century anarchist and socialist feminist theorist He-Yin Zhen, had articulated penetrating critiques of the cultural structures and social mechanisms of the *nannü* system as well as inspiring visions of women's liberation. Her insistence that "a women's revolution must go hand in hand with an economic revolution" in order to destroy the foundation of male domination was inherited by feminists who joined the Communist Revolution, which promised to accomplish both when the time was right.[1] But nonetheless, the turbulent history of the first half of the twentieth century, while laying the basis for a feminist revolution, presented plausible rationales for the male-dominated CCP to postpone feminist transformation and to posit that an economic revolution must precede a feminist revolution. The outburst of feminist energy in the first few years of the PRC, as well as persistent struggles against sexist norms and practices, expressed socialist state feminists' aspirations to seize the historical moment and their strong awareness that socialist transformation of means of production did not automatically entail the eradication of "feudal remnants."

Gender antagonisms generated within the CCP in the process of feminist-initiated cultural transformation testify to the deeply entrenched character of a male supremacist hierarchical mentality. The power of the male-dominated CCP was never threatened by the ACWF, which was structurally subordinated to the Party and headed by feminist revolutionaries who were characteristically self-effacing rather than self-aggrandizing. Party leaders' disciplinary schemes, quintessentially expressed by the Secretariat in 1957 in their effort to push women back into a traditional domestic role, revealed their unconscious resentment of the disruption of a gender order that sustained male privilege and masculine authority. While many Communist men claimed to embrace egalitarian values, few consciously examined the formation of their own gendered subjectivity. As He-Yin Zhen's insightful critiques of prominent men who advocated "equality between men and women" at the turn of the twentieth century pointed out, they embraced feminism out of a desire for social distinction rather than a genuine intention to abandon their privilege and demolish male dominance. Similarly, without consciously embracing a feminist self-reflection on male privilege and a feminist critique of male supremacy, the CCP leaders' pursuit of a Communist dream was inherently flawed, constrained, distorted, and redirected by an inner masculinist drive to reproduce male dominance. In this sense, the failure of a socialist revolution was fundamentally a failure to realize He-Yin Zhen's critical vision of the simultaneous pursuit of both a feminist revolution and an economic revolution.

The inherent flaws in the CCP motivated feminists' transformative efforts within the Party, as demonstrated in the early actions by ACWF leaders and the editors of *Women of China* criticizing Communist male officials of various ranks. However, that kind of daring behavior was viable only in the first few years of the CCP's rule, when a sense of comradeship formed in the war years combined with the euphoria of initiating a grand new epoch to produce a democratic atmosphere that encouraged dissenting or critical views from below. The 1957 Anti-Rightist Campaign decisively changed that and many Party members were punished for being outspoken, including some of the WF officials who dared to criticize their Party leaders. The feminist double task of transforming the "feudalist mentality" in and outside the Party would thereafter be severely restricted—allowing them to aim their campaign against "feudal remnants" only in the large societies.

Yet, the ACWF's efforts to focus attention on even this reduced wishlist could be frustrated when confronted with the perennial tension between "women-work" and the Party's "central tasks." The ACWF's structural subordination and marginalization as a mass organization in the state power structure, in addition to having to deal with male leaders at various levels who could not care less about "equality between men and women," were persistent obstacles to state feminists who were paid to work both on women's behalf and for the Party. It was in such a tension-ridden, uncongenial, and even perilous environment that *a politics of concealment* evolved in state feminists' daily struggles. State feminists understood that they could be most effective and obtain more state resources for their gender-specific goals only when they concealed their subversive feminist ideas and agendas in the non-gender-specific language of the official mainstream, or related them to non-gender-specific Party programs. Thus hidden feminist scripts were inscribed in socialist mainstream discourse and institutions without the acknowledgment of its original initiators. Concealing feminist authorship by openly attributing any accomplishment in the realm of gender equality to "the wise leadership of the Party" worked well to diffuse any possible envy or resentment from male party leaders. Anonymity was a key principle in the politics of concealment, with the result that many effective state feminists, willing to be self-effacing in order to advance women's interests, are unknown to us.

There were undoubtedly many successes that this strategy afforded. The Party's "anti-feudalism" agenda is an example. Deploying this legitimate agenda, state feminists engaged in widespread locally grounded practices to transform an entrenched sex / gender system and gendered power relations. But when in 1964 the *Women of China's* "anti-feudalist" forum on gender-specific topics and films critiquing traditional gender norms were denounced as "bourgeois" or "revisionist," the space for state feminists' engagement with gender-specific issues in transforming patriarchal culture and institutions was drastically reduced. A Maoist "class" struggle seriously subsumed feminist gendered practices in that particular moment, thwarting leading socialist state feminists' aspirations to combat gender and class oppression simultaneously.

The second process marking meaningful historical changes in the early PRC relates to state feminists' shifting position from grassroots organizers to state power holders. Socialist state feminists in the Women's Federation system faithfully kept to the mass line, the CCP's heritage from its revolutionary period, in their efforts to represent the majority of Chinese women. Even when their status as a "mass organization" resulted in institutional marginalization, they held to their commitment to reach out to their gender-specific constituency. Although often curtailed by masculinist power at various administrative levels as well as by an unstable political environment, the practices they adopted to hear women's voices and to represent women's interests were nonetheless meaningful. They remind us that in the early PRC many Party members had not yet shed their identities as grassroots organizers. The ACWF's rapid institutional development demonstrated Communist women's extraordinary effectiveness in mobilizing and politicizing women in both rural and urban areas. Their successful popular magazine *Women of China* testified to their ability to connect with women in a wide range of socioeconomic positions and geographic locations. Before the *Red Flag* incident in 1964, this feminist cultural front exerted its transformative power against "feudalism" and for the empowerment of laboring women. Their practice of the mass line and creation of a women's space that reflected diverse women's concerns existed alongside the process of centralizing the power of the Party, revealing one of the many contradictions of the socialist period.

However effective their organizing could be, there was also a downside to what the state feminists accomplished. As former grassroots organizers and now state officials they created an organizational mode that left little social space for those who were not state power holders to initiate alternative modes of activism. The organizational capacity of socialist state feminists led to a total "unification" of women's groups, to the point that the ACWF was the sole leader of a consolidated Chinese women's movement. As Yiching Wu in his critical study of the Cultural Revolution observes: "With the concentration of power in the state, the political movements and apparatuses once used so effectively to dismantle prerevolutionary inequalities themselves gave rise to new forms of domination."[2] The marginalization of the ACWF in the power center made its domination of the women's movement a double-edged sword. Not only did its monopoly of representative power exclude voices and interests of women that did not fit its agenda, it also exposed the vulnerability of feminist interests. Whenever the ACWF was disciplined by a masculinist power center, the entire feminist initiative suffered. At the conceptual level the "unification" of a Chinese women's movement by the ACWF had equally detrimental effects on the development of distinctive Chinese feminist theorizations based on socialist state feminists' extensive innovative practices in socialism. Such feminist intellectual work was automatically relegated to the realm of women-work, a jurisdiction of the WF. However, *the politics of concealment* seriously constrained the inside feminist agitators' ability to develop a distinctive feminist critical articulation that was not shrouded in orthodox Party language. Operating within the socialist state structure with the resources of the state—but without a social movement base to draw on or intellectual frameworks enabling critical voices from outside the state—rendered socialist state feminists both powerful and vulnerable, creating perennial dilemmas that they never resolved.

In addition to the above two features of socialist state feminist development, a third feature, although not specific to feminists alone, was crucially relevant to feminist pursuits, indeed, to all genuine pursuits of social justice and equality in the socialist period. That was the intimate and dense entanglement of the personal and political embedded in many political campaigns. This study has shown how political campaigns that seemed not to involve gender in any substantive way could be turned into an opportunity for masculinist officials to act out their resentment toward gender equality and seriously curtail socialist state feminists' endeavors. State feminists suffered in the Anti-Rightest Campaign in 1957; they not only had to replace their agenda of "women's thorough liberation" with "double-diligences" to secure the WF system, but also many a daring feminist was punished by Party leaders. The perilous environment for socialist state feminists culminated in 1964, when the anti-feudalist heritage of May Fourth New Culture was abandoned and gender issues were severely suppressed, as a consequence of personal grudges mixing with the political agenda in the Party's central leadership circle. Ironically, the time that was most devastating to socialist state feminist development was the very moment when Mao accelerated his efforts to prevent socialist China from turning capitalist and revisionist. A professedly revolutionary agenda soon evolved into a self-destructive political campaign that mobilized both idealistic passions and debased desires, creating a tragic conundrum in the socialist revolution. Elucidating incidents that occurred in 1964 involving both the ACWF and the film industry, this book illuminates a highly volatile political process that intensified the entanglement of complex tensions, ideological and personal conflicts, and ambiguous motivations in high politics, which eventually obstructed the further development of a dynamic feminist revolution.

The conceptualization of a class struggle between capitalism and socialism, which to some extent did reflect existing tendencies toward bureaucratization and the unequal distribution of political and material resources among different sectors in the socialist period (most saliently, two-tier citizenship for urban versus rural residents), was seriously undermined by Party leaders' unacknowledged desires to gain personal power and settle old accounts. That the entanglement of the personal and the political in the CCP had such negative effects is because this particular group of state power holders had a long revolutionary history in which they had formed entangled social networks, accumulated numerous personal credits or debts, and engaged in interpersonal conflicts that left lasting animosities. The abuse of power in the socialist period was not generally expressed in officials' profiteering in public assets, as is now all too common in the post-socialist period of marketization and privatization; rather, it was frequently manifested in officials' use of their power to punish their enemies and reward their allies. Driven by personal grudges, officials camouflaged their self-serving motives with a legitimizing discourse of class struggle. This type of abuse of power created ideological confusions, for the signifiers did not register the signified. Their lofty speeches and ideologically correct discourses rarely expressed the speakers' real meanings. Class, no longer employed as an analytical category in social analysis, degenerated into a powerful political club used to strike down personal rivals and enemies. Indeed, much of this duplicitous political rhetoric was created for the very purpose of attacking competitors and opponents, as Chen Boda's *Red Flag* article on the women question and Jiang Qing's fabrication of a revisionist line in the film industry illustrate. These cancerous practices could proliferate rapidly in an authoritarian political system where no space was available for open debate or the exposure of abuses.

Ultimately these malign practices within the Party contributed to the demise of the revolution. A misconceived and abusive schema of class struggle, which official discourse presented as the essence of socialist revolution after 1964, vitiated the meaning of class and delegitimized socialist state feminists' struggles against intertwined gender and class hierarchies. Its rampant excesses, in turn, became a convenient, even convincing, excuse for the CCP to switch course after Mao's death. The official mandate to move toward a society free of "class struggle" was enthusiastically supported by a general public that had long been alienated by the abusive conflicts conducted under that rhetorical banner during Mao's continuous revolution in the Cultural Revolution. A profound ideological departure from an egalitarian socialist vision and a reactionary dismantling of socialist egalitarian institutions and mechanisms were seamlessly glossed over in public discourse as the CCP's self-correction of Maoist ultra-leftist mistakes in order to redirect the country toward the "bright future" of modernity focusing on economic development and private consumption. A history of socialist state feminists' tenacious struggles for social, cultural, political, and economic empowerment of women, especially lower-class women, was thus thoroughly erased when an abusive Maoist class struggle and related crimes became what defined and constituted the socialist period in the post-Mao elite's production of knowledge and memory about that recent past. When jumping on the bandwagon of condemning a Maoist dictatorship and claiming victimhood under it became a public performance for those with discursive power to show one's avant-garde political stance, hardly any discursive space was left for narratives about genuine and serious explorations and efforts to transform multiple systems of oppression in the socialist period. The elite's direct assault on socialist feminist practices of empowering lower-class women embodied in the image of Iron Girls and strong heroines in cultural representation further succeeded in cementing the association of socialist women's liberation with the "masculinization" of Chinese women in the dominant discourse. It is not just that a socialist state feminist history is erased but also the intellectual space to investigate that recent history is sealed when such post-socialist discursive maneuvers are unrecognized and the dominant anti-socialist discourse produced is taken as *the* history of socialism.

WOMEN OF CHINA: A SIGNIFIER OF HISTORICAL RUPTURES

Nowhere was the historical rupture between state socialism and state capitalism more visibly displayed than on the covers of *Women of China* following its revival in 1978. When Hou Di returned to her leading position in the press, she continued to celebrate laboring women's participation in socialist construction. The socialist feminist aesthetic persisted until her retirement in 1983. Hou-Di's successors, who were engulfed by the rising discourse of modernization modeled after Western capitalist countries but packaged as China's New Long March, a term invoking the CCP's revolutionary history to provide an appearance of continuity, and squeezed by a competitive publishing market, fundamentally transformed the magazine. Their editorial decision to cater to urban elite women resulted in the complete erasure of peasants, factory workers, women employed in the service sector, and ethnic minority women in visual representation. Retaining its title from the social-

FIGURE 29. Cover of *Women of China,* 2007, no. 6.

ist feminist era, *Women of China* has not presented a single image of a worker or a peasant on its cover since 1998. Of the 228 issues from 1999 to 2008, entertainers are featured on 164 covers, and the rest portray successful entrepreneurs and celebrities. Like other commercial women's magazines, *Women of China* competes for market share by attracting readers with sexualized images of women's bodies (fig. 29).

On its seventieth anniversary in 2009, *Women of China* presented a seamless narrative of its history as "having consistently promoted equality between men and women, protected women's legal rights, embodied the ethos of women's self-respect, self-confidence, autonomy, self-strengthening . . . and given readers inspiring spiritual power."[3] The rhetoric of continuing to wave the flag of women's liberation sounds persuasive as long as no one notices what is missing from this representation. Class, which was overused and abused during the Mao era, has been entirely abandoned as a meaningful political concept in this magazine, as in other popular publications and academic work as well. Presenting capitalist modernity as a classless wonderland offering material abundance that everyone will be able to reach through her individual efforts, *Women of China* participates in and reproduces the collaborative political maneuver performed by the intellectual elite and the CCP, glossing over the increasing social polarization in China and the exploitation of its huge working class, which constitutes the major labor force for a global sweatshop. Rural peasants, urban migrants, laid-off workers, and anyone whose life story might disrupt the myth of a classless modernity are systematically excluded from visual representation.[4] Continued advocacy of formal gender equality goes hand-in-hand with the erasure of class in a magazine that now embodies a market feminism promoted in privatization and marketization orchestrated by the CCP as means to stabilize its rule.

The radical transformation of state feminists from socialist revolutionaries to market apostles is even more sharply demonstrated by three new magazines that the press of *Women of China* now also publishes in the market economy: *Good Housekeeper, Fashion,* and *World Women's Vision,* launched in 1993 and renamed *Self* in 2007.[5] *Good Housekeeper (Hao zhufu)* is advertised as the premier trendy magazine for middle-class families, catering to "mature intellectual women, leading an elegant lifestyle, promoting the concept of a high-quality life, and creating a warm and tender family atmosphere."[6] Its survey shows that the great majority of its readers are urban white-collar married women between ages 25 and 35. *Self,* which uses this English title alongside a Chinese title *yueji* ("pleasing oneself"), is a joint venture with the U.S. magazine of the same name. Images of Euro-white women dominate both the covers and contents (fig. 30). A fashion magazine targeting young urban professional women, it "introduces the most current trends in concepts of femininity and lifestyles of various countries, and provides the most recent information on fashion and cosmetics."[7] The third magazine, *Fashion,* whose Chinese title is "love female students" (*Ai nüsheng*), targets a younger cohort of urban women. The line on a cover of a 2009 issue reads, "Love yourself 100 percent, a magazine of stars and brand names."[8]

These three magazines aim to attract different age groups of urban middle- and upper-class women with the lure of capitalist consumerism, selling a femininity befitting a modernization modeled mostly after the United

FIGURE 30. Table of contents of *Self*, 2009, no. 4.

States. With their mixture of English and Chinese and frequent references to Western celebrities and brand names, they project a cosmopolitan flair. National boundaries appear to be dismantled by the global flow of consumer goods, but hierarchies of race, class, and gender are explicitly reproduced in both their language and their images. A new imaginary of Chinese women's position in the world is expressed in advertising that promotes consumerism; rather than sharing solidarity with global women's movements in challenging oppressive social relations, individual women are now urged to share the enjoyment of brand-name commodities and even appearance with white women celebrities in the West. Joining the huge publishing market in selling a global capitalist utopia, the three magazines represent a drastic reorientation of the press that publishes *Women of China*. Visual representations that celebrated Chinese "new women" as independent, collective-oriented, gender-neutral, working-class contributors to socialist construction have been replaced by an individualistic, privatized, and sexualized bourgeois consumer who is also commoditized simultaneously. With its ostensible goal of promoting happiness here and now, which is disguised as free of ideology and apolitical, the capitalist order has replaced a communist vision of the future, and through its pervasive propaganda mechanisms it has achieved an astonishingly rapid and sweeping transformation of popular subjectivities.

This profound capitalist transformation is also manifested in the parlance of market state feminists. The deputy chair of the ACWF, Huang Qingyi, praised the magazine on its seventieth anniversary: "Today's *Women of China* is entering a new era, with the best environment for growth and the most powerful comprehensive capacity for significant social impact. It now has the support of prominent enterprises, solid brand names, distinctive features, and it utilizes multifaceted formats that are cross-media, across different types of commerce, and transnational."[9] Her article is entitled "Progress over Time to Strive for Glory." This linear model conveniently elides ruptures, setbacks, regressions, exclusions, conflicts, displacements, and dispossessions in China's turn to global capitalism.

When I showed the recent covers of *Women of China* to Shi Yumei, the magazine's former art editor who is now in her eighties, she was so devastated that she was rendered speechless for a long moment, and her eyes moistened. Then, in a trembling voice, she asked: "Can this represent Chinese women? How many Chinese women look like this? This does not represent Chinese women. What is she doing? Sex appeal? I cannot stand this! They should not use the title *Women of China*. This insults Chinese women! It is so painful to see these images."[10] Shi Yumei's response centered on representation. She immediately grasped these covers' abandonment of representations of women of the laboring class, who still constitute the majority of women in China. The fact that she regarded this shift as tragic reveals her identification with the socialist agenda of empowering *laodong renmin,* laboring people. As one of the socialist cultural producers who worked hard to create a socialist feminist cultural front, she deeply mourned its loss.

Hou Di, the former deputy editor, also in her eighties and partially blind, was acutely aware of the drastic changes in the magazine. She had heard from other former editors that now the magazine "is no different from those in the old society," that is, the commercial magazines produced before the creation of a socialist China. She told me that her successors occasionally visited her, but added in a resigned tone, "I have long been retired and it is not appropriate for me to meddle in their work."[11]

After I gave a paper on *Women of China* at a conference of the All-China Women's Federation, I was invited to present my research findings to the press that publishes *Women of China*. About fifteen editors, including one man, attended the meeting on June 21, 2009. The editors-in-chief were in their early fifties, and the rest were in their thirties and forties; on average, they were about ten years older than the founding editors when they started the magazine in 1949. I presented the part of my paper that covered the socialist period and then invited the editors to discuss the contrast between the covers of the past and the present by giving a slide show. Showing a lively interest, the editors engaged in a fascinating and revealing debate on the meanings of visual representations of women.

Interestingly, they readily agreed that the magazine not only focuses on and promotes consumer goods, but also is itself a commodity. The male editor summarized the basic editorial tenets: "The producer of the magazines is an enterprise, a merchant. Without profit they would not go for it. . . . *Shou / lou / tou* [Thin body, revealing the body, and transparent clothing] are pursued to please the eyes of consumers. Nowadays magazines are just consumer goods." A female editor contrasted the function of the magazine in the present with that in the past: "The consumer era is different from the revolutionary era. Now it is not a matter of what we want to advocate; it is a matter of what the public wants to see." Another female editor concurred with both of her colleagues: "The cover image has to attract the eyes of consumers. In a fleeting second it should make consumers decide if they want to pay for it or not. It is just consumer goods." The legitimacy of market consumption worked like a magical invisibility cloak to render capitalist ideologies and sexist values unnoticeable and to naturalize these practices.

Since all of these popular women's magazines in today's China have sexualized urban young women on the cover, I asked whether it would make *Women of China* stand out more if the cover featured a peasant woman. "No one would buy a magazine with a cover showing a peasant," one editor claimed. "Not necessarily," another remarked, "but it is true that city people don't care about rural people at all." A third editor approached the question from a different angle, but her statement, too, reveals the association of laboring women with backwardness and outdatedness: "If we put workers and peasants on the cover, people would say, how come *Women of China* is so rustic (*tu*)?" The deputy editor-in-chief presented another reason for this absence: "Women with feminist consciousness are mostly retired with little purchasing power. The younger cohort with money is not interested in rural women. We have to update our magazine for younger women. A cover image shapes the consumer's decision. Once she buys it, she will be exposed to the healthy ideas in its contents." Her explanation significantly touches upon the reconfiguration of women's subjectivities in different historical eras. Still, what is most problematic in visual representation is interpreted as a marketing strategy rather than as a concession to the dominant capitalist ideology underpinned by social Darwinism. Lower-class laboring women, whose labor is as indispensable in a capitalist economy as it was in socialist economy, have been downgraded from their status celebrated for its centrality in socialist construction to that of a marginal social group whose physical labor and low consumption capacity determine their "backwardness" in the dominant ideology that legitimizes and conceals severe exploitation.

The editors' responses to the cover images of the 1950s and 1960s, however, were surprisingly positive, which reveals contradictory and complex sentiments about capitalist modernity. A few described them as valuable and touching, in contrast to current images that are mere commodities and do not deserve preservation. One went further: "The old images are very precious, valuable, and moving. The current ones are just consumer goods that you can see everywhere. They are spiritual trash, with no value for research." Several others, while concurring that they are "trash," protested that they are significant. "But they do reflect what people are thinking today!" one loudly declared. I was startled by the editors' negative assessment of their own cultural products right in front of their supervisor and saddened by the revelation that these editors took no pleasure, let alone pride, in their own products. As I listened to their statements, I found myself silently contrasting their stunning and depressing sense of alienation with the passion and pride expressed by the first cohort of feminist editors who devoted their labors to a revolutionary mission of cultural transformation.

One editor ardently defended the current post-socialist period: "Now the subject [*zhuti*] is independent. One can choose whatever clothing fashion she wishes, to express her independence. One does not need to wear a work uniform to express one's subjectivity. Those who read fashion magazines are usually people of three highs: high income, high pursuit, and high personality." Translated into English, this shorthand expression means that today the women the magazines serve are affluent and have enough disposable income to spend on fashionable and expensive clothing and accessories; they actively seek to fulfill their desires; and they have strong personalities and individual styles. She continued: "They pursue beauty in life. Migrant workers [who have moved from the countryside to the city] also desire the same kind of beauty. No one would want to go back to those days with no choice." Echoing mainstream discourse in China, this editor expressed the passionate faith in consumerist modernity and individual choice within the market that is embraced by the social elite.

Two editors openly declared that they were feminists. But unlike their predecessors, they conduct their feminist activities separately from their jobs at the press, working with feminist nongovernmental organizations (NGOs) in Beijing. When I pressed the question of where a feminist cultural front could be built in China today, one feminist editor replied, "This magazine embodies the values of the ACWF. It is impossible for them to be radical." The other feminist editor said: "Now the problem is that we do not have a powerful commander-in-chief. They [the ACWF officials] are all nominated and promoted by male authorities. What do they dare to say? They are much less daring than we are in terms of speaking out." These two feminist editors delineated a drastic change in the feminist landscape in China. The ACWF is no longer a leader of a unifying women's movement. Many of its officials are career-oriented bureaucrats rather than feminist fighters like their revolutionary predecessors, and they do not even command respect from their own rank and file. Those in the WF who dare to fight for feminist causes are often involved in the activities of NGOs, which have gained momentum since the Fourth UN Conference on Women held in Beijing in 1995.[12]

The loss of *Women of China* as a feminist cultural front was also due to the political environment after June 4, 1989, when peaceful popular protests in Beijing were violently suppressed by order of leader Deng Xiaoping.[13] In the aftermath of what the Chinese state calls the "June Fourth incident," the state effectively closed any public spaces for dissenting views and dissonant voices regarding the CCP's turn to global capitalism and its abuse of power that enabled the ruling class to profiteer from its privatizing public assets. Hand in hand with sealing off any space for dissenting political expressions was a massive promotion of a discourse of Chinese modernity symbolized by omnipresent images of commoditized and sexualized young women who enjoy the freedom to consume in the new material wonderland led by the CCP. Constructing and conforming to this master narrative has been the new Party line, which must be followed by all the print media in order to pass censorship. Recognizing this situation, the deputy editor-in-chief answered my question about where a feminist cultural front could be built: "Nowadays magazines are not the space for radical ideas or airing grievances, but the Internet is."

The internal dynamics of the press that publishes *Women of China* epitomize larger-scale historical processes. The magazine embodies the transformation of the CCP from a revolutionary force to an entrenched bureaucratic ruling class that caters to and benefits from a global capitalist market. The shift in the magazine and its representations of women exemplifies the reconfiguration of class and gender relations and the contribution made by urban elites with discursive power to the drastic displacement of lower-class women from not only visual representations in the mainstream media but also in socioeconomic life. At the same time, the comments of current editors reveal that people who are discontented with the status quo have been creating new social spaces outside the state and the market to take action concerning the causes they value. Not only does the magazine today resemble commercial magazines in the old society, but also the dynamics within Chinese society increasingly resemble the period before 1949 when the Communist Revolution took shape.

SOCIALIST FEMINIST LEGACIES AND NEW FIELDS OF FEMINIST ACTIVISM

For bureaucratic officials of the Women's Federation system with little feminist consciousness, actively following the Party's imperatives can be a safe passage to career mobility. They have enthusiastically embraced a capitalist consumerism that commoditizes women and actively advocated for Confucian gender differentiations and traditional feminine virtues. They sell not just the commercial magazines published by the press of *Women of China* and many local WFs, but also workshops offering trainings to shape women with "lady-like feminine virtues and etiquette" in order to hone them for "successful elite men" in the marriage market.[14]

But it is not hard to discover the legacy of socialist feminism that lives on among many of the women whose subjectivities were shaped in the period when socialist feminist discourse dominated and were beneficiaries of socialist egalitarian ideologies and policies. The equal educational and employment opportunities had opened up to them important positions in the government and academic institutions; when socialism began to be dismantled with the economic reforms begun in the 1980s, they constituted a feminist force defending women's equal rights. These urban feminists situated either in the WF system nationwide, or in academies of social sciences and universities, continued to show strong concern for lower-class women's predicament in a time of massive dislocation and displacement by initiating feminist intervention research and activist programs for migrant women workers, laid-off women workers, poverty-stricken rural women, domestic violence victims, those who experienced violations of their legal rights or psychological distress, and so on.[15]

As these feminists were situated in the official institutions and aimed to utilize state resources and intervene in public policy making, they generally operated within the tried-and-true politics of concealment, working behind the scenes without publicly claiming their authorship of feminist laws and policies. But it was this cohort of feminists who made the Fourth UN Conference on Women in 1995 a crucial breakthrough in Chinese feminist discursive and organizational development. Legitimized by the UN mandate of gender mainstreaming, they now articulate feminist agenda openly in feminist terminologies circulating globally via UN documents endorsed by the Chinese state. The term "gender equality" (*shehui xingbie pingdeng*) has been embraced by them as a sign signifying their pursuit of social justice in a time when "class" as an analytical concept has been denigrated and erased in official discourse, and "anti-feudalism" has become obsolete. "Gender equality," which for the general public parallels "equality between men and women" (*nannü pingdeng*) but implies a nuanced difference from the latter, also signifies the emergence of a legitimate feminist discourse that need not be camouflaged in Party language. "Gender" in this sense enables a feminist conceptual detachment from the male-dominated CCP, though on official occasions many feminists in this cohort would prefer to use "gender" instead of "feminist"—even today, loaded with negative connotations—to avoid the possibility of animosity on the part of male authorities. This cohort of feminists also utilized the NGO Forums accompanying the 1995 UN Conference on Women to promote the development of feminist NGOs in China, and ushered in a period of thriving development of all sorts of NGOs in China.[16]

The ACWF embodies the institutional legacy of socialist state feminism with both positive and negative implications. In the 1980s the ACWF leadership and some local WFs played a major role in resisting the massive masculinist pressure to push women back to the kitchen with the rising unemployment crisis. They invoked the fundamental socialist feminist principle that women's liberation hinged on their participation in social production. In the process they also developed a "Marxist theory of women" to consolidate socialist feminist tenets. This discursive maneuver was the state feminists' efforts to utilize the CCP's oral commitment to Marxism to hold the Party accountable to its promise of "equality between men and women" in a moment when the Party was abandoning such a commitment.[17] Moreover, in the two decades following the 1995 conference, the UN mandate of mainstreaming gender has given the ACWF legitimacy to pursue gender-specific programs. But nonetheless, the bureaucratic mass organization is still required to follow the "central tasks" of the Party Central, necessitating for conscious feminists in the WFs the same politics of concealment as always.

A revealing episode that indicates both profound changes and continuities in gender contentions took place in 2013 when the new Party leader, Xi Jinping, gave a talk to the new leading body of the ACWF. He reiterated the CCP's principles on women-work and professed his commitment to "equality between men and women," but he then tacked on a startling statement even more conservative than Deng Xiaoping's "double-diligences" in 1957. Deploying ideas that are strikingly reminiscent of what socialist state feminists had condemned as feudalist definitions of femininity, Xi declared: "Special attention should be paid to women's unique role in propagating Chinese family virtues and setting up a good family tradition. This relates to harmony in the family and in society and to the healthy development of children. Women should consciously shoulder the responsibilities of taking care of the old and young, as well as educating children."[18] Emphasizing traditional familial roles for women articulates both a masculinist imperative to restore China's pre-socialist gender order and an increasing social crisis since the state has shed its responsibilities for the care of children, the old, and the sick. The privatization of reproductive labor added new fuel to a masculinist backlash against socialist gender equality, making gender contentions ever more ferocious. Comparing the CCP leading body now with 1957, when Deng Xiaoping proposed the policy of "double-diligences"—however, for the purpose of saving the gender-based organization—the masculinist mentality of the Party leaders is all the more evident. And it is articulated with no qualms two decades after gender equality has become a UN mandate for its member states.

But the episode also clearly indicates significant changes in the ACWF. When in 1957 the ACWF top leaders complied with the "double-diligences" for a while and kept the Secretariat's sexist attack on women's liberation secret, in 2013 the ACWF publicized Xi's talk via the Internet. Did the ACWF leaders, lacking feminist consciousness, not see Xi's proposition as problematic? Or to the contrary, did some in the ACWF with gender consciousness deliberately publicize the new leader's sexism? In any case, officials of the ACWF neither followed Xi's advice nor did they critique it. Unlike in

1957, the ACWF in 2013 had the UN mandate as a backup. An even sharper contrast to the situation in 1957 was that feminists in and outside the official system instantly expressed their objections to this sexist pronouncement by China's top leader, utilizing the Internet as an open forum. The presence of loud critical feminist voices on the Internet has powerfully announced the emergence of an independent feminist force. Rather than appealing to the politics of concealment, a younger cohort of feminists has adopted the very opposite of the politics of concealment to amplify their distinctive critical voices in the public. The days of a "unified Chinese women's movement" led by the ACWF are long gone. Diverse feminists situated in different social locations initiate various agendas and adopt different strategies, significantly transforming the terrain of Chinese feminism and creating new fields of feminist activism—the silver lining in privatization and marketization.

Entering the second decade of the twenty-first century, roughly speaking, four kinds of feminist operation simultaneously function in multiple fields of activism and maneuvers. The WF system continues to serve as the most powerful institution for protecting women's rights with its official status and state resources as well as about ninety thousand paid personnel nationwide. Then there are feminist NGOs that proliferated following the UN conference with support from international donors. With their institutional networks, they tend to collaborate with the WF and other government officials in their intervention projects, targeting either state policies and laws or seeking to generate transformation in local society. The momentous success of this collaboration between feminists in and outside the official system is reflected in China's first anti–domestic violence law passed on December 27, 2015, after two decades of persistent feminist struggles following the UN conference. Collaborating with the WF dictated that the NGO leaders would also follow the politics of concealment, but even if neither ACWF nor NGO feminists could openly claim authorship of the law or publicize their decades-long efforts behind the scenes, knowledge of their work has been circulating among the enlarged circle of feminists in and outside China in the age of the Internet and globalization.

The third and fourth sites of feminist activities both operate independently from the official system: one is in the realm of developing feminist scholarship and promoting women's and gender studies curricula with financial and intellectual resources from outside China; the other is in social media, the province of a younger cohort of feminists. This younger cohort unambiguously embraces the term feminist (*nüquan zhuyizhe*), to show their defiance of the demonization of feminism in the mainstream discourse. Mostly growing up in the post–U.N. conference era and conversant with globally circulating feminist ideas and concepts enabled by the earlier feminist cohort and the Internet, they organize feminist protests and petitions online, and take a powerful and unapologetic public stance by staging sensational performance acts in public and cyber spaces. Examples such as "Occupying Men's Rooms" to demand gender equality in public facilities or wearing fake blood-stained bridal gowns in public to protest domestic violence create sharp visual images. Their public stunt against cases of domestic violence also played a significant role in the passage of the anti–domestic violence law. Their exposé of cases of sexual harassment by a college professor and mobilizing online protests pressed the university administrators and the Ministry of Education to confront this serious problem at universities. Aiming to both intervene in public policies and raise public consciousness regarding rampant gender discrimination and sexism in contemporary China, they have even created biting new terms to condemn masculinist minds. One of the terms that have gained wide currency is *zhinan ai* [straight man's cancer]. Operating skillfully via cyber space, these resources poor young feminists have nonetheless engaged in powerful discursive battles as trailblazers.

A recent case illustrating the persistence of socialist state feminism legacies took place in a moment of crisis for Chinese feminism. A group of women, naming themselves Young Feminist Activists (YFA), planned to take action against sexual harassment by posting stickers on public transportation, both to call attention to this pervasive problem and to commemorate International Women's Day in 2015. The police detained five of them on the eve of International Women's Day to thwart their action and punish them despite the legality of the action for gender equality. Their detention was a sign of the rapidly deteriorating political situation in China, which threatened to shut down the social spaces for NGO activities that had been carved out by Chinese feminists following the 1995 conference. It was also a blatantly open attack on Chinese feminism unprecedented since the founding of the PRC. For thirty-seven days a large-scale, transnational mobilization of support for their release was waged via the Internet, while protesting voices within China were systematically suppressed by police surveillance. The ACWF remained publicly silent, in seeming disregard of public and private pleas from many feminists for their open stance to defend women's legal rights. But behind the scenes, "a coalition of high-ranking members of the

All-China Women's Federation inquired in an informal letter to the Beijing Municipal Public Security Bureau about the legitimacy of the women's detention."[19] This gesture of intervention from within the official system certainly added weight to the final decision to release the Feminist Five.[20] Feminists who occupy various official positions in the state apparatus have continued to wage quiet struggles along gender lines, and the politics of concealment persists as long as the CCP perpetuates its male supremacy authoritarian political system.

Another sign of the socialist state feminist legacy is poignantly ironic. After their release, the Feminist Five began to write about their experiences in the detention center. Circulating via cellphone through the most popular app in China, WeChat, these firsthand accounts narrated the activists' emotional stress while undergoing police interrogation and enduring isolation in jail and expressed their longing to hear their four sisters' voices and the thrill of catching a glimpse of their passing shadows. Reading these touching testimonies, some young feminists instantly invoked the image of Sister Jiang in the Nationalist prison! The analogy was definitely pertinent, though beyond the wildest imagination of the socialist feminist cultural producer Xia Yan and the crew of the film *Eternity in Flames,* as well as those who produced the opera *Sister Jiang.* The image of this revolutionary heroine acquired a new political valence at a very different historical moment. Decades after the visual representation of revolutionary heroines was denounced by the postsocialist elite as signifying the masculinization of women by a patriarchal party-state, and rendered irrelevant by the ascendant public discourse of consumerism, young feminists' invocation of Sister Jiang attests to the lasting empowering effects of socialist state feminists' cultural production.

The feminists who joined the Communist Revolution would have never imagined that, in a state they had strived to create, young women in the twenty-first century would be arrested for planning to protest sexual harassment in a public space. Something certainly went seriously wrong in the course of this history. A historian does not have the luxury to contemplate the road not taken since historical processes are constituted of dynamic power-ridden conflicts and contentions as well as contingencies that are not in the range of any historical actor's conscious choice. Still, something can be learned from the rich experiences, positive and negative, of feminists in the Communist Party. Especially for a generation of young feminists who have already demonstrated their will to forge ahead with a feminist revolution in China, the socialist state feminists' perseverance through difficult conditions and their tenacious struggles for eliminating hierarchies of gender and class, as well as the historically contingent limitations of their visions and strategies, may serve as a valuable heritage. A prominent lesson from socialist state feminists' historical experiences is obvious: a feminist revolution should not be subordinated to any other campaigns for human dignity and social justice. Without a conscious and vigilant feminist critique and the systematic removal of the foundations of male dominance, any revolution, including a socialist one, sooner or later ends up reproducing unequal power relations and male dominance.

NOTES

INTRODUCTION

1. Chen Bo'er, "Nüxing zhongxin de dianying yu nanxing zhongxin de shehui" [The female-centered film and the male-centered society], *Funü shenghuo* [Women's Life] 2, no. 2 (1936): 62–64.

2. See Wendy Brown, *States of Injury: Power and Freedom in Late Modernity* (Princeton, NJ: Princeton University Press, 1995). Brown's concept of the late modern liberal state is not monolithic, but dispersed and diffused. However, women's expanding engagement with the state, although briefly acknowledged, does not figure in her conceptualization of the state.

3. Mizuyo Sudo, "Concepts of Women's Rights in Modern China," in *Translating Feminisms in China,* ed. Dorothy Ko and Wang Zheng (Oxford: Blackwell, 2007), 13–34; Ke Huiling, *Jindai Zhongguo geming yundong zhong de funü* [Women in the revolutionary movements in modern China] (Taiyuan: Shanxi Education Press, 2012), 66–67. Sudo traces early Chinese translations from Japanese texts, while Ke emphasizes the impact of Ma Junwu's selected translation from John Miller's *On the Subjection of Women* in 1902.

4. See Lydia Liu, Rebecca E. Karl, and Dorothy Ko, eds., *The Birth of Chinese Feminism: Essential Texts in Transnational Theory* (New York: Columbia University Press, 2013), 21. The volume collects important historical texts expressing diverse views on gender issues at the turn of the twentieth century, and its insightful introduction highlights He-Yin Zhen's feminist theorization of *nannü* distinction in the Chinese context. For a detailed explanation of the Chinese *nannü* system, also see Susan Mann, *Gender and Sexuality in Modern Chinese History* (New York: Cambridge University Press, 2011).

5. An earlier translation of "sexual equality" was *nannü pingquan,* "equal rights of men and women."

6. For a historical study of May Fourth feminism, see Wang Zheng, *Women in the Chinese Enlightenment: Oral and Textual Histories* (Berkeley: University of California Press, 1999).

7. For a study of radical women's participation in the inception of the CCP, see Christina K. Gilmartin, *Engendering the Chinese Revolution: Radical Women, Communist Politics, and Mass Movements in the 1920s* (Berkeley: University of California Press, 1995).

8. Marilyn J. Boxer, "Rethinking the Socialist Construction and International Career of the Concept 'Bourgeois Feminism,'" *American Historical Review* 112, no. 1 (2007): 131–58.

9. For early studies on women-work in the CCP, see Delia Davin, *Woman-Work: Women and the Party in Revolutionary China* (Oxford: Oxford University Press, 1976), and Elisabeth Croll, *Feminism and Socialism in China* (London: Routledge & Kegan Paul, 1978).

10. See Dorothy McBride Stetson and Amy G. Mazur, eds., *Comparative State Feminism* (Thousand Oaks, CA: Sage, 1995) for a detailed discussion of the evolution of the term. Beyond the scope of this work, socialist feminists have had a long history of involvement in public policies with their roots in both party-affiliated and unaffiliated women's groups.

11. See Mayfair Mei-hui Yang, "From Gender Erasure to Gender Difference: State Feminism, Consumer Sexuality, and Women's Public Sphere in China," in *Spaces of Their Own: Women's Public Sphere in Transnational China,* ed. Mayfair Mei-hui Yang (Minneapolis: University of Minnesota Press, 1999), 35–67.

12. For works best illustrating a different methodology in investigating state feminism in the West, see Stetson and Mazur, *Comparative State Feminism;* and Hester Eisenstein, *Inside Agitators: Australian Femocrats and the State* (Philadelphia: Temple University Press, 1996).

13. Judith Stacey, *Patriarchy and Socialist Revolution in China* (Berkeley: University of California Press, 1983); Kay Ann Johnson, *Women, Family, and Peasant Revolution* (Chicago: University of Chicago Press, 1983); Phyllis Andors, *The Unfinished Liberation of Chinese Women* (Bloomington: Indiana University Press, 1983); and Margery Wolf, *Revolution Postponed: Women in Contemporary China* (Stanford, CA: Stanford University Press, 1985).

14. The manifestation of the Cold War paradigm is certainly not only found in Chinese studies. For similar debates on feminist histories in European socialist countries, see Francisca de Haan, "Introduction" to Forum: "After Ten Years: Communism and Feminism Revisited," *Aspasia* 10 (2016).

15. The conceptual difference also exists in some studies on state feminism in non-Western countries. These studies assume the role of the state in changing gender relations and promoting women's social advancement without examining feminists' agitation in the state. I do not claim that my findings on China can speak for other non-Western countries, although my question on methodology may have more general implications. For studies on state feminism in non-Western countries, see Mervat Hatem, "Economic and Political Liberation in Egypt and the Demise of State Feminism," *International Journal of Middle East Studies* 24 (May 1992): 231–51; Jean Robinson, "Women, the State, and the Need for Civil Society: The Liga Kobiet in Poland," in Stetson and Mazur, *Comparative State Feminism,* 203–20; and Jenny

B. White, "State Feminism, Modernization, and the Turkish Republican Woman," *NWSA Journal* 15 (Fall 2003): 145–60.

16. See Gilmartin, *Engendering the Chinese Revolution*.

17. See Helen Praeger Young, *Choosing Revolution: Chinese Women Soldiers in the Long March* (Urbana: University of Illinois Press, 2001); and Jack Belden, *China Shakes the World* (New York: Harpers, 1949). Both books present fascinating accounts of rural women's involvement in the Communist Revolution.

18. For the growth of the CCP membership, see "Xin Zhongguo chengli 60 nianlai Zhongguo Gongchandang dangyuan zengjia 16 bei" [In the 60 years since the founding of the PRC, the number of the Chinese Communist Party members has increased 16 times], *Zhongguo Gongchandang Xinwenwang* [CPC news], June 30, 2009, http://cpc.people.com.cn/GB/64093/64387/9569767.html (accessed December 27, 2013).

19. Gilmartin, *Engendering the Chinese Revolution*.

20. See "Huang Dinghui (1907–): Career Revolutionary," in Wang Zheng, *Women in the Chinese Enlightenment*, 287–356; and Young, *Choosing Revolution*.

21. In *Jiemi shike* [Moments to reveal secrets], a Chinese language program of Voice of America (VOA), Guo Daijun interprets diaries of Chiang Kai-shek and notes this quotation from his diaries. *Riji zhongde Jiang Jieshi* [Chiang Kai-shek in his diaries], www.youtube.com/watch?v=nQiD4_vlqPc (accessed October 3, 2014).

22. Dong Bian, Cai Asong, and Tan Deshan, eds., *Women de haodajie Cai Chang* [Our good elder sister Cai Chang] (Beijing: Zhongyang wenxian chubanshe, 1992), 286–311; "The Sixth Session of the Council of the WIDF, Peking, April 24–30, 1956," International Institute of Socialist history website, https://search.socialhistory.org/Record/1057007 (accessed January 3, 2016). For a study of the WIDF, see Francisca de Haan, "Continuing Cold War Paradigms in Western Historiography of Transnational Women's Organisations: The Case of the Women's International Democratic Federation (WIDF)," *Women's History Review* 19, no. 4 (September 2010): 547–73.

23. The euphoria as well as debates among feminist drafters of the Marriage Law is vividly discussed in these books: Jin Feng, *Deng Yingchao zhuan* [A biography of Deng Yingchao], vol. 2 (Beijing: Renmin chubanshe, 1993), 457–61; Luo Qiong and Duan Yongqiang, *Luo Qiong fangtan lu* [Interviews with Luo Qiong] (Beijing: Zhongguo funü chubanshe, 2000), 119–21; Huang Chuanhui, *Tianxia hunyin: Gongheguo sanbu hunyinfa jishi* [Marriage under heaven: Three marriage laws of the PRC] (Shanghai: Wenhui Press, 2004), 33–54. An important historical document is included in an anthology, Deng Yingchao, "Guanyu Zhonghua Renmin Gongheguo hunyinfa de baogao: 1950 nian 5 yue 14 ri zai Zhangjiakou kuoda ganbu huiyi shang de jiangyan" [A report on the Marriage Law of the People's Republic of China: A speech at the expanded cadres' meeting in Zhangjiakou on May 14, 1950], in *Zhongguo funü yundong wenxian ziliao huibian* [An anthology of source materials on the Chinese women's movement], ed. Chinese Women Cadre Management School (Beijing: Zhongguo funü chubanshe, 1988), vol. 2, 49–54. (The two-volume anthology is classified as an internal document, which is not for public circulation.

Scholars may access this and many more collections of valuable source materials on Chinese women's movements in the library of the Chinese Women University in Beijing.) For the drafting of the Marriage Law, also see Luo Qiong, "Xin Zhongguo diyibu hunyinfa qicao qianhou" [Drafting the first Marriage Law of the new China], in *Kangzheng, jiefang, pingdeng: Luo Qiong wenji* [Resistance, emancipation, equality: An anthology by Luo Qiong] (Beijing: Zhongguo funü chubanshe, 2007), 427–28. Some contemporary male scholars in China claimed that the 1950 Marriage Law was motivated by CCP male officials who wanted to replace their wives, revealing both ignorance of historical evidence and assumptions of omnipresent male power. For an English translation of the 1950 Marriage Law, see Johnson, *Women, the Family and Peasant Revolution in China.* If we replace the term "reformers" in this book with "state feminists," a scene of feminist contentions in promulgating and implementing the feminist law would clearly emerge. But when Johnson wrote the book she had no idea of the key role of Deng Yingchao and the Committee of Women-Work in drafting and promoting the law, though she accurately identified the heritage of May Fourth feminism in the law.

24. See the documentary film *Small Happiness* (1984), directed by Carma Hinton.

25. See Dai Jinhua, *Cinema and Desire: Feminist Marxism and Cultural Politics in the Work of Dai Jinhua*, ed. Jing Wang and Tani E. Barlow (London: Verso, 2002); and Shuqin Cui, *Women through the Lens: Gender and Nation in a Century of Chinese Cinema* (Honolulu: University of Hawaii Press, 2003).

26. So far none of the major extant film studies scholarship in English utilizes archival research, but a PhD student of cultural studies in China in 2006 produced a solid dissertation on socialist film industry in Shanghai based entirely on his research in the Shanghai Municipal Archives. See Zhang Shuoguo, *"Shiqi nian" Shanghai dianying wenhua yanjiu* [A study of the "seventeen years" of Shanghai film culture] (Beijing: Social Sciences Press, 2014).

27. The great majority of the official posts in the new socialist state were occupied by male Communists with a military background as the takeover of the state power in one region after another was performed by the People's Liberation Army with the assistance of underground CCP members. Xia Yan, in his capacity as the top official of the cultural realm in Shanghai after the takeover, designed a test of common knowledge in the cultural field for officials of the Department of Propaganda and Department of Culture above the district level. To his dismay, 70 percent of officials failed the test and few were able to answer the question that asked the year in which the May Fourth Movement took place. It is a good indication that even officials in the cultural realm were mostly from rural backgrounds with little formal education. Xia Yan, *Lanxun jiumeng lu* [Languid recollections of old dreams] (Beijing: Sanlian Bookstore, 1985), 617–19.

28. The most famous case is how the renowned writer Ding Ling was punished for her feminist critique of sexist practices in Yan'an in 1942. See Ding Ling, "Thoughts on March 8, " in *I Myself Am a Woman: Selected Writings of Ding Ling,* ed. Tani E. Barlow with Gary J. Bjorge (Boston: Beacon Press, 1989), 316–21.

29. For the author's memoir of growing up in the socialist period, see Wang Zheng, "Call Me Qingnian But Not Funü: A Maoist Youth in Retrospect," *Feminist Studies* 27, no. 1 (Spring 2001): 9–34. The essay is also collected in Xueping Zhong, Wang Zheng, and Bai Di, eds., *Some of Us: Chinese Women Growing Up in the Mao Era* (Piscataway, NJ: Rutgers University Press, 2001).

CHAPTER ONE. FEMINIST CONTENTIONS IN SOCIALIST STATE FORMATION

1. Upon the founding of the PRC, there were three nationwide hierarchical mass organizations organized by the CCP: the Trade Union, the Youth Association, and the Women's Federation. The Trade Union organized women and men workers by workplace and included the Department of Women's Workers at the national, provincial, and municipal levels and a committee of women workers at the workplace. The Youth Association followed a similar pattern, organizing students at schools (middle school and up) and working youth in workplaces, without gender distinction, at national, provincial and municipal levels. The Women's Federation differed from the other two and paralleled the governmental administration system, with women's federations covering the national, provincial, municipal, district, street office, and neighborhood levels. Also, a woman official responsible for women-work was placed in government administration offices—down to the street offices. Officials of the various levels of the Women's Federation were appointed by the Party committee at the same administrative level (e.g, the chair of the Shanghai Women's Federation was appointed by the Shanghai Municipal Committee of the CCP rather than by the ACWF). The exceptions were: (1) the women's congress, which was elected by residents of a particular neighborhood and (2) the executive committee of the women's congress, which was in turn elected by elected representatives of the congress. Women serving on the executive committeees of the women's congresses were not on the government payroll but sometimes received subsidies for their voluntary work.

The figure of 40,000 officials appears in Deng Yingchao's report to the second Women's Federation National Congress in 1953. See "Sinianlai zhongguo funü yundong de jiben zongjie he jinhou renwu" [A summary of the Chinese women's movement in the past four years and future tasks], in *Zhongguo funü yundong wenxian ziliao huibian*, vol. 2, p. 171.

2. "Zhongguo funü yundong dangqian renwu de jueyi" [The Resolution on the current tasks of the Chinese women's movement]. Passed by the First National Women's Congress on April 1, 1949, the resolution was based on Deng Yingchao's report to the congress with a similar title. Ibid., 22–24.

3. *Jiating funü*, literally, family woman, is a term that emerged as a contrast to the new term "career woman," *zhiye funü*, in the 1930s.

4. "Shanghaishi minzhu fulian choubeihui liangge yue gongzuo gaikuang" [A summary on the two months' work of the preparatory committee for the Shanghai

Democratic Women's Federation], Shanghai Municipal Archives (hereafter SMA), 1949, C31-1-2.

5. See Cai Chang, "Guanyu nügong gongzuo de jige wenti" [A few issues about work on women workers], in *Zhongguo funü yundong wenxian ziliao huibian,* vol. 2, p. 38.

6. Because there were diverse groups of women in this one million, lumping them together into a single category might also have been an SWF strategy to gain more institutional power. "Shanghai shiwei guanyu funü gongzuo de jueding" [Shanghai Party Committee's decision on women-work], and "Tian Xin he Wang Zhiya gei Zhao Xian de xin" [The letter to Zhao Xian from Tian Xin and Wang Zhiya], SMA, 31 February 1950, C31-1-9. The letter from the two district officials to the SWF leader inquired as to whether the SWF's policy of prioritizing women workers was being changed, since they had noticed increasing reports on organizing neighborhood women in Shanghai newspapers. Obviously, the SWF leaders started pilot projects of organizing housewives before informing the lower-level WF officials of the major policy shift.

7. "Guanyu jiating funü gongzuo de jidian yijian" [Views on the work of housewives], SMA, 1949, C31-1-2.

8. Examples of urban professional women's sentiments toward the WF in the Mao era can be found in interviews of feminist urban professionals Chen Mingxia and Wang Xingjuan in the *Global Feminisms Project* conducted by University of Michigan. www.umich.edu/~glblfem/en/china.html (accessed on May 6, 2016).

9. Dong Bian, "Tan nongcun funü daibiao huiyi" [On rural women's congress] (originally published in the first issue of *Xin Zhongguo Funü* [Women of New China], July 1949), and Deng Yingchao, "Quanguo fulian fuzhuxi Deng Yingchao zai Beijingshi shoujie fudai dahui shangde jianghua" [A talk by the vice chair of the ACWF Deng Yingchao at the first municipal congress of women in Beijing], November 29, 1949, both collected in *Zhongguo funü yundong wenxian ziliao huibian,* vol. 2, pp. 32–33 and 41–42.

10. A "lane" in Shanghai usually has walls to separate it from another lane. This architectural design became the material basis for the CCP's social reorganization. One lane usually had one or several residents groups, and in the jurisdiction of a residents committee there were about one dozen residents groups from several lanes. The mode of spatial organization was not entirely an innovation of the CCP. Historically China had a *baojia* system that managed local population by residency. The system was enforced in Shanghai during the Japanese occupation in World War II and continued by the Nationalist government in the late 1940s. When the CCP took over the city, it set up local public security stations according to the spatial division of the *baojia* system. What was new in this reorganization was that women replaced men as neighborhood managers. For a detailed discussion of this gendered social transformation, see Wang Zheng, "Gender and Maoist Urban Reorganization," in *Gender in Motion: Divisions of Labor and Cultural Change in Imperial and Modern China,* ed. Bryna Goodman and Wendy Larson (Lanham, MD: Rowman and Littlefield, 2005), 189–209.

11. "Shanghaishi fuwei gongzuo gaikuang baogao" [Shanghai women's committee's work report], SMA, 1951, C31-1-31.

12. Ibid.

13. "Fuwei guanyu jinnian sanba guoji funüjie gongzuo fangan" [The women's committee's plan for the March 8 celebration], 1951; and "Quanshi sanbajie youxing renshu tongjibiao" [Citywide statistics of people in the parade on March 8], SMA, 1951, C31-1-31.

14. Committee of the Annals of Shanghai Women, ed., *Shanghai funüzhi* [The annals of Shanghai women] (Shanghai: Shanghai shehui kexueyuan chubanshe, 2000), 265. In 1996 there were 2,809 women's congresses in Shanghai. Besides the neighborhood-based women's congress, currently the Women's Federation's grassroots organization also includes a "women-work committee" in each work unit, organizing women in gainful employment. "Grassroots" may be a misnomer here since the organization did not grow spontaneously out of the local community but was part of state building. The linguistic difficulty here suggests the existence of an under-theorized phenomenon in the early PRC when former grassroots organizers were mobilizing the masses for the formation of a socialist state.

15. "Guanyu jinhou quanguo funü yundong renwu de jueyi" [Resolution on the Future Tasks of the Women's Movement in the Country], and "Zhonghua quanguo funü lianhehui zhangcheng" [The Constitution of the All-China Women's Federation], in *Zhongguo funü yundong wenxian ziliao huibian,* vol. 2, pp. 179, 181.

16. "Jiangning qu diyi paichusuo jiating funü daibiao huiyi dianxing shiyan zongjie baogao" [A summary report on the work for the housewives' congress in the first police station in Jiangning District], SMA, 1951, C31-2-57. *Yangge,* a form of folk dance in Shaanxi, was introduced to Shanghai by the CCP.

17. "Funü de zuzhi qingkuang" [The situation of organizing women], SMA, 1951, C31-2-57.

18. "Dui jinhou jiedao linong jumin weiyuanhui zuzhi de yijian" [On the future organization of residents committees], SMA, 1951, C31-2-57.

19. "Gei shiwei bangongting de baogao" [A report to the office of the municipal Party committee], SMA, 13 September 1951, C31-1-37.

20. "Guanyu muqian banshichu zuzhi jigou qingkuang ji jinhou yijian jianbao" [Briefing on the street office's organizational structure and suggestions for future work], SMA, 20 July 1953, B168-1-772.

21. Zhao Xian, the second chair of the SWF, told me unequivocally, "The women's congress came first, and the residents committee came later. The residents committee was staffed mostly by the cadres of the women's congress and neighborhood work was mostly done by women cadres." Interview with author, Eastern China Hospital, Shanghai, September 13, 2004.

22. Wu Cuichan, interview with author, Shanghai, July 1, 2002.

23. "Shanghaishi jumin weiyuanhui zhengdun gongzuo qingkuang baogao" [A report on the work on rectification of the Shanghai residents committees], SMA, 23 October 1954, B168-1-14. Cadre is an imported word from Japanese to refer to officials in modern China.

24. "Gei shiwei bangongting de baogao" [A report to the office of the municipal Party committee], SMA, 13 September 1951, C31–1–37.

25. "Shiwei pifu" [The municipal Party committee's reply], SMA, 26 September 1951, C31–1–31.

26. "Linong funü daibiao huiyi zuzhi shixing tiaoli" [Tentative Regulations on the Organization of the Women's Congress in Shanghai Neighborhoods], SMA, February 1955, B168–1–130.

27. "Benhui guanyu linong zhengdun zhong funü gongzuo de tonggao" [The women's federation's report on women-work in the rectification of the neighborhood], SMA, 1954, C31–2–235; and "Shanghaishi fulian 1954 gongzuo zhongjie" [Shanghai WF's review of work in 1954], SMA, 1955, C31–1–95.

28. In 1952 the CCP started a five-anti's campaign targeting business owners. The five anti's included anti-bribing, anti-tax evasion, anti-stealing state property, anti-fraudulence in production, and anti-stealing financial information. The SWF took considerable effort to include wives of business owners in this campaign, urging them to persuade their husbands to follow the Party's policies.

29. "Shanghai minzhu fulian 1953 nian xiabannian gongzuo zongjie" [Shanghai Democratic Women's Federation's review of work in the second half of 1953], SMA, 1954, C31–1–75.

30. "Linong funü daibiao huiyi de xingzhi renwu buke baogao" [A talk on the nature and tasks of the neighborhood women's congress], SMA, 1954, C31–2–235.

31. "Huiyi jilu" [Notes on Guan Jian's talk], SMA, 1954, C31–1–100.

32. "Linong funü daibiao huiyi de xingzhi renwu buke baogao."

33. Zhang Yun, "Guojia guodu shiqi chengshi funü gongzuo de renwu he dang-qian jixiang juti gongzuo baogao" [A talk on the tasks of urban women-work in our country's transitional period and current work], in *Zhongguo funü yundong wenxian ziliao huibian*, vol. 2, p. 216.

34. Ibid.

35. Zhao Xian, "Yi Cai dajie zai Shanghai shica" [Remembering Sister Cai's inspection in Shanghai], in *Shanghai fulian sishi nian* [Forty years of the Shanghai Women's Federation] (Shanghai: Shanghai Women's Federation, 1990), 8. Recalling Cai Chang's intervention almost forty years ago is obviously Zhao Xian's effort to write this successful behind-the-scenes feminist struggle into history.

36. "Guanyu Shanghaishi fulian jiceng fudaihui de zuzhi wenti" [On the organizational issues of Shanghai Women's Federation's women's congress], SMA, 1956, C31–1–161; "Benbu 1959 nian gongzuo jihua" [A work plan for 1959], SMA, 1959, C31–1–248.

37. Deng Yingchao was a renowned young feminist leader in the May Fourth period (1919–24) in Tianjin. She played the major role in incorporating May Fourth feminist ideas into the first Marriage Law of the PRC.

38. "Deng Yinchao tongzhi zai zhongfuwei huiyi shangde fayan" (Comrade Deng Yinchao's talk at the meeting of the Central Women's Committee), in *Zhongguo funü yundong lishi ziliao 1945–1949* [Historical documents of the Chinese

women's movement, 1945–1949] (Beijing: Zhongguo funü chubanshe, 1991), 240. A copy of Deng's talk is included in the SWF's file compiled in 1957, which indicates the conscious transmission of Deng's strategy in the WF system in a volatile time. SMA, C31-1-169.

39. Many rural women had a formal name for the first time in the land reform when they were required to register the land deeds with their own names rather than the name of a father or husband.

40. Ellen Judd, *The Chinese Women's Movement between State and Market* (Stanford, CA: Stanford University Press, 2002), observes a similar strategic pattern in the Women's Federation activities in the 1980s to 1990s.

41. Wu Xiuying, interview with author, Shanghai, March 16, 2001.

42. March 8 Flag Bearer is an honored title granted to selected exemplary female workers and professionals. The title not only expresses official recognition of a woman's remarkable accomplishments, but also comes with privileges such as those granted to labor models. March 8, International Women's Day, has been observed since the early days of the CCP, a sign of the Party's commitment to women's liberation.

43. Wu Cuichan and Cao Shunqin, interview with author, Shanghai Women's Federation, August 21, 2002.

44. Zhao Xian, interview with author, Eastern China Hospital, Shanghai, September 13, 2004. For a discussion of women's resistance to the Party's pronatalist policy, see Tyrene White, "The Origins of China's Birth Planning Policy," in *Engendering China: Women, Culture, and the State,* ed. Christina K. Gilmartin, Gail Hershatter, Lisa Rofel, and Tyrene White (Boston: Harvard University Press, 1994), 250–78.

45. "Deng Yinchao tongzhi zai zhongfuwei huiyi shangde fayan," 241.

46. James C. Scott, *Domination and the Arts of Resistance: Hidden Transcripts* (New Haven, CT: Yale University Press, 1990).

47. Wendy Brown, *States of Injury: Power and Freedom in Late Modernity* (Princeton, NJ: Princeton University Press, 1995), 173.

48. Timothy Mitchell, "Society, Economy, and the State Effect," in *State / Culture,* ed. George Steinmetz (Ithaca, NY: Cornell University Press, 1999), 77–78.

49. "1954 nian Shanghai fulian gongzuo zongjie" [A summary of Shanghai Women's Federation's work in 1954], SMA, 12 April 1955, C31-1-95.

CHAPTER TWO. THE POLITICAL PERILS IN 1957

1. For a study of the ACWF in the post-Mao era, see Ellen Judd, *The Chinese Women's Movement between State and Market* (Stanford, CA: Stanford University Press, 2002).

2. Luo Qiong and Duan Yongqiang, *Luo Qiong fangtan lu* [Interviews with Luo Qiong] (Beijing: Zhongguo funü chubanshe, 2000), 126. Mao's original phrase *san maniang* was changed by women officials into *san piping* (third, criticize) in their

public talks, perhaps because of the apparent gender offensiveness of the original and class connotation. Cursing and swearing were sometimes adopted by lower-class women as powerful weapons in their resistance, but were forbidden for women of "respectable" families.

3. Actually quite a few WF officials were labeled as "rightists" for their candid criticism of their Party leaders in 1957. For examples of such cases, see discussions of Wu Cuichan and Zhao Xian in the previous chapter.

4. See Deng Yingchao, "Zaidang lingdaoxia, tuanjie he fahui guangda funü quanzhongde liliang" [Under the Party's leadership, unite and utilize the power of women masses], and Cai Chang, "Jiji peiyang he tiba gengduo genghao de nüganbu" [Actively train and promote more and better women cadres], in *Zhongguo funü yundong wenxian ziliao huibian*, vol. 2, 262–68.

5. Delia Davin, *Woman-Work: Women and the Party in Revolutionary China* (London: Oxford University Press, 1976), 65–68.

6. See Zhang Naihua, "The All-China Women's Federation, Chinese Women and the Women's Movement: 1949–1993," PhD dissertation, Michigan State University, 1996.

7. See Elizabeth Perry, "Shanghai's Strike Wave of 1957," *China Quarterly* 137 (March 1994): 1–27; Jackie Sheehan, *Chinese Workers: A New History* (London and New York: Routledge, 1998); and Merle Goldman, *Literary Dissent in Communist China* (Cambridge, MA: Harvard University Press, 1967).

8. "Luo Qiong tongzhi chuanda zhongyang shujichu, zhongyang zhengzhiju fuze tongzhi duiyu funü gongzuo jiao zhongyao zhishi de jilu zhengli" [Notes of comrade Luo Qiong's conveying the relatively important directives on women-work by the leading comrades of the Secretariat and the Political Bureau of the Central Committee], SMA, 22 October 1957, C31–1–169.

9. *Luo Qiong fangtan lu*, 148.

10. Ibid., 144.

11. "Zhang Yun tongzhi chuanda Cai dajie he Deng dajie de zhishi" [Comrade Zhang Yun conveys instructions from elder sister Cai and elder sister Deng], ACWF archives. Since I was not allowed to access the ACWF archives, I asked friends who had access to photocopy documents relating to the preparation of the Third National Women's Congress. The dates and file numbers are unclear.

12. See All-China Women's Federation, *Huainian Zhang Yun dajie* [Remembering Sister Zhang Yun] (Beijing: Zhongguo funü chubanshe, 1996).

13. *Luo Qiong fangtan lu*, 144.

14. See the previous chapter as to how WF officials defended the necessity of a women's organization.

15. *Luo Qiong fangtan lu*, 145.

16. Ibid. The Secretariat in 1957 included Deng Xiaoping, Peng Zhen, Wang Jiaxiang, Tan Zhenlin, Tan Zheng, Huang Kecheng, and Li Xuefeng.

17. "Luo Qiong tongzhi chuanda zhongyang shujichu, zhongyang zhengzhiju fuze tongzhi duiyu funü gongzuo jiao zhongyao zhishi de jilu zhengli."

18. Ibid.

19. "Shanghai minzhu fulian 1953 nian xiabannian gongzuo zongjie" [Shanghai Democratic Women's Federation's review of work in the second half of 1953], SMA, 1954, C31–1–75. For more discussion on this critique, see chapter 1.

20. In her old age Luo Qiong wrote essays to commemorate Deng Xiaoping and Liu Shaoqi and recounted the two leaders' pivotal role at the two top meetings of the Party in 1957. She quoted directly from Deng and Liu, which confirmed the context and accuracy of the content of their speeches recorded in the document I found in the Shanghai Municipal Archives. Yet, she did not reveal a word of the Secretariat's attack on equality between men and women. See Luo Qiong, *Kangzhen, jiefang, pingdeng* [Resistance, emancipation, equality: An anthology by Luo Qiong] (Beijing: Zhongguo funü chubanshe, 2007), 491–93.

21. *Luo Qiong fangtan lu*, 145.

22. *Zhongguo funü yundong wenxian ziliao huibian,* vol. 2, p. 316.

23. "Luo Qiong tongzhi chuanda zhongyang shujichu, zhongyang zhengzhiju fuze tongzhi duiyu funü gongzuo jiao zhongyao zhishi de jilu zhengli."

24. "Zhongguo nongcun de shehuizhuyi gaochao de xuyan" [Preface to the high tide of socialism in rural China], September and December 1955, in *Mao Zedong xuanji* [hereafter *Selected Works of Mao Zedong*], vol. 5 (Beijing: Renmin chubanshe, 1955), 249.

25. "Nongye hezuohua de yichang bianlun he dangqian de jieji douzheng" [A debate on agricultural collectivization and current class struggles], October 11, 1955, in *Selected Works of Mao Zedong*, vol. 5, 213.

26. "Yijiuwuqi nian xiaji de xingshi" [The situation in summer 1957], July 1957, in *Selected Works of Mao Zedong,* vol. 5, 459.

27. *Luo Qiong fangtan lu,* 146.

28. Mao Zedong, "Duizhongyang guanyu yijiuwuqi nian kaizhan zengchan jieyue yundong de zhishi gao de piyu" [Comment on the draft directive on the Party Central launching the campaign of increasing production and practicing economy in 1957], in *Jianguo yilai Mao Zedong wengao* [Mao Zedong's papers since the founding of the PRC], vol. 6 (Beijing: Zhongyang wenxian chubanshe, 1990), 302–3.

29. *Renmin ribao* [People's Daily], March 26, 1957, p. 6.

30. "Zhang Yun tongzhi chuanda Cai dajie he Deng dajie de zhishi."

31. "Zai shengshi zizhiqu dangwei shuji huiyishang de jianghua" [Talk on the conference of provincial Party Committee secretaries], January 1957, in *Selected Works of Mao Zedong,* vol. 5, p. 335.

32. See Song Qingling, "Funü yao jianjue guohao shehuizhuyi zheyiguan" [Women should resolutely pass the test of socialism], in *Zhongguo funü yundong wenxian ziliao huibian,* vol. 2, p. 308. Song Qingling was also the vice president of the People's Congress of the PRC.

33. "Luo Qiong tongzhi chuanda zhongyang shujichu, zhongyang zhengzhiju fuze tongzhi duiyu funü gongzuo jiao zhongyao zhishi de jilu zhengli."

34. On informal relations among the Chinese elite and their influence on historical processes, see Jin Qiu, *The Culture of Power: The Lin Biao Incident in the Cultural Revolution* (Stanford, CA: Stanford University Press, 1999).

35. The ACWF's magazine *Women of China* prepared its readers for the shift in the focus of women-work by publishing an editorial in its September 1957 issue that highlighted the double diligences before the convening of the Third National Women's Congress. Starting from the February 1958 issue it also created a Forum discussing the significance of double diligences. Although the magazine increased reporting on how women in different walks creatively managed their households frugally, the topic did not dominate the magazine and women's participation in social production continued to be a prominent theme. The campaign of the double diligences impacted local WF variously. Based on her archival research on the Hebei Provincial Women's Federation, Lynda Bell presents a close examination of the process and effects of the double diligences campaign in rural Hebei in her unpublished paper, "Woman, Nation, Household Redux: Mobilizing Female Virtue in the 1950s Chinese Countryside," and discovers local state feminists' novel practices to empower peasant women. Bell's findings, in a sense, further explain Luo Qiong's genuine enthusiasm about the double diligences. I thank Lynda Bell for sharing this paper with me.

36. Luo Qiong "Deng Xiaoping tongzhi zai zhongyao de lishi shike dui funü gongzuo de zhiyin" [Comrade Deng Xiaoping's guidance of women-work at the important historical moments], in Luo Qiong, *Kangzhen, jiefang, pingdeng,* 497. See also *Luo Qiong fangtan lu,* 149–50.

37. Luo Qiong, *Kangzhen, jiefang, pingdeng,* 215, 209.

38. Susan Mann presents a vivid historical narrative of generations of women's crucial roles in sustaining large elite households as well as the civil service examination system in late imperial China in *The Talented Women of the Zhang Family* (Berkeley: University of California Press, 2007).

39. Luo Qiong, *Kangzhen, jiefang, pingdeng,* 216.

40. "Quanguo fulian guanyu 1958 nian 1yue zhaokai de sheng (shi) zizhiqu fulian zhuren huiyi de tongbao" [The ACWF's report on the conference of WF chairs of provincial, municipal, and autonomous regions in January 1958], in *Zhongguo funü yundong wenxian ziliao huibian,* vol. 2, pp. 351–56.

41. Dong Bian, "Zai quanguo funü gongzuo huiyishangde fayan" [Talk on the national conference on women-work], in *Zhongguo funü yundong wenxian ziliao huibian,* vol. 2, p. 364.

42. For a study of Women's Federation officials in the Great Leap Forward, see Kimberley Ens Manning, "Making a Great Leap Forward? The Politics of Women's Liberation in Maoist China," in *Translating Feminisms in China,* ed. Dorothy Ko and Wang Zheng (Malden, MA: Blackwell, 2007), 138–63.

43. Luo Qiong, *Kangzhen, jiefang, pingdeng,* 496.

44. Cao Guanqun, "Quanguo funü gongzuo huiyi zongjie baogao" [A summary report on the national conference of women-work], in *Zhongguo funü yundong wenxian ziliao huibian,* vol. 2, p. 376.

45. Maxine Molyneux, "Analysing Women's Movements," in *Feminist Visions of Development: Gender, Analysis and Policy,* ed. Cecile Jackson and Ruth Pearson (London: Routledge, 1998), 65–88.

46. Kimberley Ens Manning gives an account of the disbanding of local Women's Federations in 1958. See "The Gendered Politics of Woman-work: Rethinking Radicalism in the Great Leap Forward," *Modern China* 32, no. 3 (2006): 1–36. Also, see Kimberley Ens Manning, "Embodied Activisms: The Case of the Mu Guiying Brigade," *China Quarterly*, no. 204 (December 2010): 850–69 for a study of the effects of both the double diligences movement and the Great Leap Forward.

47. Luo Qiong, *Kangzhen, jiefang, pingdeng*, 497.

48. The document in the Shanghai Municipal Archives could be a leak by Zhang Yun to her old colleagues in Shanghai.

CHAPTER THREE. CREATING A FEMINIST CULTURAL FRONT

1. After the founding of the PRC, over thirty newspapers included a women's supplement and some local Women's Federations also began to publish women's journals. These publications had localized circulation and various durations of existence.

2. For studies of women's images produced in socialist China, see Tina Mai Chen, "Female Icons, Feminist Iconography? Socialist Rhetoric and Women's Agency in 1950s China," *Gender and History* 15, no. 2 (2003): 268–95, and Harriet Evans, "'Comrade Sisters': Gendered Bodies and Spaces," in *Picturing Power in the People's Republic of China: Posters of the Cultural Revolution*, ed. Harriet Evans and Stephanie Donald (Lanham, MD: Rowman and Littlefield, 1999), 63–78.

3. *Women of China* was the only national women's magazine circulating continuously until its suspension in the heat of the Cultural Revolution. Hou Di, deputy editor-in-chief of *Women of China* by the end of 1966, remembers that the magazine suspended publication after February 1967. But the electronic collection of the magazine the *Women of China* Press produced does not include the two issues in 1967 and I have not found them in any libraries. I do not claim this is a comprehensive study of the magazine, which published 238 issues from its first issue in July 1949 to the end of 1966. Many more topics can be explored from this rich and massive amount of historical source material.

4. *Zhongguo funü zazhi jianjie* [A brief introduction to *Women of China*], internal circulation of memoirs produced by the Press of *Women of China*, 1999. It is a CD without page numbers.

5. The name reflected its membership in the Women's International Democratic Federation. It changed to the All-China Women's Federation in 1957 at its third National Congress.

6. Shen Zijiu, "Nuola zuotanhui" [A symposium by Noras], in *Nüjie wenhua zhanshi Shen Zijiu* [Shen Zijiu, a woman fighter on the cultural front], ed. Dong Bian, Li Suzhen, and Zhang Jiafen (Beijing: Zhongguo funü chubanshe, 1991), 234–38.

7. Years later Shen recalled an argument between them. "When he failed to win the argument, he angrily uttered, 'A woman should not talk so much. A talkative woman is a woman with a long tongue [fond of gossip].' What an insulting remark!" Ibid., 236.

8. Shi Liangcai (1880–1934) was the most powerful media figure in the Republican period at the time of his assassination on November 13, 1934. People generally believe it was a case of state terror deployed by Chiang Kai-shek against freedom of speech, especially aimed at leftist critical views frequently published in the *Shanghai Post*.

9. Luo Qiong, "Xiang Shen Zijiu dajie zhushou de shike" [Celebrating the birthday of elder sister Shen], in Luo Qiong, *Kangzhen, jiefang, pingdeng* [Resistance, emancipation, equality: An anthology by Luo Qiong] (Beijing: Zhongguo funü chubanshe, 2007), 552.

10. Ibid., 552–53.

11. See a memoir by Shen's daughter, Zhang Lüyi, "Ta zhaodaole yaozou de lu" [She found the road she had been looking for], in Dong, Li, and Zhang, eds., *Shen Zijiu*, 204–14. For a discussion of *Women's Life*, see Louise Edwards, *Gender, Politics, and Democracy: Women's Suffrage in China* (Stanford, CA: Stanford University Press, 2008). The author does not discuss the fact that this influential women's magazine in the Nationalist-controlled areas was actually affiliated with the CCP and many CCP writers were frequent contributors.

12. For more information on Shen Zijiu, see Dong Bian's essay, "Keqin kejing de Shen dajie" [An amiable and admirable elder sister Shen], in Dong, Li, and Zhang, eds., *Shen Zijiu*, 158–65. The volume contains many essays written by former readers of *Women's Life* who became CCP officials.

13. For Dong Bian's life, see her daughters' memoirs: Zeng Li and Zeng Zi, "Women de mama Dong Bian" [Our mother Dong Bian], *Yanhuang chunqiu* [Chinese History], no. 12 (1999): 55–59; and Dong Bian, dictated to Zeng Li and Zeng Zi, "Zai Yan'an he Jiaying xiangshi xiangai de rizi" [Remembering the time in love with Jiaying in Yan'an], *Dangshi bolan* [Overviews of the Party's History] no. 3 (2010): 51–54.

14. See "Women de mama Dong Bian," 57. Deng Yingchao personally selected many Communist women to work in various posts of the ACWF, sometimes exerting quite an effort to persuade them to do women-work. Reminding women officials of the mission of women's liberation was a central point that Deng made when she recruited them. She succeeded in gathering remarkable women to work for the ACWF. In the characterization of one of my interviewees who had been a young colleague of those senior women, "Everyone of the first generation of women cadres in the ACWF could be the subject of a book." Gu Lanying's interview with author, Beijing, July 3, 2010.

15. Dong's two daughters, Zeng Li and Zeng Zi, could not recall any occasion when their mother took them to parks, shops, or hospitals. It was always their father who took them out. Respected by her husband, Dong also enjoyed the institutional childcare support assigned to official families, with a Manchu woman undertaking domestic responsibilities. The characters of the daughters' names, *zili*, mean "self-reliance."

16. Dong Bian's colleague, deputy editor-in-chief Hou Di, related details of Dong's frugality in my interview with her on July 1, 2010. Hou Di's memoir of Dong Bian, "Ren buyiding weida, dan keyi gaoshao" [One does not have to be magnificent to be noble], was published in *Women of China*, no. 12 (2001): 16–18. An unabridged version of the memoir has this story of Dong Bian refusing to take a car.

17. During the last ten months of her life, Dong Bian was hospitalized and cared for by her daughters. It was then she related her life story to them. Zeng Li and Zeng Zi's interview with author, Beijing, June 25, 2010.

18. "Jianmian hua" [Opening greetings], *Xin Zhongguo funü* [Women of New China], no. 1 (1949): 6.

19. See Dong Bian, "Keqin kejing de Shen dajie."

20. The other three were *Xuexi* [Study], *Zhongguo qingnian* [Youth of China], and *Remin wenxue* [People's Literature]. Hou Di, "Nanyi wangque de naduan lishi" [An unforgettable period of history], internal collection of memoirs produced on a CD by the Press of *Women of China* in 1999. Xuexi was renamed *Hongqi* [The Red Flag] in 1958 and *Qiushi* [Seeking Truth] in 1988. They are all official-run journals.

21. The price of a copy of the magazine at the time was twelve Chinese cents. The market success in the socialist period was not so much profit-driven since none of the members of the press benefited financially. One male editor complained to me that those elder sisters (leaders) were so frugal that they sat on the huge surplus without even purchasing a car for the press in all those years. They could have easily afforded twenty cars at the time, but instead, everyone had to either ride a bike or take a bus to run work-related errands.

22. "Zhongguo de saomang jiaoyu" [Education to eliminate illiteracy in China], by the Research Group on Education to Eliminate Illiteracy in China, in *Jiaoyu yanjiu* [Education studies], no. 6 (1997): 6.

23. By 1953 there were 40,000 women officials in the Women's Federation system nationwide. The number rose to 60,000 in the 1960s and 90,000 in the twenty-first century. The total number of women officials in the PRC was 150,000 in 1951 and 764,000 in 1956. See Dong Bian, Cai Asong, and Tan Deshan, eds., *Women de hao dajie Cai Chang* [Our good elder sister Cai Chang] (Beijing: Zhongyang wenxian chubanshe, 1992), 80.

24. The ACWDF became a member of the WIDF in 1949. Practices initiated by the WIDF became part of the political culture in the PRC, such as the annual celebration of International Children's Day on June 1. More importantly, in the Cold War era when China had few diplomatic relations with the West, the ACWDF became the most important international channel for the Chinese government, largely via the WIDF, and organized many international cultural exchanges. The international dimension of the ACWDF, an untold story, forcefully challenged the commonly held notion of "China's isolation" in the Mao era. For clues to the ACWF's heavy involvement in the diplomacy of the early PRC, see All-China Women's Federation, *Zhongguo funü yundong bainian dashi ji (1901–2000)* [Major events in a century of the Chinese women's movement (1901–2000)] (Beijing: Zhongguo funü chubanshe, 2003).

25. *Women of New China*, no. 11 (1950): 46.

26. In any case, it was Shen Zijiu who had introduced the high school graduate Li Qiyang to the Communist camp of resistance back in 1937. Li Qiyang's transfer to Beijing was because of the transfer of her husband, who was then Xi Zhongxun's secretary. Li became the deputy governor of Gansu Province in 1980 and retired in 1988. She has published two highly informative memoirs, *Huanghe dongliu* [The Yellow River running east] (Beijing: Beijing daxue chubanshe, 2003), and *Xibei liuyun* [The Northwest drifting clouds] (no publisher, which means it is not an officially registered publication, 2008). When I interviewed Li Qiyang in the summer of 2010, she could not remember writing the article, though she had a distinctive memory of creating the *Western Women's Pictorial*.

27. "The Decision on Starting Criticism and Self-criticism in Newspapers and Journals" pointed out that the Party held political power across the entire country, but that shortcomings and mistakes in its work might very easily jeopardize people's interests; its leadership position could induce conceitedness, and result in rejection and suppression of criticism. Therefore, the Central Committee decided to call for people's open criticism "of all the mistakes and shortcomings in our work in all the public occasions among the people and masses, especially in newspapers and journals," issued on April 19, 1950. See "Zhongguo gongchandang dashi ji—1950" [Major events of the CCP—1950], *E-North.com.cn,* http://news.enorth.com.cn/system /2006/06/19/001334591.shtml (accessed January 24, 2010).

28. *Women of New China*, no. 13 (1950): 14–15.

29. Ethnic minorities predominantly live in regions forming the borders of China, a heritage of a long and complex imperial history. The PRC gives an official count of fifty-six ethnic groups in China.

30. Ellen Johnston Laing alerted me to the fascinating pictures on the covers of the first volume of the *Ladies Journal* in 1915. Twelve paintings capture a range of women's work within and outside the domestic setting, including one of a woman picking mulberry leaves and two others picking tea leaves, apparently portrayed as feminine agricultural work. The pictures have vastly different significance from those in the socialist period. No class or urban / rural distinctions are suggested as they prominently extol women's virtue of diligence. The contrast between the cover images of two mainstream women's magazines in the twentieth century vividly conveys the drastic social, political, economic, and cultural changes that have reconfigured gender in China as well as continuity in terms of the celebrated importance of women's productive labor either for family or for the state.

31. Shi Yumei, interview with author, Beijing, July 20, 2009.

32. Duan Yongqiang, interview with author, Beijing, July 18, 2007.

33. Shi Yumei, interview with author, Beijing, July 20, 2009.

34. In the one-year summary published in August 1950, the editorial listed their weakness of connecting with the masses as the major problem and designed plans to address it. For readers' suggestions for improvement of the magazine, see also issue nos. 11 and 16 in 1950.

35. Hou Di, "Nanyi wangque de naduan lishi."

36. Yang Yun, "Shendajie jiaowo ban kanwu" [Elder sister Shen taught me how to run a magazine], in Dong, Li, and Zhang, eds., *Shen Zijiu*, 166–78. Yang Yun (not to be confused with the woman who committed suicide) was in charge of the editorial group for political education in the mid-1950s. In this essay she gave a detailed account of how Shen made the decision to start this forum and taught her how to select and organize readers' letters in order to incorporate readers' views.

37. See Dong Bian, "Keqin kejing de Shen dajie," 162

38. The detailed stories behind the scenes were provided by Hou Di, who was promoted to deputy editor-in-chief in the summer of 1956. See Hou Di, "Nanyi wangque de naduan lishi."

39. Hou Di, phone interview with author, March 16, 2010.

40. For an early discussion of this issue, see Davin, *Woman-Work: Women and the Party in Revolutionary China*, 102–5. For a detailed description of CCP women's debates over divorce when drafting the Marriage Law, see Jin Feng, *Deng Yingchao Zhuan* [A biography of Deng Yingchao], vol. 2 (Beijing: People's Press, 1993), 457–61. According to Jin Feng, when some women officials expressed their misgivings that the reformed divorce procedure in the law might make it easier for male officials to divorce their wives, Deng Yingchao reminded the women officials of the drafting committee that the law also made it easier for rural women to get a divorce. She emphasized that Communist women officials should prioritize the interests of the great majority of women. If, in the worst-case scenario, some official husbands should use the new law to divorce women officials, that would not be the end of the world for women officials who had the capacity to live an independent life.

41. Tina Mai Chen, "Female Icons, Feminist Iconography?"

42. For a discussion of the role of urban domestic women in socialist state building in the early 1950s, see Wang Zheng, "Gender and Maoist Urban Reorganization," in *Gender in Motion: Divisions of Labor and Cultural Change in Late Imperial and Modern China,* eds. Bryna Goodman and Wendy Larson (New York: Rowman and Littlefield, 2005), 189–209.

43. Deng Yingchao, "Guanyu funü xuanchuan jiaoyu wenti" [On the issue of women's advocacy and education work], in *Zhongguo funü yundong wenxian ziliao huibian*, vol. 2, p. 115.

44. Ibid.

45. *Women of China*, no. 8 (1956): 8–9.

46. Office of ACWF, ed., *Zhonghua quanguo funü lianhehui sishi nian* [Forty years of the All-China Women's Federation] (Beijing: Chinese Women Press, 1991), 94.

47. Kimberley Ens Manning, "Making a Great Leap Forward? The Politics of Women's Liberation in Maoist China," *Gender and History* 18, no. 3 (2006): 574–93.

48. Hou Di, phone interview with author, December 10, 2009. The reader's letter was published in no. 7 (1963).

49. Joan Judge, *Precious Raft of History: The Past, the West, and the Woman Question in China* (Stanford, CA: Stanford University Press, 2008).

50. Edwards, *Gender, Politics, and Democracy.*

51. Gail Hershatter, *The Gender of Memory: Rural Women and China's Collective Past* (Berkeley: University of California, 2011); Lisa Rofel, *Other Modernities: Gendered Yearnings in China after Socialism* (Berkeley: University of California Press, 1999).

52. Office of ACWF, ed., *Zhonghua quanguo funü lianhehui sishi nian*, 97.

53. The same point was made by Evans, in "Comrade Sisters," 72, with reference to posters of the socialist period.

54. The evidence of gender bias on the covers of *Youth of China* does not mean that the journal never used any women-centered images. It was the inconsistent practices that most clearly reveal its editors' unconscious gender bias.

55. Shi Yumei was never able to join the Party because her father had been a Nationalist army officer. Her "problematic" political background sometimes hindered her work; for example, she could not interview or photograph high-ranking officials.

56. Feminist culture in an altered variation entered the prominent mainstream media in the form of "model operas" and in newspapers such as *People's Daily* in the Cultural Revolution. See chapter 7.

CHAPTER FOUR. WHEN A MAOIST "CLASS" INTERSECTED GENDER

1. "Zhongguo gongchandang dashiji (1966)" [Major events of the Chinese Communist Party in 1966], *Renminwang People.com.cn*, http://cpc.people.com.cn /GB/64162/64164/4416081.html (accessed May 19, 2016).

2. Dong Bian, "Xiang funü xuanchuan shehui, xiang shehui xuanchuan funü: Huainian Hu Qiaomu tongzhi" [Educating women about the society, educating the society about women: Remembering comrade Hu Qiaomu], in *Zhongguo funü zazhi jianjie* [A brief introduction to *Women in China*].

3. I translate the term *airen* into "lover" instead of "spouse" to highlight a forgotten term that suggested radical transformation of conjugal relations with an emphasis on mutual affection rather than hierarchical power relations and normative roles. In the Mao era, "lover" replaced "husband and wife" in daily usage, especially in urban areas. The term has been abandoned in the post-socialist period.

4. Hou Di, "Ren buyiding weida, dan keyi gaoshang" [One does not have to be magnificent to be noble], *Women of China*, no. 12 (2001): 17.

5. Wan Muchun, "Zenyang kandai funü wenti" [How should we deal with the women question], *Red Flag*, no. 20 (1964): 23–28.

6. Ibid.

7. Ibid.

8. Ibid.

9. For an examination of the formation of this theme for the Third National Women's Congress in 1957, see chapter 2 in this volume.

10. Dong Bian, "Cai dajie—nüganbu de zhiyin he laoshi" [Elder sister Cai—women cadres' close friend and teacher], in *Women de hao dajie Cai Chang*, ed. Dong Bian, Cai Asong, and Tan Deshan (Beijing: Zhongyang wenxian chuban-she 1992), 81. At the time when editors wrote their memoirs or commemorating essays, they did not have access to old issues of *Women of China*. All the references to the magazine were from their memories, hence frequent minor inaccuracies, such as the title of Ou Mengjue's article mentioned by Dong Bian here and some quotations from the article "How Should We Deal with the Women Question" by Hou Di.

11. Ibid., 80. In this passage Dong Bian's detailed information on the name and address of the peasant family that adopted her baby son revealed her desire to get in touch with her son somehow.

12. Ibid., 81.

13. Wen Jie, "Wangshi suoji" [Reminiscences], in *Zhongguo funü zazhi jianjie*.

14. Benbao jizhe [reporter], "Ba geming shiye fangzai diyiwei" [Giving priority to the revolutionary cause], *Women of China*, no. 4 (1963): 6–7.

15. Hu Bangxiu, "Huiyi ershi duonianqian *Zhongguo funü* shangde yichang taolun" [Recalling a debate in *Women of China* over twenty years ago], in *Zhongguo funü zazhi jianjie*.

16. Ibid.

17. Ibid.

18. The Editorial, "Juexin zuo jianqiangde chedide geming nüzhanshi" [Be a strong and thoroughgoing revolutionary woman soldier resolutely], *Women of China*, no. 2 (1964): 9.

19. Ibid., 9–10.

20. Ibid., 10.

21. Ibid., 9.

22. Ibid.,9.

23. Ibid., 11.

24. Ibid., 13.

25. *Fuqi zhijian* [Between the couple] (Beijing: *Zhongguo Funü zazhishe*, 1964).

26. *Women of China*, no. 10 (1964): 21–22.

27. The reference to "nurse" and age difference between the copule in the article indicates an implied criticism of those high-ranking male officials who had replaced their old wives with young ones who, due to age and power disparity, sometimes made taking care of an official husband into a career. Ibid., 22.

28. The political stance of these state feminists may be further illustrated by an anecdote related by Dong Bian's daughters. Dong Bian's husband Tian Jiaying once commented on her being a radical leftist. Dong Bian replied that in the press she was regarded as oriented toward the right. Most of her colleagues were far more leftist than she was.

29. Hou Di, "Ren buyiding weida, dan keyi gaoshang," 17.

30. For Zhang Yun's critical letter to the Shanghai Party leader Liu Xiao, see chapter 1.

31. Peng Zhen at the time headed the "Group of Five" that had been formed in July 1964, in charge of revolutionizing the cultural realm in response to Mao's request. But in 1966 four out of five top officials in this group including Peng Zhen would be condemned and removed from their positions. The "Group of Five" was replaced by the "Central Cultural Revolution Group" headed by Chen Boda in May 1966. Peng Zhen and Chen Boda clashed at a meeting of the Party Secretariat in January 1962. When Peng suggested that all the Party leaders, including Chairman Mao and Liu Shaoqi, should take responsibility for their mistakes in policies of the previous years, Chen rebutted, "We have done a lot of messy stuff. Do we want to hold Chairman Mao responsible for all that? Do we want to check Chairman Mao's work?" See Lin Yunhui, "Zhonggong bada weishenme meiyou Peng Zhen fayan? [Why was there no Peng Zhen's speech at the Eighth Congress of the Party Central?], in *Yanhuang chunqiu* [Chinese History], no. 9 (2015): 10–15. This article traces Peng Zhen's continued insistence on the necessity to include Mao in the Party's self-criticism.

32. Dong Bian, "Cai dajie-nü ganbu de zhiying he laoshi," 82. Peng Zhen would be the first official banished from the power center by Mao in 1966 for his refusal to collaborate with the radicals in the Party who were assisting Mao in his launch of the Cultural Revolution.

33. Late in 1965 in a similar manner Peng Zhen dismissed another condemning article, "On the New Historical Play *Hai Rui Dismissed from Office*." But this time his resistance to an incriminating class analysis applied to his colleague Wu Han led to his downfall. Authorized by Mao behind the scenes, the famous article signaled Mao's offense on the "bourgeois headquarters" in the Party.

34. *Zhongnanhai* is the name of part of the royal residence and imperial court in history. When the CCP took power, it became the residential area of top party leaders as well as the site of the CCP Central Committee and the State Council. The name signifies the power center in the PRC.

35. Dong Bian had made a similar move early in 1966. She asked Tian Jiaying to submit a request for Mao's inscription for *Women of China*. But by then the relationship between Mao and Tian had already become estranged. Mao did not even open the letter sent by Tian, a gesture of contempt that contributed to Tian's despair.

36. Dong Bian, "Xiang funü xuanchuan shehui, xiang shehui xuanchuan funü."

37. Both Hu Qiaomu and Chen Boda claimed that they recommended Tian Jiaying to Mao. See Hu Qiaomu, "Wo suo zhidao de Tian Jiying" [What I know about Tian Jiaying], in *Mao Zedong he tade mishu Tian Jiaying* [Mao Zedong and his secretary Tian Jiaying], ed. Dong Bian, Tan Deshan, and Zeng Zi (Beijing: Zhongyang wenxian chubanshe, 1996), 165; and Chen Xiaonong, *Chen Boda zuihou koushu huiyi* [Chen Baoda's oral memoir in his last days] (Hong Kong: Yangguang huanqiu Press, 2005), 78, 89. In the commemorating articles by Tian Jiaying's friends and Dong Bian, only Hu Qiaomu is mentioned as the one who recommended Tian to Mao. It could be that Mao solicited a recommendation from both his secretaries.

38. Ye Yonglie, *Mao Zedong de mishumen* [Mao Zedong's secretaries] (Shanghai: Shanghai renmin chubanshe, 1994); and *Mao Zedong he tade mishu Tian Jiaying*. For

a description of Chen Boda in Yan'an, see Shi Zhe, "Wo suozhidao de Chen Boda" [What I know about Chen Boda], *Wenshi Jinghua* [Essence of culture and history], no. 8 (2002): 50–57. Shi Zhe served as Mao's Russian translator since the Yan'an period. In this piece she attributes the cause of the infamous persecution of Wang Shiwei and his "anti-Party group" to the grievances of those members of the Political Research Institute against Chen Boda, who was the director of the institute. For Chen Boda's ups and downs, see Ba Tu, "Chen Boda zai 'wenhua dageming' zhongde chen yu fu" [The ups and downs of Chen Boda in the Cultural Revolution], in *Dangshi Zongheng* [Perspectives of the Party's history], nos. 3–5 (2004): 9–12, 11–15, 20–23.

39. Peng Xianzhi, "*Mao Zedong he tade mishu Tian Jiaying*" [Mao Zedong and his secretary Tian Jiaying], in *Mao Zedong he tade mishu Tian Jiaying*, 91. This was Mao's response to Tian Jiaying's oral report that conveyed rural officials' views on how to address rural poverty and low productivity. But Tian did not heed Mao's instruction and continued to solicit support from other top party leaders, including Liu Shaoqi. Peng was Tian's assistant from 1950 until Tian's death in 1966. His eighty-page memoir of Tian constitutes one fourth of the volume that takes the title of his piece as the book title.

40. Hu Qiaomu, in *Mao Zedong he tade mishu Tian Jiaying*, 166.

41. Both Hu Qiaomu and Dong Bian remembered Chen Boda's resentment of Tian Jiaying's re-editing Mao's three volumes. Zeng Zi, email to author, October 5, 2010.

42. Zeng Zi, email to author, September 17, 2010, cited her sister Zeng Li's witness of the scene.

43. I have not found any evidence that Chen's attack was ultimately a charge against Peng Zhen, who in 1964 was entrusted by Mao to head the "Group of Five," though it could have been a stone intended to kill multiple birds.

44. No mainstream historians have paid any attention to this incident, either. No male officials, including Chen Boda, ever mentioned this incident in their memoirs.

45. See chapter 1.

46. See chapter 2.

CHAPTER FIVE. CHEN BO'ER AND THE FEMINIST
PARADIGM OF SOCIALIST FILM

An early version of this chapter was first presented in Chinese at the International Conference on *Chinese Women and Visual Representation,* Fudan University, Shanghai, December 16, 2011.

1. The Beijing Film Academy, originally called the Institute for Performing Art when Chen Bo'er founded it in June 1950, was intended to train a new generation of actors and screenwriters for a socialist film industry.

2. Chen Bo'er's tombstone gives the year of her birth as 1910, and most secondary works use that date. I follow her biographer, Wang Yongfang, who had access to

Chen's personal archive and found the date 1907 on her brief autobiography. Wang Yongfang, interview with author, December 13, 2011. Chen may have given the 1910 date herself when she was entering the film industry in 1934.

3. After her mother, her father had a second concubine.

4. This account of Chen Bo'er's early life is based on a biography of Chen, Wang Yongfang, *Mingxing, zhangshi, renmin yishujia: Chen Bo'er zhuanlue* [A star, soldier, people's artist: A biography of Chen Bo'er] (Beijing: Zhongguo huaqiao chubanshe, 1994), and a documentary film produced by the Central TV Station in 2009, *Yan'an liren* [Yan'an women], that includes an episode on Chen Bo'er. The original site has been changed to CNTV *Jishitai* [Recording History], http://jilu .cntv.cn/humhis/yananliren/classpage/video/20091109/108650.shtml (re-accessed May 22, 2016).

5. See Mei Gongyi, *Baidu.com*, http://baike.baidu.com/view/5055527.htm (accessed April 10, 2013).

6. See Ren Posheng, *Baike.com*, www.baike.com/wiki/%E4%BB%BB%E6%B3 %8A%E7%94%9F (accessed May 22, 2016). For Ren Posheng's military activities in the New Fourth Army, see "Xinsijun sishi zai Guobei" [The fourth division of the New Fourth Army in Guobei], *Guoyang online*, www.gy233600.cn/bendi/info-6346.html (accessed April 10, 2013).

7. Spoken drama was an imported form of performing art that acquired its culturally specific meaning in Chinese elite's pursuit of modernity since the early twentieth century. For an in-depth study of the relationship between avant-garde art and politics in modern China, see Liang Luo, *The Avant-Garde and the Popular in Modern China: Tian Han and the Intersection of Performance and Politics* (Ann Arbor: University of Michigan Press, 2014).

8. Xia Yan, who was an underground Communist leading cultural activities of Shanghai's left-wing artists including the SADT, narrated in detail these activities of the 1930s in his autobiography, *Lanxun jiumeng lu* [Languid recollections of old dreams] (Beijing: Sanlian shudian, 1985). For the NP's persecution of Communist artists, see 186–88. Xia Yan will be the subject of the next two chapters.

9. Xiao Chen (one of Chen Bo'er's pen names), "Nüzi de liutongbin" [Women's common errors], *Shenbao Fukan* [*Shanghai Daily Supplement*], May 9, 1934, p. 3.

10. At this period, *taitai* (Mrs.) was a term for married women of elite families. Married women of lower classes were addressed as "wife of so-and-so"; e.g., Xianglin's Wife (see chapter 6). "Miss" was also never applied to unmarried women of the poor. For a study of changing meanings of *taitai* in the Republican era, see Hou Yanxing, "Jieji, xingbie yu shenfen:minguo shiqi 'taitai' de wenhua jiangou" [Class, gender and identity: The cultural construction of "taitai" in the Republic period] in *Lanzhou xuekan* [The Journal of Lanzhou], no. 3 (2011): 178–96.

11. Chen Bo'er, "Zhongguo funü de qiantu" [The future of Chinese women], *Shenbao Fukan*, May 19, 1934, 1.

12. Ibid.

13. Chen Bo'er, "Nüzi zhiye moluo de yuanyin" [The causes of the decline of women's careers], *Shenbao Fukan*, July 16, 1934, 3.

14. Ibid.

15. Chen Bo'er, "Wuyue yougan" [Sentiments in May], *Shenbao Fukan,* May 12, 1934, 1.

16. For left-wing artists' infiltration of the film industry, see Xia Yan, *Lanxun jiumeng lu,* 231; he specifically mentions Chen Bo'er and Yuan Muzhi, 288.

17. The five films Chen starred in are *Qingchun xian* [On Youth], Shanghai Star Studio (1934); *Taoli jie* [Fate of Graduates], Shanghai Diantong Studio (1934); *Huishou dangnian* [Remembering the Past], Hong Kong Global Studio (1935); *Shengsi tongxin* [Revolutionaries], Shanghai Star Studio (1936); and *Babai zhuangshi* [Eight Hundred Heroes], Wuhan: China Film Studio (1938). Chen's role in her last film was the first resistance war heroine represented in films. Her acting as a war heroine received high acclaim.

18. Xiao Hua, "Chen Bo'er oufang" [Interview with Chen Bo'er], *Funü shenghuo* [Women's Life] 8, no. 11 (March 1940), 12.

19. Laura Mulvey, "Visual Pleasure and Narrative Cinema," *Screen* 16, no. 3 (1975): 6–18.

20. Chen Bo'er, "Nüxing zhongxin de dianying yu nanxing zhongxin de shehui" [The female-centered film and the male-centered society], *Funü shenghuo* 2, no. 2 (1936): 62–64.

21. Ibid., 66.

22. Chen Bo'er, "Guanyu Zhao Yuhua" [About Zhao Yuhua], *Mingxing banyuekan* [Star Biweekly] 7, no. 4 (1936).

23. Chen Bo'er was hailed as the first woman actor who brought the popular street theater to the front to enhance the soldiers' will to resist the Japanese invaders. Her stardom also added much publicity to the new street drama *Put Down Your Whip!* in which she played the daughter. See Xiaobing Tang, "Street Theater and Subject Formation in Wartime China: Toward a New Form of Public Art," in *Cross-Currents: East Asian History and Culture Review,* E-Journal no. 18 (March 2016): 32, https://cross-currents.berkeley.edu/e-journal/issue-18 (accessed May 12, 2016).

24. Song Qingling (1893–1981), wife of modern China's founding father Sun Yat-sen, became the vice president of the Central Government after the founding of the PRC

25. Committee of the Annals of Shanghai Women, ed., *Shanghai funüzhi* [The annals of Shanghai women] (Shanghai: Shanghai shehui kexueyuan chubanshe, 2000), 633–34.

26. He Xiangning (1878–1972), a senior member of the Nationalist Party, played a leading role in the women's movement led by the Nationalist Party during the first United Front between the NP and the CCP and chaired the Chinese Women's Resistance Association in the 1930s. She joined the Communist government after the founding of the PRC and chaired its Committee of Overseas Affairs.

27. Shen Zijiu, "Chen Bo'er cong zhandi laixin" [A letter sent by Chen Bo'er from the front], *Funü shenghuo* 8, no. 1 (1939): 11.

28. In his biography of Chen Bo'er, Wang Yongfang described the baby's death as caused by a sudden illness, but he revealed the true cause to me when I asked why

Chen always took her son with her while engaging in busy activities, instead of leaving him with his father. Wang Yong Fang, interview with author, Beijing, December 13, 2011.

29. The NP and CCP formed a Second United Front to resist the Japanese invasion in 1937, which meant that the NP stopped both military combat against the CCP-controlled base areas and its arrests of underground CCP members. But the CCP's new recruits from NP-controlled areas kept their affiliation secret, given what the CCP had learned from the first alliance with the NP. After the First United Front was broken, the NP hunted down many CCP members. Keeping its members' identity confidential also allowed them to function in NP-controlled institutions and in the larger society as nonpartisan figures.

30. Edgar P. Snow (1905–1972), an American journalist who interviewed Mao Zedong and other Communist leaders in Yan'an and published books and articles on the Communist Revolution, the most famous of which was *Red Star over China* (1937), screened his documentary at Peking University, an event Chen Bo'er attended during her trip to the North in 1937.

31. Chen Bo'er, "Sange xiaojiao daibiao yinxiangji" [Impressions of three representatives with bound-feet], *Funü shenghuo* 8, no. 11 (1940): 15.

32. Ibid., 17.

33. Ibid., 19.

34. Ibid., 20.

35. Ibid., 20.

36. Yao, Zhongming, Chen Bo'er, et al. *Tongzhi, ni zoucuole lu!* [Comrade, you are on the wrong road], in *Beifang wenyi* [Northern literature and arts], ed. Zhou Erfu, vol. 3 (Beijing: Xin Zhongguo chubanshe, 1949). Chen Bo'er's article "Directing" in the volume gives a detailed review of the process of creating this highly acclaimed experimental drama and her rationale for many innovations.

37. "Zhonghua quanguo wenxue yishujie lianhehui changwu weiyuan Ding Ling tongzhi jianghua" [A talk by comrade Ding Ling, standing committee member of the All-China Literature and Art Association], in *Renmin yishujia Chen Bo'er tongzhi jinian teji* [A memorial series on the people's artist comrade Chen Bo'er] (Beijing: Xin dianying chubanshe, 1952), 12. The CCP had an internal hierarchy in Yan'an. "The big pot" meal and "the middle pot" meal were different qualities and quantities of food provided for the lowest-ranking and mid-ranking officials; "the small pot meal" was reserved for the top leaders.

38. Lu Ming, interview with author, Beijing, July 18, 2012. Chen Bo'er's niece, Chen Tilan, also made the same remark about Chen being a perfect person without a flaw in my phone interview with her (June 3, 2012).

39. Liang Luo, *The Avant-Garde and the Popular in Modern China*.

40. Xiaobing Tang, "Street Theater and Subject Formation in Wartime China," 45. In this illuminating study of the historical origins of Mao's Yan'an Talks, Tang notes that many urban, left-wing artists experienced "culture shock" when they traveled into rural areas to present street theater during the resistance war and real-

ized the necessity of two-way transformations, similar to what Chen Bo'er experienced in the war.

41. Examining the left-wing films in a critical light, Vivian Shen also shows that what appeared in Mao's Yan'an Talks for the most part had already surfaced in left-wing artists' ideas and practices in the 1930s. Vivian Shen, *The Origins of Left-Wing Cinema in China, 1932–1937* (New York: Routledge, 2005).

42. Many CCP couples were separated during the long war and had no means of communicating or even hearing about each other. Ren Posheng became an officer in the New Fourth Route Army in the resistance war, operating mainly in base areas in East China.

43. Chen Bo'er and Yuan Muzhi played couples in the films of the 1930s and remained close friends since their first film together. Yuan was invited by Zhou Enlai to Yan'an to make films. He collaborated with Chen in the production of some stage dramas before he went to the Soviet Union to study filmmaking.

44. Shanghai-based director Xie Jin told Greg Lewis in an interview, "We learned a great deal about how to make *gongnongbing* (worker-peasant-soldier) films from the Dongbei (later Changchun) Film Studio." See Greg Lewis, "The History, Myth, and Memory of Maoist Chinese Cinema, 1949–1966," *Asian Cinema* 16, no. 1 (Spring / Summer 2005): 171–72. In this article Lewis expresses his disagreement with Paul Clark's conceptualization of Yan'an versus Shanghai to explain the conflicts in the socialist film industry, as his interviewees did not reveal such tension. If Lewis knew who led the Northeast Film Studio, he would have a strong argument against Clark. The top leaders Chen Bo'er and Yuan Muzhi were both from the Shanghai film community of the 1930s and went to Yan'an later. The experiences of the leading couple of the socialist film industry disrupted Clark's thesis. Changchun Film Studio no longer exists. But on the site of the studio a film museum has been built. A group statue of founders of the studio is placed in the introductory hall with Chen Bo'er in the center.

45. Lu Ming (who worked with Chen Bo'er in NFS), interview with author, Beijing, July 18, 2012. See Lu Ming, *Zhongguo dianying qishizai: Qinli, shilu* [Seventy years of Chinese film: Personal experience and recording] (Beijing: Zhongguo dianying chubanshe, 2012), 346. Xingshan is the location where the Northeast Film Studio was first established. In 1946 the CCP expected additional military engagement with the NP in Changchun; therefore, the equipment left by Japanese in the Manchuria Film Studio was hurriedly shipped by train to the remote coal-mining town of Xingshan. Meanwhile, the CCP also maneuvered to have the NP send the CCP underground members, the movie star couple Jin Shan and Zhang Ruifang, to represent the NP to take over the Manchuria Film Studio after the equipment had been safely shipped away. The tremendous takeover efforts of a film studio demonstrate the importance of film industry in the envisioning of a socialist state by the CCP leaders. Zhou Enlai was directly involved in planning the takeover of the film studio.

46. Most of the technical personnel who had worked in the Japanese-owned Manchuria Film Studio stayed at their posts after the CCP's takeover, including many Japanese technicians.

47. Yan Yiyan, "Diyici xuexi: *Zhonghua Nüer* de xiezuo jingguo" [The first learning experience: The process of writing *Daughters of China*], in *Zhonghua nüer dianying wenxue juben* [The script of *Daughters of China*] (Beijing: Zhongguo dianying chubanshe, 1958), 53; and "Mianhuai Chen Bo'er tongzhi" [Remembering comrade Chen Bo'er], *Xin wenxue shiliao* [Historical Sources on New Literature] 4 (1980): 181.

48. Yan Yiyan, "Guanghui de dianfan" [A glorious paragon], *Dazhong dianying* [Popular Film] 1–2 (1952).

49. "Lin Zifeng Koushu: Dajia guanwojiao feng daoyan" [Interview of Lin Zifeng: People called me a crazy director], in *Women de yanyi shengya* [Our performing careers], ed. Lian Jing, Lu Hua, and Guo Jinhua (Beijing: Zhongguo shudian, 2008): 106–33. Also, Lu Ming, interview with author, Beijing, July 18, 2012. Lu Ming still remembers the big fight between Yan and Lin over the narrative structure of the script. Yan did not want to delete any of the touching stories of the heroines she collected. Only Chen Bo'er was able to convince her of the necessity of sacrificing those stories.

50. Dai Jinhua, *Cinema and Desire: Feminist Marxism and Cultural Politics in the Work of Dai Jinhua*, ed. Jing Wang and Tani E. Barlow (London: Verso, 2002), 102. But without historical research, Dai assumed that the heroines were not narrated in the gaze of male desire but in the gaze of authorities ("this gaze is of course male"). This assumption led to her famous thesis of patriarchal masculinization of women in socialist cultural representation.

51. Yu Hua, "Lishishang yongyuan liuzhe tamende mingzi: *Zhonghua nüer* guanhou" [Their names are forever engraved in history: After viewing *Daughters of China*], *Dianying wenxue* [Film Literature], no. 3 (1959): 82; Ya Su, "*Zhonghua nüer* guanhou" [After viewing *Daughters of China*], *Xin Zhongguo funü* [Women of New China], no. 7 (1950): 17.

52. Meng Liye, *Xin Zhongguo dianying yishushi: 1949–1965* [A history of cinematic art in the new China: 1949–1965] (Beijing: Zhongguo dianying chubanshe, 2011), 43. Hung Liu, an overseas Chinese artist who had watched *Daughters of China* in her childhood in China, revisited this film half a century later on her research trip to China. Still deeply moved by it, she decided to create a series of large-scale paintings based on the screen images of *Daughters of China* depicting how the heroines carried their dead comrade while wading through the roaring river, which she completed in 2008. The power of the heroines conveyed by Hung Liu can be accessed via her website: www.hungliu.com/daughters-of-china.html. This work is in the permanent collection at the Denver Art Museum.

53. The film received high acclaim in the Soviet Union as well. Film critics there recognized the similarities between *Daughters of China* and *Chapaev* right away, hailing it as a landmark in the move toward realism in Chinese cinema. See "Su gedi shangying *Zhonghua nüer*: Qian Xiaozhang baogao canjia guoji yingzhan qingkuang" [On the screenings of *Daughters of China* in the Soviet Union: Qian Xiaozhang's report on the situation of participating in the international film festival], *Wenhui bao* [Wenhui Daily], September 5, 1950, p. 3; "*Zhonghua nüer* zai

Sulian" [*Daughters of China* in the Soviet Union], Li He, reporter of Xinhua news agency in Moscow, *Wenhui bao,* August 11, 1950, p. 3. For a study of the impact of Soviet film on socialist films in China, see Lu Ming, "Sulian dianying zai Zhongguo gaishu" [On Soviet films in China], in *Zhongguo dianying qishizai: qingli, shilu,* 149–50.

54. In addition to *Daughters of China,* the other three films with revolutionary heroines are *Baiyi zhanshi* [Soldiers in White Coats], *Zhao Yiman,* and *Liu Hulan. Baimao nü* [The White-Haired Girl] was based on a popular opera originally created in Yan'an depicting a poor young peasant woman's resistance against sexual violence and oppression of a landlord.

55. Chen Bo'er, "Gushipian congwudaoyou de biandao gongzuo" [Scriptwriting and directing feature films from the scratch], in *Zhongguo dianying yanjiu ziliao: 1949–1979* [Source material on Chinese film studies: 1949–1979], vol. 1, ed. Wu Di (Beijing: Wenhua yishu chubanshe, 2006), 64 (hereafter cited as Wu Di).

56. Lu Ming, interview with author, Beijing, July 18, 2012.

57. Chen Bo'er, "Gushipian congwudaoyou de biandao gongzuo."

58. Private film studios still managed their own production in the early 1950s.

59. When *Zhao Yiman,* a biographical film about a Communist woman leader who was captured, brutally tortured, and eventually killed by the Japanese, had immediately followed *Daughters of China,* some film critics expressed disapproval of making two films featuring revolutionary heroines. See Zhong Dianfei, "Kanle *Zhao Yiman* yihou" [After watching *Zhao Yiman*], *Renmin ribao* [People's Daily], July 9, 1950, p. 3.

60. Cao Jisan, "Chizha fengyun Chen Bo'er" [An all-powerful Chen Bo'er], *Tianjin ribao* [Tianjin Daily], May 15, 2009, p. 15.

61. The Karlovy Vary International Film Festival drew many filmmakers from socialist countries. Having just emerged from long and brutal struggles against fascism, many shared a commitment to films representing anti-fascist and anti-imperialist struggles. In that context, the extraordinary Chinese revolutionary heroines touched a highly sympathetic chord in viewers and judges.

62. Mao Zedong, "Yingdang zhongshi dianying *Wu Xun Zhuan* de taolun" [We should pay attention to the discussions of *The Life of Wu Xun*], *Renmin ribao,* May 10, 1951, p. 1. The article appeared as the editorial without Mao's name. Collected in Wu Di, vol. 1, pp. 92–93.

63. For more discussion of the impact of the criticism of *The Life of Wu Xun* and Mao's wife Jiang Qing's involvement in this event, see chapters 6 and 7.

64. Chen Bo'er, "Cong *Wu Xun Zhuan* tandao dianying chuangzuo shangde wenti" [On issues of filmmaking based on *The Life of Wu Xun*] *Xin Dianying* [New Film] 1, no. 7 (1951): 10–13.

65. Actor Zhong Xinghuo (who was present at the meeting with Chen Bo'er), interview with author, Shanghai, August 29, 2012. Also see Zhong Jingzhi, "Zhuiyi Chen bo'er tongzhi zuihou de rizi" [Recalling the last few days of comrade Chen Bo'er's life], *Dianying yishu* [Film Art], no. 3 (1991): 49.

66. Xia Yan, "Daonian Chen Bo'er tongzhi" [Remembering comrade Chen Bo'er], *Wenhui bao,* November 29, 1951, p. 8.

67. Deng Yingchao, "Daonian Chen Bo'er tongzhi" [Remembering comrade Chen Bo'er], *Renmin ribao,* November 13, 1951, p. 3.

68. Sheng Zijiu, "Zhonghua quanguo minzhu funü lianhehui daibiao Sheng Zijiu tongzhi de jianghua" [The talk by comrade Sheng Zijiu, representative of the All-China Democratic Women's Federation], in *Renmin yishujia Chen Bo'er tongzhi jinian teji* [A memorial series on the people's artist comrade Chen Bo'er] (Beijing: Xin dianying chubanshe, 1952), 14.

69. The lopsided scholarly treatment of Chinese women in the first versus second half of the twentieth century is best illustrated in a book that surveys the English scholarship produced in recent decades. See Paul J. Bailey, *Women and Gender in Twentieth-Century China* (New York: Palgrave Macmillan), 2012.

70. Chen Wenjing, interview with author, Beijing, July 19, 2012. See also the conference volume edited by Chen Wenjing, *Women zai zheli chengzhang* [We grew up here], in the Beijing Film Academy library.

71. See "Zhongguo dianying jiaoyu dianjizhe, kaituozhe tongxiang jiemu yishi zai woyuan longzhong juxing" [Our Academy holds the grand ceremony for unveiling the bronze statues of the founders and pioneers of Chinese film education], Beijing Film Academy website: www.bfa.edu.cn/news/2012–12/22/content_57470.htm (accessed January 14, 2016).

CHAPTER SIX. FASHIONING SOCIALIST VISUAL CULTURE

An early version of this chapter was first presented at the "Conference on Nines," University of Michigan, December 5, 2009.

1. The Shanghai Municipal Archives has made available over two thousand volumes of the Shanghai Film Bureau from 1949 to 1966. The collection contains a wealth of primary sources, ranging from meeting minutes of Shanghai film studios and the Film Bureau and five-year plans about making films to notes on numerous interactions between the central leadership in the film industry and actors, directors, producers, and studio managers in Shanghai and elsewhere. Not everything related to film is accessible, but the archives nonetheless demonstrate the complexity of situations in the film industry and often yield surprises. For the first study that systematically researched archival documents on Shanghai film industry, see Zhang Shuoguo, *"Shiqi nian" Shanghai dianying wenhua yanjiu* [A study of the "seventeen years" of Shanghai film culture] (Beijing: Shehui kexue chubanshe, 2014). In the 2011 anthology *The Chinese Cinema Book,* edited by Song Hwee Lim and Julian Ward (London: Palgrave Macmillan), socialist films receive the attention of one chapter, "The Remodeling of a National Cinema: Chinese Films of the Seventeen Years (1949–1966)" by Julian Ward, but there is still no trace of archival research by film scholars cited in the chapter. See pp. 87–93.

2. The cultural dimension of the Cultural Revolution is rarely examined in scholarship on China. Paul Clark, *The Chinese Cultural Revolution: A History* (New York: Cambridge University Press, 2008), captures the importance of the cultural transformation agenda in the history of the CCP.

3. See Paul G. Pickowicz, "Zheng Junli, Complicity and the Cultural History of Socialist China, 1949–1976," in *The History of the PRC (1949–1976)*, special issue of *China Quarterly* 7 (2007), ed. Julia Strauss (Cambridge: Cambridge University Press), 194–215; Paul G. Pickowicz, "Acting Like Revolutionaries: Shi Hui, the Wenhua Studio, and Private-Sector Filmmaking, 1949–52," in *Dilemmas of Victory: The Early Years of the People's Republic of China,* by Jeremy Brown and Paul G. Pickowicz (Cambridge, MA: Harvard University Press, 2007), 256–87. Both articles focus on artists who were persecuted during the Mao era. Film historian Paul Clark's careful research in the 1980s yielded a complex picture of making socialist films and a re-periodization of the Cultural Revolution. Although he astutely pointed out that "divisions within the creative ranks served as warning against a simplistic differentiation of Party versus artists," he nevertheless organized the book around the framework of a tripartite relationship among party, artists, and audiences. The insertion of audiences significantly complicates power relations in a so-called totalitarian regime, but the dichotomy of party versus artists remains at the conceptual level. Paul Clark, *Chinese Cinema: Culture and Politics since 1949* (New York: Cambridge University Press, 1987), 53. In Clark's more recent work with a much more complex analytical framework, he recognized that "[f]ilm was prominent from the early rumblings of what became the Cultural Revolution storm in 1964." However, without archival research, he missed the opportunity to trace Xia Yan's pivotal role in the contentions of the cultural realm and only mentioned him briefly as a film writer. See Clark, *Chinese Cultural Revolution*, 110. Greg Lewis noticed a meaningful discrepancy between historiography of Chinese socialist films and the film artists' memories of their experiences in making socialist films as a result of his interviews of film artists. However, he again missed the opportunity to dig deep into the discrepancy by conducting archival research to verify his interviewees' memories and to understand the discrepancy in the context of historical ruptures rather than simply in the differences of cohorts. See Greg Lewis, "The History, Myth and Memory of Maoist Chinese Cinema, 1949–1966," *Asian Cinema* 6, no. 1 (2005): 162–83.

4. Yingjin Zhang, *Cinema and Urban Culture in Shanghai, 1922–1943* (Stanford, CA: Stanford University Press, 1999), 207.

5. Film historian Paul Clark characterized Xia Yan as an important artist who held a merely nominal official position. See Clark, *Chinese Cinema*. To date, Xia Yan's central role in socialist film production has received attention outside China only in a brief study of non-Chinese language: Sergei Toroptsev, "Xia Yan and the Chinese Cinema," *Far Eastern Affairs* 4 (1985): 126–31 (Institute of the Far East, USSR Academy of Sciences).

6. A sixteen-volume anthology of Xia Yan's works (9.2 million words) was published in China in 2005; many collections of his works edited by himself or his

friends have been published since the early 1980s. Chinese sources characterize him as a renowned writer, scriptwriter, playwright, literary critic, literary artist, translator, journalist, and public figure. A major biography, *Xia Yan zhuan* [A biography of Xia Yan] by Chen Jian and Chen Qijia (Beijing: Zhongguo xiju chubanshe, 2015), is a revision of an earlier edition (Beijing: Beijing Shiyue wenyi chubanshe, 1998).

7. "Xia Yan" was one of his many pen names when he worked underground in the Republican era.

8. The surname Shen suggests that Xia Yan was a descendant of a large, prestigious clan in Zhejiang that had produced many famous figures in modern Chinese history. Xia Yan's paternal grandmother was a cousin of Zhang Taiyan, the renowned scholar and anti-Qing revolutionary. His grandfather was captured by the Taiping army and served as General Chen Yucheng's secretary. He was released before Chen's final defeat in Shouzhou, Anhui, in 1862. Because of this political "stain" he could not take the civil service examination, which ended a genealogy of scholar-officials in this branch of the Shen clan. Xia Yan's father did not pass the civil service examination and became a doctor. When Xia Yan was born, the family lived in a tumbledown compound inherited from his wealthy ancestors. The huge house with a tall wall had been designed for over three hundred people. Local legend claimed that the compound had been used as the headquarters of the Taiping army. In Xia Yan's childhood, the rent from two rooms facing the street was an important part of the family income.

9. An anthology of renowned literary figures' recollections of their mothers suggests the public recognition of this phenomenon: Li Yucun and Peng Guoliang, eds., *Zhongguo wenhua mingren yi muqin* [Chinese cultural celebrities' recollections of their mothers] (Changsha: Hunan Wenyi chubanshe, 1995).

10. Xia Yan, *Lanxun jiumeng lu* [Languid recollections of old dreams] (Beijing: Sanlian shudian, 1985), 23. This autobiography narrates his life from 1900 to 1949.

11. Ibid., 24.

12. Ibid., 25.

13. Susan Mann, in *The Talented Women of the Zhang Family* (Berkeley: University of California Press, 2007), illuminates the significant role women played in sustaining the elite status of scholarly families and the drastic decline of the elite class in the lower Yangzi region in the aftermath of the Taiping Rebellion. The prevalence of male literati's memory of their virtuous mothers has been a subject of historical research. See Hsiung Ping-chen, "Constructed Emotions: The Bond between Mothers and Sons in Late Imperial China," *Late Imperial China* 15, no. 1 (June 1994): 87–117. Also Yu-Ying Chen has argued that motherly love [*ci*] became a Confucian moral principle in the works of Ming Confucian philosopher Luo Rufang because of the powerful role played by his mother. See Susan Mann and Yu-Yin Chen, eds., *Under Confucian Eyes: Writings on Gender in Chinese History* (Berkeley: University of California Press, 2001), 103–7.

14. Here I revise one of my major points in *Women in the Chinese Enlightenment: Oral and Textual Histories* (Berkeley: University of California Press, 1999). Most men among the Chinese elite in contemporary China have no qualms about

claiming a modern subject position while openly being misogynist and anti-feminist. In light of contemporary gender politics, the May Fourth New Culturalists' pro-feminist position cannot simply be interpreted as based on their need to claim a modern identity. That cohort's psychological composition should be further historicized and contextualized.

15. *New Youth* 7, no. 2 (1920); Xia Yan, *Lanxun jiumeng lu*, 48.

16. For information on Zhang Xichen, see Wang Zheng, *Women in the Chinese Enlightenment*, chap. 2. Also see Xia Yan, "Huainian Zhang Xichen xiansheng" [Remembering Mr. Zhang Xichen], in *Xia Yan Qishinian Wenxuan* [A selected anthology of Xia Yan's seventy years of works], ed. Li Ziyun (Shanghai: Wenyi chubanshe, 1996), 509–14. Cited hereafter as Li Ziyun, this anthology includes a number of essays on women's issues written before 1949.

17. August Bebel (1840–1913), *Women and Socialism,* trans. Meta L. Stern (Hebe) (New York: Socialist Literature, 1910). Bebel was one of the founders of the Social Democratic Workers' Party of Germany, a leading figure of the social democratic movement in Germany, and served as chairman of the Social Democratic Party of Germany from 1892 until his death.

18. See Zhang Xichen, "Fuyin tiji" [Notes before printing], in *Furen yu shehuizhuyi* [*Women and Socialism*], by August Bebel, trans. Shen Duanxian (Shanghai: Kaiming Bookstore, 1927), xxii–xxvi.

19. The quotation is from the English text. Bebel, *Women and Socialism,* 7.

20. Ibid., 507.

21. Xia Yan was a frequent contributor to the left-wing women's magazine *Funü shenghuo* [Women's Life] run by Shen Zijiu. Xia Yan had close friendships with Shen Zijiu and her younger brother, Shen Xilin, a renowned filmmaker in the 1930s. Shen Zijiu's close friend and roommate in Japan, Cai Shuxin, married Xia Yan in 1930.

22. The editor-in-chief of *Nüsheng* [Women's Voice], Wang Yiwei, recalled that Xia Yan visited her in the 1930s and gave her a copy of *Women and Socialism.* See Wang Zheng, *Women in the Chinese Enlightenment*, 230.

23. See *Xia Yan zhuan,* 84.

24. *Indentured Women Workers* (*Baoshengong*) remains the most famous of Xia Yan's writings because it has long been included in high school textbooks in the PRC. Ironically, the reportage was removed from textbooks in 2004 for fear that readers might identify it with the severe exploitation of women migrant workers in contemporary capitalist China. An article circulated widely on the Internet poignantly elaborates the irony of Xia Yan's exposé in the contemporary context: "Xia Yan, nide baoshenggong henbu jingdian, gai tuichu lishi wutai le" [Xia Yan, your indentured women workers were not classic, they should exit the historical stage], by Wei wenqian, *Tiexue.net,* http://bbs.tiexue.net/post2_4287287_1.html (accessed May 21, 2016).

25. Xia Yan, "*Sai Jinhua* yuhua" [Remaining words on *Sai Jinhua*], written in September 1936, originally published in *Nüzi yuekan* [Women's monthly] 4, no. 9, 1936, citation from *Xia Yan shu hua* [Xia Yan's writings], ed. Jiang Deming (Beijing: Beijing chubanshe, 1998), 4–5.

26. Qiu Jin (1875–1907) was a feminist revolutionary who promoted feminism at the turn of the twentieth century and was committed to the overthrow of the Qing Empire as the precondition for Chinese women's liberation. Her martyrdom in 1907 made her the number-one heroine of modern China via generations of writers' and politicians' writings and commemorations. Xia Yan started to think about writing a play on Qiu Jin when he was translating *Women and Socialism*. See Chen Jian and Chen Qijia, *Xia Yan zhuan*, 215–16.

27. Xia Yan, "*Qiu Jin* zaiban daixu" [Preface to the reprint of *Qiu Jin*], in Li Ziyun, 312. In this passage "they" is a feminine pronoun.

28. Ibid.

29. Xia Yan, "Qiangzhe a, nide mingzi jiaozuo nüren," in Li Ziyun, 767–68.

30. Film scholar Laikwan Pang depicts the shifting sentiments among the urban cinema audience: "The spectators had lost their appetite for martial arts in cinema while violence was all too real and too close for them." See Laikwan Pang, *Building a New China in Cinema: The Chinese Left-Wing Cinema Movement, 1932–1937* (Lanham, MD: Rowman and Littlefield, 2002), 29.

31. Ibid., 41.

32. Xia Yan's adaptation of Tian Han's story *Children of a Troubled Time* (*Fengyun ernü*) and the play *Sai Jinhua* were both produced in 1935 when he was in hiding. See Xia Yan, *Lanxun jiumeng lu*, 277–87.

33. Yingjin Zhang, *Cinema and Urban Culture*, 87. The phrase "small men and women" refers to people of the lower classes.

34. Zhang Zhen, *An Amorous History of the Silver Screen: Shanghai Cinema, 1896–1937* (Chicago: University of Chicago Press, 2005), 247.

35. The Diantong Film Company was forced to close in 1935 after it produced a few influential films.

36. Xia Yan, "Cong 'Baoshengong' suo yinqide huiyi" [Reminiscences from "the indentured workers"], in Li Ziyun, 43. Xia Yan's famous reportage based on the same research material was written when he went into hiding in 1935 and published in 1936.

37. Private film studios were nationalized in 1953, partly due to the political campaign against *The Life of Wu Xun* and partly due to the financial difficulties they encountered. The film industry was the first industry to be nationalized in socialist China. See Zhang Shuoguo, "*Shiqi nian" Shanghai dianying wenhua yanjiu*, chap. 1.

38. See a documentary on Xia Yan in which his son recalls his father's voluntary work on revising scripts: "Xia Yan yibian dang buzhang, yibian gaibian xiju" [Xia Yan managed to serve as a minister while revising scripts for plays and films], *v.ifeng. com*, http://v.ifeng.com/history/shishijianzheng/201105/b53953e7-e29f-404a-b330-e54e014af26c.shtml (accessed May 21, 2016). On this site the documentary on Xia Yan runs five episodes. Xia Yan helped to revise many scripts, including the script that was turned into the popular film *Wuduo Jinhua* [Five Golden Flowers] in 1959. The romantic musical film, in the genre of light comedy, depicts five ethnic minority women's active participation in rural collective work set against beautiful Yunnan landscapes.

39. Xia Yan's warm relations with filmmakers as well as the reverence he enjoyed in the industry are reflected in many memoirs of filmmakers, and most vividly described in a self-criticism made by Chen Huangmei, the director of the Film Bureau of the Ministry of Culture, who worked closely with him in the effort to develop socialist film. Even though Chen was supposed to criticize filmmakers' "wrong tendency" of treating Xia Yan as a higher authority than the Party, the whole piece is read more like a confirmation of his own respect for Xia Yan than a condemnation of him. "Chen Huangmei tongzhi zai wenhuabu quanti dangyuan he zhishu danwei fuze ganbu huishangde jiancha" [Comrade Chen Huangmei's self-criticism at the Ministry of Culture's meeting for all the party members and major cadres of the affiliated units], Shanghai Municipal Archives (hereafter SMA), 21 January 1965, B177–1–303–21.

40. Xia Yan, *Lanxun jiumeng lu,* 610–11.

41. Ibid., 637.

42. In Xia Yan's analysis, Jiang Qing sought to silence filmmakers who might gossip about this former movie star's life in Shanghai before she became Mao's wife. See Xia Yan, "*Wu Xun Zhuan* shijian shimo" [The cause of the incident of *The Life of Wu Xun*], in *Zhongguo dianying yanjiu ziliao: 1949–1979* [Source materials for Chinese film studies: 1949–1979], ed. Wu Di, vol. 1 (Beijing: Wenhua yishu chubanshe, 2006), 195–200. In the view of one of Jiang Qing's biographers, condemning *The Life of Wu Xun* was Jiang Qing's revenge directed against the director Sun Yu and other filmmakers who slighted her in the 1930s. See Zhong huamin, *Jiang Qing zhengzhuan* [A biography of Jiang Qing] (Hong Kong: Youlian yanjiusuo, 1967), 50–53. According to another biographer, Roxane Witke, Jiang Qing told her that Mao "disapproved of her action, an argument ensued, and she walked out on him." See Roxane Witke, *Comrade Chiang Ch'ing* (Boston: Little, Brown, 1977), 240. See the next chapter for further discussion of Jiang Qing. In any case, Jiang Qing boasted about her role in bringing *The Life of Wu Xun* to Mao's attention to military officials when she was hosting the seminar on literature and the arts in 1966, years before she did the same in her interviews with Witke. The consistency in language and tone when narrating the event years apart may prove the validity of her claim. See Liu Zhijian, "Budui wenyi zuotanhui jiyao chansheng qianhou" [Before and after the production of the notes on the seminar on literature and arts in the military], collected in Wu Di, vol. 3, p. 19.

43. Mao Zedong, "Yingdang zhongshi dianying Wu Xun zhuan de taolun" [We should pay attention to discussions of *The Life of Wu Xun*], in Wu Di, vol. 1, pp. 92–93.

44. Chen Huangmei, ed., *Dangdai Zhongguo dianying* [Contemporary Chinese film], vol. 1 (Beijing: Zhongguo shehui kexue chubanshe, 1989), 28. Given their prominent role in the CCP-owned film studio in 1948, Yuan Muzhi and Chen Bo'er surely contributed to this directive. Yuan Muzhi's total withdrawal from his leading post after Chen Bo'er's death might also have been an expression of his profound disappointment with Mao's criticism of *The Life of Wu Xun.*

45. See Chen Huangmei and Chen Bo, eds., *Zhou Enlain yu dianying* [Zhou Enlai and films] (Beijing: Zhangyang wenxian chubanshe, 1995). This volume of

recollections of filmmakers and officials in the film industry reveals Zhou Enlai's close relationship with artists and his mitigation of harmful thrusts of Mao's and his radical associates' attacks on cultural producers. All the major filmmakers' autobiographies published since the late twentieth century mention Zhou's efforts in maintaining a more relaxed political atmosphere for artistic creativity.

46. "1954–1957 nian dinaying gushipian zhuti, ticai tishi caoan" [A draft brief on suggested topics for themes and subject matters of feature films to be made in 1954–1957], October 1, 1953, in Wu Di, vol. 1, p. 356.

47. For a study of the historical process of producing *Liu Qiao'er,* see Xiaoping Cong, *Marriage, Law and Gender in Revolutionary China* (Cambridge: Cambridge University Press, 2016); and for a study of socialist feminist films produced by women directors in the early PRC, see Lingzhen Wang, "Wang Ping and Women's Cinema in Socialist China: Institutional Practice, Feminist Cultures, and Embedded Authorship," *Signs: Journal of Women in Culture and Society* 40, no. 3 (2015): 589–622.

48. Because of his official responsibilities in Shanghai, Xia Yan did not move to Beijing until July 1955.

49. For instance, Shanghai mayor Ke Qingshi in 1963 insisted that film production should focus on the "thirteen years" of the socialist period. In his unpublished article written in June 1956, Zhong Dianfei criticized the first Film Bureau head, Yuan Muzhi, for transforming Mao's call for literature and art to serve the masses into a narrow agenda of only making "workers / peasants / soldiers films"; Zhong Dianfei, "Lun dianying zhidao sixiang zhong de jige wenti" [On a few issues in guiding concepts in film], in Wu Di, vol. 1, pp. 20–29.

50. Those who had worked with the progressives (CCP or CCP sympathizers) in the film industry before 1949 were hired by the state-run studios after the industry's nationalization.

51. Film scholar Zhang Shuoguo insightfully points out this contradiction in *"Shiqinian" Shanghai dianying wenhua,* 163–66.

52. When a non-CCP writer asked him if literature and art could also serve the petty bourgeoisie, Xia Yan, who was in charge of the Shanghai film industry at that time, gave an affirmative answer without any hesitation. The rumor soon circulated through the grapevine that Xia Yan was "promoting" the idea that literature and art should serve the petty bourgeoisie. His close friend warned him to be more cautious in his statements. See Xia Yan, *Lanxun jiumeng lu,* 619–20.

53. See Xia Yan, "Zai dianying daoyan huiyi shangde jianghua" [Talks on the conference of film directors], September 24, 1979, in Wu Di, vol. 3, pp. 575–85.

54. Jin Jiang's work on the history of Yue opera gives a detailed account of the adaptation of Lu Xun's short story into a Yue opera. See chapter 4 in *Women Playing Men: Yue Opera and Social Change in Twentieth-Century Shanghai* (Seattle: University of Washington Press, 2009). My translation of the character Xianglin Sao differs from hers as Xianglin was the name of her husband and the nameless character only acquired a name as Xianglin's Wife. Lu Xun's penetrating understanding of Chinese gender system was also expressed in the naming of his character. Yue opera

is one of many operas based on local dialects in China. Yue opera was the first to adapt Lu Xun's short story, as his hometown is in Zhejiang and the story was situated in his hometown. If the short story had an audio version, Xianglin's Wife would speak the Shaoxing dialect on which Yue opera developed.

55. Xia Yan's prominent role in making adaptations of the New Cultural literature was noted by Paul Clark in his early study of socialist film, though in his reading of visual texts such efforts of adaptations were an act of "remembrance of times past." See Clark, *Chinese Cinema*, 109–13.

56. Xia Yan, "Zatan gaibian" [On adaptation], in Li Ziyun, 712.

57. Ibid., 711.

58. Xia Yan, "Cong miwuzhong kan yimian jingzi" [Looking at a mirror in the fog], in Li Ziyun, 644.

59. Contemporary critics think the voice-over is evidence of Xia Yan's sacrificing artistic standards in order to comply with political demands of the time. See Wei Jiankuan, "Xia Yan xiansheng gaibian Zhufu de baibi" [Failures in Xia Yan's adaptation of *New Year's Sacrifice*], *Yuwen beike dashi* [Master of teaching Chinese language], www.xiexingcun.com/dushu/HTML/11294.html (accessed May 21, 2016).

60. This critique of the May Fourth New Culturalist portrayal of women as victims of feudal society was first made in Dorothy Ko's *Teachers of the Inner Chambers: Women and Culture in Seventeenth-Century China* (Stanford, CA: Stanford University Press, 1994); see her introduction for a critical analysis of the rise of the "May Fourth story" of the Chinese tradition. My own book, *Women in the Chinese Enlightenment* (cited above), also challenges the CCP's dominant representation of women pre-1949 as victims without agency.

61. For a detailed study of the implementation of the 1950 Marriage Law in the PRC in English, see Kay Ann Johnson, *Women, the Family and Peasant Revolution in China*, especially 132. For Chinese studies and sources on the 1950 Marriage Law, see a list of citations in note 23 in the Introduction.

62. For analyses of socialist state feminists' deployment of the concept of feudalism, see chapters 1 and 3.

63. For a description of the production process of the film, see Zhu Anping, "Zhufu yongyou duoge 'diyi' de huihuang jilu" [*The New Year's Sacrifice* has many glorious number ones], *Mtime*, http://i.mtime.com/4020546/blog/7374617/ (accessed August 15, 2014). To view the film online, see "Zhufu: Zhongguo jingdian huaijiu dianying" [*The New Year's Sacrifice*: A Chinese classic film] www.youtube .com/watch?v=qjNSt9V4Zhw (accessed May 16, 2016).

64. To view the two films, see *Geming Jiating* [A revolutionary family], *Tengxun Shipin, v.qq.com*, http://v.qq.com/cover/s/s24zzkfxpu2ulao/b00154rfggn.html; and Beiying dianying 65 *Liehuo zhong yongsheng* [Beijing Film Studio films 65 *Eternity in Flames*], www.youtube.com/watch?v=7wTmd8RmXwA (accessed May 22, 2016).

65. *Wode yijia* [My family], dictated by Tao Cheng and written by He Jiadong and Zhao Jie (Beijing: Zhongguo gongren chubanshe, 1959). It sold 6 million copies.

66. The magazine *Women of China* published a similar story of an underground Communist woman who played the role of a caring mother to many young Communists who separated from their families. The story was received with overwhelmingly emotional responses from many readers who had encountered such surrogate mothers when working underground. Huang Gang, "Geming muqin Xia Niangniang" [A revolutionary Mother Xia], was published as a serial in numbers 1–8 in 1957. The Communist movie star Zhang Ruifang, in her memoir, also narrated her mother's role in the underground work. See Jin Yifeng, *Suiyue youqing: Zhang Ruifang huiyilu* [Sentiments in times: A memoir by Zhang Ruifang], from Zhang Ruifang's oral narration (Beijing: Zhongyang wenxian chubanshe, 2005).

67. Kang Sheng, a CCP leader who had also worked underground in Shanghai, objected to the adaptation by Xia Yan on the ground that he had never heard of this underground woman. Xia Yan insisted on the production of the film by giving the heroine a name different from that in the original autobiography. See Meng Liye, *Xin Zhongguo dianying yishushi: 1949–1965* [A history of cinematic art in the new China: 1949–1965] (Beijing: Zhongguo dianying chubanshe, 2011), 323.

68. The author's own viewing experience of this film in her childhood is recorded in a memoir entitled "Call Me Qingnian But Not Funü: A Maoist Youth in Retrospect," *Feminist Studies* 27, no. 1 (Spring 2001): 9–34. It also appears in the volume of collective memoirs *Some of Us: Chinese Women Growing Up in the Mao Era,* ed. Xueping Zhong, Wang Zheng, and Bai Di (Piscataway, NJ: Rutgers University Press, 2001).

69. One of the three original authors, Liu Debin, was categorized as a "rightist" in 1957, which led to the omission of his name in the final publication.

70. Yu Lan, "Wo shige xinyun de yanyuan" [I am a lucky actor], *Dianying yishu* [Cinematic Art] 4 (1999): 20. In this article Yu Lan recalls her roles in three of Xia Yan's four adaptations, all regarded as classics.

71. Yu Lan revealed this reservation when I interviewed her on July 24, 2012, at her home in Beijing.

72. "Zhongguo gongchandang dashiji: 1963nian" [Important events of the CCP in 1963], *People.com*, http://cpc.people.com.cn/GB/64162/64164/4416060.html (accessed April 20, 2015).

73. Yu Lan, interview by author, Beijing, July 24, 2012.

74. Both *Eternity in Flames* and *A Revolutionary Family* have been generally listed as classics of the socialist period in Chinese film studies for their successful portrayal of heroines. See Li Suyuan, Hu Ke, and Yang Yuanyin, eds., *Xin Zhongguo dianying 50 nian* [Fifty years of film in the new China] (Beijing: Beijing guangbo xueyuan chubanshe, 2000), 78.

75. Some film critics in post-socialist China criticized the film as a precursor of the style of "Model Theaters" produced by Jiang Qing for its romantic portrayal of revolutionary heroes. Film critic Meng Liye gave a more balanced assessment. For a complex art, film had to strike a balance between the filmmaker's own penchants and the political demands of the time. Meng pointed out the realism in the script and the directing for the most part, but also commented on the exaggerated acting

of the main male character in his effort to conform to revolutionary romanticism. See Meng Liye, *Xin Zhongguo dianying yishushi: 1949–1965*, 459.

76. On a famous TV talk show hosted by Lu Yu in the episode on *Yu Lan and Sister Jiang* in 2010, Yu Lan's close friend Zhu Xiaoou revealed that Yu Lan strove to live up to the ethical and spiritual standards Sister Jiang had set. See "Yu Lan ban *Jiangjie* zao Jiang Qing pipan" [Yu Lan's Sister Jiang was condemned by Jiang Qing], *vifeng.com*, http://v.ifeng.com/society/201007/da6ef300-d9fd-411f-97d9-c50ca483356d.shtml (accessed April 24, 2015).

77. In the sensational detention of "the Feminist Five" in China in March 2015, a young generation of feminists invoked the image of Sister Jiang to express their commitment to the feminist cause and their defiance against the threat of imprisonment by the CCP. What a sad and ironic twist!

78. For a discussion of gender implications of the socialist films of revolutionary heroines, see chapter 8.

CHAPTER SEVEN. THE CULTURAL ORIGINS OF THE CULTURAL REVOLUTION

1. Xia Yan, "Cong *Wuxun Zhuan* de pipan jiantao wozai shanghai wenhua yishujie de gongzuo" [A self-criticism of my work in Shanghai's arts and culture, starting from the criticism of *The Life of Wu Xun*], *People's Daily*, August 26, 1951, in Wu Di, ed., *Zhongguo dianying yanjiu ziliao 1949–1979* [Source materials for Chinese film studies: 1949–1979], vol. 1 (Beijing: wenhua yichu chubanshe, 2006), 190–94. As to why he accepted Zhou Yang's demand, see Xia Yan, "*Wu Xun Zhuan* shijian shimo" [The causes of the incident of *The Life of Wu Xun*], in Wu Di, vol. 1, pp. 197–98.

2. See Editorial, "Jianjue hanwei shehuizhuyi de dianyig shiye" [Resolutely defend the cause of socialist film], *Popular Film*, September 1957, in Wu Di, vol. 1, pp. 146–48. Xia Yan joined the criticism of Zhong Dianfei, one of the first "rightists" in the film industry.

3. Chen Jian and Chen Qijia, *Xia Yan Zhuan* [A biography of Xia Yan] (Beijing: Zhongguo xiju chubanshe, 2015), 528–34. The biographers make a particular note that this emotional charge against Feng Xuefeng was an anomaly in Xia Yan's behavioral pattern.

4. "Xia buzhang baogao (11 yue 1 ri zai taolun yishupian fang wenxing zuotanhui shang de baogao)" [A talk by Minister Xia (at the forum on launching art film satellites on November 1)], Shanghai Municipal Archives (hereafter SMA), 1958, B177-1-216-1. The phrase "launching satellites" was coined during the Great Leap Forward to describe setting exceptionally high goals for achievement. Xia Yan embraced the term when urging filmmakers to create outstanding films to celebrate the tenth anniversary of the PRC. Art film production leaped from 42 in 1957 to 105 in 1958. See also Xia Yan, "Wei dianying shiye de jixu dayuejin er fendou" [Strive for the continuous Great Leap Forward of the film industry], *People's Daily*, February 2,

1960, in which he continued the condemnation of "rightists" and adopted Mao's class analysis in his depiction of the film industry. The article is collected in Wu Di, vol. 2, pp. 275–80.

5. See Xia Yan, "Zai quanguo gushipianchang changzhang huiyi shangde jianghua" [Talks on the national conference of directors of film studios], February 13, 1979, in Wu Di, vol. 3, p. 534.

6. Xia Yan, *Lanxun jiumeng lu* [Languid recollections of old dreams] (Beijing: Sanlian shudian, 1985): 642.

7. "Guanyu woju dangqian gaoji zhishifenzi de qingkuang baogao" [A report by the Shanghai Film Bureau on the current state of senior level intellectuals], SMA, 1960, B177–1–144, p. 11. The party committee's survey of filmmakers in 1960 reveals that 31 of 67 senior-level intellectuals had applied to join the CCP. "The great majority of intellectuals demonstrate high enthusiasm toward Party's policies and all kinds of political campaigns."

8. Qin Yi, phone interview with author, Shanghai, August 24, 2012.

9. Xia Yan, "Guanyu Zhongguo dianying wenti" [On issues in Chinese films], 1983, in *Xia Yan tan dianying* [Xia Yan on film], ed. Lin Man and Li Ziyun (Beijing: Chinese Film Press, 1993), 117–18. He characterized the acting in his famous 1933 film *Spring Silkworms* as "urbanites playing country folks."

10. The awards were entirely based on viewers' votes. The process of producing the film is recorded in *Li Shuangshuang: Cong xiaoshuo dao dianying* [*Li Shuangshuang*: From a novel to a film] (Beijing: Zhongguo dianying chubanshe, 1963). For an analysis of the cultural significance of this film, see Xiaobing Tang, "Rural Women and Social Change in New China Cinema: From *Li Shuangshuang* to *Ermo*," *Positions* 11, no. 3 (Winter 2003), 647–74; and a new discussion on the "rural film" in socialist China in Xiaobing Tang, *Visual Culture in Contemporary China: Paradigms and Shifts* (Cambridge: Cambridge University Press, 2015), chap. 3.

11. "Haiyanchang bianju, bianji disanci zuotanhui jilu" [Minutes of the third forum for screenwriters and editors of Haiyan Studio], SMA, 2 August 1961, B177–1–243, p. 5.

12. Xia Yan, "Wei dinaying shiye de jixu dayuejin er fendou," in Wu Di, vol. 2, p. 280.

13. During the "honeymoon" in relations between the USSR and the PRC in the early 1950s, the Chinese film industry replaced the Hollywood model with the Soviet one. See Cai Chusheng, "Sulian dianying dui Zhongguo dianying shiye de yingxiang he bangzhu" [Soviet films' impact on and help with Chinese films], *People's Daily*, November 7, 1951. The article is collected in Wu Di, vol. 1, pp. 228–30.

14. Chinese opera films were welcomed not only by Chinese peasants but also by overseas Chinese, who were a target audience for socialist films. Overseas Chinese constituted a sizable film market that generated much-needed foreign currency.

15. A 2004 film directed by Jiang Xiao, *Electric Shadows,* vividly captures the film culture of a small town from the 1960s to the 1980s.

16. Xia Yan, "Wei dianying shiye de jixu dayuejin er fendou," Wu Di, vol. 2, p. 275.

17. Xia Yan, "Zai dianying gongzuo huiyi shang de zongjie baogao" [A summary of the film working conference], April 16, 1959, in Wu Di, vol. 2, p. 265.

18. "Ji Hong juzhang jianghua" [Director Ji Hong's talk], SMA, 3 July 1964, B177–1–30, p. 63.

19. This anecdote of viewing experience was relayed to me by Jin Yihong in a private communication.

20. "Xia Yan tongzhi dui Shangying lingdao ganbu ji zhuyao chuangzuo renyuan zuotan jilu" [Notes on comrade Xia Yan's talk to leading cadres and major filmmakers of Shanghai film studios], SMA, 19 June 1960, B177–1–288, p. 6.

21. "Shanghaishi dianyingju chuangzuo zuotanhui zongjie lingdao jianghua" [A summary of leaders' talks at the forum on filmmaking by the Shanghai Film Bureau], SMA, 11 September 1961, B177–1–235, p. 29.

22. *Chuangxin dubai yu Qu Baiyin* [The monologue of innovations and Qu Baiyin] (Beijing: Chinese Film Press, 1982). This collection includes Qu's original essay and his colleagues' memories of Qu.

23. "Mao Zedong dui wenxue yishu de pishi" [Mao Zedong's directives on literature and the arts: December 12, 1963], in Wu Di, vol. 2, pp. 418–19.

24. Roxane Witke, *Comrade Chiang Ch'ing* (Boston: Little, Brown, 1977), 238–44.

25. For Jiang Qing's connection with Shanghai radicals, see Shi Yun, *Zhang Chunqiao Yao Wenyuan shizhuan: Zizhuan, riji, gongci* [Biographies of Zhang Chunqiao and Yao Wenyuan: Autobiographies, diaries, confessions] (Hong Kong: Sanlian shudian, 2012), 150–63; and Witke, *Comrade Chiang Ch'ing*, 307.

26. The marriage was highly controversial inside the CCP. It was Mao's fourth marriage while he and his third wife, the revolutionary He Zizhen who had accompanied him on the Long March, were not formally divorced. It was Jiang Qing's third marriage. Many in the CCP were concerned about Jiang Qing's complicated social and sexual relations in Shanghai when she was an actor. Many were displeased that Mao replaced a senior revolutionary woman with a young actor who had little revolutionary credentials.

27. Zhong Huamin, *Jiang Qing Zhengzhuan* [A biography of Jiang Qing] (Hong Kong: Youlian yanjiusuo, 1967), 46–47. After Jiang Qing rose to power in the mid-1960s, quite a few biographies of Jiang Qing appeared in Taiwan and Hong Kong, often with an obvious misogynist position but with little scholarly qualification. Zhong's, in comparison, was a more serious study with quite solid research. Not including Jiang Qing in this prestigious event of the cultural realm, in my view, could be an expression of fairness by those in charge of the invitee list since Jiang Qing at that time was not known for any prominent artistic accomplishments. It could also indicate the integrity of the conference organizers, be they women or men, as none of them used this opportunity to woo the wife of new China's top leader out of self-interest.

28. Witke, *Comrade Chiang Ch'ing*, 489, 384. The main points from Jiang Qing's interviews presented in Witke's biography corroborate well with Jiang Qing's secretary's memoirs published in China. See Yang Yinlu, "Wo suozhidao de Jiang

Qing yu Weiteke furen de tanhua" [The talks between Jiang Qing and Madam Witike that I know of], *Gejie* [All Fields], no. 9 (2011): 11–14; and "Wo suozhidao de Jiang Qing yu Weiteke furen tanhua de qingkuang" [The situation of the talks between Jiang Qing and Madam Witike that I know of], *Dangshi zonglan* [Overview of the Party's History], no. 10 (2010): 46–48.

29. For Jiang Qing's relationship with her allies in Shanghai, see Xu Jingxian, *Shinian yimeng* [Ten years a dream: A Shanghai ex-mayor's memoir of the Cultural Revolution] (Hong Kong: Time International, 2005). See also Li Song, "'Yangbanxi' de gongguo shifei" [The merits and faults of "model theater"], in *Guojia renwen lishi* [Culture and History of the State], no. 12 (2013): 35–37.

30. This and many more detailed descriptions of animosities between the Shanghai leaders and leaders of the film industry are presented in "Chen Huangmei tongzhi zai wenhuabu quanti dangyuan he zhishu danwei fuze ganbu huishangde jiancha." "Xia Gong" was how filmmakers addressed Xia Yan to show their reverence.

31. Huang Zongying (narrator) and Hu Xiaoqiu, "Jiafeng zhongde Zhao Dan, Huang Zongying fufu" [The couple Zhao Dan and Huang Zongying surviving in a tight corner], in *Dangan Chunqiu* [History in Archives], no. 4 (2006): 33–34. Zhao Dan and Zheng Junli were good friends of Jiang Qing when she was an actor in Shanghai before she went to Yan'an. The artists' insensitivity to Jiang Qing's recruitment cost them dearly. Both Zhao Dan and Zheng Junli were persecuted in the Cultural Revolution. In this piece Huang Zongying also reveals how Ke Qingshi blocked the making of a film, *Mao Liying* (based on the life of a Communist woman martyr who conducted underground work in Shanghai), that Chen Huangmei approved of in 1964. Ke was angry at Huang and other Shanghai filmmakers who did not follow his instruction of "writing the thirteen years."

32. Mao's information on operas obviously came from Jiang Qing, who claimed to have watched over 1,300 Peking operas in the early 1960s while she was on sick leave. See Xiao Donglian, *Qiusuo Zhongguo: Wenge qianshinian shi* [Exploring China: A history of the decade before the Cultural Revolution], vol. 2 (Beijing: Zhonggong dangshi chubanshe, 2011), 767.

33. Ke Qingshi made the announcement when giving a speech to leading artists in Shanghai at a New Year's party. Not all the artists who were present grasped the political significance of his proposal. See Shi Yun, *Zhang Chunqiao Yao Wenyuan shizhuan*, 153–55. Also see Yan Zhifeng, "Ke Qingshi tichang daxie shisannian suo yingqide yichang fengbo" [The storm stirred up by Ke Qingshi's representing the "thirteen years"], in *Dangshi Bocai* [Collections from the Party's history], no. 5 (2010): 32–34; Zhu Anping, "'Daxie shisannian' kouhao de youlai" [The background of the slogan "representing the thirteen years"], in *Dangshi Bolan* [Overviews of the Party's History], no. 1 (2015): 30–33; Wang Cuncheng, "Guanyu 'xie shisannian' zhenglun de liangfen neibu cailiao" [Two internal documents on the debates on "representing the thirteen years"], in *Xinwenxue Shiliao* [Historical Sources of New Literature], no. 1 (2015): 17–24; Li Zhi, "Huiyi yu sikao: 'daxie shisannian' de dazhenglun jiqi Beijing" [Remembering and thinking: The huge

debate on and background of "representing the thirteen years"], in *Xinwenxue Shiliao* [Historical Sources of New Literature], nos. 3–4 (1997): 123–28, 136, and 53–60, 119.

34. In dismay, Chen Huangmei sent a telegraph to Xia Yan from the conference venue in Nanjing, reporting on the disputes and his insistence on the position on a broader definition of socialist culture. See Chen Jian and Chen Qijia, *Xia Yan Zhuan,* 571. On the context of Mao's revising of the stages from "new democracy" to "socialist revolution," recent scholarship indicates that besides the domestic success of the first few years of the CCP rule, the death of Stalin was a crucial factor in Mao's acceleration of entering a new historical stage. See Alexander V. Pantsov and Steven Levine, *Mao: The Real Story* (New York: Simon and Schuster, 2012).

35. Witke, *Comrade Chiang Ch'ing,* 327.

36. Ibid., 103.

37. For a detailed narrative of Jiang Qing's fight for the role of Sai Jinhua, see Wang Suping, *Ta haimei jiao Jiang Qing de shihou* [Before she became Jiang Qing] (Beijing: Shiyue wenyi chubanshe, 1993), 223–30.

38. For Jiang Qing's revenge against Wang Ying, see Li Runxin, *Jiebai de mingxing: Wang Ying* [A pure star: Wang Ying] (Beijing: Zhongguo qingnian chubanshe, 1987), 112–14. This biography narrates how Jiang Qing put Wang Ying in prison during the Cultural Revolution, where she died. Also see Xia Yan, *Lanxun jiumeng lu,* 335–36.

39. Given that socialist China had banned Hollywood films a decade before and was starting to reject the Soviet model as "revisionist," filmmakers may have revisited films from the thirties to look for pedagogical models for the new generation of filmmakers.

40. Fu Xiaohong, *Liangbu kua pingsheng: Xie Tieli koushu shilu* [Two steps going through life's journey: An interview of Xie Tieli] (Beijing: Zhongguo dianying chubanshe, 2005), 80–103. In October 1964 the film was among the first to be circulated nationwide as a "bourgeois poisonous weed" produced by the "Xia-Chen revisionist line." Jiang Qing condemned the film but expressed her appreciation of the director's artistic creativity by entrusting him with filming her model operas in the Cultural Revolution.

41. The evidence of the "Xia-Chen revisionist line" was collected in a file in SMA, B177-1-303. The thick file includes self-criticisms from Xia Yan and Chen Huangmei, the original screen script *Early Spring in February* with the marks of Xia Yan's heavy revision, Qu's "Monologue" with Xia Yan's editorial marks, and investigation of the screenings of the 1930s films. Both Xia Yan and Chen Huangmei's many suggestions and comments on how to revise *Early Spring in February* during their multiple visits to Beijing Film Studio are also noted in detail in this file. It also includes a report written in 1957 by Cai Chusheng on the survey trip to Europe by the Chinese filmmakers' delegation, "Guowai dianying shiye zhong kegong cankao gaijin de yixie zuofa" [Some methods in foreign film industries that can be referenced or improved]. The valuable file, which originally functioned as material for the condemnation of Xia-Chen, is the best evidence of how a so-called revisionist line was fabricated in 1964. The Shanghai Film Bureau in September 1964 compiled

a detailed document that collected Chen Huangmei's talks to various groups in the Shanghai film industry from 1959 to 1963, which was "submitted to leaders as a reference." It was classified as highly confidential. Obviously, Shanghai officials also actively collected "evidence" of "the Xia-Chen line" for Jiang Qing. "Chen Huangmei tongzhi zai Shangying xitong fabiao de mouxie zhongyao yanlun" [Some of Comrade Chen Huangmei's important comments given to the Shanghai film system], SMA, September 1964, B177–1–21.

42. For Jiang Qing's role in shaping Mao's opinions on the cultural realm, see Xiao Donglian, *Qiusuo Zhongguo: Wenge qian shinian shi,* 765–80.

43. Zhou Yang, Xia Yan's friend since the 1930s, changed his position after he sensed Jiang Qing's animosity against Xia Yan. He was the first to criticize *Early Spring in February* at the time when watching the rushes (see Fu Xiaohong, *Liangbu kua pingsheng*), and later described Xia Yan as "not only lacking hatred against capitalism, but also being attracted to it." See "Zhou Yang tongzhi baogao" [Comrade Zhou Yang's talk], SMA, B177–1–308, p. 49. The original document is undated; it was probably made during the rectification campaign between late 1964 and early 1965. The excerpt of another talk he gave on November 19, 1965, in which he claimed that opposition to writing the thirteen years was in effect opposition to writing socialism, is collected in Wu Di, vol. 2, pp. 501–13.

44. "Xia Yan tongzhi zai wenhuabu quanti dangyuan he zhishu danwei fuze ganbu huishang de jiancha" [Xia Yan's self-criticism at the meeting of Party members of the Ministry of Culture and the leaders of the affiliated units], SMA, 19 January 1965, B177–1–303, p. 32.

45. She also contended that the film portrayed the Party secretary of Chongqing, who was allegedly a traitor. Jiang Qing, "Guanyu dianying de wenti" [On the issue of film], a talk in May 1965, collected in a volume for internal circulation without the name of the editors and press, *Jiang Qing tongzhi lun wenyi* [Comrade Jiang Qing on literature and the arts], May 1968, p. 101. The volume collects three talks addressing film given by Jiang Qing, one without a date, and two with similar contents. In these talks she condemned all films with Xia Yan's direct and indirect involvement as evidence of a thick revisionist line in the cultural realm. Some contents in these talks are cited in Yan Donglian, *Qiusuo Zhongguo.*

46. Ibid. In the same talk, Jiang Qing also criticized the roles played by Yu Lan and Zhao Dan. Yu Lan's Sister Jiang, in Jiang Qing's view, "lacks heroism." For a more detailed account of Jiang Qing's hostile reaction to the rushes in December 1964 at the Beijing Film Studio, and how Yu Lan had to appeal to Zhou Enlai to come to rescue the film, see Zhang Shuihua and Yu Lan, "Yichang teshu de zhandou" [A special battle], in *Zhou Enlai yu dianying* [Zhou Enlai and film], ed. Chen Huangmei and Chen Bo (Beijing: Zhongyang wenxian chubanshe, 1995), 347–52. Zhou Enlai defended the film against Jiang Qing's charges and suggested the title for the film as well.

47. For Jiang Qing's attempt to adapt *Red Crag* into a Peking opera, see He Shu, "'Yangbanxi' 'Hongyan' yaozheji" [The aborted attempt on "model opera" "Red Crag"], *Wenshi Jinghua,* no. 10 (2003): 29–35. The opera *Red Crag* was completed in

1967 when Jiang Qing decided to give it up for political reasons; that is, according to He Shu, the complexity of historical figures in the story might implicate Jiang Qing in a politically volatile time in the Cultural Revolution.

48. For Mao's response to the opera *Sister Jiang,* see http://blog.sina.com.cn/s /blog_4c3b65fb0102uxni.html?tj = 2 (accessed May 2, 2015). When Mao heard that the audience cried over Sister Jiang's martyrdom, he said, "Then don't let Sister Jiang die." In her Peking opera adaptation of *Red Crag,* Jiang Qing followed Mao's "instruction" to keep Sister Jiang alive. According to this article, it was Jiang Qing who banned the opera because its popularity outshined her "model theaters." After the Cultural Revolution, the opera *Sister Jiang* was restaged. It has remained the most influential opera in the PRC.

49. Significantly, after Xia Yan's rehabilitation after the Cultural Revolution, continuing an agenda of anti-feudalism was the most emphasized theme in his numerous talks.

50. Unaware of Xia Yan's central role in the film industry, Paul Clark nevertheless noted the rupture in the film industry by suggesting the periodization of 1956–64 and 1964–78. See his *Chinese Cinema: Cultural and Politics since 1949* (New York: Cambridge University Press, 1987).

51. See "Guanyu qingli yishupian sucai de tongzhi" [An announcement on sorting out art films], issued by the CCP Committee of the Shanghai Film Bureau, SMA, 25 May 1965, B177–1–314. The top confidential document offered three categories for special teams organized by Shanghai's two film studios to sort out 195 films produced after 1949. The first category referred to films with both correct ideologies and good artistic qualities; the second included films that were healthy overall but with some minor problems; and the third were those films that had serious political problems. But until May 30, 1966, the confidential reviewing teams were unable to finish watching all the films. Among the finished, they listed 31 films as basically good, 19 were poisonous, 8 had serious problems, and 43 were problematic that needed further analysis.

52. "Qiyue ershiwu ri shangwu yubeihuiyi qingkuang" [A report on the preparatory meeting during the morning of July 25, 1965], SMA, B177–1–32. The document recorded the instructions regarding the film industry issued by Peng Zhen, who headed the "five-people group" of the Cultural Revolution. He emphasized the importance of filmmakers going to the country to serve peasants.

53. "Zhou Zongli ting wenhuabu dangzu huibao dianying gongzuo shide chahua" [Premier Zhou commented on the reports on film work presented by the Party group of the Ministry of Culture], SMA, 5 August 1965, B177–1–32. His comments on this exclusive occasion were actually an outline of the key points for his long talk to the conference of filmmakers on August 11, 1965. The only difference was that he did not mention the impending war at all! The excerpt of Zhou's long talk is collected in Wu Di, vol. 2, pp. 496–501. But the lengthy section of the war threat in the original is omitted in this collection.

54. A few days before Zhou Enlai's speech, the new deputy minister of culture Liu Baiyu gave a long talk to the conference of filmmakers. He still elaborated on

how to follow Mao's proletarian line in film production. See "Liu Baiyu tongzhi baogao" [A report by comrade Liu Baiyu], SMA, 7 August 1965, B177–1–32. In this talk, Xia Yan's artistic style of realism was also condemned as bourgeois opposition to the combination of revolutionary romanticism and revolutionary realism.

55. "Zhou Zongli zai renda huitang baogao jilu" [A record of Premier Zhou's talk in the People's Hall], SMA, 11 August 1965, B177–1–32, p. 8.

56. Ibid., 10

57. Zhang Ruifang, *Suiyue youqing*, 341.

58. Zhou Enlai protected Xia Yan, who had worked directly under his leadership on many confidential missions before 1949, by transferring him to the commission for cultural exchange with foreign countries after Xia Yan's removal from his position in the Ministry of Culture. But Xia Yan then fell ill and did not go to his new post. See Chen Jian and Chen Qijia, *Xia Yan Zhuan,* 590.

59. Along with Jiang Qing's increasing political power promoted by Mao, Zhou Enlai amplified his open praise of Jiang. He emphasized that the achievement of revolutionary theater was the result of Jiang Qing's hard struggle against the "revisionist black line in the cultural realm from the 1930s to 1960s." See "Zai shoudu wenyijie wuchanjieji wenhua dageming dahui shangde jianghua" [Talk at the meeting of the fields of literature and the arts in Beijing on the Cultural Revolution], January 28, 1966, *Jiang Qing tongzhi lun wenyi,* 17–18. At a mass gathering with a hundred thousand participants on March 27, 1968, Zhou took pains to defend Jiang Qing by claiming the materials collected by reactionaries on Jiang Qing's 1930s activities were all slanderous. "In her youth," Zhou claimed, "Jiang Qing already had a spirit as unyielding as Lu Xun, daring to fight back against persecution, oppression, abuse, slandering, and rumors." In "Zhou Zongli zai 1968 nian 3 yue 27 ri de zhongyao jianghua" [Premier Zhou's important talk on March 27, 1968], in the same volume, 203–5.

60. Jiang Qing, *On the Revolution of Peking Opera* (Beijing: Foreign Language Press, 1968), 2. This talk was not published until 1967 when Jiang Qing became one of the top leaders of the Cultural Revolution. It is collected in Wu Di, vol. 2, pp. 444–47.

61. Yue opera staged the modern opera *Sister Xianglin* in 1946. Also, see Rosemary A. Roberts, *Maoist Model Theatre: The Semiotics of Gender and Sexuality in the Chinese Cultural Revolution (1966–1976)* (Leiden: Koninklijke Brill NV, 2010). The author gives a brief historical account of the development of modern theater prior to Jiang Qing's efforts.

62. Wang Suping, *Ta haimei jiao Jiang Qing de shihou,* 67–78.

63. Zhen Guangjun, "Wenge qijian Jiang Qing yu Hebei bangzi" [Jiang Qing and Hebei opera during the Cultural Revolution], *Wenshi jinghua* [Essence of culture and history], no. 5 (2010): 57–60.

64. Jiang Qing, *On the Revolution of Peking Opera,* 2.

65. For a detailed study of Mao's tactful moves behind the scenes in launching Jiang Qing to her powerful position in the Cultural Revolution, see Chen Zhao, "Budui wenyi zuotanhui 'jiyao' pouxi: Bo 'Lin Biao Jiang Qing' goujie lun'" [An

analysis of "records" of seminars on literature and the arts in the military: Refuting the thesis of "the collaboration between Ling Biao and Jiang Qing"], in Ding Kai-wen, ed., *Bainian Linbiao* [The centennial of Lin Biao] (New York: Mirror Books, 2007): 220–59; and also Yu Ruxin, "Daodi shi Lin weituo, haishi Mao weituo?" [Authorized by Lin or Mao?], in the same volume, 195–219. Both articles center on the historical process of producing the crucial document in February 1966, "The Notes on the Seminars on Literature and the Arts in the Military that Comrade Lin Biao Authorized Comrade Jiang Qing to Host." It was the first time Jiang Qing appeared in the Party Central's formal document.

66. "Bada Yangbanxi" [Eight model works], *Baidu baike*, http://baike.baidu.com/view/126013.htm (accessed May 3, 2015). The site contains images from these "model works."

67. "The Notes on the Seminars on Literature and the Arts in the Military that Comrade Lin Biao Authorized Comrade Jiang Qing to Host" evidenced Jiang Qing's parallel maneuvers. In the "seminars" she hosted, Jiang Qing focused on condemning films made under Xia Yan's leadership. In the process of producing the "Notes," Chen Boda highlighted Jiang Qing's efforts at "model operas," making the "two-line struggle" in the cultural realm prominent. See Liu Zhijian, "Budui wenyi gongzuo zuotanhui jiyao chansheng qianhou," in Wu Di, vol. 3, pp. 19–22.

68. Tang Jixiang (one of the participating artists), interview with author, Guang-dong Academy of Arts, Guangzhou, December 5, 2011. The set of paper cuts was produced for sale at the Canton Fair that opened twice a year as an outlet for China's international trading. It could be 1969 or 1970. He could not remember the exact date for producing this specific set as they were often commissioned art works for the Canton Fair in the Cultural Revolution. But since Lin Biao was also portrayed in this set, the production date and its circulation must be before his plane crash on September 13, 1971.

69. The name of the character, Aqing sao, is more commonly translated Sister Aqing. For the same reason as my translation of Xianglin sao as Xianglin's Wife, here I translate Aqing sao as Aqing's Wife. The playwright understood that the character's status as Aqing's Wife gave her legitimacy to function as a respected figure in the rural village in her time.

70. Roberts, *Maoist Model Theatre*.

71. Rosemary A. Roberts gives an excellent critique of the thesis of "gender erasure and masculinization of women" in "Introduction: Gender and Model Works" in her book. However, her perceptive critique of an essentialized notion of masculinization of women prevalent among literary critics is weakened by her insist-ence on "masculinization" and "feminization" as an overarching analytical device. Also, in citing Chinese scholars' thesis of "gender erasure," she does not make a distinction between "gender" and "sex." Chinese scholars' critiques of the socialist women's liberation and representation were made before the feminist concept of "gender" had a designated Chinese translation. In their expression in Chinese, "*mosha xingbie chayi*," *xingbie* should be more faithfully translated as "sex" since their emphasis was on innate biological difference between men and women, hence

revealing a clear essentialized understanding of "femininity" and "masculinity" in their assumed "naturalness" of gender roles and norms. The fact that their "pre-gender" critique is translated into English as "gender erasure" demonstrates difficulties in cross-cultural theoretical communication.

72. A rare moment that distinctively refers to gender in these "model works" appears in *Azalea Mountain*. A group of self-fashioned guerrillas wants to find a Communist to lead them so they attempt to rescue a Communist who is about to be executed. But when the guerrilla leader hears that the Communist is a woman, he is startled, "A woman?!" He anguishes for a while before he finally decides with reluctance to rescue her. This part of the opera never failed to arouse laughter among the audience who knew perfectly well the underlying meaning in his hesitation. The scene prepares the implied gender tension in the opera that is never explicitly addressed.

73. An excellent film in this regard that is much neglected by film critics is *Spring Forever* [*Wanziqianhong zongshichun*], screenplay by Shen Fu, Qu Baiying (author of "The Monologue on Innovation"), and his wife Tian Nianxuan, directed by Shen Fu, Shanghai Haiyan Film Studio (1959). The film depicted how housewives in Shanghai broke traditional gender and domestic constraints to join the collective production activities organized in neighborhoods. A team of top-ranking actors starred in the film. The All-China Women's Federation promoted the film on International Women's Day nationwide in 1960 and invited foreign women in Beijing to the screening. According to Zhang Ruifang who played the leading role, a Japanese woman was moved to tears, saying, "When will we be able to enjoy that? ... The thorough liberation of Chinese women is way ahead of countries with higher productivity." See Zhang Ruifang's memoir coauthored with Jin Yifeng, *Suiyue youqing* [Affective years] (Beijing: Zhongyang wenxian chubanshe, 2005), 305–8. The film was also selected to be among the exported films from China, and the Party branch in the crew was awarded special honors for producing a film with high artistic quality while reducing the costs of production by relying on the masses. "Shanghaishi dianyingju chuxi shiwenjiao qunyinghui daibiaotuan fenzu mingdan" [The name list of the group that represents the Shanghai Film Bureau to attend the conference of labor models in Shanghai culture and education fields], SMA, 20 January 1960, B177-1-8.

74. One exception is the ballet *The White-Haired Girl,* a revolutionary opera created in the Yan'an period. In the original opera as well as in the film adapted under Chen Bo'er's leadership, the leading female protagonist, a peasant girl, was raped by the landlord. In the ballet the plot was changed to depict her successful resistance to sexual violence.

75. The author was selected to play a leading role in the first film made since the Cultural Revolution and thus had the opportunity to observe how filmmakers consciously catered to Jiang's Qing's paradigm.

76. In the interviews conducted by Roxane Witke, Jiang Qing frequently discussed examples of sexist norms and male chauvinism; see Witke, *Comrade Chiang Ch'ing,* 191, 220, 230, 251–53, 442.

77. While Witke also noted how Jiang Qing compared herself with Deng Yingchao and Cai Chang, the quotation here is cited from the article by Jiang Qing's secretary. See Yang Yinlu, "Wo suozhidao de Jiang Qing yu Weiteke furen de tan-hua," *Gejie* [All Fields], p. 11.

78. See Zhang Ruifang with Jin Yifeng, *Suiyue youqing,* 382–84.

79. China's socialist revolution had been undone by the time Jiang Qing committed suicide in prison in 1991. Her theatrical heroines, however, survived her. A whole cohort of Chinese who were accustomed to model operas and ballets during their formative years have nostalgically revisited these revolutionary works in a time of capitalist globalization, and some in the younger generation who have grown up in a banal, materialistic world have been fascinated and excited by the strange novelty in these works. Jiang Qing was correct when she confided to Roxane Witke that revolutionizing theatrical works would be her real contribution. Witke, *Comrade Chiang Ch'ing,* 317. Kevin Latham predicts, "Unlike much of the propaganda of the Cultural Revolution period, model operas are likely to have a much longer lifetime and will find a new secure place for themselves in the repertoire of national Chinese theatrical performance." See Kevin Latham, *Pop Culture China! Media, Arts, and Lifestyle* (Santa Barbara, CA: ABC-CLIO, 2007), 321–22.

CHAPTER EIGHT. THE IRON GIRLS

1. In the development of Chinese state capitalism all of the social gaps have widened even though many people's material lives have been improved considerably in the market economy. This study does not examine the increasing gaps between the dominant Han ethnic group and ethnic minorities, and between the coastal cities and inland peripheral regions. But the ideological logic of neoliberalism and social Darwinism in denigrating the Iron Girls is being consistently applied to other social hierarchies and power relations in the post-socialist reconfiguration of society and values.

2. Faced with the state-sponsored denigration of Dazhai after Deng Xiaoping decided to abolish collective agriculture, some scholars worked to resist the post-Mao master narrative by collecting oral histories of Dazhai villagers, county officials, and reporters who originally reported on Dazhai. In these works Dazhai villagers continue to express their pride in building their village under the leadership of Chen Yonggui and refute rumors that their accomplishments were a result of state subsidies. The most valuable source material on the history of the Iron Girls Brigade in Dazhai is in a two-volume collection of oral histories of 150 villagers. Sun Liping and Liu Xiaoli, eds., *Koushu Dazhai shi* [hereafter *Oral Histories of Dazhai*] (Guangzhou: South Daily Press, 2008). Many websites provide valuable visual and written sources on the leader of the Iron Girls Brigade, Guo Fenglian. For instance, "Guo Fenglian yi Dazhai Tieguniang" [Guo Fenglian recalls Dazhai Iron Girls], *Tudou.net,* www.tudou.com/programs/view/gkcBBnHwNB4/ (accessed on May 18, 2016).

3. *Oral Histories of Dazhai*, 99, 102–4. Also, "Bangyang—Guo Fenglian" [A role model—Guo Fenglian], *Banbiantian* [Half the Sky], *CCTV*, no. 67, 2009, http://tv.cntv.cn/video/C10305/97ea6621ecff407747a2f58821e0b9c3 (accessed May 20, 2014; now only accessible in China). *Half the Sky* was a CCTV talk show program in which the host Zhang Yue interviewed women from diverse backgrounds. The program started after the Fourth UN Conference of Women held in Beijing and was cancelled in July 2010.

4. *Oral Histories of Dazhai*, 127, 129.

5. For more images of the Dazhai Iron Girls, see Zhang Yi, "Dazhai Tieguniang de huiyi" [Reminiscences of the Dazhai Iron Girls], January 1, 2015, *China.net*, http://club.china.com/data/thread/1015/2775/67/59/1_1.html?5 (accessed January 19, 2015).

6. Gail Hershatter, *The Gender of Memory: Rural Women and China's Collective Past* (Berkeley: University of California Press, 2011). The renowned poet of the Tang Dynasty, Du Fu (712–770), wrote about how robust women plowed the fields in times of war. See Hugh Grigg, "Translation: Ballad of the Army Carts, by Dufu," March 30, 2011, *EastAsiaStudent.net*, https://eastasiastudent.net/china/classical/du-fu-bing-che-xing/ (accessed May 18, 2016).

7. See Bao Shu and Gao Qi, "Gege saiguo Mu Guiying" [Everyone surpasses Mu Guiying], *Women of China*, no. 4 (April 1958): 4; Jing Dao, "Jiaohua yaozuo Mu Guiying" [Jiaohua wants to be Mu Guiying], *Women of China*, no. 5 (May 1958): 5; Corresponding Group of the Xu County Committee, "Turang geming zhongde 'Hua Mulan' zhandouying" ["Hua Mulan" battalion in the soil revolution], *Women of China*, no. 14 (October 1958): 3.

8. See *Li Shuangshuang: Cong xiaoshuo dao dianying* [*Li Shuangshuang*: From a novelette to a film], edited and published by Beijing Chinese Film Press (1979). The volume was first published in 1963 without an editor's name. It includes the film script, essays by the screenwriter, director, and actors discussing the production process, and commentary by film critics. See also Zhang Ruifang with Jin Yifeng, *Suiyue youqing: Zhang Ruifang huiyi lu* [Affective years: A memoir of Zhang Ruifang] (Beijing: Zhongyang wenxian chubanshe, 2005): 318–35. In her memoir, the actor Zhang Ruifang details the process of her fieldwork when she lived in a village with a woman activist as her model and also recalls her interactions with rural women after the film was screened nationwide to hear their feedback.

9. *Oral Histories of Dazhai*, 89.

10. Ibid., 235.

11. See CCTV talk show featuring Guo Fenglian, *Feichang Xiangshang* [Striving upwards], *Sohu.net*, http://tv.sohu.com/20130510/n375487819.shtml (accessed September 20, 2013; now only accessible in China).

12. Jin Yihong, "Rethinking the 'Iron Girls': Gender and Labour during the Chinese Cultural Revolution," in *Translating Feminisms in China*, ed. Dorothy Ko and Wang Zheng (Oxford: Blackwell, 2007), presents the mixed assessments of former participants. Complaints of damage to some women's health because of heavy physical labor were common, especially in urban industries. Yet Jin empha-

sizes that the spirit of the Iron Girls, taken as a challenge to traditional gender divisions of labor, was emulated by many women of that generation, including those who did not join Iron Girls brigades.

13. Gayatri Chakravorty Spivak, "Can the Subaltern Speak?" in *Marxism and the Interpretation of Culture*, ed. Cary Nelson and Lawrence Grossberg (Urbana: University of Illinois Press, 1988), 271–313.

14. Here I borrow an insight from Pierre Bourdieu that the principle of the "magic efficacy" of the official language does not lie in the language itself, "but in the group that authorizes and recognizes it and, with it, authorizes and recognizes itself." Pierre Bourdieu, *The Logic of Practice* (Stanford, CA: Stanford University Press, 1990), 110.

15. Emily Honig and Gail Hershatter, *Personal Voices: Chinese Women in the 1980's* (Stanford, CA: Stanford University Press, 1988), vividly captures the discursive shift in that historical moment. For their discussion of the Iron Girls, see 23–31.

16. For a biographical article that describes Guo Fenglian's ups and downs, see Caoshangfei, *Guo Fenglian*, August 17, 2014, *360doc.net*, www.360doc.com/content /14/0817/12/7966463_402560400.shtml (accessed May 18, 2016). The course of Guo Fenglian's career constitutes a fascinating account of China's history over the past five decades.

17. Honig and Hershatter, *Personal Voices*, 25. Guo Fenglian, however, had many suitors, including some men who were urban residents. Some Iron Girls of Dazhai even married men from other villages who came to live there, reversing the usual pattern of patrilocal residence.

18. See the interview with a male writer in the documentary film *Morning Sun*, directed by Carma Hinton, 2003.

19. Honig and Hershatter, *Personal Voices*, 25.

20. Liu, Lydia, Rebecca Karl, and Dorothy Ko, eds., *The Birth of Chinese Feminism: Essential Texts in Transnational Theory* (New York: Columbia University Press, 2013), 250.

21. Xueping Zhong, *Masculinity Besieged? Issues of Modernity and Male Subjectivity in Chinese Literature of the Late Twentieth Century* (Durham, NC: Duke University Press, 2000), 11.

22. See Zhong's close reading of a group of famous male writers' literary texts in *Masculinity Besieged?*, including Zhang Xianliang's "Half of Men Is Women."

23. Meng Xiaoyun, "Dangdai Zhongguo funü mianmian guan" [Perspectives on contemporary Chinese women], *People's Daily* (overseas version), January 8–10, 1986. This summary of public debates and surveys on women's roles contends that a woman is confronted with three choices: the choice of the state that requires a woman to contribute to society; the choice of men that demands from a woman a pleasing appearance, a gentle personality, and a strong competence in domesticity; and a woman's own choice. The author emphasizes that many women's rejection of just being a good wife and mother is in sharp conflict with men's expectations. For a discussion of increasing gender conflicts in the economic reform, see Wang Zheng, "Gender, Employment and Women's Resistance," in *Chinese Society: Change,*

Conflict and Resistance, 2nd edition, ed. Elizabeth J. Perry and Mark Selden (London and New York: RoutlegeCurzon, 2003), 159–82.

24. Zheng Yefu, "Nannü pingdeng de shehuixue sikao" [Sociological thinking on equality between men and women], *Shehuixue yanjiu* [Sociological Studies], no. 2 (1994): 110.

25. Pan Jintang, "Funü jiefang de shizhi yu biaozhi tanxi" [Analyzing the substance and sign of women's liberation], *Zhongguo funübao* [China Women's News], May 27, 1988.

26. Chang Leren, "Youhua peizhi he zuijia fenpei" [Optimization and the best distribution], *Zhongguo funübao* [China Women's News], July 11, 1988.

27. Zhang Xiaosong, "Dui 'nannü pingdeng kouhao de zhiyi'" [Interrogating the slogan of "equality between men and women"], *Zhongguo funübao* [China Women's News], May 16, 1988.

28. Feng Chujun, "Wei minzu fazhan xuyao xisheng" [The national development requires sacrifice], *Zhongguo funü* [Women of China], no. 9 (1988): 16. At a banquet during my lecture tour in China in July 2013 my host, a high-level male university administrator, asked me to explain "gender studies." After hearing my brief explanation, he offered his solution to tensions in gender relations: "To maintain harmony and balance in conjugal relations, wives should return home and their salaries should be paid to their husbands."

29. Pan Suiming, "Zhongguo xinnüxing mianlin de xuanze yu deshi" [New choice and gain-and-loss confronted by Chinese new women], *Zhongguo funübao* [China Women's News], January 19, 1987.

30. Zheng Yefu, "Nannü pingdeng de shehuixue sikao," 111.

31. See Wang Xia, *Haipai zhangfu mianmianguan* [An overview of Shanghai husbands] (Shanghai: Shanghai Social Sciences Press, 1991), 2.

32. For an early examination of how socialist women's liberation benefited women, written by one of the beneficiaries, see Li Xiaojiang, *Xiawa de tansuo* [Eve's exploration] (Zhengzhou: Henan People's Press, 1988), 165–69. Her assessment aligns with the prevailing male intellectuals' concept that the level of women's liberation outpaced socioeconomic conditions and that gender equality was bestowed on Chinese women by the state.

33. Zhang Xinxin, "Wo zainaer cuoguole ni?" [Where did I miss you?]. It was originally published in *Shouhuo* [Harvest], no. 5 (1980). Citation from Zhang Xinxin, *Zhang Xinxin daibiaozuo* [Representative works by Zhang Xinxin] (Zhengzhou: Huanghe wenyi chubanshe, 1988), 23.

34. Li Xiaojiang, *Eve's Exploration,* 288.

35. Ibid.

36. Examples of English-language scholarship that circulated the thesis of "the masculinization of Chinese women" include: Mayfair Mei-Hu Yang, *Spaces of Their Own: Women's Public Sphere in Transnational China* (Minneapolis: University of Minnesota Press, 1999): 1–33; Shuqin Cui, *Women through the Lens: Gender and Nation in a Century of Chinese Cinema* (Honolulu: University of Hawaii Press, 2003); Mayfair Mei-Hui Yang, director, *Through Chinese Women's Eyes,* documen-

tary film, 1997; and Dai Jinhua, *Cinema and Desire: Feminist Marxism and Cultural Politics in the Work of Dai Jinhua*, ed. Jing Wang and Tani E. Barlow (London: Verso, 2002). In Dai's influential work, she claims that in socialist films "because the image of Woman no longer served as an object of the gaze of male desire, women also ceased to exist as a gender group distinct from men" (p. 102). For a strong critique of Chinese women literary scholars' thesis of socialist gender erasure, including Meng Yue and Dai Jinhua's influential works centering on this thesis, see Rosemary A. Roberts, *Maoist Model Theatre: The Semiotics of Gender and Sexuality in the Chinese Cultural Revolution (1966–1976)* (Leiden: Koninklijke Brill NV, 2010).

37. Rural men highly value women with strong physiques. In some rural areas in Fujian the value of betrothal gifts (bride-price) given to a bride by the groom's family was determined by her body weight, a practice that persisted even through the Cultural Revolution.

38. Ou Yansheng, ed., *Visual Voices: 100 Photographs of Village China by the Women of Yunnan Province* [*Zhongguo Yunnan nongcun funü ziwo xiezhen ji*] (Kunming: Yunnan People's Publishing House, 1995).

39. For discussions of changing gender discourses in twentieth-century China, see Ko and Wang Zheng, *Translating Feminisms in China*.

40. For a critical examination of the relationship between the post-socialist ascendancy of the discourse of "scientific modernity" and the rapidly increasing political power of scientists, see Susan Greenhalgh's penetrating study, *Just One Child: Science and Policy in Deng's China* (Berkeley: University of California Press, 2008).

41. For an analysis of women intellectuals' promotion of essentialism, see Wang Zheng, "Research on Women in Contemporary China," in *Guide to Women's Studies in China,* ed. Gail Hershatter et al. (Berkeley: Institute of East Asian Studies, 1998), 1–43.

42. *Through Chinese Women's Eyes.*

43. "Iron Lady" was a nickname for Prime Minister Margaret Thatcher of the United Kingdom. Here the Chinese usage connotes recognition of Guo Fenglian's current social status as a successful entrepreneur. See "Guo Fenglian: 'Tieguniang' de huali zhuanshen" [Guo Fenglian: An Iron Girl's magnificent turn], *China.net*, www.china.com.cn/economic/zhuanti/xzgjjlsn/2009–07/24/content_18200659 .htm (accessed August 19, 2014).

44. Guo Fenglian was first appointed to the Standing Committee of the Fifth National Congress in 1978. She was removed from all her official positions in 1980 after Deng Xiaoping's decision to abandon collectivization of the rural economy. She resumed her membership in the Standing Committee of the National Congress in 2003, not because of her past glory as a model peasant from a rural village but due to her present accomplishment as a CEO of a sizable enterprise in the market economy.

45. Interview of Guo Fenglian, "Striving Upwards," *Souhu.net*, http://tv.sohu .com/20130510/n375487819.shtml (accessed September 20, 2013; now only accessible in China).

46. For stories and images of Guo Fenglian's contemporary role as a CEO, see "Dazhai dongshizhang Guo Fenglian lai Han zhaoshang" [Dazhai's CEO Guo Fenglian comes to Wuhan to do businesss], *163.com*, http://news.163.com/10/1024/02/6JNQJMJ000014AED.html (accessed January 19, 2015).

47. "Zhongguo de xingbie gongzi chayi" [Income difference by gender in China], *Wageindicator.cn*, www.wageindicator.cn/main/salary/753759735de58d445dee8ddd; and "Shouru xingbiecha" [Gender difference in income], *Hudong Baike* [Interactive encyclopedia], www.baike.com/wiki/收入性别差 (both accessed August 25, 2014).

48. See Zha Jianying, *Bashi niandai fangtanlu* [Interviews of the 1980s] (Beijing: Sanlian shudian, 2006). The literary scholars and artists included in the volume present fascinating memories of and comments about what they experienced during the 1980s. Tellingly, neither gender nor class is deployed as an analytical category in their narratives.

49. Many Chinese websites have reported Ma Hu's suit against the Beijing Post Office and her eventual victory. In November 2015 the Shunyi district court in Beijing ruled that delivering packages does not fall into the category of jobs "unsuitable for women" stipulated by the state. Ma Hu is her pseudonym. For a detailed report of the case, see Feminist Voices, "Tashi zhongguo diyige zhuanggao guoqi jiuye xingbie qishi de nüsheng, ranhou yingle" [She is the first woman student who has ever sued a state enterprise for gender discrimination in employment, and she won], November 2, 2015, http://chuansong.me/n/1867398 (accessed January 1, 2016).

CONCLUSION

1. Lydia H. Liu, Rebecca E. Karl, and Dorothy Ko, eds., *The Birth of Chinese Feminism: Essential Texts in Transnational Theory* (New York: Columbia University Press, 2013), 103.

2. Yiching Wu, *The Cultural Revolution at the Margins: Chinese Socialism in Crisis* (Cambridge, MA: Harvard University Press, 2014), 228.

3. This evaluation is by Hong Tianhui, deputy chair of the ACWF, who was in charge of its publicity work. See *Women of China,* the first issue in June 2009, p. 18. In 2000 the magazine became bimonthly, with one issue each month devoted to legal advice in response to urban women's increasing demand for knowledge of civil law, mostly about property and marriage. That is the ground for its claim to protect women's legal rights.

4. For a penetrating study of the interplay of gender and class in China's merging with global capitalism, see Pun Ngai, *Made in China: Women Factory Workers in a Global Workplace* (Durham, NC: Duke University Press, 2005).

5. Information on the new publications can be accessed online; see *Hao Zhufu* [Good Housekeeper], *GotoRead.net*, www.gotoread.com/mag/585/emag.html and Yueji [Self], www.gotoread.com/mag/13286/order.html (both accessed May 20, 2016).

6. *Hao Zhufu*, www.gotoread.com/mag/585/ (originally accessed March 2, 2009). It has been changed to www.gotoread.com/mag/585/emag.html with a different home page without the introduction of the magazine.

7. *Yueji*, http://cn.qikan.com/JournalDetails.aspx?issn = 1005–1872 (originally accessed March 2, 2009). The site has been changed to www.gotoread.com /mag/13286/order.html with a different home page (accessed May 20, 2016).

8. *Ai Nüsheng* [Fashion], www.gotoread.com/magazine/12560/issue/17933 /cover.jpg (originally accessed March 2, 2009). The site has been changed to www .gotoread.com/mag/12560/order.html with a different home page (accessed May 20, 2016).

9. Huang Qingyi, "Fengyu licheng zoukaige, yushijujin zhu huihuang" [Songs of triumph during stormy journeys, progress over time while striving for glory], *Women of China* (June 2009): 1.

10. Shi Yumei, interview by author, Beijing, July 20, 2009.

11. Hou Di, interview by author, Beijing, July 1, 2010.

12. For studies of recent feminist activities in China, see Wang Zheng, "Research on Women in Contemporary China," in *Guide to Women's Studies in China,* ed. Gail Hershatter et al. (Berkeley: Institute of East Asian Studies, 1998), 1–43; Wang Zheng, "Feminist Networks," in *Reclaiming Chinese Society: Politics of Redistribution, Recognition, and Representation,* ed. Ching Kwan Lee, (London: Routledge Curzon, 2010), 101–18; Wang Zheng and Ying Zhang, "Global Concepts, Local Practices: Chinese Feminism since the Fourth UN Conference on Women," *Feminist Studies* 36, no. 1 (Spring 2010): 40–67.

13. Recent scholarship emphasizes diverse aspects of the massive popular protests in 1989, other than the previously highlighted theme of a demand for political democracy by intellectuals and students. The working class's discontent with its downward mobility engendered in privatization and marketization and accompanying corruption of the party officials constituted a major factor in the popular support of student demonstrations. See Wu Yiching, *The Cultural Revolution at the Margins,* 227–38.

14. Many local WFs have promoted such "lady training workshops." See a report on Xingtai WF: "Xingtai 'shunüban' kaijiangla" [Xingtai's "ladies' class" has begun], *Paigu.com*, http://news.paigu.com/a/335/2090316.html, and a survey of "lady training workshops" including those run by universities, "'Shunüban' diaocha: 'bianlian' duo, dingshang younü shaonü" [An investigation of "ladies' class": Multiple faces, turning attention to female children and adolescents], *Guangdong Nüxing e jiayuan* [E-home for Guangdong females], www.gdwomen.org.cn /jdgz/201006/t20100621_99412.htm (accessed January 14, 2016).

15. The prominent feminists among this group include Tan Shen, who pioneered research on migrant women workers in sweatshops in the South China; Liang Jun, who persevered in organizing rural women to achieve the alleviation of poverty and the cultural transformation of their villages' patriarchal norms in Henan; Gao Xiaoxian, who initiated rural women's political participation in village elections in Shaanxi; Wang Xingjuan, who opened China's first women's hotline in Beijing to

provide psychological counseling to women in distress; Chen Mingxia, Ge Youli, Bu Wei, Feng Yuan and the many others who dedicated themselves to bringing domestic violence against women out of the closet and into the law; and He Zhonghua, who initiated projects to research and empower ethnic minority women in Yunnan. And the full list is much longer than this brief one. For more detailed information on NGO feminists' struggles, see interviews of ten Chinese feminists by the University of Michigan's Global Feminisms Project, China site, www.umich.edu/~glblfem/en/china.html (accessed April 20, 2015).

16. For a detailed discussion of differences between "gender equality" and "equality between men and women," and feminist NGO activities, see Wang Zheng and Ying Zhang, "Global Concepts, Local Practices."

17. For a detailed discussion of the WF's role in fighting for women's equal rights in employment when Deng Xiaoping's regime began to privatize urban enterprises, see Wang Zheng, "Gender, Employment and Women's Resistance," in *Chinese Society: Change, Conflict and Resistance,* second edition, ed. Elizabeth J. Perry and Mark Selden (London and New York: RoutledgeCurzon, 2003), 158–82.

18. Xi Jinping, "Jianchi nannü pingdeng jiben guoce, fahui woguo funü weida zuoyong" [Upholding the fundamental state policy of equality between men and women, exerting women's great role in our country], *Xinhua.net*, October 31, 2013, http://news.xinhuanet.com/politics/2013–10/31/c_117956150.htm (accessed May 20, 2015).

19. Nozom Hayashi (correspondent), "Outcry at Home and Abroad Leads to Release of Chinese Female Activists," April 18, 2015, *Asahi Shimbun*, http://ajw.asahi.com/article/asia/china/AJ201504180045 (accessed April 20, 2015). (The website has moved to the following new site that only carries the correspondent's postings since May 25, 2015: http://sitesearch.asahi.com/.cgi/ajwsitesearch/sitesearch.pl?Keywords=Nozom%20Hayashi&page=3 [accessed May 20, 2016]).

20. For an analysis of the event, see Wang Zheng, "Detention of the Feminist Five in China," *Feminist Studies* 41, no. 2 (2015): 476–82. The five young feminists are Li Tingting, Wei Tingting, Zheng Churan, Wu Rongrong, and Wang Man.

GLOSSARY

AIREN 爱人

AI NÜSHENG 《爱女生》

ANBU 庵埠

BABAI ZHUANGSHI 《八百壮士》

BAI YANG 白杨

BAOJIA 保甲

BAOSHENGONG 《包身工》

BEIDAIHE 北戴河

BINGTUAN JI 兵团级

CAI CHANG 蔡畅

CAI HESEN 蔡和森

CAO GUANQUN 曹冠群

CAO SHUNQIN 曹舜琴

CHANG LEREN 常乐人

CHAOQIAN 超前

CHAOZHOU 潮州

CHEN BODA 陈伯达

CHEN BO'ER 陈波儿

CHEN DUXIU 陈独秀

CHENG GANG 成岗

CHEN HUANGMEI 陈荒煤

CHEN JIHUA 陈季华

CHEN SHUNHUA 陈舜华

CHEN WENJING 陈文静

CHEN YI 陈毅

CHEN YONGGUI 陈永贵

CHIANG KAI-SHEK 蒋介石

DA DUCAO 大毒草

DAZHAI 大寨

DENG XIAOPING 邓小平

DENG YINGCHAO 邓颖超

DING LING 丁玲

DONG BIAN 董边

DU FU 杜甫

DUAN YONGQIANG 段永强

FANG HAIZHEN 方海珍

FEIXINGHUA 非性化

FENG CHUJUN 冯楚军

FENGJIAN 封建

FENGJIAN SIXIANG 封建思想

FENGJIAN ZHUYI 封建主义

FENG XUEFENG 冯雪峰

FOSHAN 佛山

FUDAIHUI 妇代会

FUNÜ GONGZUO 妇女工作

FUNÜ JIEFANG 妇女解放

FUNÜ QUANLI 妇女权利

FUNÜ SHENGHUO 《妇女生活》

FUNÜ WENTI 妇女问题

FUNÜ WENTI DE TICHU HE JIEJUE 妇女问题的提出和解决

FUNÜ YUANDI 《妇女园地》

FUQI ZHIJIAN 《夫妻之间》

GAO QI 高奇

GENG RUZHANG 耿如璋

GONGNONGBING 工农兵

GUAN JIAN 关建

GUO FENGLIAN 郭凤莲

HAO ZHUFU 《好主妇》

HE LAOLIU 贺老六

HE XIANGNING 何香凝

HE-YIN ZHEN 何殷震

HOU DI 侯荻

HU BANGXIU 胡邦秀

HU QIAOMU 胡乔木

HU XIUZHI 胡秀芝

HU YUZHI 胡愈之

HUA MULAN 花木兰

HUANG CHEN 黄晨

HUANG QINGYI 黄晴宜

HUANG YECAI 黄叶裁

HUANG ZONGYING 黄宗英

HUISHOU DANGNIAN 《回首当年》

JIA CUNSUO 贾存锁

JIATING FUNÜ 家庭妇女

JIANG SHUIYING 江水英

JIANG QING 江青

JIANG ZHUJUN 江竹筠

JIEFANG RIBAO 《解放日报》

JIEMEIMEN 姐妹们

JIN 斤

JIN SHAN 金山

KANG KEQING 康克清

KE QINGSHI 柯庆施

KE XIANG 柯湘

KONG QINGFEN 孔庆芬

LAN PING 蓝萍

LAO POZI 老婆子

LAO TOUZI 老头子

LAODONG RENMIN 劳动人民

LEI FENG 雷锋

LI DAZHAO 李大钊

LI FUCHUN 李富春

LINONG 里弄

LI QIYANG 李屺阳

LI SHUANGSHUANG 《李双双》

LI TIEMEI 李铁梅

LI XIAOJIANG 李小江

LI ZHUN 李准

LING ZIFENG 凌子风

LIU LANTAO 刘澜涛

LIU LEQUN 刘乐群

LIU QIAOER 《刘巧儿》

LIU SHAOQI 刘少奇

LIU XIAO 刘晓

LONG DONGHUA 龙冬花

LU MING 鲁明

LU XUN 鲁迅

LUO BAOYI 罗抱一

LUO QIONG 罗琼

MA HU 马户

MAKESI ZHUYI WUCHAN JIEJI FUNÜ JIEFANG LILUN 马克思主义无产阶级妇女解放理论

MAO ZEDONG 毛泽东

MEI GONGYI 梅公毅

MEI JIWEN 梅基文

MU GUIYING 穆桂英

NANNÜ 男女

NANNÜ PINGDENG 男女平等

NANNÜ SHOUSHOU BUQIN 男女授受不亲

NANNÜ YOUBIE 男女有别

NANZHUWAI, NÜZHUNEI 男主外，女主内

NAO DULIXING 闹独立性

NEIWAI 内外

NIU YUFEN 牛玉芬

NÜQUAN 女权

NÜQUAN ZHUYI 女权主义

NÜQUAN ZHUYIZHE 女权主义者

NÜREN HUOZHE WEI SHENME 女人活着为什么

NÜXING DE NAHAN 《女性的呐喊》

NÜXING TEZHI 女性特质

OU MENGJUE 欧梦觉

PAN JINTANG 潘锦棠

PAN SUIMING 潘绥铭

PEIHE GONGZUO 配合工作

PENG ZHEN 彭真

PENGZHUANG 碰撞

QIAN XINGCUN 钱杏邨

QILÜ HUANMA 骑驴换马

QIN YI 秦怡

QINGCHUN XIAN 《青春线》

QINJIAN JIANGUO, QINJIAN CHIJIA 勤俭建国，勤俭持家

QIU JIN 秋瑾

QU BAIYIN 瞿白音

QUNZHONG LUXIAN 群众路线

REN POSHENG 任泊生

ROU SHI 柔石

SAI JINHUA 《赛金花》

SANBA HONGQISHOU 三八红旗手

SANBAOYIDAO 三饱一倒

SANG HU 桑弧

SANGE MODENG NÜXING 《三个摩登女性》

SANGE XIAOJIAO DAIBIAO YINXIANGJI 三个小脚代表印象记

SANJIEHE 三结合

SANZHI DUIWU 三支队伍

SHA YEXIN 沙叶新

SHAN-GAN-NING 陕甘宁

SHANGGUAN YUNZHU 上官云珠

SHEHUI XINGBIE PINGDENG 社会性别平等

SHENBAO FUKAN 《申报副刊》

SHEN NAIXI 沈乃熙

SHENNÜ 《神女》

SHEN XILING 沈西苓

SHEN ZIJIU 沈兹九

SHENGSI TONGXIN 《生死同心》

SHI LIANGCAI 史量才

SHI YUMEI 时玉梅

SHISHI LEIBIAN 《时事类编》

SHUI HUA 水华

SONG MEILING 宋美龄

SONG QINGLING 宋庆龄

SUN YAT-SEN 孙中山

SUN YU 孙瑜

TAITAI 太太

TAMEN 她们

TAO CHENG 陶承

TAOLI JIE 《桃李劫》

TIAN GUIYING 田桂英

TIAN JIAYING 田家英

TU 土

WANG DANFENG 王丹凤

WANGFUJING 王府井

WANG GUILAN 王桂兰

WANG MUCHUN 万木春

WANG YING 王莹

WEN JIE 文杰

WU CUICHAN 吴翠婵

WU GUIHUA 吴桂花

WU XIUYING 吴秀英

WU XUN ZHUAN 《武训传》

XI JINPING 习近平

XIBAIPO 西柏坡

XIA GONG 夏公

XIA SHENGHUO 下生活

XIA YAN 夏衍

XIANGLIN SAO 祥林嫂

XIANGSHENG 相声

XIE JUEZAI 谢觉哉

XIE TIELI 谢铁骊

XIE XUEGONG 解学恭

XIAO JIANQIU 肖涧秋

XINGBIE 性别

XIN NÜXING 《新女性》

XU YUNFENG 许云峰

XUANZE AIREN DE BIAOZHUN SHI SHENME 选择爱人的标准是什么

YAN'AN 延安

YAN YIYAN 颜一烟

YANG FUZHEN 杨富珍

YANGGE 秧歌

YANG HANSHENG 阳翰笙

YANG HUIMIN 杨惠敏

YANG YUN 杨云

YANG YUN 杨蕴

YANG ZHIHUA 杨之华

YAOWO BUGEMING, CHUFEI TAIYANG CONG XIBIAN CHULAI 要我不革命，除非太阳从西边出来

YI SONG ER CUI SAN MANIANG 一送二催三骂娘

YINSHENG YANGSHUAI 阴盛阳衰

YU LAN 于蓝

YUAN LIANFANG 苑莲芳

YUAN MUZHI 袁牧之

YUEJI 《悦己》

ZAOYUAN XIGOU 枣园西沟

ZENG LI 曾立

ZENG ZI 曾自

ZENGCHAN JIEYUE 增产节约

ZHANG CHUNQIAO 张春桥

ZHANGFU BIANZOUQU 《丈夫变奏曲》

ZHANG LIZHU 张丽珠

ZHANG QINGYUN 张青云

ZHANG RUIFANG 张瑞芳

ZHANG SHUFENG 张树凤

ZHANG WUZHEN 张悟真

ZHANG XIAOSONG 张晓崧

ZHANG XICHEN 章锡琛

ZHANG XINXIN　张欣辛

ZHANG YUN　章蕴

ZHAO DAN　赵丹

ZHAO MANCANG　赵满仓

ZHAO XIAN　赵先

ZHAO YIMAN　《赵一曼》

ZHEJIANG XINCHAO　《浙江新潮》

ZHENG BOQI　郑伯奇

ZHENG JUNLI　郑君里

ZHENG YEFU　郑也夫

ZHINAN AI　直男癌

ZHONGHUA NÜER　《中华女儿》

ZHONGNANHAI　中南海

ZHONGXINGHUA　中性化

ZHOU ENLAI　周恩来

ZHOU LIAN　周莲

ZHOU YANG　周扬

ZHU DE　朱德

ZIBEI SIXIANG　自卑思想

ZHU FU　《祝福》

ZHUTI　主体

ZUO FUNÜ GONGZUO　做妇女工作

ZUO FUYUN GONGZUO　做妇运工作

LIST OF INTERVIEWS

Cao Shunqin, Shanghai, August 21, 2002; December 2, 2003; and September 3, 2004.
Chen Huizhen, Shanghai, June 19, 2010.
Chen Jihua, by phone, December 15, 2012.
Chen Manqian, Shanghai, January 3, 2001.
Chen Tilan, by phone, June 3, 2012.
Chen Wenjing, Beijing, July 19, 2012.
Duan Yongqiang, Beijing, July 18, 2007.
Fan Ximei, Shanghai, March 15, 2001.
Feng Qi, Shanghai, August 25, 2008.
Gao Danzhu, Xi'an, August 11, 2009.
Gao Shilan, by phone, May 30, 2012.
Gu Lanying, Beijing, July 3, 2010.
Guo Liwen, Beijing, September 2, 2007.
Guo Nanning, Beijing, June 27 and July 1, 2010.
Guo Wenlin, Shanghai, November 11 and November 13, 1996.
Hou Di, Beijing, August 29 and August 31, 2007; July 1, 2010.
Hou Di, by phone, December 10, 2009 and March 16, 2010.
Huang Ganying, Beijing, August 29, 2007.
Huang Zhun, Shanghai, August 29, 2008.
Ji Shufen, Beijing, October 30, 2012.
Jin Ruiying, Beijing, July 6, 2010.
Li Qiyang, Xi'an, July 7, 2010.
Lin Ruwei, Beijing, July 20, 2012.
Liu Jing, Beijing, June 30, 2010.
Liu Zhonglu, Beijing, September 3, 2007.
Lu Ming, Beijing, July 18 and December 14, 2012.
Lu Zhengmin, Beijing, July 21, 2009.
Mao Yaqing, Shanghai, June 7, 2000.
Meng Liye, Beijing, December 13, 2012 and July 13, 2013.

Qin Xiaomei, Shanghai, March 19, 2001.
Qin Yi, by phone, August 24, 2012.
Shang Shaohua, Beijing, August 28, 2007.
Shen Yanglian, Shanghai, June 22, 2010.
Shi Yumei, Beijing, July 20, 2009.
Song Ningqi, Shanghai, June 8, 2012.
Su Ping, Beijing, August 30 and September 3, 2007.
Sun Yu, Beijing, July 25, 2012.
Sun Zhilan, Shanghai, July 10, 2002.
Tang Jixiang, Guangzhou, December 5, 2011.
Tao Chunfang, Beijing, July 27, 2007.
Wang Qingshu, Beijing, September 1, 2007.
Wang Suhua, Shanghai, June 17, 2010.
Wang Yongfang, Beijing, December 13, 2011.
Wang Yun, Beijing, August 30, 2005.
Wu Cuichan, Shanghai, July 1 and August 21, 2002.
Wu Xiuying, Shanghai, March 16, 2001.
Xiang Mei, Shanghai, August 28, 2008.
Xu Jingxin, Shanghai, August 11, 2012.
Yang Qixian, Anbu Town, December 8, 2011.
Yu Lan, Beijing, July 24, 2012.
Zeng Li and Zeng Zi, Beijing, June 25, 2010.
Zhang Hui, Beijing, June 30, 2010.
Zhang Jiexun, Beijing, July 20, 2009.
Zhang Ruifang, August 29, 2008.
Zhao Huanzhang, Shanghai, August 17, 2012
Zhao Wei, Beijing, August 28, 2005.
Zhao Xian, Shanghai, September 13, 2004 and July 10, 2005.
Zhong Xinghuo, Shanghai, August 29, 2012.

BIBLIOGRAPHY

"1950 nian minzhu jianzheng gongzuo chubu zongjie" [A preliminary summary of the work on democratically building the government in 1950]. Shanghai Municipal Archives, n.d., B168-1-745.

"1954 nian Shanghai fulian gongzuo zongjie" [A summary of Shanghai Women's Federation's work in 1954]. Shanghai Municipal Archives, 12 April 1955, C31-1-95.

ACWF's Institute for Research on Women, ed. *Zhongguo funü yanjiu nianjian 1996–2000* [Chinese women's studies yearbook 1996–2000]. Beijing: Zhongguo funü chubanshe, 2004.

Ai Nüsheng [Fashion]. *GotoRead.com.* www.gotoread.com/mag/12560/order.html (accessed May 20, 2016).

All-China Women's Federation. *Huainian Zhang Yun dajie* [Remembering elder sister Zhang Yun]. Beijing: Zhongguo funü chubanshe, 1996.

————. *Zhongguo funü yundong bainian dashi ji (1901–2000)* [Major events in a century of the Chinese women's movement (1901–2000)]. Beijing: Zhongguo funü chubanshe, 2003.

Andors, Phyllis. *The Unfinished Liberation of Chinese Women.* Bloomington: Indiana University Press, 1983.

"Ba geming shiye fangzai diyiwei" [Giving priority to the revolutionary cause]. *Zhongguo Funü* [Women of China], no. 4 (1963): 6–7.

Ba, Tu. "Chen Boda zai 'wenhua dageming' zhongde chen yu fu" [The ups and downs of Chen Boda in the Cultural Revolution]. In *Dangshi Zongheng* [Perspectives of the Party's History], nos. 3–5 (2004): 9–12, 20–23, and 11–15.

"Bada Yangbanxi" [Eight model works]. *Baidu baike.* http://baike.baidu.com /view/126013.htm (accessed May 21, 2016).

Bailey, Paul J. *Women and Gender in Twentieth-Century China.* New York: Palgrave Macmillan, 2012.

Banbiantian [Half the Sky]. "Bangyang—Guo Fenglian" [A role model—Guo Fenglian]. *CCTV*, no. 67, 2009. http://tv.cntv.cn/video/C10305/97ea6621ecff40 7747a2f5882ieob9c3 (accessed May 20, 2014; now only accessible in China).

"Bannian minzhu jianzheng gongzuo jihua" [A plan for the work on democratically establishing the government in the next six months, November 1950–April 1951]. Shanghai Municipal Archives, 1950, B168–1–745.

Bao, Shu, and Gao Qi. "Gege saiguo Mu Guiying" [Everyone surpasses Mu Guiying]. *Women of China* (1958): 4.

Bebel, August. *Women and Socialism.* Translated by Meta L. Stern (Hebe). New York: Socialist Literature, 1910.

Beiying dianying 65 *Liehuo zhong yongsheng* [Beijing Film Studio films 65 *Eternity in Flames*]. www.youtube.com/watch?v=7wTmd8RmXwA (accessed May 22, 2016).

Belden, Jack. *China Shakes the World.* New York: Harpers, 1949.

Bell, Lynda. "Woman, Nation, Household Redux: Mobilizing Female Virtue in the 1950s Chinese Countryside." Unpublished paper.

"Benbu 1959 nian gongzuo jihua" [A work plan for 1959]. Shanghai Municipal Archives, 1959, C31–1–248.

"Benju guanyu Huangpu deng shijiugeque linong gongzuo zongjie" [A summary of neighborhood work in Huangpu and eighteen other districts by the department of civil affairs]. Shanghai Municipal Archives, 1950, B168–1–751.

"Benhui guanyu linong zhengdun zhong funü gongzuo de tonggao" [The women's federation's report on women-work in the rectification of the neighborhood]. Shanghai Municipal Archives, 1954, C31–2–235.

"Benju guanyu zhengquan jianshe yu zuzhi jianshe baogao" [The department of civil affairs' reports on building political power and organizations]. Shanghai Municipal Archives, 1953, B168–1–772.

Benton, Gregor, and Lin Chun, eds. *Was Mao Really a Monster?* London: Routledge, 2010.

Berry, Chris, ed. *Perspectives on Chinese Cinema.* London: British Film Institute, 1991.

Bourdieu, Pierre. *The Logic of Practice.* Stanford, CA: Stanford University Press, 1990.

Boxer, Marilyn J. "Rethinking the Socialist Construction and International Career of the Concept 'Bourgeois Feminism.'" *American Historical Review* 112, no. 1 (2007): 131–58.

Brown, Jeremy, and Paul G. Pickowicz, eds. *Dilemmas of Victory: The Early Years of the People's Republic of China.* Cambridge, MA: Harvard University Press, 2007.

Brown, Wendy. *States of Injury: Power and Freedom in Late Modernity.* Princeton, NJ: Princeton University Press, 1995.

Brownell, Susan, and Jeffrey N. Wasserstrom, eds. *Chinese Femininities/Chinese Masculinities.* Berkeley: University of California Press, 2002.

Cai, Chang. "Guanyu nügong gongzuo de jige wenti" [A few issues about work on women workers]. In *Zhongguo funü yundong wenxian ziliao huibian* [An anthology of source material on the Chinese women's movement], edited by Chinese Women Cadres Management School, vol. 2, 34–38. Beijing: Zhongguo funü chubanshe, 1988.

———. "Jiji peiyang he tiba gengduo genghao de nüganbu" [Actively train and promote more and better women cadres]. In *Zhongguo funü yundong wenxian ziliao huibian* [An anthology of source material on the Chinese women's movement], edited by Chinese Women Cadres Management School, vol. 2, 262–68. Beijing: Zhongguo funü chubanshe, 1988.

Cai, Chusheng. "Sulian dianying dui Zhongguo dianying shiye de yingxiang he bangzhu" [Soviet films' impact on and help with Chinese films]. *People's Daily,* November 7, 1951.

Cao, Guanqun, "Quanguo funü gongzuo huiyi zongjie baogao" [A summary report on the national conference of women-work]. In *Zhongguo funü yundong wenxian ziliao huibian* [An anthology of source material on the Chinese women's movement], edited by Chinese Women Cadres Management School, vol. 2, 376. Beijing: Zhongguo funü chubanshe, 1988.

Cao, Jisan. "Chizha fengyun Chen Bo'er" [An all-powerful Chen Bo'er]. *Tianjin ribao* [Tianjin Daily], May 15, 2009.

"Cao Manzhi juzhang guanyu dachengshi qude jianzheng wenti zai quanguo minzheng huiyishang fayan tigang" [An outline of director Cao Manzhi's talk about establishing government at the disctrict level in large cities at the national conference of civil affairs]. Shanghai Municipal Archives, 17 August 1950, B168–1–745.

Caoshangfei. *Guo Fenglian. 360docnet,* August 17, 2014. www.360doc.com/content /14/0817/12/7966463_402560400.shtml (accessed May 18, 2016).

Chang, Leren. "Youhua peizhi he zuijia fenpei" [Optimization and the best distribution]. *Zhongguo funübao* [China Women's News], July 11, 1988.

Chen, Bo'er. "Bei shang laojun de jingguo yu ganxiang" [Experience and feelings of consoling troops in the North]. *Guan sheng* [Sound Off], no. 9 (1937).

———. "Cong 'shengguan tu' zhong xuexi" [Learning from the "Promotion Picture"]. *Qingming* [Pure Bright], no. 1 (1946): 51.

———. "Cong *Wu Xun Zhuan* tandao dianying chuangzuoshang de jige wenti" [From *The Life of Wu Xun* to a few issues on filmmaking]. *Xin dianying* [New Film], no. 7 (1951): 10–13.

———. "Cong Shanghai dao kangzhan zui qianxian" [From Shanghai to the forefront of the resistance]. *Linglong,* no. 17 (1937).

———. "Cong Shanghai dao kangzhan zui qianxian (xu wan)" [From Shanghai to the forefront of the resistance (continued)]. *Linglong,* no. 18 (1937).

———. "Dao biye ge zuoquzhe" [Mourning the composer of the "Graduation"]. *Qingqing dianying* [Green Movie] 2, no. 5 (1935): 1.

———. "Dianying yu fanzhan yundong" [Film and the anti-war movement]. *Dianying huabao* [Film Pictorial] 26 (1936): 20.

———. "Duiyu xinnian de xiwang" [Wishes for the New Year]. *Dian sheng* [Electro-acoustic] 6, no. 1 (1937): 45.

———. "Dujue ji: Qianxian weilao guilai" [Rebuff: Returning from consolation of soldiers on the frontline]. *Xin xueshi* [The New Knowledge], no. 4 (1937).

———. "Gedi tongxun: Sange xiaojiao daibiao yinxiang ji (shang)" [Correspondence: Impressions of three representatives with bound feet (first half)]. *Funü shenghuo* [Women's Life] 8, no. 11 (1940): 15–17.

———. "Gedi tongxun: Sange xiaojiao daibiao yinxiang ji (xia)" [Correspondence: Impressions of three representatives with bound feet (second half)]. *Funü shenghuo* [Women's Life] 8, no. 12 (1940): 19–21.

———. "Guanju suibi: Cong 'shengguan tu' zhong xuexi" [Viewing essay: Learning from the "Promotion Picture"]. *Shidai dianying* [Movie Times] 1, no. 16 (1946): 4.

———. "Guanyu Zhao Yuhua" [About Zhao Yuhua]. *Mingxing banyuekan* [Star Biweekly] 7, no. 4 (1936).

———. "Gushipian congwudaoyou de biandao gongzuo" [Screenwriting and directing feature films from scratch]. In *Zhongguo dianying yanjiu ziliao: 1949–1979* [Source material on Chinese film studies: 1949–1979], edited by Wu Di, 58–66. Beijing: Wenhua yishu chubanshe, 2006.

———. "Hei zhuaxia de huabei wenhua" [The North China culture under the black claw]. *Ouya wenhua* [Eurasian Culture], nos. 5–6 (1940).

———. "Hushang beige" [Elegy on the lake]. *Wuxiandian tekan* [Radio Special] 1, nos. 1–12 (1940): 70.

———. "Lülin youhui" [Greenwood tryst]. *Da feng* [Gale], no. 69 (1940): 2159–61.

———. "Nüxing zhongxin de dianying yu nanxing zhongxin de shehui" [The female-centered film and the male-centered society]. *Funü shenghuo* [Women's Life] 2, no. 2 (1936): 59–66.

———. "Nüzi zhiye moluo de yuanyin" [The causes of the decline of women's careers]. *Shen Bao Fukan* [Shanghai Post Supplement], July 16, 1934.

———. "Shangbing qu (dianying juben)" [Song of wounded (film script)]. *Chuangzuo yuekan* [Creation Monthly], no. 2 (1942).

———. "Wo de lian'ai guan" [My views on love]. *Dianying huabao* [Film Pictorial], no. 17 (1935): 47.

———. "Wuyue yougan" [Sentiments in May]. *Shenbao Fukan* [Shanghai Daily Supplement], May 12, 1934.

———. "Xinnian ganxiang" [New Year thoughts]. *Dianying huabao* [Film Pictorial], no. 17 (1935): 19.

———. "Xueye zhong: yige duanpian" [On a snowy night: A fragment]. *Shehui yuebao* [Society Monthly] 1, no. 3 (1934): 52.

———. "Yuan bieli" [Lamenting parting]. *Wuxiandian tekan* [Radio Special] 1, nos. 1–12 (1940): 70.

———. "Zai guofang qianxian yan guofang jü" [Played defense dramas in the defense frontline]. *Yuebao* [Monthly] 1, no. 4 (1937): 889–94.

———. "Zai guofang qianxian yan guofang jü" [Played defense dramas in the defense frontline]. *Silujun yuekan* [Fourth Military Monthly], no. 10 (1937): 249–52.

———. "Zhongguo funü de qiantu" [The future of Chinese women]. *Shenbao Fukan* [Shanghai Daily Supplement], May 19, 1934.

———. "Zhudangde danchen he renmin dianying de shengli" [Celebrating the birthday of the Party and the victory of people's films]. *Xin dianying* [New Film], no. 7 (1951): 5–6.

———. *Babai zhuangshi* [Eight Hundred Heroes]. Wuhan: China Film Studio, 1938.

———. *Guangmang wan zhang* [Shine]. *Zhongguo dianying yu yishushi ziliao*, 1950.

———. *Huishou dangnian* [Remembering the Past]. Hong Kong Global Studio, 1935.

———. *Qingchun xian* [On Youth]. Shanghai Star Studio, 1934.

———. *Shengsi tongxin* [Revolutionaries]. Shanghai Star Studio, 1936.

———. *Taoli jie* [Fate of Graduates]. Shanghai Diantong Studio, 1934.

———, et al. *Zhongguo dianying pinglun ji* [A collection of reviews on Chinese films]. Beijing: Zhongguo dianying chubanshe, 1957.

——— and Chen Junmei. "Suiyuan laojun jingguo" [An experience of consoling the troops in Suiyuan]. *You xun* [Friends News], no. 15 (1937): 6–10.

——— and Shen Zijiu. "Chen Bo'er cong zhandi de laixin" [Chen Bo'er's letter from the battlefield]. *Funü shenghuo* [Women's Life] 8, no. 1 (1939): 10–11.

Chen, Boda (Wanmuchun), "Zenyang kandai funü wenti" [How should we deal with the women question]. In *Hongqi* [Red Flag], no. 20 (1964): 23–27.

Chen, Huangmei. "Chen Huangmei tongzhi zai Shangying xitong fabiao de mouxie zhongyao yanlun" [Some of comrade Chen Huangmei's important comments given to Shanghai film system]. Shanghai Municipal Archives, September 1964, B177-1-21.

——— "Chen Huangmei tongzhi zai wenhuabu quanti dangyuan he zhishu danwei fuze ganbu huishangde jiancha" [Comrade Chen Huangmei's self-criticism at the Ministry of Culture's meeting for all Party members and major cadres of the affiliated units]. Shanghai Municipal Archives, 22 January 1965, B177-1-303-21.

———, ed. *Dangdai Zhongguo dianying* [Contemporary Chinese film]. Beijing: Zhongguo shehui kexue chubanshe, 1989.

———, and Chen Bo, eds. *Zhou Enlai yu dianying* [Zhou Enlai and films]. Beijing: Zhongyang wenxian chubanshe, 1995.

Chen, Jian, and Chen Qijia. *Xia Yan zhuan* [A biography of Xia Yan]. Beijing: Zhongguo xiju chubanshe, 2015.

———. *Xia Yan zhuan* [A biography of Xia Yan]. Beijing: Beijing Shiyue wenyi chubanshe, 1998.

Chen, Muhua. *Zhonghua quanguo funü lianhehui sishi nian* [Forty years of the All-China Women's Federation]. Beijing: Zhongguo funü chubanshe, 1991.

Chen, Tina Mai. "Female Icons, Feminist Iconography? Socialist Rhetoric and Women's Agency in 1950s China." *Gender and History* 15, no. 2 (2003): 268–95.

Chen, Wenjing. *Women zai zheli chengzhang* [We grew up here]. Beijing Film Academy library (internally circulated material).

Chen, Xiaonong. *Chen Boda zuihou koushu huiyi* [Chen Baoda's oral memoir in his last days]. Hong Kong: Yangguang huanqiu chubanshe, 2005.

Chen, Ya-Chen. *The Many Dimensions of Chinese Feminism*. New York: Palgave Macmillan, 2011.

Chen, Yaoting, and Chen Bo'er. "Chen Bo'er she Wang Renmei liangfu (zhaopian)" [Chen Bo'er took two photographs of Wang Renmei (photographs)]. *Dianying shenghuo* [Film Life], no. 4 (1935): 36.

Chen, Youxin. "Tuichu yinmu de zhishi fenzi xingxiang: yi 'liehuo zhong yongsheng' weili tan 'shiqinian' dianying fanshi" [The image of intellectuals exiting the screen: Using *Eternity in Flames* as an example to discuss the "seventeen-year" movie paradigm]. *Dianying wenxue* [Film Literature], no. 11 (2012): 37–39.

Chen, Zhao. "Budui wenyi zuotanhui 'jiyao' pouxi: Bo 'Lin Biao Jiang Qing' goujie lun'" [An analysis of "records" of seminars on literature and the arts in the military: Refuting the thesis of "the collaboration between Ling Biao and Jiang Qing"]. In Ding Kaiwen, ed., *Bainian Linbiao* [The centennial of Lin Biao], 220–59. New York: Mirror Books, 2007.

"Chengshi jumin weiyuanhui gongzuo" [The work on urban residents committees]. Shanghai Municipal Archives, 1955, B168-1-783.

Chiang, Ching. *On the Revolution of Peking Opera*. Peking: Foreign Languages Press, 1968.

Chinese Filmmakers Association, ed. *Lun Xiejin dianying* [A discussion of Xie Jin's films]. Beijing: Zhongguo dianying chubanshe, 1998.

Chinese Women Cadres Management School, ed. *Zhongguo funü yundong wenxian ziliao huibian* [An anthology of source material on the Chinese women's movement], vols. 1 and 2. Beijing: Zhongguo funü chubanshe, 1988.

Chuangxin dubai yu Qu Baiyin [The monologue of innovations and Qu Baiyin]. Beijing: Zhongguo dianying chubanshe, 1982.

Clark, Paul. *Chinese Cinema: Culture and Politics since 1949*. New York: Cambridge University Press, 1987.

———. *The Chinese Cultural Revolution: A History*. New York: Cambridge University Press, 2008.

Committee of the Annals of Shanghai Women, ed. *Shanghai funüzhi* [The annals of Shanghai women]. Shanghai: Shanghai shehui kexueyuan chubanshe, 2000.

Cong, Xiaoping. *Marriage, Law and Gender in Revolutionary China*. Cambridge: Cambridge University Press, 2016.

Corresponding Group of the Xu County Committee. "Turang geming zhongde 'Hua Mulan' zhandouying" ["Hua Mulan" battalion in the soil revolution]. *Women of China*, no. 14 (1958): 3.

Croll, Elisabeth. *Feminism and Socialism in China*. London: Routledge and Kegan Paul, 1978.

Cui, Shuqin. *Women through the Lens: Gender and Nation in a Century of Chinese Cinema*. Honolulu: University of Hawaii Press, 2003.

Dai, Jinhua. *Cinema and Desire: Feminist Marxism and Cultural Politics in the Work of Dai Jinhua,* edited by Jing Wang and Tani E. Barlow. London: Verso, 2002.

Dai, Xiu, and Zhuang Xin. *Xie Jin zhuan* [A biography of Xie Jin]. Shanghai: Hua-dong shifan daxue chubanshe, 1997.

"Daonian Chen Bo'er tongzhi" [Remembering comrade Chen Bo'er]. *Wenhui bao* [Wenhui Daily], November 13, 1951.

Davin, Delia. *Woman-Work: Women and the Party in Revolutionary China.* London: Oxford University Press, 1976.

Deng Yingchao shuxin xuanji [A selection of correspondence written by Deng Yingchao]. Beijing: Zhongyang wenxian chubanshe, 2000.

Deng, Yingchao. "Deng Yinchao tongzhi zai zhongfuwei huiyi shangde fayan" [Comrade Deng Yinchao's talk at the meeting of the Central Women's Committee]. In *Zhongguo funü yundong lishi ziliao 1945–1949* [Historical documents of the Chinese women's movement, 1945–1949], 238–43. Beijing: Zhongguo funü chubanshe, 1991.

"Daonian Chen Bo'er tongzhi" [Remembering comrade Chen Bo'er]. *Renmin ribao* [People's Daily], November 13, 1951.

———. "Guanyu funü xuanchuan jiaoyu wenti" [On the issue of women's advocacy and education work]. In *Zhongguo funü yundong wenxian ziliao huibian* [An anthology of selected source materials on the Chinese women's movement], edited by Chinese Women Cadres Management School, vol. 2, 114–17. Beijing: Zhongguo funü chubanshe, 1988.

———. "Guanyu Zhonghua Renmin Gongheguo hunyinfa de baogao: 1950 nian 5 yue 14 ri zai Zhangjiakou kuoda ganbu huiyi shangde jiangyan" [A report on the Marriage Law of the People's Republic of China: A speech at the expanded cadres' meeting in Zhangjiakou on May 14, 1950]. In *Zhongguo funü yundong wenxian ziliao huibian* [An anthology of source materials on the Chinese women's movement], edited by Chinese Women Cadres Management School, 49–54. Beijing: Zhongguo funü chubanshe, 1988.

———. "Quanguo fulian fuzhuxi Deng Yingchao zai Beijingshi shoujie fudai dahui shangde jianghua" [A talk by the vice chair of the ACWF Deng Yingchao at the first municipal congress of women in Beijing], November 29, 1949. In *Zhongguo funü yundong wenxian ziliao huibian* [An anthology of source material on the Chinese women's movement], edited by Chinese Women Cadres Management School, vol. 2, 41–42. Beijing: Zhongguo funü chubanshe, 1988.

———. "Sinianlai zhongguo funü yundong de jiben zongjie he jinhou renwu" [A summary of the Chinese women's movement in the past four years and future tasks]. In *Zhongguo funü yundong wenxian ziliao huibian* [An anthology of source material on the Chinese women's movement], edited by Chinese Women Cadres Management School, vol. 2, 171–78. Beijing: Zhongguo funü chubanshe, 1988.

———. "Zaidang lingdaoxia, tuanjie he fahui guangda funü quanzhong de liliang" [Under the Party's leadership, unite and exert the power of women masses]. In *Zhongguo funü yundong wenxian ziliao huibian* [An anthology of source material on the Chinese women's movement], edited by Chinese Women Cadres Management School, vol. 2, 262–65. Beijing: Zhongguo funü chubanshe, 1988.

Denning, Michael. *The Cultural Front: The Laboring of American Culture in the Twentieth Century.* London: Verso, 1996.

Ding, Ling. "Thoughts on March 8." In *I Myself Am a Woman: Selected Writings of Ding Ling,* edited by Tani E. Barlow with Gary J. Bjorge, 316–21. Boston: Beacon Press, 1989.

Dirlik, Arif. *Marxism in the Chinese Revolution.* Lanham, MD: Rowman and Littlefield, 2005.

Dissanayake, Wimal. *Cinema and Cultural Identity: Reflections on Films from Japan, India, and China.* Lanham, MD: University Press of America, 1988.

Dong, Bian. "Cai dajie—nü ganbu de zhiying he laoshi" [Elder sister Cai—women cadres' close friend and teacher]. In *Women de haodajie Cai Chang,* edited by Dong Bian, Cai Asong, and Tan Deshan, 79–84. Beijing: Zhongyang wenxian chubanshe, 1992.

———. "Keqin kejing de Shen dajie" [An amiable and admirable elder sister]. In *Nüjie wenhua zhanshi Shen Zijiu* [Shen Zijiu, a woman fighter on the cultural front], edited by Dong Bian, 158–65. Beijing: Zhongguo funü chubanshe, 1991.

———. "Tan nongcun funü daibiao huiyi" [On rural women's congress]. In *Zhongguo funü yundong wenxian ziliao huibian* [An anthology of source material on the Chinese women's movement], edited by Chinese Women Cadres Management School, vol. 2, 32–33. Beijing: Zhongguo funü chubanshe, 1988.

———. "Xiang funü xuanchuan shehui, xiang shehui xuanchuan funü: Huainian Hu Qiaomu tongzhi" [Educating women about the society, educating the society about women: Remembering comrade Hu Qiaomu]. In *Zhongguo funü zazhi jianjie* [A brief introduction to *Women of China*], internal circulation of memoirs produced by the Press of *Women of China,* 1999.

———. "Zai quanguo funü gongzuo huiyi shangde fayan" [Talk at the national conference on women-work]. In *Zhongguo funü yundong wenxian ziliao huibian* [An anthology of source material on the Chinese women's movement], edited by Chinese Women Cadres Management School, vol. 2, 363–65. Beijing: Zhongguo funü chubanshe, 1988.

———, ed. *Nüjie wenhua zhanshi Shen Zijiu* [Shen Zijiu, a woman fighter on the cultural front]. Beijing: Zhongguo funü chubanshe, 1991.

Dong, Bian, Cai Asong, and Tan Deshan, eds. *Women de hao dajie Cai Chang* [Our good elder sister Cai Chang]. Beijing: Zhongyang wenxian chubanshe, 1992.

Dong, Bian, Tan Deshan, and Zeng Zi, eds. *Mao Zedong he tade mishu Tian Jiaying* [Mao Zedong and his secretary Tian Jiaying]. Beijing: Zhongyang wenxian chubanshe, 1996.

Dong Bian. Dictated to and recorded by Zeng Li and Zeng Zi. "Zai Yan'an he Jiaying xiangshi xiangai de rizi" [Remembering the time in love with Jiaying in Yan'an]. *Dangshi bolan* [Overviews of the Party's history], no. 3 (2010): 51–54.

Dong, Zhujun. *Wo de yige shiji* [One of my century]. Beijing: Sanlian shudian, 1997.

"Dui jinhou jiedao linong jumin weiyuanhui zuzhi de yijian" [On the future organization of residents committees]. Shanghai Municipal Archives, 1951, C31-2-57.

Edwards, Louise. *Gender, Politics, and Democracy: Women's Suffrage in China*. Stanford, CA: Stanford University Press, 2008.

Einhorn, Barbara, and Eileen Janes Ye, eds. *Women and Market Societies: Crisis and Opportunity*. Alderson, UK: Edward Elgar, 1995.

Eisenstein, Hester. *Inside Agitators: Australian Femocrats and the State*. Philadelphia: Temple University Press, 1996.

Esherick, Joseph W., Paul G. Pickowicz, and Andrew G. Walder, eds. *The Chinese Cultural Revolution as History*. Stanford: Stanford University Press, 2006.

Evans, Harriet. "'Comrade Sisters': Gendered Bodies and Spaces." In *Picturing Power in the People's Republic of China: Posters of the Cultural Revolution*, edited by Harriet Evans and Stephanie Donald, 63–78. Lanham, MD: Rowman and Littlefield, 1999.

———. *Women and Sexuality in China: Female Sexuality and Gender since 1949*. New York: Continuum, 1997.

Fei, Honghuan, Zhao Chunsheng, and Liu Chunxiu. *Tongzhou fengyu lu: Zhou enlai Deng Yingchao aiqing shujian jiedu* [On the same boat through storms: Interpretation of love letters of Zhou Enlai and Deng Yingchao]. Beijing: Zhongyang wenxian chubanshe, 2001.

Feminist Voices, "Tashi zhongguo diyige zhuanggao guoqi jiuye xingbie qishi de nüsheng, ranhou yingle" [She is the first woman student who has ever sued a state enterprise for gender discrimination in employment, and then she won], November 2, 2015. http://chuansong.me/n/1867398 (accessed January 1, 2016).

Fu, Xiaohong. *Liangbu kua pingsheng: Xie Tieli koushu shilu* [Two steps going through life's journey: An interview of Xie Tieli]. Beijing: Zhongguo dianying chubanshe, 2005.

"Funü de zuzhi qingkuang" [The situation of organizing women]. Shanghai Municipal Archives, 1951, C31-2-57.

Fuqi zhijian [Between the couple]. Beijing: *Zhongguo Funü* zazhishe, 1964.

"Fuwei guanyu jinian sanba guoji funüjie gongzuo fangan" [The women's committee's plan for the March 8 celebration]. Shanghai Municipal Archives, 1951, C31-1-31.

"Gei shiwei bangongting de baogao" [A report to the office of the municipal Party committee]. Shanghai Municipal Archives, 13 September 1951, C31-1-37.

Geming Jiating [A revolutionary family]. *Tengxun Shipin*, v.qq.com. http://v.qq .com/cover/s/s24zzkfxpu2ulao/b00154rfggn.html (accessed May 22, 2016).

Gilmartin, Christina K. *Engendering the Chinese Revolution: Radical Women, Communist Politics, and Mass Movements in the 1920s*. Berkeley: University of California Press, 1995.

Global Feminisms Project. University of Michigan. www.umich.edu/~glblfem/en /china.html (accessed May 6, 2016).

Goldman, Merie. *Literary Dissent in Communist China*. Cambridge, MA: Harvard University Press, 1967.

Greenhalgh, Susan. *Just One Child: Science and Policy in Deng's China*. Berkeley: University of California Press, 2008.

Gu, Xiulan, ed. *Ershi shiji Zhongguo funü yundongshi* [A history of the twentieth-century Chinese women's movement], vol. 1. Beijing: Zhongguo funü chubanshe, 2008.

———, ed. *Ershi shiji Zhongguo funü yundongshi* [A history of the twentieth-century Chinese women's movement], vols. 2 and 3. Beijing: Zhongguo funü chubanshe, 2013.

"Guanyu chengshi jiceng zhengquan wenti diaocha baogao" [An investigative report on the issue of urban grassroots' political power]. Shanghai Municipal Archives, 1950, B168–1–745.

"Guanyu jiating funü gongzuo de jidian yijian" [Views on the work of housewives]. Shanghai Municipal Archives, 1949, C31–1–2.

"Guanyu jinhou quanguo funü yundong renwu de jueyi" [Resolution on the future tasks of the women's movement in the country]. In *Zhongguo funü yundong wenxian ziliao huibian* [An anthology of source material on the Chinese women's movement], edited by Chinese Women Cadres Management School, vol. 2, 179–80. Beijing: Zhongguo funü chubanshe, 1988.

"Guanyu minzhu jianzheng gongzuo: yijiuwuyi nian siyue zhi shiyue" [On the work of democratically establishing the government: from April to October, 1951]. Shanghai Municipal Archives, 1951, B168–1–763.

"Guanyu muqian banshichu zuzhi jigou qingkuang ji jinhou yijian jianbao" [Briefing on the street office's organizational structure and suggestions for future work]. Shanghai Municipal Archives, 20 July 1953, B168–1–772.

"Guanyu renmin minzhu jianzheng gongzuo baogao" [On the work on democraticly establishing the government by the people] (no date, but placed with documents dated between 1950 and 1951). Shanghai Municipal Archives, B168–1–745.

"Guanyu Shanghaishi fulian jiceng fudaihui de zuzhi wenti" [On the organizational issues of the Shanghai Women's Federation's women's congress at the grassroots]. Shanghai Municipal Archives, 1956, C31–1–161.

"Guanyu woju dangqian gaoji zhishifenzi de qingkuang baogao" [A report by the Shanghai Film Bureau on the current state of intellectuals]. Shanghai Municipal Archives, 1960, B177–1–144, 11.

Guo, Daijun. *Riji zhongde Jiang Jieshi* [Chiang Kai-shek in his diaries], *Jiemi shike* [Moments to reveal secrets]. *Voice of America*. www.youtube.com/watch?v= nQiD4_vlqPc (accessed October 3, 2014).

Guo, Fenglian, an interview. *Feichang Xiangshang* [Striving upwards], *Sohu.net*. http://tv.sohu.com/20130510/n375487819.shtml (accessed September 20, 2013; now only accessible in China).

"Guo Fenglian: 'Tieguniang' de huali zhuanshen" [Guo Fenglian: An Iron Girl's magnificent turn]. *China.net*. www.china.com.cn/economic/zhuanti/xzgjjlsn /2009–07/24/content_18200659.htm (accessed August 19, 2014).

"Guo Fenglian yi Dazhai Tieguniang" [Guo Fenglian remembers Dazhai Iron Girls]. *Tudou.com*. www.tudou.com/programs/view/gkcBBnHwNB4/ (accessed May 18, 2016).

Guo, Jianmin. "Gemin lishi xushi: Zhongguo dangdai geming lishi xiaoshuo (1949–1966) de yiyi shengcheng" [Revolutionary history narratives: The formation of meaning in contemporary Chinese revolutionary historical novels (1949–1966)]. PhD dissertation, Zhejiang University, 2005.

Haan, Francisca de. "Continuing Cold War Paradigms in Western Historiography of Transnational Women's Organisations: The Case of the Women's International Democratic Federation (WIDF)." *Women's History Review* 19, no. 4 (2010): 547–73.

———. "Introduction" to Forum: "After Ten Years: Communism and Feminism Revisited." *Aspasia* 10 (2016).

"Haiyanchang bianju, bianji disanci zuotanhui jilu" [Minutes of the third forum for scriptwriters and editors of Haiyan Studio]. Shanghai Municipal Archives, 2 August 1961, B177–1–243, 5.

Han, Wei, and Chen Xiaoyun. *Xin zhongguo dianying shihua* [Chinese film since 1949]. Hangzhou: Zhejiang daxue chubanshe, 2003.

Hao Zhufu [Good housekeeper]. *GotoRead.net*. www.gotoread.com/mag/585/emag .html (accessed May 20, 2016).

Hatem, Mervat. "Economic and Political Liberation in Egypt and the Demise of State Feminism." *International Journal of Middle East Studies* 24 (May 1992): 231–51.

Hayashi, Nozom (correspondent). "Outcry at Home and Abroad Leads to Release of Chinese Female Activists." *Asahi Shimbun*, April 18, 2015. http://ajw.asahi .com/article/asia/china/AJ201504180045 (accessed April 20, 2015). (This site no longer available. The new site only carries correspondent's postings since May 25, 2015. http://sitesearch.asahi.com/.cgi/ajwsitesearch/sitesearch.pl?Keywords= Nozom%20Hayashi&page=3 [accessed May 20, 2016].)

Hershatter, Gail. *The Gender of Memory: Rural Women and China's Collective Past*. Berkeley: University of California, 2011.

History Compiling Committee of the Women's College in the Second Field of Army. *Erye Nüda* [A women's college in the second field of army]. Beijing: Zhongyang wenxian Press, 1999.

Honig, Emily, and Gail Hershatter. *Personal Voices: Chinese Women in the 1980's*. Stanford, CA: Stanford University Press, 1988.

Hou, Di. "Nanyi wangque de naduan lishi" [An unforgettable period of history]. In the electronic collection *Zhongguo funü 60 zhounian jinian* [Commemorating sixty years of *Women of China*], compiled by the Press of *Women of China*, 1999. Internal circulation.

———. "Ren buyiding weida, dan keyi gaoshang: Shenqie huainian Dong Bian tongzhi" [One does not have to be magnificent to be noble: Remembering comrade Dong Bian with deep feelings]. *Women of China*, no. 12 (2001): 16–18.

Hou Yanxing. "Jieji, xingbie yu shenfen: minguo shiqi 'taitai' de wenhua jiangou" [Class, gender and identity: The cultural construction of 'taitai' in the Republic period]. In *Lanzhou xuekan* [The journal of Lanzhou], no. 3 (2011): 178–96.

Hsiung, Ping-chen. "Constructed Emotions: The Bond between Mothers and Sons in Late Imperial China." *Late Imperial China* 15, no. 1 (1994): 87–117.

Hu, Bangxiu. "Huiyi ershi duonianqian *Zhongguo funü* shangde yichang taolun" [Recalling a debate in *Women of China* over twenty years ago]. In *Zhongguo funü zazhi jianjie* [A brief introduction to *Women of China*]. Internal circulation of memoirs produced by the Press of *Women of China*, 1999.

Hu, Qiaomu. "Wo suo zhidao de Tian Jiying" [What I know about Tian Jiaying]. In *Mao Zedong he tade mishu Tian Jiaying* [Mao Zedong and his secretary Tian Jiaying], edited by Dong Bian, Tan Deshan, and Zeng Zi, 165–66. Beijing: Zhongyang wenxian chubanshe, 1996.

Huang, Chuanhui. *Tianxia hunyin: Gongheguo sanbu hunyinfa jishi* [Marriage under heaven: Three marriage laws of the PRC]. Shanghai: Wenhui Press, 2004.

Huang, Gang. "Geming muqin Xia Niangniang" [Revolutionary Mother Xia]. *Women of China*, vols. 1–8 (1957).

Huang, Ganying. *Huang Ganying zi zhuan* [A biography of Huang Ganying]. Unpublished manuscript.

Huang, Mulan. *Huang Mulan zizhuan* [A biography of Huang Mulan]. Beijing: Zhongguo da baike quanshu chubanshe, 2004.

Huang, Qingyi. "Fengyu licheng zoukaige, yushijijin zhu huihuang" [Songs of triumph in stormy journeys, progress over time while striving for glory]. *Women of China* (June 2009): 1.

Huang, Zongying (narrator) and Hu Xiaoqiu. "Jiafeng zhongde Zhao Dan, Huang Zongying fufu" [The couple Zhao Dan and Huang Zongying surviving in a tight corner]. In *Dangan Chunqiu* [History in archives], no. 4 (2006): 33–34.

Hugh, Grigg. "Translation—Ballad of the Army Carts, by Dufu." *EastAsiaStudent.net*, March 30, 2011. https://eastasiastudent.net/china/classical/du-fu-bing-che-xing/ (accessed May 18, 2016).

Hung, Liu. *Daughters of China* [Large-scale paintings]. www.hungliu.com/daughters-of-china.html (accessed May 10, 2015).

"Huiyi jilu" [Notes on Guan Jian's talk]. Shanghai Municipal Archives, 1954, C31–1–100.

"Ji Hong juzhang jianghua" [Director Ji Hong's talk]. Shanghai Municipal Archives, 3 January 1964, B177–1–30, 63.

Jiang, Qing. "Guanyu dianying de wenti" [On the issues of film]. In *Jiang Qing tongzhi lun wenyi* [Comrade Jiang Qing on literature and the arts], May 1965, 101. Publisher unknown, 1968.

———. "Tan jingju geming" [On the revolution of Peking opera]. In *Zhongguo dianying yanjiu ziliao: 1949–1979* [Source materials for Chinese film studies: 1949–1979], edited by Wu Di, vol. 2, 444–47. Beijing: Wenhua yishu chubanshe, 2006.

———. "Zai shoudu wenyijie wuchanjieji wenhua dageming dahui shangde jianghua" [Talk at the meeting of the fields of literature and the arts in Beijing on the Cultural Revolution]. In *Jiang Qing tongzhi lun wenyi* [Comrade Jiang Qing on literature and the arts], January 28, 1966, 17–18. Publisher unknown, 1968.

———. *Jiang Qing tongzhi jianghua xuanbian* [A selection of Comrade Jiang Qing's talks]. Wuhan: Hebei renmin chubanshe, 1969.

———. *On the Revolution of Peking Opera*. Beijing: Foreign Language Press, 1968.

"Jiangning qu diyi paichusuo jiating funü daibiao huiyi dianxing shiyan zongjie baogao" [A summary report on the work for the housewives' congress in the first police station in Jiangning District]. Shanghai Municipal Archives, 1951, C31–2–57.

"Jianjue hanwei shehuizhuyi de dianying shiye" [Resolutely defend the cause of socialist film], *Popular Film* (September 1957). In *Zhongguo dianying yanjiu ziliao: 1949–1979* [Source materials for Chinese film studies: 1949–1979], edited by Wu Di, vol. 1, 146–48. Beijing: Wenhua yishu chubanshe, 2006.

"Jianmian hua" [Opening greetings]. *Xin Zhongguo funü* [Women of New China] 1 (1949): 6.

"Jiedao linong juweihui tongji" [Statistics of neighborhood and street residents committees]. Shanghai Municipal Archives, October 1951, B168–1–770.

Jin, Feng. *Deng Yingchao Zhuan* [A biography of Deng Yingchao]. Beijing: Renmin chubanshe, 1993.

Jin, Jiang. *Women Playing Men: Yue Opera and Social Change in Twentieth-Century Shanghai*. Seattle: University of Washington Press, 2009.

Jin, Qiu. *The Culture of Power: The Lin Biao Incident in the Cultural Revolution*. Stanford, CA: Stanford University Press, 1999.

Jin, Ruiying, ed. *Deng Yingchao: Yidai weida de nüxing* [Deng Yingchao: A great woman of her generation]. Taiyuan: Shanxi renmin chubanshe, 1989.

Jin, Yihong. "Rethinking the 'Iron Girls': Gender and Labour during the Chinese Cultural Revolution." In *Translating Feminisms in China,* edited by Dorothy Ko and Wang Zheng. Oxford: Blackwell, 2007.

Jin, Yutong. "Youxian de qingjie kaijue: zaikan 'hongse jingdian' 'liehuo zhong yongsheng'" [Limited plot explorations: A second look at the "red classic" *Eternity in Flames*]. *Dianying pingjie* [Film Review], no. 7 (2007): 39.

Jing, Dao. "Jiaohua yaozuo Mu Guiying" [Jiaohua wants to be Mu Guiying]. *Women of China*, no. 5 (1958): 5.

Johnson, Kay Ann. *Women, the Family and Peasant Revolution in China*. Chicago: University of Chicago Press, 1983.

"Juexin zuo jianqiangde chedide geming nüzhanshi" [Be a strong and thoroughgoing revolutionary woman soldier resolutely]. *Women of China*, no. 2 (1964): 9.

Judd, Ellen. *The Chinese Women's Movement between State and Market*. Stanford, CA: Stanford University Press, 2002.

Judge, Joan. *Precious Raft of History: The Past, the West, and the Woman Question in China*. Stanford, CA: Stanford University Press, 2008.

Kangri zhanzheng shiqi de Chongqing dianying (1937–1945) [Chongqing films during the war against Japan (1937–1945)]. Chongqing: Chongqing Press, 1991.

Kantola, Johanna. *Feminists Theorize the State*. New York: Palgrave Macmillan, 2006.

Karl, Revecca E. *Mao Zedong and China in the Twentieth-Century World: A Concise History*. Durham, NC: Duke University Press, 2010.

Ke, Huiling. *Jindai Zhongguo geming yundongzhong de funü: 1900–1920* [Women in the revolutionary movements in modern China: 1900–1920]. Taiyuan: Shanxi jiaoyu chubanshe, 2012.

Ko, Dorothy. *Teachers of the Inner Chambers: Women and Culture in Seventeenth-Century China*. Stanford, CA: Stanford University Press, 1994.

———, ed., with Jahyun Kim Harboush and Joan R. Piggott. *Women and Confucian Cultures in Premodern China, Korea, and Japan*. Berkeley: University of California Press, 2003.

———, ed., with Wang Zheng. *Translating Feminisms in China*. Malden, MA: Blackwell, 2007.

Latham, Kevin. *Pop Culture China! Media, Arts, and Lifestyle*. Santa Barbara, CA: ABC-CLIO, 2007.

Lee, Ching Kwan, and Guobin Yang, eds. *Re-envisioning the Chinese Revolution: The Politics and Poetics of Collective Memories in Reform China*. Stanford, CA: Stanford University Press, 2007.

Lewis, Greg. "The History, Myth and Memory of Maoist Chinese Cinema, 1949–1966." *Asian Cinema* 6, no. 1 (2005): 162–83.

Li Shuangshuang: Cong xiaoshuo dao dianying [Li Shuangshuang: From a novel to a film]. Beijing: Zhongguo dianying chubanshe, 1979.

Li, He. "*Zhonghua nüer* zai Sulian" [*Daughters of China* in the Soviet Union]. *Wenhui bao* [Wenhui Daily], August 11, 1950.

Li, Qiyang. *Huanghe dongliu* [The Yellow River running east]. Beijing: Beijing University Press, 2003.

———. *Xibei liuyun* [The northwest drifting clouds]. No publisher, 2008.

Li, Runxin. *Jiebai de mingxing: Wang Ying* [A pure star: Wang Ying]. Beijing: Zhongguo qingnian chubanshe, 1987.

Li, Song, "'Yangbanxi' de gongguo shifei" [The merits and faults of "model theater"]. In *Guojia renwen lishi* [Culture and History of the State], no. 12 (2013): 35–37.

Li, Suyuan, Hu Ke, and Yang Yuanyin, eds. *Xin Zhongguo dianying 50 nian* [Fifty years of film in the new China]. Beijing: Beijing guangbo xueyuan chubanshe, 2000.

Li, Xiaojiang. *Xiawa de tansuo* [Eve's exploration]. Zhengzhou: Henan renmin chubanshe, 1988.

Li, Yucun, and Peng Guoliang, eds. *Zhongguo wenhua mingren yi muqin* [Chinese cultural celebrities' recollections of their mothers]. Changsha: Hunan wenyi chubanshe, 1995.

Li, Zhi. "Huiyi yu sikao: 'daxie shisannian' de dazhenglun jiqi beijing" [Remembering and thinking: The huge debate on and background of "representing the thirteen years"]. In *Xinwenxue Shiliao* [Historical Sources of New Literature], nos. 3–4 (1997): 123–128, 136, and 53–60, 119.

Li, Zhuozhuo, and Chen Bo'er. "Su-Hang qiriji" [Seven days in Suzhou and Hangzhou]. *Dianying shenghuo* [Film Life], no. 1 (1935): 1–4.

Li, Ziyun, ed. *Xia Yan Qishinian Wenxuan* [A selected anthology of Xia Yan's seventy years of works]. Shanghai: Wenyi chubanshe, 1996.

Lian, Jing, Lu Hua, and Guo Jinhua eds. "Lin Zifeng Koushu: Dajia guanwojiao feng daoyan" [Interview of Lin Zifeng: People called me a crazy director]. In *Women de yanyi shengya* [Our performing careers], 108–33. Beijing: Zhongguo shudian, 2008.

Lin, Hanbiao. "Ping ju 'zai liehuo zhong yongsheng' de gaibain he yanchu" [The adaptation and performance of the Ping opera *Eternity in Flames*]. *Xijü Bao* [Drama News], no. 12 (1962).

Lin, Man, and Li Ziyun, eds. *Xia Yan tan dianying* [Xia Yan on film]. Beijing: Zhongguo dianying chubanshe, 1993.

Lin, Yunhui. "Zhonggong bada weishenme meiyou Peng Zhen fayan?" [Why was there no Peng Zhen's speech at the Eighth Congress of the Party Central?]. In *Yanhuang chunqiu* [Chinese History], no. 9 (2015): 10–15.

"Linong funü daibiao huiyi de xingzhi renwu buke baogao" [A talk on the nature and tasks of the neighborhood women's congress]. Shanghai Municipal Archives, 1954, C31–2–235.

"Linong funü daibiao huiyi zuzhi shixing tiaoli" [Tentative Regulations on the Organization of the Women's Congress in Shanghai Neighborhoods]. Shanghai Municipal Archives, February 1955, B168–1–130.

"Linong zhengdun xuanchuan gongzuo zongjie" [A summary of the publicitiy work on rectifying neighborhoods]. Shanghai Municipal Archives, 30 March 1955, B168–1–780.

"Linong zhengdun shidian zuzhi jianshe jieduan funü gongzuo xiaojie" [A summary of the women-work in the period of the pilot projects of neighborhood rectification and organizational building]. Shanghai Municipal Archives, 14 September 1954, B168–1–780.

"Linong zhengdun yundong cailiao gongzuo zongjie" [A summary of the work on collecting the material on the campaign of neighborhood rectification]. Shanghai Municipal Archives, 15 February 1955, B168–1–780.

"Linong zhengdun zhunbei gongzuo qingshi baogao" [A report to request instructions on preparing for the work on neighborhood rectification]. Shanghai Municipal Archives, 20 April 1954, B168–1–014.

"Liu Baiyu tongzhi baogao" [A report by comrade Liu Baiyu]. Shanghai Municipal Archives, 7 August 1965, B177–1–32.

Liu, Chunxiu. *Zhou Enlai he Deng Yingchao* [Zhou Enlai and Deng Yingchao]. Xi'an: Shanxi renmin chubanshe, 2004.

Liu, Lydia, Rebecca E. Karl, and Dorothy Ko, eds. *The Birth of Chinese Feminism: Essential Texts in Transnational Theory.* New York: Columbia University Press, 2013.

Liu, Zhijian. "Budui wenyi zuotanhui jiyao chansheng qianhou" [Before and after the production of the notes on the seminar on literature and arts in the military], collected in Wu Di, ed., *Zhongguo dianying yanjiu ziliao 1949–1979* [Source materials for Chinese film studies: 1949–1979], vol. 3, 14–35. Beijing: Wenhua yishu chubanshe, 2006.

Lu, Hongshi. *Zhongguo dianying: Miaoshu yu chanshi* [Chinese films: Description and interpretation]. Beijing: Zhongguo dianying chubanshe, 2002.

Lu, Ming. *Zhongguo dianying qishizai: Qinli, shilu* [Seventy years of Chinese film: Personal experience and recording]. Beijing: Zhongguo dianying chubanshe, 2012.

Luo, Liang. *The Avant-Garde and the Popular in Modern China: Tian Han and the Intersection of Performance and Politics.* Ann Arbor: University of Michigan Press, 2014.

"Luo Qiong tongzhi chuanda zhongyang shujichu, zhongyang zhengzhiju fuze tongzhi duiyu funü gongzuo jiao zhongyao zhishi de jilu zhengli" [Notes of comrade Luo Qiong's conveying the relatively important directives on women-work by the leading comrades of the Secretariat and the Political Bureau of the Central Committee]. Shanghai Municipal Archives, 22 October 1957, C-31-1-169.

Luo, Qiong. "Deng Xiaoping tongzhi zai zhongyao de lishi shike dui funü gongzuo de zhiyin" [Comrade Deng Xiaoping's guidance of women-work at the important historical moments]. In *Kangzhen, jiefang, pingdeng: Luo QIong wenji* [Resistance, emancipation, equality: An anthology by Luo Qiong], 497. Beijing: Zhongguo funü chubanshe, 2007.

———. "Xiang Shen Zijiu dajie zhushou de shike" [Celebrating the birthday of elder sister Shen]. In *Kangzhen, jiefang, pingdeng: Luo Qiong wenji* [Resistance, emancipation, equality: An anthology by Luo Qiong], 552–53. Beijing: Zhongguo funü chubanshe, 2007.

———. "Xin Zhongguo diyibu hunyinfa qicao qianhou" [Drafting the first Marriage Law of the new China]. In *Kangzheng, jiefang, pingdeng: Luo Qiong wenji* [Resistance, emancipation, equality: An anthology by Luo Qiong], 427–28. Beijing: Zhongguo funü chubanshe, 2007.

———. *Funü jiefang wenti jiben zhishi* [On the basics of women's liberation]. Beijing: Renmin chubanshe, 1986.

———. *Kangzheng, jiefang, pingdeng: Luo Qiong wenji* [Resistance, emancipation, equality: An anthology by Luo Qiong]. Beijing: Zhongguo funü chubanshe, 2007.

——— and Duan Yongqiang. *Luo Qiong fangtan lu* [Interviews with Luo Qiong]. Beijing: Zhongguo funü chubanshe, 2000.

Lü, Xiaoming. *Zhang Junxiang zhuan* [A biography of Zhang Junxiang]. Shanghai: Shanghai renmin chubanshe, 2010.

Ma, Shexiang. *Yi ge nügemingzhe de lishi jianzheng.* [Historical witness from a woman revolutionary]. Beijing: Zhonggong dangshi chubanshe, 2003.

Mann, Susan L. *Gender and Sexuality in Modern Chinese History.* New York: Cambridge University Press, 2011.

———. *The Talented Women of the Zhang Family.* Berkeley: University of California Press, 2007.

———, ed. *Women and Gender Relations.* Ann Arbor: Association for Asian Studies, 2004.

———, and Yu-Yin Chen, eds. *Under Confucian Eyes: Writings on Gender in Chinese History.* Berkeley: University of California Press, 2001.

Manning, Kimberley Ens. "Embodied Activisms: The Case of the Mu Guiying Brigade." *China Quarterly* no. 204 (2010): 850–69.

———. "Making a Great Leap Forward? The Politics of Women's Liberation in Maoist China." In *Translating Feminisms in China,* edited by Dorothy Ko and Wang Zheng, 138–63. Malden, MA: Blackwell, 2007.

———. "The Gendered Politics of Woman-work: Rethinking Radicalism in the Great Leap Forward." *Modern China* 32, no. 3 (2006): 1–36.

"Mao Zedong dui wenxue yishu de pishi" [Mao Zedong's directives on literature and the arts: December 12, 1963]. In *Zhongguo dianying yanjiu ziliao: 1949–1979* [Source materials for Chinese film studies: 1949–1979], edited by Wu Di, vol. 2, 418–19. Beijing: Wenhua yishu chubanshe, 2006.

Mao, Zedong. "Dui zhongyang guanyu yijiuwuqi nian kaizhan zengchan jieyue yundong de zhishi gao de piyu" [Comment on the draft directive on the Party Central launching the campaign of increasing production and practicing economy in 1957]. In *Jianguo yilai Mao Zedong wengao* [Mao Zedong's papers since the founding of the PRC], vol. 6, 302–3. Beijing: Zhongyang wenxian chubanshe, 1990.

———. "Nongye hezuohua de yichang bianlun he dangqian de jieji douzheng" [A debate on agricultural collectivization and current class struggles], October 11, 1955. In *Selected Works of Mao Zedong,* vol. 5, 213. Shanghai: Renmin chubanshe, 1977.

———. "Yijiuwuqi nian xiaji de xingshi" [The situation in summer 1957], July 1957. In *Mao Zedong xuanji* [Selected works of Mao Zedong], vol. 5, 456–65. Shanghai: Renmin chubanshe, 1977.

———. "Yingdang zhongshi dianying *Wu Xun zhuan* de taolun" [We should pay attention to discussions of *The Life of Wu Xun*]. In *Zhongguo dianying yanjiu ziliao: 1949–1979* [Source materials for Chinese film studies: 1949–1979], edited by Wu Di, vol. 1, 92–93. Beijing: Wenhua yishu chubanshe, 2006.

———. "Zai shengshi zhizhiqu dangwei shuji huiyi shang de jianghua" [Talk on the conference of provincial Party Committee secretaries], January 1957. *Mao Zedong xuanji* [Selected works of Mao Zedong], vol. 5, 330–62. Shanghai: Renmin chubanshe, 1977.

———. "Zhongguo nongcun de shehuizhuyi gaochao de xuyan" [Preface to the high tide of socialism in rural China], September and December 1955. In *Mao Zedong xuanji* [Selected works of Mao Zedong], vol. 5, 249. Beijing: Renmin chubanshe, 1955.

Martin, Gloria. *Socialist Feminism: The First Decade 1966–1976,* second edition. Seattle: Freedom Socialist, 1986.

Mei Gongyi. *Baidu.com.* http://baike.baidu.com/view/5055527.htm (accessed April 10, 2013).

Meisner, Maurice. *Mao's China and After: A History of the People's Republic.* New York: Free Press, 1999.

Meng, Liye. *Shi zhi shang* [Intellectuals' early death]. Beijing: Shidai wenhua chubanshe, 2012.

———. *Xin zhongguo dianyiing yishu shigao 1949–1959* [A history of cinematic art in New China: 1949–1959]. Beijing: Zhongguo dianying chubanshe, 2002.

———. *Xin zhongguo dianying yishushi: 1949–1965* [A history of cinematic art in New China: 1949–1965]. Beijing: Zhongguo dianying chubanshe, 2011.

Meng, Xiaoyun. "Dangdai Zhongguo funü mianmian guan" [Perspectives on contemporary Chinese women]. *People's Daily* (overseas version), January 8–10, 1986.

Meng, Xing. "Xia Yan de kutong yu zixing" [Pains and self-reflection of Xia Yan]. *Tongzhou gongjin* [The same boat together], no. 2 (2013): 57–60.

"Minzhu jianzheng" [Democratically establshing the government]. Shanghai Municipal Archives, 27 March 1951, B168-1-763.

Mitchell, Timothy. "Society, Economy, and the State Effect." In *State/Culture,* edited by George Steinmetz. Ithaca, NY: Cornell University Press, 1999.

Molyneux, Maxine. "Analysing Women's Movements." In *Feminist Visions of Development: Gender, Analysis and Policy,* edited by Cecile Jackson and Ruth Pearson, 65–88. London: Routledge, 1998.

Morning Sun. Directed by Carma Hinton. 2003.

Mulvey, Laura. "Visual Pleasure and Narrative Cinema." *Screen* 16, no. 3 (1975): 6–18.

Nochlin, Linda. *Women, Art, and Power and Other Essays.* New York: Harper and Row, 1988.

Office of ACWF, ed. *Funü ertong gongzuo wenxuan (1998.8–1999.12)* [Selected works on women and children (1998.8–1998.12)]. Beijing: Zhongguo funü chubanshe, 2000.

———. *Funü ertong gongzuo wenxuan (2000.1–2000.12)* [Selected works on women and children (2000.1–2000.12)]. Beijing: Zhongguo funü chubanshe, 2001.

———. *Funü ertong gongzuo wenxuan (2001.1–2001.12)* [Selected works on women and children (2001.1–2001.12)]. Beijing: Zhongguo funü chubanshe, 2002.

———. *Funü ertong gongzuo wenxuan (2002.1–2002.12)* [Selected works on women and children (2002.1–2002.12)]. Beijing: Zhongguo funü chubanshe, 2003.

———. *Funü ertong gongzuo wenxuan (2003.1–2003.12)* [Selected works on women and children (2003.1–2003.12)]. Beijing: Zhongguo funü chubanshe, 2004.

———. *Funü ertong gongzuo wenxuan (2004.1–2004.12)* [Selected works on women and children (2004.1–2004.12)]. Beijing: Zhongguo funü chubanshe, 2005.

———. *Funü ertong gongzuo wenxuan (2005.1–2005.12)* [Selected works on women and children (2005.1–2005.12)]. Beijing: Zhongguo funü chubanshe, 2006.

———. *Funü ertong gongzuo zhongyao wenjian huibian* [A compilation of important documents on women and children (1988–1996)]. Internal circulation, 1997.

———. *Qida yilai funü ertong gongzuo wenxuan (1993.9–1988.6)* [Selected works on women and children since the seventh National Women's Congress (1993.9–1988.6)]. Internal circulation. 1998.

———. *Zhonghua quanguo funü lianhehui sishi nian* [Forty years of the All-China Women's Federation]. Beijing: Zhongguo funü chubanshe, 1991.

Ou, Yansheng, ed. *Visual Voices: 100 Photographs of Village China by the Women of Yunnan Province [Zhongguo Yunnan nongcun funü ziwo xiezhen ji]*. Kunming: Yunnan minzu chubanshe, 1995.

Pan, Jintang. "Funü jiefang de shizhi yu biaozhi tanxi" [Analyzing the substance and signs of women's liberation]. *Zhongguo funübao* [China Women's News], May 27, 1988.

Pan, Sheng. "'Shiqinian' geming huiyilu shuxie zhongde lishi xushi yu gonggong jiyi" [Historical narratives and public memory in the revolution memoirs of "Seventeen Years"]. Master's thesis, Nanjing Normal University, 2006.

Pan, Suiming. "Zhongguo xinnüxing mianlin de xuanze yu deshi" [New choices and gain-and-loss confronted by new Chinese women]. *Zhongguo funübao* [China Women's News], January 19, 1987.

Pang, Laikwan. *Building a New China in Cinema: The Chinese Left-Wing Cinema Movement, 1932–1937*. Lanham, MD: Rowman and Littlefield, 2002.

Pantsov, Alexander V., and Steven Levine. *Mao: The Real Story*. New York: Simon and Schuster, 2012.

Peng, Peiyun. *Pingdeng, fazhan, heping* [Equality, development, peace]. Beijing: Zhongguo funü chubanshe, 2005.

Peng, Xianzhi. *"Mao Zedong he tade mishu Tian Jiaying"* [Mao Zedong and his secretary Tian Jiaying]. In *Mao Zedong he tade mishu Tian Jiaying*, edited by Dong Bian, Tan Deshan, and Zeng Zi, 28–109. Beijing: Zhongyang wenxian chubanshe, 1996.

Perry, Elizabeth J. "Shanghai's Strike Wave of 1957." *China Quarterly*, no. 137 (March 1994): 1–27.

——— and Mark Selden, eds. *Chinese Society: Change, Conflict and Resistance*, second edition. London: RoutledgeCurzon, 2000.

Pickowicz, Paul G. "Acting Like Revolutionaries: Shi Hui, the Wenhua Studio, and Private-Sector Filmmaking, 1949–52." In *Dilemmas of Victory: The Early Years of the People's Republic of China*, edited by Jeremy Brown and Paul G. Pickowicz, 256–87. Cambridge, MA: Harvard University Press, 2007.

———. "Zheng Junli, Complicity and the Cultural History of Socialist China, 1949–1976." In *The History of the PRC (1949–1976)*, special issue of *China Quarterly* 7, edited by Julia Strauss, 194–215. Cambridge: Cambridge University Press, 2007.

Pun, Ngai. *Made in China: Women Factory Workers in a Global Workplace*. Durham, NC: Duke University Press, 2005.

Qian, Zhengwen. "Zuowei zhengzhi wenhua de lishi jiangshu: yi *Hongyan* xiezuo 'Qianshi'" [Historically narrated as political culture: Using *Red Crag* to write "Previous History"]. *Wenhua yu shixue* [Culture and Poetry], no. 2 (2008).

"Qiyue ershiwu ri shangwu yubeihuiyi qingkuang" [A report on the preparatory meeting during the morning of July 25, 1965]. Shanghai Municipal Archives, B177-1-32.

"Quanguo fulian guanyu 1958 nian 1 yue zhaokaide sheng (shi) zizhiqu Fulian zhuren huiyi de tongbao" [The ACWF's announcement on the conference of WF chairs of provincial, municipal, and autonomous regions in January 1958]. In *Zhongguo funü yundong wenxian ziliao huibian* [An anthology of source material on the Chinese women's movement], edited by Chinese Women Cadres Management School, vol. 2, 351–56. Beijing: Zhongguo funü chubanshe, 1988.

"Quanshi sanbajie youxing renshu tongjibiao" [Citywide statistics of people in the parade on March 8]. Shanghai Municipal Archives, 1951, C31–1–31.

Ren, Posheng. *Baike.com*. www.baike.com/wiki/%E4%BB%BB%E6%B3%8A%E7%94%9F (accessed May 22, 2016).

Research Group on Education to Eliminate Illiteracy in China. "Zhongguo de saomang jiaoyu" [Education to eliminate illiteracy in China]. *Jiaoyu yanjiu* [Education Studies], no. 6 (1997): 5–16.

Research Institute of the Party Central of the CCP, ed. *Women de Deng dajie* [Our elder sister Deng]. Chongqing: Chongqing chubanshe, 2004.

Roberts, Rosemary A. *Maoist Model Theatre: The Semiotics of Gender and Sexuality in the Chinese Cultural Revolution (1966–1976)*. Leiden: Koninklijke Brill NV, 2010.

Rofel, Lisa. *Desiring China: Experiments in Neoliberalism, Sexuality, and Public Cutlure*. Durham. NC: Duke University Press, 2007.

———. *Other Modernities: Gendered Yearnings in China after Socialism*. Berkeley: University of California Press, 1999.

Schoenhals, Michael, ed. *China's Cultural Revolution, 1966–1969: Not a Dinner Party*. New York: M.E. Sharpe, 1996.

Scott, James C. *Domination and the Arts of Resistance: Hidden Transcripts*. New Haven, CT: Yale University Press, 1990.

Sha, Ting. "Guanyu dianying *zai liehuozhong yongsheng* de huiyi" [Memories of the film *Eternity in Flames*]. *Kaifang shidai* [Open Times] no. 4 (1994).

"Shanghai minzhu fulian1953 nian xiabannian gongzuo zongjie" [Shanghai Democratic Women's Federation's review of work in the second half of 1953]. Shanghai Municipal Archives, 1954, C31–1–75.

"Shanghai shiwei guanyu funü gongzuo de jueding" [Shanghai Party committee's decision on women-work]. Shanghai Municipal Archives, 31 March 1950, C31–1–9.

Shanghai Xie Jin Film Techonology Corporation and Shanghai University Xie Jin Film Museum, eds. *Xie Jin hua zhuan* [A pictorial biography of Xie Jin]. Shanghai: Fudan daxue chubanshe, 2008.

"Shanghaishi dianyingju 1960 nian chuangzuo huiyi tongzhi, jihua, dianbao, bianhan, baogao" [Documents by the Shanghai Film Bureau on the 1960 filmmaking meetings]. Shanghai Municipal Archives, 12 January 1960, B177–1–223.

"Shanghaishi dianyingju 1961 nian chuangzuo gongzuo zuotanhui, huiyi jiyao, baogao" [Meeting minutes by the Shanghai Film Bureau on the 1961 filmmaking forum]. Shanghai Municipal Archives, 9 February 1961, B177–1–232.

"Shanghaishi dianyingju 1963 nian dianying chuangzuo zuotan huiyi qingkuang baogao, jianbao" [A summary by the Shanghai Film Bureau on the 1963 filmmaking discussion forum]. Shanghai Municipal Archives, 12 February 1963, B177–1–284.

"Shanghaishi dianyingju 1963 nian gongzuo zongjie" [A summary by the Shanghai Film Bureau on the year of 1963]. Shanghai Municipal Archives, February 1964, B177–1–31.

"Shanghaishi dianyingju 1964 nian xianjin jingyan jiaoliu huiyi wenjian" [An anthology by the Shanghai Film Bureau on the meeting for exchange experiences]. Shanghai Municipal Archives, 23 April 1964, B177–1–33.

"Shanghaishi dianyingju 1965 nian dangwei kuoda huiyi qingkuang fanying" [Report by the Shanghai Film Bureau on the 1965 expanded Party committee meeting]. Shanghai Municipal Archives, 8 August 1965, B177–1–180.

"Shanghaishi dianyingju 1965 nian gushipian shengchan renwu, ticai, jumu, ji juben chuangzuo jihua" [Plans by the Shanghai Film Bureau for the making, subjects, topics, and writing of feature films in 1965]. Shanghai Municipal Archives, 26 January 1965, B177–1–309.

"Shanghaishi dianyingju canjia geji zhaokai de dianying zuotanhui renyuan mingdan" [List by the Shanghai Film Bureau on participants in the film forum held at all levels]. Shanghai Municipal Archives, 25 July 1961, B177–1–237.

"Shanghaishi dianyingju chuangzuo renyuan yewu qingkuang dengji biao" [A record of productive activities of filmmakers by the Shanghai Film Bureau]. Shanghai Municipal Archives, 9 August 1957, B177–1–213.

"Shanghaishi dianyingju chuangzuo zuotanhui zongjie lingdao jianghua" [A summary of leaders' talks at the forum on filmmaking by the Shanghai Film Bureau]. Shanghai Municipal Archives, 11 September 1961, B177–1–235, 29.

"Shanghaishi dianyingju chuxi shiwenjiao qunyinghui daibiaotuan fenzu mingdan" [The list of members of the group that represents the Shanghai Film Bureau to attend the conference of labor models in Shanghai culture and education fields]. Shanghai Municipal Archives, 20 January 1960, B177–1-8.

"Shanghaishi dianyingju chuxi zhonggong Shanghai shiwei kuoda huiyi bufen daibiao zai xiaozu taolunhui shangde fayan jilu" [A summary by the Shanghai Film Bureau on the panel discussion at an expanded meeting of the CCP Shanghai Municipal Committee attended by some representatives]. Shanghai Municipal Archives, 23 May 1958, B177–1–127.

"Shanghaishi dianyingju disici dianying chuangzuo zuotan huiyi jilu" [Meeting minutes by the Shanghai Film Bureau for the fourth filmmaking forum]. Shanghai Municipal Archives, 5 August 1961, B177–1–244.

"Shanghaishi dianyingju dianying chuangzuo zuotanhui dahui fayan huibian" [A collection of talks on the filmmaking forum compiled by the Shanghai Film Bureau]. Shanghai Municipal Archives, September 1961, B177–1–250.

"Shanghaishi dianyingju dianying chuangzuo zuotanhui taolun qingkuang, huiyi jilu" [Meeting minutes by the Shanghai Film Bureau for the filmmaking discussion forum]. Shanghai Municipal Archives, 29 July 1961, B177–1–241.

"Shanghaishi dianyingju guanyu 'Shangying nianjian' de chugao" [A draft of "Shanghai Film Yearbook" by the Shanghai Film Bureau]. Shanghai Municipal Archives, January 1961, B177–1–11.

"Shanghaishi dianyingju guanyu 'taoli man tianxia' deng yingpian de shencha tongguo ling" [A report by the Shanghai Film Bureau on the approval of films such as *With Pupils All over the World*]. Shanghai Municipal Archives, 22 August 1950, B177–1–209.

"Shanghaishi dianyingju guanyu 1959 nian dangwei kuoda huiyi jilu" [A summary by the Shanghai Film Bureau on the 1959 expanded Party committee meeting]. Shanghai Municipal Archives, 16 May 1959, B177–1–137.

"Shanghaishi dianyingju guanyu 1959 nian dangwei kuoda huiyi jilu" [A summary by the Shanghai Film Bureau on the 1959 expanded Party committee meeting]. Shanghai Municipal Archives, 22 August 1959, B177–1–140.

"Shanghaishi dianyingju guanyu 1963 nian dangwei huiyi jilu" [A summary by the Shanghai Film Bureau on the 1963 Party committee meeting]. Shanghai Municipal Archives, 15 January 1963, B-177–1–163.

"Shanghaishi dianyingju guanyu anpai 1965 nian zhipian renwu de baogao" [A report by the Shanghai Film Bureau on the plan of film production tasks for the year 1965]. Shanghai Municipal Archives, 14 November 1964, B177–1–299.

"Shanghaishi dianyingju guanyu bufen daibiao chuxi zhonggong Shanghai shiwei kuoda huiyi xiaozu taolun de qingkuang huibao" [A report by the Shanghai Film Bureau on the panel discussion at an expanded meeting of the CCP Shanghai Municipal Committee attended by some representatives]. Shanghai Municipal Archives, 22 June 1958, B177–1–128.

"Shanghaishi dianyingju guanyu caiwu gongzuo de yijian" [Suggestions by the Shanghai Film Bureau on the accounting work]. Shanghai Municipal Archives, 5 February 1960, B177–1–16.

"Shanghaishi dianyingju guanyu caiwu gongzuo de yijian, tongzhi" [Suggestions by the Shanghai Film Bureau on the accounting work]. Shanghai Municipal Archives, 23 January 1964, B177–1–29.

"Shanghaishi dianyingju guanyu caiwu gongzuo de yijian, yewu zhibiao zanxing tiaoli" [Suggestions of temporary rules for the accounting work by the Shanghai Film Bureau]. Shanghai Municipal Archives, 22 January 1964, B177–1–24.

"Shanghaishi dianyingju guanyu Chen Bo'er de shengping ji zaiqi zhuidaohuishang de daoci" [The biography of Chen Bo'er and the euology for her by the Shanghai Film Bureau]. Shanghai Municipal Archives, November 1951, B177–1–3.

"Shanghaishi dianyingju guanyu Chen Huangmei fubuzhang zai zongjiehuishang de buchong fayan" [A report by the Shanghai Film Bureau on the additional comments made by deputy director Chen Huangmei at the wrap-up meeting]. Shanghai Municipal Archives, 23 March 1964, B177–1–298–61.

"Shanghaishi dianyingju guanyu Chen Huangmei juzhang dui xinkan 'dazhong dianying' de jidian yijian" [Several suggestions made by director Chen Huangmei on the new magazine *Popular Film* issued by the Shanghai Film Bureau]. Shanghai Municipal Archives, August 1962, B177–1–298–2.

"Shanghaishi dianyingju guanyu Chen Huangmei tongzhi jianghua: Wenhua shiye kaifa deng" [A summary by the Shanghai Film Bureau on the talk given by comrade Chen Huangmei on cultural undertakings and so on]. Shanghai Municipal Archives, 10 January 1964, B177–1–298–16.

"Shanghaishi dianyingju guanyu chengli Shanghaishi dianying zhipianchang de baogo" [A report by the Shanghai Film Bureau on the establishment of Shanghai Film Studio]. Shanghai Municipal Archives, 16 November 1949, B177–1–1.

"Shanghaishi dianyingju guanyu chouban Shanghai dianying xuexiao de jihua fang'an, huiyi jiyao" [The plan and meeting minutes by the Shanghai Film Bureau on establishing the Shanghai Film Academy]. Shanghai Municipal Archives, 31 March 1959, B177–1–74.

"Shanghaishi dianyingju guanyu dangwei gongzuo de baogao, jueyi" [A report and decisions by the Shanghai Film Bureau on the work of the Party committee]. Shanghai Municipal Archives, 15 March 1962, B177–1–159.

"Shanghaishi dianyingju guanyu dangwei gongzuo de baogao" [A report by the Shanghai Film Bureau on the work of the Party committee]. Shanghai Municipal Archives, 6 May 1962, B177–1–160.

"Shanghaishi dianyingju guanyu dangwei gongzuo de jiancha, baogao" [A report and inspections by the Shanghai Film Bureau on the work of the Party committee]. Shanghai Municipal Archives, 14 October 1964, B177–1–182.

"Shanghaishi dianyingju guanyu dangwei gongzuo de jihua, baogao, yijian" [Plans and suggestions by the Shanghai Film Bureau on the work of the Party committee]. Shanghai Municipal Archives, 5 June 1959, B177–1–138.

"Shanghaishi dianyingju guanyu dangwei gongzuo de jihua, yaodian, zanxing fangfa" [Plans, main points, and provisional methods by the Shanghai Film Bureau on the work of the Party committee]. Shanghai Municipal Archives, 7 January 1965, B177–1–196.

"Shanghaishi dianyingju guanyu dangwei gongzuo de jihua, yaodian" [Plans and key points by the Shanghai Film Bureau on the work of the Party committee]. Shanghai Municipal Archives, 14 January 1960, B177–1–145.

"Shanghaishi dianyingju guanyu dangwei gongzuo de jihua, yaodian" [Plans and key points by the Shanghai Film Bureau on the work of the Party committee]. Shanghai Municipal Archives, 18 June 1963, B177–1–176.

"Shanghaishi dianyingju guanyu dangwei gongzuo de jueyi, jueding, huiyi jilu" [Decisions and meeting minutes by the Shanghai Film Bureau on the work of the Party committee]. Shanghai Municipal Archives, 15 February 1962, B177–1–156.

"Shanghaishi dianyingju guanyu dangwei gongzuo de qingshi, baogao, jihua, jueyi" [Requests and plans of the Party committee required by the Shanghai Film Bureau]. Shanghai Municipal Archives, 25 November 1961, B177–1–154.

"Shanghaishi dianyingju guanyu dangwei gongzuo de qingshi, baogao" [A report and requests of the Party committee required by the Shanghai Film Bureau]. Shanghai Municipal Archives, 28 February 1963, B-177–1–164.

"Shanghaishi dianyingju guanyu dangwei gongzuo de yaodian, gangyao" [A platform and key points for the work of the Party committee by the Shanghai Film Bureau]. Shanghai Municipal Archives, 22 January 1965, B177–1–197.

"Shanghaishi dianyingju guanyu dangwei gongzuo de yaodian, huiyi jiyao" [Key points and meeting minutes by the Shanghai Film Bureau on the work of the Party committee]. Shanghai Municipal Archives, 24 September 1963, B177–1–171.

"Shanghaishi dianyingju guanyu dangwei gongzuo de yaodian, zongjie, baogao" [A summary by the Shanghai Film Bureau on the work of the Party committee]. Shanghai Municipal Archives, 30 October 1965, B177–1–208.

"Shanghaishi dianyingju guanyu dangwei gongzuo de zongjie, baogao" [A summary by the Shanghai Film Bureau on the work of the Party committee]. Shanghai Municipal Archives, 12 March 1959, B177–1–142.

"Shanghaishi dianyingju guanyu dangwei zuzhi gongzuo de yijian, jihua, tongzhi" [Suggestions and plans by the Shanghai Film Bureau on the organizational work of the Party committee]. Shanghai Municipal Archives, 29 March 1961, B177–1–152.

"Shanghaishi dianyingju guanyu dianying bianji gongzuo de zongjie, lingdao jianghua, baogao" [A summary by the Shanghai Film Bureau on the work of film editing and leaders' talks]. Shanghai Municipal Archives, 1 July 1959, B177–1–301.

"Shanghaishi dianyingju guanyu dianying bianji shengchan de baogao, lingdao jianghua" [A report by the Shanghai Film Bureau on film editing and production]. Shanghai Municipal Archives, 2 July 1959, B177–1–219.

"Shanghaishi dianyingju guanyu dianying chuangzuo gongzuo de baogao, lingdao jianghua, zuotan jilu" [A report and meeting minutes by the Shanghai Film Bureau on filmmaking]. Shanghai Municipal Archives, 9 January 1963, B177–1–282.

"Shanghaishi dianyingju guanyu dianying chuangzuo shengchan de guihua, yaodian, gongzuo zongjie, baogao" [A report by the Shanghai Film Bureau on planning film production]. Shanghai Municipal Archives, 14 January 1960, B177–1–313.

"Shanghaishi dianyingju guanyu dianying chuangzuo shengchan de jihua, tongzhi, zongjie" [A summary by the Shanghai Film Bureau on planning film production]. Shanghai Municipal Archives, 6 May 1959, B177–1–218.

"Shanghaishi dianyingju guanyu dianying chuangzuo shengchan de qingkuang baogao yijian" [A report by the Shanghai Film Bureau on film production]. Shanghai Municipal Archives, 31 March 1962, B177–1–265.

"Shanghaishi dianyingju guanyu dianying chuangzuo shengchan gongzuo de yijian, tongzhi, dafu, huiyi baogao" [A report by the Shanghai Film Bureau on film production]. Shanghai Municipal Archives, May 1962, B177–1–266.

"Shanghaishi dianyingju guanyu dianying chuangzuo shengchan gongzuo de qingshi, pifu, tongzhi, baogao" [Miscellaneous documents of the Shanghai Film Bureau on film production]. Shanghai Municipal Archives, 2 May 1957, B177–1–270.

"Shanghaishi dianyingju guanyu dianying chuangzuo shengchang de jihua, diaocha baogao, yijian" [Plans and suggestions by the Shanghai Film Bureau on film production]. Shanghai Municipal Archives, 4 May 1961, B177–1–236.

"Shanghaishi dianyingju guanyu dianying chuangzuo wenti de qingshi, baogao" [A report by the Shanghai Film Bureau on filmmaking issues]. Shanghai Municipal Archives, 20 May 1961, B177–1–302.

"Shanghaishi dianyingju guanyu dianying chuangzuo zuotanhui dongtai (di liu qi–di shisan qi)" [A report by the Shanghai Film Bureau on the filmmaking forum (vols. 3–13]. Shanghai Municipal Archives, 10 August 1961, B177–1–246.

"Shanghaishi dianyingju guanyu dianying chuangzuo zuotanhui taolun qingkuang, huiyi jilu" [Meeting minutes by the Shanghai Film Bureau for the filmmaking discussion forum]. Shanghai Municipal Archives, 31 July 1961, B177–1–242.

"Shanghaishi dianyingju guanyu dianying chuangzuo, shengchan de yijian, cao'an, guihua, tongzhi" [Plans and suggestions by the Shanghai Film Bureau on film production]. Shanghai Municipal Archives, 21 October 1961, B177–1–261.

"Shanghaishi dianyingju guanyu dianying chuangzuo, zhipian shengchan de jihua, cuoshi, lingdao jihua, huiyi jiyao" [Plans and meeting minutes by the Shanghai Film Bureau on film production]. Shanghai Municipal Archives, 17 January 1961, B177–1–231.

"Shanghaishi dianyingju guanyu dianying gongzuo de jianghua, baogao" [A report by the Shanghai Film Bureau on film work]. Shanghai Municipal Archives, 14 November 1964, B177–1–306.

"Shanghaishi dianyingju guanyu dianying gushipian chuangzuo shengcha de baogao, lingdao jianghua" [A report by the Shanghai Film Bureau on the production of feature films and leaders' talks]. Shanghai Municipal Archives, 17 February 1961, B177–1–233.

"Shanghaishi dianyingju guanyu dianying juben gelei gaochou wenti de qingshi, huibao, pifu, zanxing fangfa" [Provisional methods by the Shanghai Film Bureau on the issues of screenplay payments]. Shanghai Municipal Archives, 1 January 1963, B177–1–281.

"Shanghaishi dianyingju guanyu dianying shengchan jingying guanli de zuotan jilu" [Meeting minutes by the Shanghai Film Bureau for the discussion on film production and management]. Shanghai Municipal Archives, 6 July 1962, B177–1–268.

"Shanghaishi dianyingju guanyu dianying shengchan jingying guanli de qingshi, pifu, yijian, tongzhi, gongzuo zongjie" [Miscellaneous documents of the Shanghai Film Bureau on film production and management]. Shanghai Municipal Archives, 3 August 1961, B177–1–274.

"Shanghaishi dianyingju guanyu dianying shiye fazhan de guihua, jihua, yaodian" [Plans and main points by the Shanghai Film Bureau on the development of the film industry]. Shanghai Municipal Archives, 14 April 1965, B177–1–312.

"Shanghaishi dianyingju guanyu dianying shiye fazhan de guihua, yijijan, gongzuo yaodian" [Plans and key points by the Shanghai Film Bureau on the development of the film industry]. Shanghai Municipal Archives, 22 October 1959, B177–1–221.

"Shanghaishi dianyingju guanyu dianying shiye fazhan gongzuo de guihua, gong-zuo yaodian, jiaobao" [Plans and key points by the Shanghai Film Bureau on the development of the film industry]. Shanghai Municipal Archives, April 1963, B177–1–311.

"Shanghaishi dianyingju guanyu dianying xuanti guihua, chuangzuo shengchan gongzuo de yijian, cao'an, guihua, tongzhi" [Plans and suggestions by the Shanghai Film Bureau on planning film topics and filmmaking]. Shanghai Municipal Archives, July 1961, B177–1–262.

"Shanghaishi dianyingju guanyu dianying yishu de lilun yanjiu cankao ziliao" [Reference materials on the theoretical study of film arts by the Shanghai Film Bureau]. Shanghai Municipal Archives, February 1962, B177–1–275.

"Shanghaishi dianyingju guanyu dianying yishu gongzuo de qingkuang huibao huiyi jilu" [A report and meeting minutes by the Shanghai Film Bureau on the work of film arts]. Shanghai Municipal Archives, 7 August 1961, B177–1–245.

"Shanghaishi dianyingju guanyu dianying yishupian qingli gongzuo de tongzhi, qingkuang baogao" [A report by the Shanghai Film Bureau on the cleanup of art films]. Shanghai Municipal Archives, 28 May 1965, B177–1–314.

"Shanghaishi dianyingju guanyu dianying zhipian shengchan gongzuo de jihua, yijian, tongzhi, tongbao" [Plans and suggestions by the Shanghai Film Bureau on the work of film production]. Shanghai Municipal Archives, June 1962, B177–1–277.

"Shanghaishi dianyingju guanyu fazhan dianying shiye de jucuo, guihua, jianyi" [Plans and suggestions by the Shanghai Film Bureau on the development of the film industry]. Shanghai Municipal Archives, 14 April 1958, B177–1–217.

"Shanghaishi dianyingju guanyu gaijin he jiaqiang dangwei dui chuangzuo shengchan lingdao de yijian" [Suggestions by the Shanghai Film Bureau on improving and strengthening the Party's leadership in film production]. Shanghai Municipal Archives, 25 November 1961, B177–1–153.

"Shanghaishi dianyingju guanyu dianying chuangzuo shengchan de guanli zhidu guiding" [Management systems and regulations by the Shanghai Film Bureau on filmmaking systems]. Shanghai Municipal Archives, June 1961, B177–1–238.

"Shanghaishi dianyingju guanyu gushipian shengchan guanli de wuzhong zhidu ji dianying zhipian, gongye shengchan anquan tiaoli" [Regulations by the Shanghai Film Bureau on the feature film production management system, and filmmaking and industrial production safety]. Shanghai Municipal Archives, 10 February 1964, B177–1–291.

"Shanghaishi dianyingju guanyu jiaqiang zhipian jishu guanli de yijian guiding" [Regulations by the Shanghai Film Bureau on strengthening the management of production technology]. Shanghai Municipal Archives, 17 August 1961, B177–1–249.

"Shanghaishi dianyingju guanyu juben chuangzuo, yangpian shencha gongzuo shixing tiaoli, yijian" [Trial regulations and suggestions by the Shanghai Film Bureau on screenwriting and film rushes reviews]. Shanghai Municipal Archives, 10 August 1961, B177–1–248.

"Shanghaishi dianyingju guanyu niandu gongzuo de jihua, yaodian, jianbao, zongjie" [A plan and summary by the Shanghai Film Bureau on the annual work]. Shanghai Municipal Archives, 24 March 1961, B177–1–27.

"Shanghaishi dianyingju guanyu niandu gongzuo jihua, zongjie, anpai" [An annual working summary and seasonal working plan by the Shanghai Film Bureau]. Shanghai Municipal Archives, 2 April 1963, B177–1–23.

"Shanghaishi dianyingju guanyu Situ Huimin juzhang de zongjie baogao: Wenhua gongzuo de fangmian" [A report by the Shanghai Film Bureau on the wrap-up report given by director Situ Humin on the aspects of cultural undertakings]. Shanghai Municipal Archives, 23 March 1964, B177–1–298–64.

"Shanghaishi dianyingju guanyu Xia Yan buzhang dui xinkan Dazhong dianying de jidian yijian" [Several suggestions to the Shanghai Film Bureau made by minister Xia Yan on the new magazine *Popular Film*]. Shanghai Municipal Archives, August 1962, B177–1–298–1.

"Shanghaishi dianyingju guanyu yishupian chang jiaqiang chuangzuo shengchan zerenzhi de ruogan guiding" [Several provisions by the Shanghai Film Bureau on strengthening accountability for the film production by art film studios]. Shanghai Municipal Archives, 15 August 1961, B177–1–247.

"Shanghaishi dianyingju guanyu zhaokai dianying chuangzuo huiyi de baogao dahui fayan" [A report by the Shanghai Film Bureau on holding filmmaking conferences]. Shanghai Municipal Archives, 31 October 1961, B177–1–252.

"Shanghaishi dianyingju guanyu zhaokai guishipian changzhang huiyi de baogao, jianghua, jilu" [A report by the Shanghai Film Bureau on holding meetings of directors of feature film studios]. Shanghai Municipal Archives, 16 January 1960, B177–1–230.

"Shanghaishi dianyingju guanyu zhipian shengchan gongzuo de jihua, yijian, tongzhi, qingshi baogao" [Plans and suggestions by the Shanghai Film Bureau on the work of film production]. Shanghai Municipal Archives, 7 November 1962, B177–1–279.

"Shanghaishi dianyingju guanyu zhipian shengchan gongzuo de jihua, qingshi, baogao, tongzhi" [Documents by the Shanghai Film Bureau on film production]. Shanghai Municipal Archives, 1959, B177–1–300.

"Shanghaishi dianyingju guanyu zhipian shengchan renwu de yijian, baogao" [A report by the Shanghai Film Bureau on film production tasks]. Shanghai Municipal Archives, 21 October 1964, B177–1–305.

"Shanghaishi dianyingju juzhang Zhang Junxiang zai dianying chuangzuo huiyishang de jianghua jilu" [A talk by the Shanghai Film Bureau director Zhang Junxiang at the filmmaking meeting]. Shanghai Municipal Archives, 23 September 1961, B177–1–240.

"Shanghaishi dianyingju zhaokai dianying zuotanhui de jihua, baogao zongjie" [A summary by the Shanghai Film Bureau on holding a film forum]. Shanghai Municipal Archives, 4 February 1963, B177–1–283.

"Shanghaishi dianyingju zhaokai gexiang dianying zhuanye zuotanhui de jiyao" [Meeting minutes by the Shanghai Film Bureau for holding various professional filmmaking forums]. Shanghai Municipal Archives, 16 February 1962, B177–1–263.

"Shanghaishi dianyingju zuzhi bufen daibiao chuxi Shanghai shiwei kuoda huiyi xiaozu taolun de qingkuang jilu" [A summary on the panel discussion at an expanded meeting of the Shanghai Municipal Committee organized by the Shanghai Film Bureau attended by some representatives]. Shanghai Municipal Archives, 12 July 1958, B177–1–129.

"Shanghaishi fulian 1954 gongzuo zhongjie" [Shanghai WF's review of work in 1954]. Shanghai Municipal Archives, 1955, C31–1–95.

"Shanghaishi fuwei gongzuo gaikuang baogao" [Shanghai women's committee's work report]. Shanghai Municipal Archives, 1951, C31-1-31.

"Shanghaishi jiefangqian renmin tuanti tongjibiao" [A survey of the people's organizations before liberation in Shanghai]. Shanghai Municipal Archives, 1950, B168–1–742.

"Shanghaishi jumin weiyuanhui zhengdun gongzuo qingkuang baogao" [A report on the work of rectification of the Shanghai residents committees]. Shanghai Municipal Archives, 23 October 1954, B168–1–14.

"Shanghaishi jumin weiyuanhui zuzhi zanxing banfa" [Temorary methods for organizing Shanghai residents committees]. Shanghai Municipal Archives, 1950, B168–1–749.

"Shanghaishi linong qunzhong zuzhi gongzuo zongjie"[A summary of the work on organizing masses in Shanghai neighborhoods], Shanghai Municipal Archives, 1950, B168–1–750.

"Shanghaishi linong zhengdun zuzhi jianshe gongzuo zongjie" [A summary of the work on Shanghai neighborhood rectification and organizational building]. Shanghai Municipal Archives, April 1955, B168–1–780.

"Shanghaishi linong zuzhi he zhengdun gongzuo qingkuang" [The situation of neighborhood organization and rectification in Shanghai]. Shanghai Municipal Archives, 1953, B168–1–772.

"Shanghaishi minzhu fulian choubeihui liangge yue gongzuo gaikuang" [A summary on the two months' work of the preparatory committee for the Shanghai Democratic Women's Federation]. Shanghai Municipal Archives, 1949, C31–1–2.

"Shanghaishi renmin zhengfu minzhengju zuzhi guicheng" [Organizational regulations of the department of civil affairs of the Shanghai municipal people's government]. Shanghai Municipal Archives, August 1949, B168–1–382.

"Shanghaishi shiqu linong jiedao jumin zuzhi shixing fangan" [A trial plan for organizing residents in lanes and streets in Shanghai urban districts]. Shanghai Municipal Archives, 18 October 1950, B168–1–749.

"Shanghai shiqu minzhu jianzheng gongzuo zongjie" [A summary of the work on Shanghai urban disctricts democraticly establishing the government]. Shanghai Municipal Archives, 1951, B168–1-763.

"Shanghai shiwei guanyu funü gongzuo de jueding" [Shanghai Party Committee's decision on women-work]. Shanghai Municipal Archives, 1950, C31–1–9.

Sheehan, Jackie. *Chinese Workers: A New History*. London and New York: Routledge, 1998.

Shen, Vivian. *The Origins of Left-Wing Cinema in China, 1932–1937*. New York: Routledge, 2005.

Shen, Yun. "Wo suo zhidao de Xia Yan yu Huangmei" [What I know about Xia Yan and Huangmei]. *Dangdai dianying* [Contemporary Film], no. 12 (2013): 41–43.

Shen, Zijiu. "Chen Bo'er cong zhandi laixin" [A letter sent by Chen Bo'er from the front]. *Funü shenghuo* [Women's Life] 8, no. 1 (1939): 11.

———. "Nuola zuotanhui" [A symposium by Noras]. In *Nüjie wenhua zhanshi Shen Zijiu* [Shen Zijiu, a woman fighter on the cultural front], edited by Dong Bian, 235–38. Beijing: Zhongguo funü chubanshe, 1991.

———. "Zhonghua quanguo minzhu funü lianhehui daibiao Shen Zijiu tongzhi de jianghua" [The talk by comrade Shen Zijiu, representative of the All-China Democratic Women's Federation]. In *Renmin yishujia Chen Bo'er tongzhi jinian teji* [A memorial series on the people's artist comrade Chen Bo'er]. Beijing: Xin Zhongguo dianying, 1952.

Shi, Yun. *Zhang Chunqiao Yao Wenyuan shizhuan: Zizhuan, riji, gongci* [Biographies of Zhang Chunqiao and Yao Wenyuan: Autobiographies, diaries, confessions]. Hong Kong: Sanlian shudian, 2012.

Shi, Zhe. "Wo suozhidao de Chen Boda" [What I know about Chen Boda]. *Wenshi Jinghua* [Essence from Culture and History], no. 8 (2002): 50–57.

"Shiwei guanyu linong zhengdun gongzuo de zhishi" [The municipal Party committee's instruction on the work on rectifying lanes]. Shanghai Municipal Archives, 20 April, 1954, B-168-1-780.

"Shiwei pifu" [The municipal Party committee's reply]. Shanghai Municipal Archives, 26 September 1951, C31-1-31.

"Shouru xingbiecha" [Gender difference in income]. *Hudong Baike* [Interactive encyclopedia]. www.baike.com/wiki/收入性别差 (accessed August 25, 2014).

"'Shunüban' diaocha: 'bianlian' duo, dingshang younü shaonü" [An investigation of "ladies' class": Multiple faces, turning attention to female children and adolescents]. *Guangdong Nüxing e jiayuan* [E-home for Guangdong females]. www.gdwomen.org.cn/jdgz/201006/t20100621_99412.htm (accessed January 14, 2016).

"The Sixth Session of the Council of the WIDF: Peking: April 24–30, 1956." International Institute of Socialist History website: https://search.socialhistory.org/Record/1057007 (accessed January 3, 2016).

Small Happiness. Directed by Carma Hinton. 1984.

Smedley, Agnes. *Portraits of Chinese Women in Revolution,* edited by Jan MacKinnon and Steve Mackinnon. New York: Feminist Press at the City University of New York, 1976.

Song, Qingling, "Funü yao jianjue guohao shehuizhuyi zheyiguan" [Women should resolutely pass the test of socialism]. In *Zhongguo funü yundong wenxian ziliao huibian* [An anthology of source materials on the Chinese women's movement], edited by Chinese Women Cadres Management School, vol. 2, 308. Beijing: Zhongguo funü chubanshe, 1988.

Spivak, Gayatri Chakravorty. "Can the Subaltern Speak?" In *Marxism and the Interpretation of Culture,* edited by Cary Nelson and Lawrence Grossberg. Urbana: University of Illinois Press, 1988.

Spring Forever [*Wanziqianhong zongshichun*]. Directed by Shen Fu. Shanghai Haiyan Film Studio, 1959.

Stacey, Judith. *Patriarchy and Socialist Revolution in China*. Berkeley: University of
California Press, 1983.

Stern, Meta L. (Hebe), trans. *August Bebel (1840–1913), Women and Socialism*. New
York: Socialist Literature, 1910.

Stetson, Dorothy McBride, and Amy G. Mazur, eds. *Comparative State Feminism*.
Thousand Oaks, CA: Sage, 1995.

"Su gedi shangying *Zhonghua nüer*: Qian Xiaozhang baogao canjia guoji yingzhan
qingkuang" [On the screenings of *Daughters of China* in the Soviet Union: Qian
Xiaozhang's report on the situation of participating in the international film
festival]. *Wenhui bao* [Wenhui Daily], September 5, 1950.

Sudo, Mizuyo. "Concepts of Women's Rights in Modern China." In *Translating
Feminisms in China,* ed. Dorothy Ko and Wang Zheng, 13–34. Oxford: Blackwell, 2007.

———. *Zhongguo "nüquan" gainian de bianqian* [Changes in the concept of "feminism" in China], translated by Mizuyo Sudo and Yao Yi. Beijing: Social Sciences
and Academic Press, 2010.

Sun, Liping, and Xiaoli Liu. *Koushu Dazhai shi* [Oral histories of Dazhai].
Guangzhou: South Daily Press, 2008.

Tang, Mingsheng. *Qing Yi zhuan* [A biography of Qin Yi]. Beijing: People's Daily
Press, 2012.

Tang, Xiaobing. *Chinese Modern: The Heroic and the Quotidian*. Durham, NC:
Duke University Press, 2000.

———. "Rural Women and Social Change in New China Cinema: From *Li
Shuangshuang* to *Ermo.*" *Positions* 11, no. 3 (2003): 647–74.

———. "Street Theater and Subject Formation in Wartime China: Toward a New
Form of Public Art." *Cross-Currents: East Asian History and Culture Review*,
E-Journal no. 18 (March 2016): 21–50. https://cross-currents.berkeley.edu/e-
journal/issue-18 (accessed May 12, 2016).

———. *Visual Culture in Contemporary China: Paradigms and Shifts*. Cambridge:
Cambridge University Press, 2015.

Tao, Cheng, Jiadong He, and Jie Zhao. *Wode yijia* [My family]. Beijing: Zhongguo
gongren chubanshe, 1959.

Tao, Chunfang, and Fan Aiguo. *Zhimian xiagang* [Facing being laid-off]. Beijing:
Contempory China Press, 2001.

Tao, Jie, Zheng Bijun, and Shirley, L. Mow. *Holding Up Half of the Sky: Chinese
Women Past, Present, and Future*. New York: Feminist Press at the City University of New York, 2004.

Tian, He. *Laomo Shen Jilan* [Model worker Shen Jilan]. Taiyuan: Shanxi jiaoyu
chubanshe [Shanxi Education Press], 1999.

"Tian Xin he Wang Zhiya gei Zhao Xian de xin" [The letter to Zhao Xian from
Tian Xin and Wang Zhiya]. Shanghai Municipal Archives, 31 February 1950,
C31-1-9.

"Tongzhi, 6 yue 15 ri zhengwu jieguan weiyuanhui" [Announcement by the political takeover committee]. Shanghai Municipal Archives, 15 June 1949, B168–1–382.

Toroptsev, Sergei. "Xia Yan and the Chinese Cinema." *Far Eastern Affairs* 4 (1985): 126–31.

Wang, Ban. *The Sublime Figure of History: Aesthetics and Politics in Twentieth-Century China.* Stanford, CA: Stanford University Press, 1997.

Wang Cuncheng. "Guanyu 'xie shisannian' zhenglun de liangfen neibu cailiao" [Two internal documents on the debates on "representing the thirteen years"]. *Xinwenxue Shiliao* [Historical Sources of New Literature], no. 1 (2015): 17–24.

Wang, Lingzhen, ed. *Chinese Women's Cinema: Transnational Contexts.* New York: Columbia University Press, 2011.

———. "Wang Ping and Women's Cinema in Socialist China: Institutional Practice, Feminist Cultures, and Embedded Authorship." *Signs: Journal of Women in Culture and Society* 40, no. 3 (2015): 589–622.

Wang, Shiqiang. "'Hongse meixue' de shengcheng: Dui du 'hong yan' yu 'liehuo zhong yongsheng'" [The generation of "red aesthetics": Comparing *Red Crag* and *Eternity in Flames*]. *Changcheng* [Great Walls], July 15, 2011.

Wang, Suping. *Ta haimei jiao Jiang Qing de shihou* [Before she became Jiang Qing]. Beijing: Shiyue wenyi chubanshe, 1993.

Wang, Xia. *Haipai zhangfu mianmianguan* [An overview of Shanghai husbands]. Shanghai: Shanghai Social Sciences Press, 1991.

Wang, Yongfang. *Mingxing, zhangshi, renmin yishujia: Chen Bo'er zhuanlue* [A star, soldier, people's artist: A biography of Chen Bo'er]. Beijing: Zhongguo huaqiao chubanshe, 1994.

Wang, Zheng. "Call Me Qingnian But Not Funü: A Maoist Youth in Retrospect." *Feminist Studies* 27, no. 1 (2001): 9–34.

———. "Detention of the Feminist Five in China." *Feminist Studies* 41, no. 2 (2015): 476–82.

———. "Feminist Networks." In *Reclaiming Chinese Society: Politics of Redistribution, Recognition, and Representation,* edited by Ching Kwan Lee, 101–18. London: RoutledgeCurzon, 2010.

———. "Gender and Maoist Urban Reorganization." In *Gender in Motion: Divisions of Labor and Cultural Change in Imperial and Modern China,* edited by Bryna Goodman and Wendy Larson, 189–209. Lanham, MD: Rowman and Littlefield, 2005.

———. "Gender, Employment and Women's Resistance." In *Chinese Society: Change, Conflict and Resistance,* 2nd edition, edited by Elizabeth J. Perry and Mark Selden, 159–82. London and New York: RoutlegeCurzon, 2003.

———. "Research on Women in Contemporary China." In *Guide to Women's Studies in China,* edited by Gail Hershatter et al., 1–43. Berkeley: Institute of East Asian Studies, 1998.

———. *Women in the Chinese Enlightenment: Oral and Textual Histories.* Berkeley: University of California Press, 1999.

———— and Ying Zhang. "Global Concepts, Local Practices: Chinese Feminism since the Fourth UN Conference on Women." *Feminist Studies* 36, no. 1 (Spring 2010): 40–67.

Wang, Zhimin, Yang Yuanying, and Ding Ning. "Cong zongli mishu dao zhipian zhuren: Beijing dianying zhipian chang Wang Zhimin fangtan" [From prime minister's secretary to production manager: Interview with Wang Zhimin of Beijing Film Studio]. *Dianying Yishu* [Film Arts], no. 5 (2010).

Ward, Julian. "The Remodeling of a National Cinema: Chinese Films of the Seventeen Years (1949–1966)." In *The Chinese Cinema Book,* edited by Song Hwee Lim and Julian Ward, 87–93. London: Palgrave Macmillan, 2011.

Wei, Jiankuan, "Xia Yan xiansheng gaibian *Zhufu* de baibi" [Failures in Xia Yan's adaptation of *New Year's Sacrifice*]. *Yuwen beike dashi* [Master of teaching Chinese language]. http://www.xiexingcun.com/dushu/HTML/11294.html (accessed May 21, 2016).

Wei, Wenqian. "Xia Yan, nide baoshenggong henbu jingdian, gai tuichu lishi wutai le" [Xia Yan, your indentured women workers were not classic, they should exit the historical stage]. *Tiexue net.* http://bbs.tiexue.net/post2_4287287_1.html (accessed May 21, 2016).

Wen, Jie. "Wangshi suoji" [Reminiscences]. In *Zhongguo funü zazhi jianjie* [A brief introduction to *Women of China*]. Internal circulation of memoirs produced by the Press of *Women of China*, 1999.

White, Jenny B. "State Feminism, Modernization, and the Turkish Republican Woman." *NWSA Journal* 15 (Fall 2003): 145–60.

White, Tyrene. "The Origins of China's Birth Planning Policy." In *Engendering China: Women, Culture, and the State,* edited by Christina K. Gilmartin, Gail Hershatter, Lisa Rofel, and Tyrene White, 250–78. Boston: Harvard University Press, 1994.

Witke, Roxane. *Comrade Chiang Ch'ing.* Boston: Little, Brown, 1977.

Wolf, Margery. *Revolution Postponed: Women in Contemporary China.* Stanford, CA: Stanford University Press, 1985.

Women of China (1939–1942, 1956–2010). Yan'an and Beijing: *Zhongguo Funü* zazhishe.

Women of New China (1949–1955). Beijing: *Xin Zhongguo Funü* zazhishe.

Wu, Di, ed. *Zhongguo dianying yanjiu ziliao 1949–1979* [Source materials for Chinese film studies: 1949–1979]. Beijing: wenhua yishu chubanshe, 2006.

Wu, Hui. *Once Iron Girls: Essays on Gender by Post-Mao Chinese Literary Women.* Lanham, MD: Rowman and Littlefield, 2010.

Wusi shiqi funü wenti wen xuan [A collection of articles on women's issues during the May Fourth period]. Bejing: Zhongguo funü chubanshe, 1981.

Wu, Yiching. *The Cultural Revolution at the Margins: Chinese Socialism in Crisis.* Cambridge, MA: Harvard University Press, 2014.

Xi Jinping, "Jianchi nannü pingdeng jiben guoce, fahui woguo funü weida zuoyong" [Upholding the fundamental state policy of equality between men and women, asserting women's great role in our country]. *Xinhua net*, October 31, 2013. http://news.xinhuanet.com/politics/2013-10/31/c_117956150.htm (accessed May 20, 2015).

"Xia buzhang baogao (11 yue 1 ri zai taolun yishupian fang weixing zuotanhuishang de baogao)" [A talk by Minister Xia (at the forum on launching art film satellites on November 1)]. Shanghai Municipal Archives, 1958, B177-1-216-1.

"Xia Yan buzhang zai 1962 nian 9 yue 8 ri tingqu Shanghaishi dainyingju guanyu 1963 zhi 1964 nian de jumu anpai huibao hou de jianghua" [Minister Xia Yan's talk on September 8, 1962, after listening to the report by the Shanghai Film Bureau on the film production plan for years 1963 to 1964]. Shanghai Municipal Archives, 1 December 1958, B177-1-288.

"Xia Yan fu buzhang 5 yue 18 ri zai gushipianchang changzhang, dangweishuji hui-yishang de fayan zhaiyao" [A summary of deputy minister Xia Yan's talk at the meeting with directors of feature film studios and Party secretaries on May 18]. Shanghai Municipal Archives, 21 May 1963, B177-1-285.

"Xia Yan tongzhi dui Shangying lingdao ganbu ji zhuyao chuangzuo renyuan zuotan jilu" [Notes on comrade Xia Yan's talk to leading cadres and major filmmakers of Shanghai film studios]. Shanghai Municipal Archives, 19 June 1960, B177-1-288, 6.

"Xia Yan tongzhi zai wenhuabu quanti dangyuan he zhishu danwei fuze ganbu huishang de jiancha" [Xia Yan's self-criticism at the meeting of Party members of the Ministry of Culture and the leaders of the affiliated units]. Shanghai Municipal Archives, 19 January 1965, B177-1-303, 32.

"Xia Yan yibian dang buzhang, yibian gaibian xiju" [Xia Yan managed to serve as a minister while revising scripts for plays and films]. *v.ifeng.com*. http://v.ifeng.com/history/shishijianzheng/201105/b53953e7-e29f-404a-b330-e54e014af26c.shtml (accessed May 21, 2016)

Xia, Yan. "Cong 'Baoshengong' suo yinqide huiyi" [Reminiscences from "the inden-tured workers"]. In *Xia Yan Qishinian Wenxuan* [A selected anthology of Xia Yan's seventy years of works], edited by Li Ziyun, 43. Shanghai: Wenyi chuban-she, 1996.

———. "Cong miwuzhong kan yimian jingzi" [Looking at a mirror in the fog], in *Xia Yan Qishinian Wenxuan* [A selected anthology of Xia Yan's seventy years of works], edited by Li Ziyun, 644–49. Shanghai: Wenyi chubanshe, 1996.

———. "Cong *Wuxun Zhuan* de pipan jiantao wozai shanghai wenhua yishujie de gongzuo" [A self-criticism of my work in Shanghai's arts and culture, starting from the criticism of *The Life of Wu Xun*], *People's Daily*, August 26, 1951. In *Zhongguo dianying yanjiu ziliao: 1949–1979* [Source materials for Chinese film studies: 1949–1979], edited by Wu Di, vol. 1, 190–94. Beijing: Wenhua yishu chubanshe, 2006.

———. "Guanyu Zhongguo dianying wenti" [On issues in Chinese films], 1983. In *Xia Yan tan dianying* [Xia Yan on film], edited by Lin Man and Li Ziyun, 117–18. Beijing: Zhongguo dianying chubanshe, 1993.

———. "Huainian Zhang Xichen xiansheng" [Remembering Mr. Zhang Xichen]. In *Xia Yan Qishinian Wenxuan* [A selected anthology of Xia Yan's seventy years of works], edited by Li Ziyun, 509–14. Shanghai: Wenyi chubanshe, 1996.

———. *Lanxun jiumeng lu* [Languid recollections of old dreams]. Beijing: Sanlian shudian, 1985.

———. "Qiangzhe a, nide mingzi jiaozuo nüren" [Stronger, your name is woman]. In *Xia Yan Qishinian Wenxuan* [A selected anthology of Xia Yan's seventy years of works], edited by Li Ziyun, 767–68. Shanghai: Wenyi chubanshe, 1996.

———. "*Qiu Jin* zaiban daixu" [Preface to the reprint of *Qiu Jin*]. In *Xia Yan Qishinian Wenxuan* [A selected anthology of Xia Yan's seventy years of works], edited by Li Ziyun, 311–13. Shanghai: Wenyi chubanshe, 1996.

———. *Shenghuo, ticai, chuangzu* [Life, theme, creation], edited by Cheng Yi. Changsha: Hunan renmin chubanshe, 1981.

———. "Wei dianying shiye de jixu dayuejin er fendou" [Strive for the continuous Great Leap Forward of the film industry]. *People's Daily*, February 2, 1960.

———. "*Wu Xun Zhuan* shijian shimo" [The causes of the incident of *The Life of Wu Xun*]. In *Zhongguo dianying yanjiu ziliao: 1949–1979* [Source materials for Chinese film studies: 1949–1979], edited by Wu Di, vol. 1, 195–200. Beijing: Wenhua yishu chubanshe, 2006.

———. *Xia Yan shu hua* [Xia Yan's writings], edited by Jiang Deming. Beijing: Beijing chubanshe, 1998.

———. "Zai dianying daoyan huiyi shangde jianghua" [Talks on the conference of film directors, September 24, 1979]. In *Zhongguo dianying yanjiu ziliao: 1949–1979* [Source materials for Chinese film studies: 1949–1979], edited by Wu Di, vol. 3, 575–85. Beijing: Wenhua yishu chubanshe Press, 2006.

———. "Zai dianying gongzuo huiyi shang de zongjie baogao" [A summary of the film working conference], April 16, 1959. In *Zhongguo dianying yanjiu ziliao: 1949–1979* [Source materials for Chinese film studies: 1949–1979], edited by Wu Di, vol. 2, 262–68. Beijing: Wenhua yishu chubanshe Press, 2006.

———. "Zai quanguo gushipianchang changzhang huiyi shangde jianghua" [Talks on the national conference of directors of film studios], February 13, 1979. In *Zhongguo dianying yanjiu ziliao: 1949–1979* [Source materials for Chinese film studies: 1949–1979], edited by Wu Di, vol. 3, 526–41. Beijing: Wenhua yishu chubanshe, 2006.

———. "Zatan gaibian" [On adaptation]. In *Xia Yan Qishinian Wenxuan* [A selected anthology of Xia Yan's seventy years of works], edited by Li Ziyun, 704–15. Shanghai: Shanghai wenyi chubanshe, 1996.

Xiao, Chen (one of Chen Bo'er's pen names). "Nüzi de liutongbin" [Women's common errors]. *Shenbao Fukan* [Shanghai Daily Supplement], May 9, 1934.

Xiao, Donglian. *Qiusuo Zhongguo: Wenge qianshinian shi* [Exploring China: A history of the decade before the Cultural Revolution]. Beijing: Zhonggong dangshi chubanshe, 2011.

Xiao, Hua. "Chen Bo'er oufang" [Interview with Chen Bo'er]. *Funü shenghuo* [Women's Life] 8, no. 11 (1940): 12.

"Xie buzhang koutou baogao jiyao" [Notes on Minister Xie's talk]. Shanghai Municipal Archives, 16 July 1950, B168–1–745.

"Xingtai 'shunüban' kaijiangla" [Xingtai's "ladies' class" has begun]. *Paigu.com.* http://news.paigu.com/a/335/2090316.html (accessed January 14, 2016).

"Xingzheng gongzuo chubu zongjie: 1949, 6–12" [A preliminary summary of administrative work: From June–December, 1949]. Shanghai Municipal Archives, 1950, B168–1–742.

"Xinsijun sishi zai Guobei" [The fourth division of the New Fourth Army in Guobei]. *Guoyang online.* www.gy233600.cn/bendi/info-6346.html (accessed April 10, 2013).

"Xin Zhongguo chengli 60 nianlai Zhongguo Gongchandang dangyuan zengjia 16 bei" [In the 60 years since the founding of the PRC, the number of the Chinese Communist Party members has increased 16 times]. *Zhongguo Gongchandang Xinwenwang* [CPC News], June 30, 2009. http://cpc.people.com.cn/GB/64093 /64387/9569767.html (accessed December 27, 2013).

Xu, Jingxian. *Shinian yimeng* [Ten years a dream: A Shanghai ex-mayor's memoir of the Cultural Revolution]. Hong Kong: Time International, 2005.

Xue, Xiaohe, ed. *Baguo fangzai jia qianmian: Luo Qiong shishi yi zhounian jinian wenji* [Prioritizing the country over the family: Anthology of the first anniversary of Luo Qiong's death]. Beijing: Zhongguo funü chubanshe, 2007.

Ya, Su. *"Zhonghua nüer* guanhou" [After viewing *Daughters of China*]. *Xin Zhongguo funü* [Women of New China], no. 7 (1950): 17.

Yan, Ping. "Xia Yan de 1964" [Xia Yan in 1964]. *Shouhuo* [Harvest] 1 (2014): 73–89.

Yan, Yiyan. "Diyici xuexi: *Zhonghua nüer* de xiezuo jingguo" [The first learning experience: The process of writing *Daughters of China*]. In *Zhonghua nüer dianying wenxue juben* [The script of *Daughters of China*]. Beijing: Zhongguo dianying chubanshe, 1958.

———. "Guanghui de dianfan" [A glorious paragon]. *Dazhong dianying* [Popular Film] 1–2 (1952).

———. "Mianhuai Chen Bo'er tongzhi" [Remembering comrade Chen Bo'er]. *Xin Wenxue Shiliao* [Historical Sources on New Literature] no. 4 (1980): 181.

Yan, Zhifeng. "Ke Qingshi tichang daxie shisannian suo yingqide yichang fengbo" [The storm stirred up by Ke Qingshi's representing the "thirteen years"]. In *Dangshi Bocai* [Collections from the Party's History], no. 5 (2010): 32–34.

Yan'an liren [Yan'an women]. CNTV documentary. http://jilu.cntv.cn/humhis /yananliren/classpage/video/20091109/108650.shtml (accessed May 22, 2016).

Yang, Jinfu. *Shanghai dianying bainian tushi* [A hundred-year graphical history of Shanghai film]. Shanghai: Weihui chubanshe, 2006.

Yang, Mayfair Mei-Hui. *Spaces of Their Own: Women's Public Sphere in Transnational China.* Minneapolis: University of Minnesota Press, 1999.

———. *Through Chinese Women's Eyes.* Documentary film. 1997.

Yang, Yinlu. "Wo suozhidao de Jiang Qing yu Weiteke furen de tanhua" [The talks between Jiang Qing and Madam Witike that I know of]. *Gejie* [All Fields], no. 9 (2011): 11–14.

———. "Wo suozhidao de Jiang Qing yu Weiteke furen tanhua de qingkuang" [The situation of the talks between Jiang Qing and Madam Witike that I know of]. *Dangshi zonglan* [Overviews of the Party's History], no. 10 (2010): 46–48.

Yang, Yun. "Shendajie jiaowo ban kanwu" [Elder sister Shen taught me how to run a magazine]. In *Nüjie wenhua zhanshi Shen Zijiu* [Shen Zijiu, a woman fighter on the cultural front], edited by Dong Bian, 166–78. Beijing: Zhongguo funü chubanshe, 1991.

Yao, Zhongming, Chen Bo'er, et al. *Tongzhi, ni zoucuole lu!* [Comrade, you are on the wrong road]. In *Beifang wenyi* [Northern literature and arts], vol. 3, edited by Zhou Erfu. Xin Zhongguo chubanshe, 1949.

Ye, Weili, and Xiaodong Ma. *Dongdang de qingchun: Hongse dayuan de nü'er men* [Unrest among youth: Daughters of the red compound]. Beijing: Xinhua Press, 2008.

Ye, Yonglie. *Mao Zedong de mishumen* [Mao Zedong's secretaries]. Shanghai: Shanghai renmin chubanshe, 1994.

Yi Deng dajie Editorial Committee, ed. *Yi Deng dajie* [Memoirs of elder sister Deng]. Beijing: Zhongyang wenxian chubanshe, 1994.

Ying, Hong, and Ling Yan. *Xin Zhongguo dianying shi* [A history of Chinese cinema: 1949–2000]. Changsha: Hunan meishu chubanshe, 2002.

Young, Helen Praeger. *Choosing Revolution: Chinese Women Soldiers on the Long March*. Urbana: University of Illinois Press, 2001.

Yu, Hua. "Lishishang yongyuan liuzhe tamende mingzi: *Zhonghua nüer* guanhou" [Their names are forever engraved in history: After viewing *Daughters of China*]. *Dianying wenxue* [Film Literature] 3 (1959): 82.

Yu, Lan. "Wo shige xinyun de yanyuan" [I am a lucky actor]. *Dianying yishu* [Cinematic Art] no. 4 (1999): 20.

"Yu Lan ban *Jiangjie* zao Jiang Qing pipan" [Yu Lan's Sister Jiang was condemned by Jiang Qing]. *vifeng.com*. http://v.ifeng.com/society/201007/da6ef300-d9fd-411f-97d9-c50ca483356d.shtml (accessed April 24, 2015).

Yu, Ruxin, "Daodi shi Lin weituo, haishi Mao weituo?" [Authorized by Lin or Mao?]. In *Bainian Linbiao* [The centennial of Lin Biao], edited by Ding Kaiwen, 195–219. New York: Mirror Books, 2007.

Yuan, Chengliang. "Dianying *Liehuo zhong yongsheng* dansheng ji" [The birth of the film *Eternity in Flames*]. *Dangshi zonglan* [History Overview] 6 (2008).

Yueji [Self]. www.gotoread.com/mag/13286/order.html (accessed May 20, 2016).

Zeng, Delin. "Du *Liehuo zhong yongsheng*: Gongchan zhuyi jiaoyu de shengdong jiaocai" [*Eternity in Flames*: Lively textbook of Communist education]. *Dushu* [Reading] 7 (1959).

Zeng Li and Zeng Zi. "Women de mama Dong Bian" [Our mother Dong Bian]. *Yanhuang chunqiu* [Chinese History], no. 12 (1999): 55–59.

Zha, Jianying. *Bashi niandai fangtanlu* [Interviews of the 1980s]. Beijing: Sanlian shudian, 2006.

Zhang, Jin. *Changchun ying shi: Dongbei juan* [Changchun film stories: Dongbei volume]. Beijing: Minzu chubanshe, 2011.

Zhang, Lüyi. "Ta zhaodaole yao zoude lu" [She found the road she had been looking for]. In *Nüjie wenhua zhanshi Shen Zijiu* [Shen Zijiu, a woman fighter on the cultural front], edited by Dong Bian, 204–14. Beijing: Zhongguo funü chubanshe, 1991.

Zhang, Naihua. "The All China Women's Federation, Chinese Women and the Women's Movement: 1949–1993." PhD dissertation, Michigan State University, 1996.

Zhang, Ruifang, and Jin Yifeng. *Suiyue youqing: Zhang Ruifang huiyi lu* [Affective years: A memoir of Zhang Ruifang]. Beijing: Zhongyang wenxian chubanshe, 2005.

Zhang, Shuihua, and Yu Lan. "Yichang teshu de zhandou" [A special battle]. In *Zhou Enlai yu dianying* [Zhou Enlai and film], edited by Chen Huangmei, and Chen Bo, 347–52. Beijing: Zhongyang wenxian chubanshe, 1995.

Zhang, Shuoguo. *"Shiqi nian" Shanghai dianying wenhua yanjiu* [A study of the "seventeen years" of Shanghai film culture]. Beijing: Shehui kexue chubanshe, 2014.

Zhang, Xiaosong. "Dui 'nannü pingdeng kouhao de zhiyi'" [Interrogating the slogan of "equality between men and women"]. *Zhongguo funübao* [China Women's News], May 16, 1988.

Zhang, Xichen. "Fuyin tiji" [Notes before printing]. In *Furen yu shehuizhuyi* [*Women and Socialism*], by Bebel, translated by Shen Duanxian. Shanghai: Kaiming Bookstore, 1927.

Zhang, Xinxin, "Wo zainaer cuoguole ni?" [Where did I miss you?]. In *Zhang Xinxin daibiaozuo* [Representative works by Zhang Xinxin], 1–32. Zhengzhou: Huanghe wenyi chubanshe, 1988.

Zhang, Yi. "Dazhai Tieguniang de huiyi" [Reminiscences of the Dazhai Iron Girls], January 1, 2015. *china.com*. http://club.china.com/data/thread/1015/2775/67/59/1_1.html?5 (accessed January 19, 2015).

Zhang, Yingjin. *Cinema and Urban Culture in Shanghai, 1922–1943*. Stanford, CA: Stanford University Press, 1999.

Zhang, Yun. "Guojia guodu shiqi chengshi funü gongzuo de renwu he dangqian jixiang juti gongzuo baogao" [A talk on the tasks of urban women-work in our country's transitional period and current work]. In *Zhongguo funü yundong wenxian ziliao huibian* [An anthology of source material on the Chinese women's movement], edited by Chinese Women Cadres Management School, vol. 2, 209–18. Beijing: Zhongguo funü chubanshe, 1988.

"Zhang Yun tongzhi chuanda Cai dajie he Deng dajie de zhishi" [Comrade Zhang Yun conveys instructions from elder sister Cai and elder sister Deng]. All-China Women's Federation Archives (no date and file numbers).

Zhang, Zhen. *An Amorous History of the Silver Screen: Shanghai Cinema, 1896–1937*. Chicago: University of Chicago Press, 2005.

Zhang, Zige. *Zai Song Meiling shenbian de rizi* [Working alongside Mayling Soong]. Beijing: Tuanjie chubanshe, 2003.

Zhao, Wei. *Xihuating suiyue: Wozai Zhou Enlai Deng Yingchao Shenbian Sanshiqi nian* [Years of Xihuating: I worked with Zhou Enlai and Deng Yingchao for thirty-seven years]. Beijing: Zhongyang wenxian chubanshe, 2004.

Zhao, Xian. "Yi Cai dajie zai Shanghai shica" [Remembering elder sister Cai's inspection in Shanghai]. In *Shanghai fulian sishi nian* [Forty years of the Shanghai Women's Federation], 8. Shanghai: Shanghai Women's Federation, 1990.

Zhao, Yunsheng, and Honghui Wang. *Jiangjun furen zhuan* [A collection of biographies of wives of generals]. Beijing: Zhonggong dangshi chubanshe, 2003.

Zhen, Guangjun. "Wenge qijian Jiang Qing yu Hebei bangzi" [Jiang Qing and Hebei opera during the Cultural Revolution]. *Wenshi jinghua* [Essence of Culture and History], no. 5 (2010): 57–60.

Zheng, Yefu. "Nannü pingdeng de shehuixue sikao" [Sociological thinking on equality between men and women]. *Shehuixue yanjiu* [Sociological Studies], no. 2 (1994): 108–113.

Zhong, Dianfei. "Kanle *Zhao Yiman* yihou" [After watching *Zhao Yiman*]. *Renmin ribao* [People's Daily], July 9, 1950.

———. "Lun dianying zhidao sixiang zhong de jige wenti" [On a few issues among guiding concepts in film]. In *Zhongguo dianying yanjiu ziliao 1949–1979* [Source materials for Chinese film studies: 1949–1979], edited by Wu Di, vol. 1, 20–29. Beijing: wenhua yishu chubanshe, 2006.

Zhong, Jingzhi. "Zhuiyi Chen bo'er tongzhi zuihou de rizi" [Recalling the last few days of comrade Chen Bo'er's life]. *Dianying yishu* [Film Art] 3 (1991): 49.

Zhong, Huamin. *Jiang Qing zhengzhuan* [A biography of Jiang Qing]. Hong Kong: Youlian yanjiusuo, 1967.

Zhong, Xueping. *Masculinity Besieged? Issues of Modernity and Male Subjectivity in Chinese Literature of the Late Twentieth Century*. Durham, NC: Duke University Press, 2000.

———, Wang Zheng, and Bai Di, eds. *Some of Us: Chinese Women Growing Up in the Mao Era*. Piscataway, NJ: Rutgers University Press, 2001.

"Zhonggong Shanghaishi dianyingju dangwei guanyu shinianlai Shanghai dianying shiye de juda fazhan he bianhua" [A report by the Shanghai Film Bureau Party committee on the tremendous growth and change in the film industry in the last decade]. Shanghai Municipal Archives, 25 September 1959, B177–1–220.

"Zhonggong Shanghaishi dianyingju dangwei kuoda huiyi jilu" [A summary of the Shanghai Film Bureau Party committee's expanded meeting]. Shanghai Municipal Archives, 14 August 1959, B177–1–139.

"Zhonggong Shanghaishi dianyingju dangwei kuoda huiyi qingkuang fanying" [Reflections of the CPC Shanghai Film Bureau Party committee's expanded meeting]. Shanghai Municipal Archives, 8 August 1964, B177–1–181.

"Zhongguo de xingbie gongzi chayi" [Income difference by gender in China]. *Wageindicator.cn*. www.wageindicator.cn/main/salary/753759735de58d445dee8ddd (accessed August 25, 2014).

"Zhongguo dianying jiaoyu dianjizhe, kaituozhe tongxiang jiemu yishi zai woyuan longzhong juxing" [Our Academy holds the grand ceremony for unveiling the bronze statues of the founders and pioneers of Chinese film education]. Beijing Film Academy website: www.bfa.edu.cn/news/2012–12/22/content_57470.htm (accessed January 14, 2016).

"Zhongguo funü yundong dangqian renwu de jueyi" [The resolution on the current tasks of the Chinese women's movement]. In *Zhongguo funü yundong wenxian ziliao huibian* [An anthology of source material on the Chinese women's movement], edited by Chinese Women Cadres Management School, vol. 2, 22–24. Beijing: Zhongguo funü chubanshe, 1988.

Zhongguo funü zazhi jianjie [A brief introduction to *Women of China*]. Internal circulation of memoirs produced by the Press of *Women of China*, 1999.

"Zhongguo gongchandang dashi ji—1950" [Major events of the CCP—1950]. *Beifangwang* E-North.com.cn. http://news.enorth.com.cn/system/2006/06/19 /001334591.shtml (accessed January 24, 2010).

"Zhongguo gongchandang dashiji: 1963 nian" [Important events of the CCP in 1963]. *Renminwang* People.com.cn. http://cpc.people.com.cn/GB/64162/64164 /4416060.html (accessed April 20, 2015).

"Zhongguo gongchandang dashiji (1966)" [Major events of the Chinese Communist Party in 1966]. *Renminwang* People.com.cn. http://cpc.people.com.cn /GB/64162/64164/4416081.html (accessed May 19, 2015).

"Zhonghua quanguo funü lianhehui zhangcheng" [The Constitution of the All-China Women's Federation]. In *Zhongguo funü yundong wenxian ziliao huibian* [An anthology of source material on the Chinese women's movement], edited by Chinese Women Cadres Management School, vol. 2, 180–82. Beijing: Zhongguo funü chubanshe, 1988.

"Zhonghua quanguo wenxue yishujie lianhehui changwu weiyuan Ding Ling tongzhi jianghua" [The talk of comrade Ding Ling, standing committee member of the All-China Literature and Art Association]. In *Renmin yishujia Chen Bo'er tongzhi jinian teji* [A memorial series on the people's artist comrade Chen Bo'er], 12. Beijing: Xin dianying chubanshe, 1952.

Zhongtian Feihong. "Geju 'Jiangjie' wengezhong zao jinyan de zhenshi neimu" [The real story of the banning of the opera Sister Jiang in the Cultural Revolution]. *Sina blog.* http://blog.sina.com.cn/s/blog_4c3b65fb0102uxni.html?tj = 2 (accessed May 2, 2015).

Zhou Enlai Deng Yingchao tongxin xuanji [A selected collection of correspondances between Zhou Enlai and Deng Yingchao]. Beijing: Zhongyang wenxian chubanshe, 1998.

Zhou, Jinghao. *Remaking China's Public Philosophy and Chinese Women's Liberation: The Volatile Mixing of Confucianism, Marxism, and Feminism.* Lewiston, ME: Edwin Mellon Press, 2006.

Zhou, Xi. *Haishang yingzong: Shanghai juan* [Trace of film over the sea: Shanghai volume]. Beijing: Minzu Press, 2011.

"Zhou Yang tongzhi baogao" [Comrade Zhou Yang's talk]. Shanghai Municipal Archives, B177–1–308, p. 49, undated (1964 or 1965).

"Zhou Zongli ting wenhuabu dangzu huibao dianying gongzuoshi de chahua" [Premier Zhou comments on the reports on film work presented by the Party group of the Ministry of Culture]. Shanghai Municipal Archives, 5 August 1965, B177–1–32.

"Zhou Zongli zai 1968 nian 3 yue 27 ri de zhongyao jianghua" [Premier Zhou's important talk on March 27, 1968]. In *Jiang Qing tongzhi lun wenyi* [Comrade Jiang Qing on literature and the arts], 203–5. Publisher unknown, 1968.

"Zhou Zongli zai renda huitang baogao jilu" [A record of Premier Zhou's talk in the People's Hall]. Shanghai Municipal Archives, 11 August 1965, B177–1–32.

Zhu, Aijun. *Feminism and Global Chineseness: The Cultural Production of Controversial Women Authors.* Youngstown, OH: Cambria Press, 2007.

Zhu, Anping, " 'Daxie shisannian' kouhao de youlai" [The background of the slogan "representing the thirteen years"]. *Dangshi Bolan* [Overviews of the Party's History], no. 1 (2015): 30–33.

Zhu, Anping, "*Zhufu* yongyou duoge 'diyi' de huihuang jilu" [The New Year's Sacrifice has many glorious "number ones"]. *Mtime.* http://i.mtime.com/4020546/blog/7374617/ (accessed August 15, 2014).

"Zhufu: Zhongguo jingdian huaijiu dianying" [The New Year's Sacrifice: A Chinese classic film]. www.youtube.com/watch?v=qjNSt9V4Zhw (accessed May 16, 2016).

INDEX

Chinese Democratic Alliance, 84

Chinese Films, 190

class: realignment of, 93, 221, 229, 238–39; gendered, 240

class struggle, 139, 199, 205, 218; conceptualization, 248–49; gendered, 128–30, 220, 238, 246; Mao on, 114, 137–38; Maoist, 19, 24, 112, 196, 250; misuse of, 249; replacing anti-feudalism, 19; *Women of China* and, 106, 113–17, 128

Collection of Current Affairs (Shishi leibian), 80

Communist morality, 95–96, 110

Communist Revolution, 1, 6, 8, 25, 70, 169, 219, 258; anti-feudalism, 130; base areas, 17; Chen Bo'er and, 149, 151, 163; Edgar Snow, 288n30; mass line, 110; socialist films and, 185; women's participation in, 8–9, 11, 20, 29, 80, 85, 120, 244, 263, 267n17

Comrade Chiang Ch'ing, 206. *See also* Roxane Witke

Comrade, You Are on the Wrong Road! (Tongzhi, ni zoucuole lu!), 156

Confucianism: feudalism, 4; gender system, 3, 188, 231, 258; on motherly love, 294n13; revival of, 19, 233

conjugal relations, 83, 95, 118–19, 128–29, 134, 282n3, 314n28

Constitution of the People's Republic of China, 16, 135

Cries of Women, The (Nüxing de nahan), 178

cultural front, 2, 12–14, 79, 85, 109–11, 114, 138–39, 143, 182, 243, 247, 257

Cultural Revolution: affecting ACWF, 139; "Central Cultural Revolution Group," 284n31; condemnation of, 229, 249; cultural production in, 25, 215–17, 282n56, 293n2, 293n3, 305n40, 311n79; Dong Bian during, 92, 133; international factor of, 305n34; Jiang Qing as the vanguard of, 206, 214–18, 216*fig,* 220, 307n47, 307n48, 308n60, 308n65, 309n68, 310n75; Mao's cultural agenda, 183; Mao's images during, 109; Peng Zhen in, 284n32, 307n52; persecutions in, 304n31, 305n38; prelude to, 19, 205;

Women of China during, 277n3; Xia Yan and, 170–71, 212. *See also* Jiang Qing; Mao Zedong

Dai Jinhua, 162, 290n50, 315n36

Daughters of China (Zhonghua nüer), 155, 161–64, 162*fig,* 290n52, 290n53, 291n54, 291n59. *See also* Chen Bo'er; Ling Zifeng; Yan Yiyan

Davin, Delia, 55

Dazhai, 222–26, 229, 234, 239–40, 311n2, 312n3

Deng Xiaoping: denouncing the Cultural Revolution; "double diligences" and, 67, 74–76, 229, 260; hosting meetings of the Secretariat in 1957; instructions to ACWF officials, 56–57, 61, 64–65, 68–70; turning to global capitalism, 257

Deng Yingchao: commemoration of Chen Bo'er, 167; comment by Jiang Qing on, 218, 311n77; Deng Xiaoping and, 61, 64, 68–69; feminist strategies, 46, 50; land reform and, 46–47; leadership in ACWF, 9, 13*fig,* 14, 21, 269n1,n2, 278n14; Marriage Law and, 14, 267–68n23, 272n37, 281n40; on feudalist mentality in the CCP, 101–2; on women's liberation and women-work, 83–84, 99–100; promoting women's participation in politics, 55; protecting the ACWF, 69; recruiting feminists, 83, 269n1, 278n14; work report in 1957 and, 58–59, 61, 64, 67–68, 268n23

Department of Civil Administration, 32, 36–42

Diantong Film Company, 149, 296n35

Ding Ling, 79, 156, 157*fig,* 268n28

domesticity, 21, 37, 48, 71, 75, 83, 119–20, 122, 128, 146, 233, 313n23

Dong Bian: Cai Chang and, 120–21; Chen Boda and, 135–36; condemnation of, 133–34; drafting the 1957 ACWF work report, 57, 64, 73, 77; editing the forum of *Women of China,* 119–21, 123, 132; in charge of *Women of China,* 84–85, 94, 106, 279n16, 283n11,n28; in Yan'an, 135; joining the CCP, 82–83; leadership in ACWF, 10; life, 278n13, 279n17; on

55–56, 59–61, 73–77, 103–4, 125, 184, 244, 278n14. *See also* feminism

funü wenti (the women question, or, women's problem): subordination of, 115–16. See also *Red Flag*; Chen Boda

gender: awareness, 47, 60; based, 41, 43, 53, 54, 59, 60, 64, 66, 73, 76, 132; blind, 137; class and, 16, 25, 48–49, 104, 112, 119, 163, 189, 229, 241, 264, 316n4; concept of, 259; conflict, 45, 53; democracy, 110; discourse, 14, 78, 187, 194, 230, 237, 315n39; differentiation, 19, 229, 231, 233, 239–40, 258; disparity in income, 240; division of work, 65, 219, 231, 313n12; equality (*shehui xingbie pingdeng*), 8, 21, 25, 50, 228, 259–60, 318n16; erasure, 24, 236, 309n71, 315n36; gap, 64; hierarchy, 4, 18, 25, 63, 106, 110, 130, 217; identity, 42, 148; line, 2, 8, 77, 242, 263; mainstreaming, 259–60; norms, 25, 42, 103, 128, 154, 187, 190, 198, 215, 223, 241, 310n71; interests (practical and strategic), 75; oppression, 11, 60, 127, 130, 177, 217; performativity, 15; positions, 63; regime, 100, 103, 231; representation, 15; sameness, 19, 229, 234; segregation, 4, 104; social space and, 48.; specific, 36, 42, 51, 66, 102, 119, 148, 246; state and, 266n15, 314n32; stratification, 240; struggles, 24, 76, 77–78, 101, 110–11, 128, 130; subordination, 106; system, 3, 11, 130, 244, 246, 298n54; unmarked, 116, 160. *See also* feminism; *funü jiefang*; *nannü pingdeng*

Geng Ruzhang, 154

Gilmartin, Christina K., 10, 266n7

Goddess, The (Shennü), 179

going to the people, 158

gongnongbing (worker/peasant/soldier), articles on, 134; making films of, 160–61, 163–64, 183, 185–87, 200–2, 204, 289n44, 298n49; Mao's 1964 directives on literature and art, 210; revolutionizing theatres for, 213–14; visual representation of, 106, 107*fig*; watching films, 203; women, 135; *xiashenghuo*, 200–1, 212

Good Housekeeper (Hao zhufu), 252

Great Leap Forward, 44, 120, 136; ACWF during, 72–75, 90, 276n42, 277n46; significance in women's liberation, 101–2, 118, 224, 236

Guo Fenglian: attacks on the Iron Girls, 229; becoming CEO, 239–40, 316n46; in the media, 312n3, 312n11; meeting Zhou Enlai, 226*fig*, 234; personal life, 313n17; promotion, 225; remembering her youth, 240; rise and fall, 222, 313n16, 315n44; shouldering physical labor, 236; symbol, 226; team member and, 227*fig*, 236; visual images of, 311n2. *See also* Iron Girls; Iron Girls Brigade

Hamlet, 176

Harbor, The, 215

Hershatter, Gail, 104, 223, 230, 312n6, 313n15, 313n17

He Xiangning, 152, 287n26

He-Yin Zhen, 244–45, 265n4

hidden transcripts, 50, 111

History of the Development of Film in China, A, 209

Honig, Emily, 230, 313n15, 313n17

Hou Di: editing *Women of China*, 95–96, 102–3, 115, 131, 250, 254, 277n3; image of, 88*fig*; on Dong Bian, 94, 113, 131–32, 279n16; on the mass line, 136; on Red Flag article, 113

housewives: associations, 30–32, 36, 38, 270n5; committees, 32, 34; film representation of, 310n73; in neighborhood work, 36–37; mobilizing, 20, 36, 40, 52; parade, 33; redefining, 31; representatives, 35; socialist construction and, 118; Women's Federation and, 21, 43, 48

housework: discussions in *Women of China*, 122–23, 128–29; during the double diligences campaign, 71; socialization of, 72–75, 102

Hu Bangxiu, 123–24

Hu Qiaomu: Chen Boda and, 135–37, 284n37, 285n41; Tian Jiaying and, 135–37, 284n37, 285n41

Hu Xiuzhi, 161, 162*fig*

Hu Yuzhi, 82

Liu Lantao, 74

Liu Qiaoer, 184–5

Liu Shaoqi, Peng Zhen and, 284n31; protecting ACWF, 66, 69, 275n20; Tian Jiaying and, 285n39

Liu Xiao, 38–39

Liu Ying, 160*fig*

Long March, 9; Mao's marriages, 303n26

Lu Xun: adaptation of "New Year's Sacrifice," 188–90, 193, 298n54; "New Year's Sacrifice," 187–88, 193. See also *New Year's Sacrifice* (film); Xianglin's Wife

Luo, Liang, 158, 286n7

Luo Qiong: double diligences and, 71–76, 276n35; drafting the work report in 1957, 57, 61–66; editing *Women of China,* 79, 124–29; leadership in ACWF, 10, 21, 44; the Marriage Law and, 267–68n23, 281n40; remembering Deng Xiaoping, 57, 275n20; on Shen Zijiu, 81; theorizing gendered class struggle, 128–130

male-centeredness, political order, 116, 126; visual representation, 106, 150–51

male chauvinism, 14, 18, 63, 217, 310n76

male domination: economic foundation of, 244; in employment, 101; in neighborhood organization, 36; in power structure, 7, 18, 24, 50, 60, 63, 70, 132–33, 206, 219, 245, 259; in society, 1, 151, 169

male gaze, 150, 162

Manchuria Film Studio, 1, 289n45, 289n46

Manchurian Incident, 9, 80, 145

Mao Zedong, 9, 19, 25, 54, 59, 68, 83, 90, 114, 122, 126, 198, 234, 273n2, 288n30, 297n45, 304n32, 305n34; Anti-Rightest Campaign and, 59–60; the CCP after, 248–49; criticism of *The Life of Wu Xun,* 165, 170, 181–83, 186, 205, 291n62, 291n63, 297n42, 297n44; Dazhai and, 222, 225–26; directives on literature and arts, 205, 210; "double diligences," 67; Chen Boda and, 136–37; Hu Qiaomu and, 135–36, 284n37; inscription for *Women of China,* 134–35, 284n35; instructing ACWF leaders, 53; marriages, 303n26; on class struggle, 137–38; on continuous revolution, 126, 129, 131;

comments on the cultural realm, 306n42, 307n48, 308n54; Peng Zhen and, 284n31, 284n32, 284n33, 285n43; praise of Jiang Qing, 308n59; *Selected Works,* 135; "Things Are Beginning to Change," 60; Tian Jiaying and, 135–36, 284n35, 284n37, 285n39; visual images, 108–9; Yan'an Talks, 157–60, 157*fig*, 164, 183, 185–86, 212, 288n40, 289n41, 295n49

March 8 Flag Bearer *(sanba hongqishou),* 49, 273n42

Marxism, 4, 115, 125–26, 145, 153, 173, 177, 243, 259

Marxist theory of proletarian women's liberation, 5, 21, 31, 50, 125

masculinist, attack, 77, 117; desire, 245, 260; discourse, 241; expressions, 219; hostility, 220, 248; mentality, 168, 219, 260, 262; power, 2, 16, 49, 53, 69, 110, 138, 247; pressure, 259; practices, 116; sentiment, 233; values, 218

masculinity: essentialization of, 216, 309n71; hegemonic, 241; in male writings, 230–31

"masculinization" of women, 15, 163, 228, 250, 309n71; critique of, 235–37; cultural representation of, 234, 263, 290n50; the Iron Girls and, 221, 228–31, 233, 236, 239–40. *See also* Iron Girls

mass line *(qunzhong luxian),* 11, 53, 78, 85, 94, 110–11, 133, 136, 156; in filmmaking, 201–2

mass organization, 17, 43, 52–54, 74, 79, 110, 132, 138, 246–47, 260, 269n1

May Fourth Movement, 185, 200, 268n27; anti-feudalism, 14, 25, 130, 211, 244, 248; feminism, 50, 81, 82, 110, 130, 143, 146, 148, 154, 171, 243, 265n6, 268n23, 295n14; feminists, 46, 80, 173–77, 218, 272n37; Lu Xun, 187; theme of "love revolution," 151; May Fourth story, 299n60. *See also* New Cultural Movement

Mei Gongyi, 144–45, 148

Mexico International Film Festival, 193

Mingxing film studio, 177

Ministry of Education, 262

politics of concealment: anonymity of state feminists, 18, 228, 246, 259; articulation, 50–51; cases of, 78, 261; discursive strategy, 17–18, 111, 246, 259; effects of, 248; in post-socialist China, 221; opposite of, 261; political system and, 22, 24, 260, 263

politics of erasure: effects, 18–20; historical context of, 18, 221; political dynamics in, 18; resistance to, 26, 85

proletarian line, 215, 218, 308n54

psychoanalysis, 150

Qian Xingcun, 177

qilü huanma (replacing a donkey with a horse), 95

Qin Yi, 201

Qu Baiyin, 204–5

Red Crag, 194–96, 211; Jiang Qing and, 306n47. See also *Eternity in Flames*

Red Flag, 112–114, 118, 122, 125, 131–35, 137, 139, 247, 249, 279n20. *See also* Chen Boda

Red Lantern, The (*Hongdeng ji*), 215

Ren Posheng, 144–45, 152, 159, 286n6, 289n.42. *See also* Chen Bo'er

residents committee, emergence in Shanghai, 32–34, 36–39; rectification of, 39; women's congress and, 34, 36–39, 41–44, 48, 52, 271n21

revisionist line, 25, 198, 205, 210, 212, 214, 218, 249, 305n40, 306n45. *See also* Xia Yan

Revolutionaries (*Shengsi tongxin*), 151, 287n17

Revolutionary Family, A (*Geming jiating*), 194–96, 195*fig*, 211, 299n64, 300n74

revolutionary outlook, 94, 95, 119, 121–22, 124–5, 127, 130

Roberts, Rosemary A., 216, 308n61, 309n71, 315n36

Rofel, Lisa, 104

Rosie the Riveter, 241

Rou Shi, 209

rustic (*tu*), 93, 255

Sai Jinhua, 175–76, 208–9, 296n32, 305n37. *See also* Jiang Qing; Xia Yan

sanbao yidao (three fulls and one down), 128

Sang Hu, 193

sanjiehe (collaboration among officials, filmmakers, and the masses), 202

Scott, James C., 50

Self (*Yueji*), 252, 316n5, 317n7

self-effacement, 18, 85, 111. *See also* politics of concealment; politics of erasure

Sha Yexin, 233

Shajia Village (*Shajia bang*), 215

Shangguan Yunzhu, 201

Shanghai Art Drama Troupe (SADT), 145, 286n8

Shanghai Arts College, 145

Shanghai Film Bureau, 201, 204, 292n1, 302n7, 305n41, 307n51, 310n73

Shanghai Film Studio, 202, 292n1

Shanghai Housewives Association, 31–32

Shanghai Incident, 145

Shanghai lanes: organizing residents in, 32; spatial organization, 270n10; women's congresses in, 34

Shanghai Women's Federation (SWF), critical voices in, 40–41; contestation with male officials, 49; DCA and, 38–41; five-anti's campaign and, 272n28; founding and development of, 30–35; hostilities towards, 35, 37–39; institutional boundaries, 52; neighborhood work, 36–37, 48, 270n5; mission of, 40; organizing housewives, 30–32, 270n6; organizing parade, 33–34; redefining women-work, 39, 42; women's congresses and, 34, 36–37, 39, 42–44, 271n21

Shanghai Women's National Salvation Association, 152, 154

Shen Xiling, 80, 178

Shen Zijiu: as a third-cohort feminist, 10; Dong Bian and, 84; early career, 80–82; education, 80; Li Qiyang and, 280n26; marriages, 80; *Women's Life*, 1, 82, 278n12; *Women of China* and, 80, 84–86, 94, 110; Xia Yan and, 295n21. See also *Women of China*

Shenbao (*Shanghai Daily*), 80–81, 145

Shi Liangcai, 81, 278n8

Shi Yumei, 92, 94, 105–8, 254, 282n55
Shui Hua, 195
Sister Jiang (Jiang Zhujun): as a revolutionary heroine, 211; the image of, 263, 301n77; representation in *Eternity in Flames,* 196–198, 210; Yu Lan and, 301n76, 306n46. See also *Eternity in Flames*
Sister Jiang (opera), 211, 263, 307n48
Snow, Edgar, 153, 288n30
socialism: the Anti-Rightist Campaign and, 66; capitalism and, 248, 250; China's departure from, 19, 21, 235, 258; condemnation of, 220, 232, 237–38, 241, 243, 250; cultural productions of, 185, 209, 306n43; international, 5; socialist construction, 6, 8, 42, 56, 63–64, 69; socialist revolution, 2, 114; women's liberation and, 8, 25, 45, 54, 68–69, 72–73, 86, 101, 146, 174, 193, 223, 225, 236, 247. *See also* feminism
socialization of housework, 72, 102
Sociological Studies, 231
Song of the Dragon River, 255
Song Qingling, 68, 152, 287n24
South Sea Press, 82
Soviet Revolution, 145
spatial organization, 32, 270n10
Spivak, Gayatri, 227
Spring Forever (Wanziqianhong zongshichun), 310n73
Spring Silkworms, 171, 302n9
street office, 32, 36–38, 43, 269n1
Sun Yat-sen, 173, 287n24
Sun Yu, 165, 181–82, 297n42. See also *The Life of Wu Xun*
Swan Lake, 204
symbolic order, 90, 228

Tang, Xiaobing, 158, 287n34, 288n40, 302n10
Tao Cheng, 194, 299n65
three big mountains, 6, 83, 130
Three Modern Girls (Sange modeng nüxing), 179
three troops (*sanzhi duiwu*), 93
"Three Women Are Not Equal to One Man," 100, 101*fig*

Tian Han, 158, 296n32
Tian Jiaying: Chen Boda and, 135–37, 284n37, 285n41; Dong Bian and, 83, 84*fig,* 283n28; Hu Qiaomu and, 135–37, 284n37, 285n41; Mao Zedong and, 284n35, 285n39
Trade Union, 9, 12, 21, 30, 35, 269n1
two-line struggle: impacts on film, 25, 205, 218, 309n67; Jiang Qing's framing of, 205, 211, 218; Mao on, 137, 205, 210

United Nations (UN), 259

visual representation: of ethnic minority women, 90, 92*fig,* 93; of Chairman Mao, 108; of "new women," 253–58; of revolutionary heroines, 155, 160–65; of rural women, 89–90; of women militia, 107, 109*fig;* of women role models, 92, 105; omission of political campaign, 106. See also *Women of China*

Wang Danfeng, 201
Wang Guilan, 97*fig*
War of Resistance (also known as the second Sino-Japanese War), 9–10; mobilization of women in the base areas, 79; rural women in, 224–25; urban women in, 154–55. *See also* national salvation
"What Should Women Live For," 113, 116, 119, 121, 127, 134. See also *Women of China*
"white terror," 178
Wild Torrents, 171
Witke, Roxane, 205–6, 208, 218, 297n42, 303n28, 310n76, 311n77, 311n79. *See also* Jiang Qing
Women and Socialism, 174, 197, 295n17, 296n26. *See also* August Bebel; Xia Yan
women militia, 107, 108*fig,* 109*fig*
Women of China, 1, 78; after the *Red Flag* incident, 131–39; attack from Chen Boda, 112–17, 124–27, 131, 133–38; cartoon in, 101*fig,* 102; circulation, 86, 247, 277n3; content of, 70, 94–96, 102, 224, 276n35, 300n66; cover of, 89–93, 90*fig,*